The Ends and Means of Welfare
Coping with economic and social change in Australia

The Ends and Means of Welfare explores the relation between economic liberalism and social policy in Australia. How do social policies operate in a fiercely individualist market economy, and if the market is expected to provide solutions to social problems, what role ought the government take to ensure that it does so? Why is it that quality of life in Australia has diminished as the economy has undergone sustained growth? These are just a few of the key questions Peter Saunders asks. He draws upon the most up-to-date research, including recent national surveys conducted by the Social Policy Research Centre. The book covers the key trends in economic and social policy over the past 25 years, showing how economic liberalism, despite all positive economic indicators, has contributed to an increase in unemployment, inequality, social dysfunction and alienation.

Peter Saunders is Professor of Social Policy and Director of the Social Policy Research Centre at the University of New South Wales. He is the author of *Welfare and Inequality* (Cambridge University Press, 1994).

The Ends and Means of Welfare
Coping with economic and social change in Australia

Peter Saunders
University of New South Wales

CAMBRIDGE UNIVERSITY PRESS
Cambridge, New York, Melbourne, Madrid, Cape Town,
Singapore, São Paulo, Delhi, Mexico City

Cambridge University Press
The Edinburgh Building, Cambridge CB2 8RU, UK

Published in the United States of America by Cambridge University Press, New York

www.cambridge.org
Information on this title: www.cambridge.org/9780521524438

© Peter Saunders 2002

This publication is in copyright. Subject to statutory exception
and to the provisions of relevant collective licensing agreements,
no reproduction of any part may take place without the written
permission of Cambridge University Press.

First published 2002

A catalogue record for this publication is available from the British Library

National Library of Australia Cataloguing in Publication Data
Saunders, Peter (Peter Gordon), 1948– .
The ends and means of welfare: coping with economic and
social change in Australia.
Bibliography.
Includes index.
ISBN 0 521 81892 3.
ISBN 0 521 52443 1 (pbk.).
1. Capitalism – Australia. 2. Australia – Social policy –
1976–1990. 3. Australia – Social policy – 1990– .
4. Australia – Social conditions – 1976–1990. 5. Australia –
Social conditions – 1990– . 6. Australia – Economic policy
– 1976–1990. 7. Australia – Economic policy – 1990– .
I. Title.
361.250994

ISBN 978-0-521-81892-6 Hardback
ISBN 978-0-521-52443-8 Paperback

Cambridge University Press has no responsibility for the persistence or
accuracy of URLs for external or third-party internet websites referred to in
this publication, and does not guarantee that any content on such websites is,
or will remain, accurate or appropriate. Information regarding prices, travel
timetables, and other factual information given in this work is correct at
the time of first printing but Cambridge University Press does not guarantee
the accuracy of such information thereafter.

Contents

Preface	*page* vi
List of Figures	x
List of Tables	xi
Introduction	1
1 The paradox of affluence	3
Part I Economic and Social Performance	21
2 Has the economy delivered?	23
3 Legitimacy of the welfare state	59
Part II The Changing Socioeconomic Landscape	85
4 Employment and unemployment	87
5 Income and living standards	114
6 Poverty and exclusion	143
7 Inequality	177
Part III Reform Directions and Strategies	213
8 Welfare reform	215
9 Re-mapping the contours of welfare	242
Appendix: Details of the Coping with Economic and Social Change (CESC) Survey	266
References	273
Index	293

Preface

Most books are a long time coming and this one is no exception. The original idea of conducting a survey of community attitudes to social issues, social change and the social policy response grew out of discussions with colleagues at the Social Policy Research Centre (SPRC) in 1997. It was already apparent by then that disquiet was growing in the community about the threats posed by market-oriented economic reforms to many aspects of people's lives, to their families and communities. The welfare system – the provision of income and other forms of support for working-age people – was at the centre of these debates because it sits at the interface between the family, the state and the market. The idea of examining attitudes to *specific* aspects of social change and social policy seemed a useful way to tap into community opinion in a way that could inform the broader intellectual and policy debates.

After more than a decade of intensive reform, the Australian welfare system is still seen by those driving the neo-liberal economic reform agenda as an obstacle whose shape and purpose need to conform to the new reform imperatives. The focus has shifted away from the powerful distributional impact of welfare to its alleged detrimental effects on incentives, yet an increasing proportion of the population is reliant on welfare benefits to supplement increasingly insecure and dispersed market incomes. The issue of 'welfare dependency' (a term, like welfare itself imported from the United States) has emerged as the main focus of the welfare reform agenda.

These developments were unfolding against a backdrop in which market forces were driving global integration and as a flourishing economy proved unable to put to rest the murmurings of social discontent. The role and significance of social cohesion and equality no longer feature on a policy agenda focused exclusively on providing individuals with the 'right' incentive signals and 'sending the right messages' to those whose behaviour does not conform with the prevailing ideology of individualism and self-reliance. The notion of a 'Fair Go' (recently described by journalist Paul Kelly as 'the two most abused words in

Australia today') has been abandoned, along with the basis of Australia's egalitarian tradition. Although there has been some acknowledgment that social exclusion prevents some people from participating in the fruits of economic success, policies to combat exclusion have been strong on rhetoric but weak on action and resources, as fiscal discipline has severely constrained what governments can do (other than provide tax cuts to the better-off).

In addressing these issues, it has been necessary to take a thorough look at what we require of the welfare system, including its ends and means – what it is expected to achieve and how. This leads inevitably into a discussion of the impact of the various instruments of social policy in the welfare field and how these have responded to broader social changes. This, in turn, involves exploring how the welfare system conforms to community values about the problems it is trying to combat. Above all, it involves examining the potentially negative consequences of welfare provision while acknowledging its positive effects on incomes, living standards and inequality. Only once these have been fully documented is it possible to understand and interpret the nature of community attitudes to social change and social policy.

One of the hallmarks of social policy is complexity. The issues with which it deals, its avenues of response, its design and impact, its technicalities and judgments, its economics and sociology, its history and institutions, its programs and politics, all guarantee this. The point at which these ideas and forces come together provides a challenging but exciting intellectual climate, not always noted for the clarity of its argument, but rarely lacking in spirit and insight. Those economists intent on reducing the analysis of social policy to the simplistic arithmetic of differential calculus fail the basic tests of social research *and* sound economics. Their theories will never touch the underlying reality, yet they continue to have unwarranted influence on those responsible for policy development. Social policy deserves better and my hope is that this book will represent a small step in that direction.

The research project that produced the results reported throughout this book formed part of the core research agenda of the SPRC between 1998 and 2000. In fact, it was one of the last of those projects, because the Commonwealth Government withdrew the Centre's core funding from the end of 2000, replacing it by a project-focused, contractual funding arrangement spread across three research institutes (including SPRC) from the beginning of 2001. These new contracts were awarded after a process of open tender and competitive bidding; social policy research has not been isolated from the broader trends in government funding! It is still too soon to assess how effective the new arrangements will be, but this book and the research on which it is based provide an example of what can be achieved under the core-funding model. Many of the issues it addresses are not popular under the current policy regime and it is doubtful whether the research would have been funded under the new arrangements. A way must be found of combining research that addresses specific issues of immediate policy interest with basic, curiosity-motivated research that raises longer-term fundamental questions not currently at the forefront of the reform agenda. Social policy research can do so much more than helping to resolve current policy quandaries.

As always, many people have contributed to the research reported here. I have been enormously fortunate to be associated with the SPRC and have benefited from the wisdom and insight of its many excellent researchers. Among my colleagues who have, directly and indirectly, contributed to this book are Michael Bittman, Bruce Bradbury, Tony Eardley, Ceri Evans, George Matheson and Cathy Thomson. Others who have helped me to formulate my ideas and provided critical insight into the issues discussed (often unknowingly and unintentionally!) include Jonathan Bradshaw, Frank Castles, Bob Goodin, Bob Gregory, Bob Haveman, John Nevile, Sue Richardson, Tim Smeeding and Peter Whiteford. My intellectual debt to two great pioneers of Australian social policy research – Fred Gruen and Ronald Henderson – will, I hope, be apparent. None of those mentioned above have commented on the manuscript and they are in no way responsible for the use I have made of what I have learnt from them. A small army of excellent researchers has assisted me through my own data manipulation inadequacies. A special thanks is due to Judy Brown, Ceri Evans, George Matheson, Kate Norris, Tony Salvage, Cathy Thomson, Merrin Thompson, Rob Urquhart and Matthew Williams. Diana Encel produced the Index with her customary no-fuss efficiency, picking up several typographical errors in the process. I must accept full responsibility for those that remain.

I have also benefited from the many comments received in response to my preliminary reporting of the research findings. I would, in particular, like to acknowledge the valuable suggestions provided by participants in seminars or conferences held at SPRC, the Australian National University, the University of Melbourne, the University of Western Sydney, the University of Hong Kong, Sung Kyun Kwan University in Seoul, Korea, the Australian Institute of Health and Welfare, the Australian Institute of Family Studies and the 2000 Research Seminar of the Foundation for International Studies on Social Security (FISS) held in Sigtuna, Sweden. Most of the first draft of the manuscript was completed in the first half of 2001 when I was an F. H. Gruen Visiting Professorial Fellow in the Economics Program, Research School of Social Sciences at the Australian National University. I am grateful to the generous hospitality, peaceful contemplation and creative intellectual environment that this provided me with.

Finally, a word of sincere thanks to my partner Janet Chan, who has been a constant source of advice and encouragement while fully engaged on her own intellectual tasks. She has been a source of inspiration and wise counsel as well as a trusted friend and respected colleague.

Figures

2.1 Movements in real household disposable income per
    capita, 1959–60 to 1998–99 ($ 1997–98 prices) *page* 31
2.2 Movements in real household final consumption expenditure
    per capita, 1959–60 to 1998–99 ($ 1997–98 prices) 31
2.3 Trend in the unemployment rate, 1966–2001 33
3.1 Framework linking values, beliefs and attitudes 68
3.2 Alternative foundations of attitudes to the unemployed 68
3.3 Public opinion on taxes and spending on social services 74
7.1 The burden of unemployment on family units aged 15
    and over, 1979–2000 200
7.2 Where Australians think their incomes place them relative
    to the incomes of others 204
8.1 Views on penalties for not meeting social security
    requirements 240

Tables

2.1	Comparisons of Australian and OECD macroeconomic performance	page 26
2.2	Comparisons of government spending and receipts in Australia and the OECD (percentages of GDP)	27
2.3	General government outlays, welfare state spending and taxation in OECD countries, 1997 (percentages)	29
2.4	Trends in household size, 1947–96	32
2.5	Selected characteristics of the long-term unemployed, April 2001	35
2.6	Incidence of financial stress by household income quintile, 1998–99 (percentage of households reporting each indicator)	40
3.1	Overall attitudes to economic and social change (percentages)	77
3.2	Questions used to determine the value framework of CESC respondents	79
3.3	Demographic characteristics of the value sub-samples (percentages)	81
3.4	Subjective well-being and value position (percentages)	83
4.1	The distribution of hours worked by employed persons, March 2001	93
4.2	Subjective well-being, attitudes and employment status	99
4.3	Indicators of economic insecurity (percentages)	101
4.4	Incidence of job insecurity by socioeconomic characteristics (percentages)	102
4.5	Estimates of the current unemployment rate (percentages)	103
4.6	Estimates of the level of long-term unemployment (percentages)	104
4.7	Explanations for high unemployment (percentages)	105
4.8	Views on the responsibility for solving the unemployment problem (percentages)	107
4.9	The role of government in solving unemployment	108

4.10	Views on levels of government support for unemployed people (percentages)	111
4.11	Views on levels of government support for unemployed people among different value groupings (percentages)	112
5.1	The changing composition of household income, 1959–60 to 1999–2000 (percentages of gross income)	126
5.2	The effects of government benefits and taxes on household income, 1984–94	130
5.3	Social wage benefits and taxes, by household gross income quintile, 1993–94 (average weekly $ value)	131
5.4	Past and future changes in standards of living (percentages)	134
5.5	Standard of living and happiness (percentages of total)	136
5.6	Trends in satisfaction and happiness, 1983–1999 (percentages)	137
5.7	Self-assessments of happiness and subjective health status (percentages of total)	137
5.8	Income levels and income adequacy (percentages)	138
5.9	Relationship between equivalent income and income adequacy (percentages)	140
5.10	Income levels and satisfaction with standard of living (percentages)	140
5.11	Income levels and overall happiness (percentages)	141
5.12	Income levels and self-assessed health status (percentages)	141
6.1	Community perceptions of the meaning of poverty (percentages)	150
6.2	Overall descriptions of poverty (percentages)	151
6.3	Perceptions of the causes of Australian poverty in 1973 (Adelaide survey)	153
6.4	Community views on the causes of poverty (percentages)	154
6.5	Reasons for poverty by adequacy of family income (percentages in each managing category who strongly agree or agree)	156
6.6	Estimates of income poverty in Australia, 1989–90 to 1996–97	159
6.7	Consensual poverty lines (CPL) and consensual poverty, 1988 and 1999	164
6.8	Perceptions of income adequacy (percentages)	166
6.9	Comparing consensual and subjective poverty rates, 1999 (percentages)	167
6.10	Identification of necessities and indicators of social exclusion	174
7.1	Changes in income distribution among families, 1968–69 to 1999–2000	189
7.2	Changes in the distribution of weekly income, 1985–86 to 1999–2000	192

7.3	Earnings distribution ratios for full-time adult employees, 1985–98	194
7.4	International comparisons of earnings differentials (percentile ratios)	197
7.5	Labour force status of husband and wife in married couple families aged 15 and over, June 2000 (numbers in thousands and percentage distribution in brackets)	198
7.6	Comparison of perceived and actual distributional ranking (row percentages)	205
7.7	Income distribution in selected countries around 1995	209
7.8	Differences in income distribution changes between countries, 1980s–1990s	210
8.1	Community views on the nature of welfare support (percentages)	234
8.2	Levels of support for activity test requirements (percentages)	236
8.3	Support for mutual obligation across different value categories (mean values)	238
8.4	Attitudes to social security penalties by value position (percentages)	240
A.1	Survey sample and responses	267
A.2	The composition of the CESC sample and the general population	268
A.3	Characteristics of the sample compared with 1996 Census data (percentages)	269
A.4	Survey and population estimates of the income distribution	271
A.5	Numbers satisfying alternative value variable cut-off scores	272

Introduction

1   The Paradox of Affluence

Seen from the long sweep of history, the 1990s will be remembered as a decade when unprecedented prosperity was accompanied by rising economic insecurity, social alienation and growing unease. The 'success story' recorded in official statistics on productivity growth, real incomes and budget consolidation was overshadowed by a widespread perception of growing inequality, institutional decline and uncertain prospects. The constant drumbeat of the market – price signals, profitability and competitiveness – shook the foundations of social institutions as disparate as the family, the welfare system and wage arbitration and raised challenges for how social policies could smooth the interface between them.

The political response to these pressures did little to comfort the cynics. Political leaders strove to imitate each other in the relentless quest for the 'sound economic management credentials' on which the confidence (and votes!) of middle Australia was assumed to depend. Their unwillingness to resist or influence change was expressed through a combination of deceit and denial. They preached egalitarianism while introducing policies that generated rising inequality, compassion while denying it to the victims of their own policies, and calmness in an increasingly frenzied economic world. The most commonly claimed characteristic of Australian society is its emphasis on the 'fair go' egalitarian spirit. The sentiment remains strong and the perceptions enduring, but the statistics tell a story of deep poverty amid growing affluence, of deprivation and wealth, of exclusion and privilege, of discrimination and opportunity.

The 1990s were marked by a growing realisation that the future prospects were similarly bleak under alternative policy regimes. Public perceptions are harder to capture in a single statistic than objective economic and social indicators. Community attitudes are difficult to measure, subject to wild swings and open to alternative interpretation. Public opinion does not always satisfy the simple rules of arithmetic and consistency and cannot therefore be analysed using conventional logic. This applies not only to the nature of beliefs and attitudes, but also to the factors and the information flows on which they are based. In giving greater prominence to the role of subjective perceptions (as reflected in community attitudes) about the nature, causes and consequences of economic and social change, we cannot ignore the objective indicators. By combining the two, we might better understand current conditions, the nature of change and the concerns that accompany it.

These beliefs motivate this book's emphasis on the impact that social and economic change have had on living standards and the fabric of contemporary Australian society. At the heart of the argument is the institutional apparatus of state, market, family and community that comprises civil society. Beneath this lie the building blocks on which they rest and the linkages that bind them together: the labour market and the welfare and tax systems. These are all subject to the same pressures for change, but contrary to the prevailing public policy orthodoxy, change can be resisted or manipulated to comply with social preferences (the 'will of the people'). There are alternative ways of responding to externally driven change, but to make these choices, we need to understand the nature of change and to identify shared values and aspirations.

Prosperity and progress?

Between the recession of the early 1990s and the end of the millennium, the Australian economy grew at an average rate of over 4 per cent a year. The extra output produced was sufficient for national income to increase by more than one-third, even after allowing for higher prices. By 2000, many Australians had incomes that could buy more than a decade before – often substantially more. Yet rather than contentment with the fruits of this increased prosperity, there were signs of increasing community discontent. Some Australians have paid a high price for economic success, while increasing numbers have been denied the benefits of increased affluence by unemployment and other factors.

Data from the latest population census provides a snapshot of the nation's circumstances in the midst of growing economic affluence. In 1996, those living in the most disadvantaged areas of the country faced an unemployment rate almost twice the national average, were more then three times as likely to live in public housing and had almost one-third lower household incomes than the population as a whole. Indigenous Australians had a life expectancy around 20 years below that of non-Indigenous people, an imprisonment rate 12 times higher and unemployment 2.5 times higher than the national rate. Close to 700,000 workers had been retrenched in the three years to July 1997, by 1999 almost 200,000 Australians had been unemployed for more than a year and almost 70,000 people were living permanently in caravan parks (ABS,

2000a). The deprivation of these families and many of the associated disadvantages are likely to be passed on to their children, perpetuating inequality across the generations.

When asked in May 1999 about changes in the quality of life in Australia, over one-third (36 per cent) of those surveyed thought that it was getting worse, 38 per cent saw little change and only a quarter (24 per cent) thought that it was improving (Eckersley, 1999). These figures contrast disturbingly with the rise in gross domestic product (GDP) over the 1990s but they are in fact a lot better than those reported in a similar survey conducted two years earlier. When asked to identify important national priorities, over 80 per cent mentioned factors such as good education, health care, broad access to work and an acceptable society – particularly for children. Only slightly more than half referred to maintaining a high standard of living and keeping up with changes in technology as important priorities (Eckersley, 1999: Table 3). Increased material prosperity has not satisfied many of the needs that people regard as important to their well-being. The objective and subjective indicators are diverging, along with the economic and social statistics.

Several reasons have been advanced to explain the discontentment revealed by the subjective quality-of-life indicators. Some argue that, whereas increasing individual affluence brings ever-smaller increases in satisfaction, the sacrifices that individuals have to make to secure a rising income rise disproportionately in terms of time commitments, pressures and anxieties. Over time, these processes weaken the link between material prosperity and overall well-being. There is a similar set of forces acting at the level of society, where increasing inequality and social dislocation, along with damage inflicted on the natural environment are the most commonly cited casualties of economic progress. These have fundamental and far-reaching consequences for the social context within which people live their lives and mediate the satisfaction obtained from increasing material resources. Finally, not everyone shares in the increased affluence that economic growth brings. Some are excluded entirely while others gain disproportionately, leading to a widening gap in economic fortunes that disturbs prevailing notions of fairness – particularly in the context of a 'fair go' society.

The standard response to resolving these forms of social disaffection is politics. Democracy provides the means to realign the priorities of those who hold political power. However, the current political system has tended to produce a narrowing set of options, all of which emphasise the need for more stringent, market-oriented economic policies, ignoring the electorate's increased misgivings about the longer-term wisdom of such strategies. We view our politicians with increasing dismay yet seem unable to deny them office when they seek it. Resolving this apparent paradox involves looking at how economic decisions affect the social infrastructure and why these effects are rarely given the prominence and attention that they warrant. Central to this nexus of pressures and responses is the network of relationships between economic and social choices and constraints.

This book explores the paradox between economic success and social decline, with a view to identifying its causes and developing responses. My basic purpose is to question the wisdom of continuing down a path in which economic forces, factors and arguments dominate thinking about the ends and means of 'the good society' (Galbraith, 1996). Crucial to this questioning is the notion of choice. What does it mean in practice for individuals and how are the factors that influence the agenda of social choices manipulated to preserve a specific set of interests and power relations? To answer these questions, we must explore economic and social ideas, how they are portrayed in public debate and how they influence public attitudes and perceptions. The role of research in influencing the climate of public opinion through its engagement with the media is also important.

Perceptions matter. When people are asked to choose between alternative responses to extremely complex issues – as they are each time they enter a polling booth – the judgments they express reflect their values and understanding of the issues involved. Both are greatly influenced by external forces, including public debate surrounding the nature, causes and consequences of the major policy challenges. While politicians and the 'spin doctors' who advise them have long understood the role of perceptions in determining the popularity of alternative social choices, researchers have often assumed that the world is occupied by rational beings with the ability to process the information needed to make optimal choices. By ignoring the factors that determine how perceptions are formed and the mechanisms through which they can be influenced, social research has been unable to provide a complete understanding of the relationship between economic and social choice.

Some of the tables in later chapters report findings from a nationally representative sample of Australian adults, undertaken in mid-1999, which explored community attitudes to change, perceptions of the nature and causes of economic and social issues and what should be done about them. Data from the survey provide a refreshing contrast with the official statistics bandied about in the daily struggles of political debate. The problem is not that economic success alone cannot generate contentment and social stability. The principle that, *other things constant*, people always prefer more to less, at least in terms of material goods, services and activities remains an important source of motivation and understanding. Rather, the issue is that in striving to maximise economic outcomes, many of the things that have to be sacrificed are more highly valued *at the level of society* than the resulting increase in economic prosperity for individuals.

The conventional economic response to this situation is inadequate because in seeking to establish the conditions for increased affluence, the social conditions that people value will be further eroded, thus worsening the problem. It is necessary to break out of this cycle and begin from a perspective that sees economic success not as an end in itself but as a means of achieving social progress. This in turn involves investigating what is meant by social progress – a task made difficult by the fact that social performance is complex and multi-dimensional, with no common metric against which success can be measured, or alternative outcomes ranked. There are no comprehensive social accounts in which performance can be documented and summarised in a single figure: 'The economy grew by 4 per cent last year, but statistics released yesterday reveal that society was 2 per cent worse by the end of the year'. The juxtaposition is bizarre, yet the circumstances described conform to a common perception of what is actually happening.

In order to encourage those responsible for public policy to give attention to social progress, we must identify, at least in broad terms, the main ingredients of what constitutes a 'good society'. We can only do this at the most general level, because *social conditions* require input from society as a whole to identify and prioritise them. Despite this, it is useful to try to articulate what it is about the nature of social conditions that people value. The actions taken to promote increased material prosperity are transforming two important aspects of society that need to be considered. The first relates to the issue of *sustainability*, the ability to maintain current material and non-material living conditions into the future. The second is concerned with the changing nature and consequences of the *social relations* that people face in their lives.

Sustainability has been the focus of attention in discussions of the environmental consequences of economic growth. Although this is an extremely important aspect of sustainability, the emphasis here is on how the social conditions that shape and are shaped by the economy can be made more sustainable, both in their own right and as a way of achieving political sustainability. Social policy has a key role to play in promoting sustainability and unless it can ameliorate the conditions that threaten social cohesion and stability, the fruits of economic prosperity will be temporary.

The nature and consequences of social relations comprise a huge topic that can be addressed at many different levels. This study directs attention to how the development of society affects how individuals relate to each other and to institutions. The main argument is that the increased emphasis given to how people relate to each other as economic actors has seen a lack of attention paid to other relational factors that are also highly valued. The relations between people and the institutions of state and market have become increasingly based on a form of economic rationality that emphasises choice, self-interest and profit. As this process has encroached into more and more areas, the effect has been to replace cooperation by competition and notions of the public good by self-interest.

These shifts have required the state to play an increasing role in enforcement of private property rights so that markets can function effectively to translate choices into commodities and opportunities into resources. Increasingly, the role of the state has shifted from that of provider to that of regulator. This change, in conjunction with the increased competition necessary to realise the benefits of the 'invisible hand', has been necessary to promote trust in the instruments of, and participants in, the market.

At the same time as public confidence in the functioning of markets has increased, other aspects of trust have been eroded by the emphasis given to individualism and commercialism. It is ironic that the decline of trust in other people (as social beings rather than as economic agents) as well as in social institutions generally reduces the ability of government to work with the market sector to promote social capital and economic development (Putnam, 1993). Trust and engagement affect social well-being. We promote social well-being by promoting social and civic trust, where 'social trust is the measure of relationships with strangers and those who are not familiar [and] civic trust is the trust in the institutions of governance which set the rules of engagement' (Cox, 1998, p. 164).

The importance of social capital, as reflected in levels of trust and engagement, has found expression in the emphasis given in the McClure Report on welfare reform to promoting equity through broadening economic and social participation (Reference Group on Welfare Reform, 2000a, 2000b). Yet, there appears to be little recognition that that the restoration of trust will require a reversal of the dominance of economics in policy development. People may trust the information provided by price signals in a free market, but be very cautious about how the functioning of that market will affect their future. The key to improving social relations lies in abandoning the idea of market supremacy in favour of an approach that sees the market as one of the means of achieving social objectives, not as an end in itself.

The neo-liberal agenda

Most of the concerns described above are not new. Trying to ensure that economic activity and the processes that underlie it are consistent with good social outcomes has long been a core policy objective in liberal democracies (Gruen, 1996). In Australia, this trend is reflected in the emergence of economic rationalism as the dominant policy paradigm. This is a doctrine which states, 'that markets and prices are the *only reliable* means of setting a value on anything, and, further, that markets and money can *always*, at least in principle, deliver better outcomes that states and bureaucracies' (Pusey, 1993, p. 14; italics in the original). Implicit in this definition is a challenge to all forms of state intervention, including the policies and programs of the welfare state. Yet the term 'economic rationalism' is inappropriate, as Brennan (1993) and Nevile (1998) have argued. Its propositions are not derived from a rational application of economic principles to policy problems, but reflect a social philosophy that is founded on the idea of a libertarian state. It is this underlying philosophy rather than its application of economic reasoning that makes economic rationalism so hostile to state intervention.

This point is also emphasised by Argy (1998, Chapter 5) who argues that the term 'hard economic liberalism' is more apt, primarily because it draws attention to the importance of philosophical ideas that have little to do with mainstream neo-classical economics. Hard economic liberalism not only regards economic decisions as best left to markets, but also sees the state's role as being kept to a strict minimum, even where there is evidence of market failure or to correct macroeconomic problems. The state should also not attempt to redistribute resources but leave the pattern of economic outcomes to those generated by market forces in response to the choices made by individual consumers and producers motivated by self-reliance and personal responsibility.

These ideas have a historical basis in classical libertarian social philosophy, but give rise to new policy ideas in the context of the extensive state intervention that evolved during the post-war period. For this reason, it is useful to distinguish recent liberal ideas from their classical forebears, and the term 'economic neo-liberalism' can be used for this purpose. (The adjective emphasises the strong reliance on economic reasoning that accompanies most practical policy proposals, although it will be omitted henceforth for ease of exposition). There is a tension between the traditional and radical strands of neo-liberalism that reflects a contradiction between its hostility to and dependence on, traditional conservative values 'in the areas of nation, religion, gender and family' (Giddens, 1994, p. 9). This contradiction reflects a commitment to a fundamentalist conservative philosophy within a framework that is hostile to tradition in its emphasis on market forces and individual responsibility.

However, the attack on neo-liberalism will not succeed if the solutions it offers represent a return to collective provision within a bureaucratically organised and centrally controlled welfare state underpinned by a large public sector. Many of the assumptions underlying the development of the welfare state are no longer valid in a world dominated by *laissez-faire* competition. Some of its ideas were inadequately explored, while many of its programs have not achieved what was expected of them. In its emphasis on identifying and promoting a set of citizens' 'rights' that offered protection against unexpected but largely unavoidable misfortune, the welfare state paid too little attention to the role of individual responsibility and its connection with personal autonomy (Giddens, 1994, Chapter 2).

As these deficiencies have been exposed by the limited effectiveness of welfare programs, so too has the idea of retracing a policy pathway back to a welfare state of earlier decades been abandoned. A crucial element in the attack on neo-liberalism must thus involve theorising, designing and implementing policies that draw upon new ideas that span the traditional left–right divide. There is no going back to a bureaucratic model of standardised state provision because it is not possible to unravel the choices and market mechanisms that are now intertwined in the social fabric. Instead, we need to explore new ways of drawing positively on market forces while allowing individuals to express and achieve their choices in ways that also address traditional concerns with discrimination, poverty and inequality.

Such an exercise must begin from a position informed by the current ideas and policies of neo-liberalism, since it is here that the forces of freedom and responsibility have found concrete expression. We must reflect on the nature and influence of neo-liberal ideas over the last three decades. We must ask how these ideas gained prominence over the traditional arguments that had been used to justify state intervention, not only among those responsible for policy, but also in the hearts and minds of citizens.

Perceptions, priorities and politics

Because social policy rests on value judgments (about ends as well as means) its development is an outcome of the political process. This is not true of economic policy to anything like the same extent, because economists have been able to propagate the myth that economic policy is primarily concerned with technical, rather than normative questions. This does not deny the inevitability of having to face conflicts between the different ends and means of economic policy, but these choices are treated as if they too are technical matters that do not involve value judgments. Social policy, in contrast, cannot avoid confronting moral principles and value judgments and is thus a natural terrain for the playing out of political forces.

These processes extend beyond the debates between political parties that are the lifeblood of representative democracy. The political system is the instrument through which political disputes are resolved and decisions made. But it is the ideals and practical possibilities of different groups in society and how these influence and play out in the context of existing social structures, class interests and power relations that drive the political process. The role of party politics is to articulate ideas, develop programs and mobilise support for the necessary ameliorative legislation and compensatory interventions. This support takes two forms, support within the political system (having 'the numbers') and broad support within the community for the policies and programs that are linked to specific goals. This latter form of support for policy is generally referred to as 'legitimacy'.

The support provided for alternative policies by different community groups depends upon how those policies influence power relations and social status. This in turn depends upon the stated goals of policy (whose interests does it claim to serve?) and the means through which these are achieved (whose interests are threatened?). Both are influenced by the perceptions of participants in the political process about the current state of society and how it will change in response to a change in policy. These perceptions have a critical impact on the design of policy and on the degree of community support and thus legitimacy attached to different options. So it is important to study community perceptions of social (and economic) problems and the likely impact of responses to them in order to understand the nature of political support for policy reforms.

This does not mean that community perceptions cannot be influenced by what happens in the political process. Indeed, one of the main goals of political debate is to influence and shape public opinion in order to gain backing for specific policies or programs. How successful this will be is constrained by the nature of existing perceptions and understandings. Political skill is required to lead the debate, but not to get too far ahead of public opinion, gradually closing the gap between perceptions and possibilities. Policy change is thus generally an incremental process and even 'radical' reforms often turn out to involve only relatively minor (but nonetheless necessary) changes from the *status quo*.

To attract the support of public opinion, it is necessary to understand the nature of public opinion and the perceptions that underpin it. This is part of the bread and butter of party politics, where public opinion surveys and focus group discussions are regularly used to monitor community attitudes to various issues and the potential policy responses to them. The media too, investigates and utilises public opinion to assess the performance of political actors, as well as to explore the degree of support for policy proposals. When reported, these findings can have a powerful influence on public debate and thus on policy development and they are often generated and released for precisely this purpose.

Although public opinion surveys are often influential, the validity of many of them can and should be questioned. Rarely do those who undertake such surveys provide details of the sampling methods and response rates required to check the robustness and general applicability of findings. Often, questions are clumsily constructed or asked in such a way as to produce a desired response from the respondent, and few if any details are provided (or sought) about the characteristics of the respondent, beyond basic demographic information on their age, sex and political affiliation. This makes it very difficult to explore how perceptions vary with the circumstances of those who hold them, so there is no analysis of the structural determinants of the attitudes expressed. Most media-driven sample surveys are undertaken for a specific purpose, have a focus on immediate issues and concentrate primarily on *describing* public opinion rather than *understanding* it.

These features do not prevent these surveys from making a valuable contribution to public debate on contemporary social and economic issues. The surveys still alert politicians (and others) to the nature of public opinion and how it is changing and can provide valuable feedback on emerging social trends and new ideas. However, many public opinion surveys reported in the mainstream media are limited in scope and cannot withstand the rigour expected of academic research. This is beginning to change, though only slowly. The *Australian Social Monitor* published by the Melbourne Institute of Applied Economic and Social Research (MIAESR) attempts to bridge the gap between the attitudinal studies reported in the popular media and the more academic studies of public opinion that are found in the professional research literature (MIAESR, 2001).

In order to generate public opinion data that can contribute to a more informed and reflective understanding of social issues and policies, surveys need to have a specific research focus. Research questions need to be clearly specified and a research instrument needs to be developed that is capable of eliciting information in an informative, but unbiased manner. The survey instrument must be capable of describing current community perceptions and providing a basis for exploring how they relate to the nature of the issues addressed and the circumstances of respondents. Many of the findings reported in this book are based on a survey that was designed to meet these objectives.

The nature and role of social research

Social research is in a state of flux, reflecting changes in perceived priorities, current issues, available expertise and the extent and sources of funding. Australian researchers do not have access to funding from large charitable foundations like the Joseph Rowntree or Nuffield Foundations in the United Kingdom or similar philanthropic institutions in the United States and other countries. As a consequence, Australian social research is heavily dependent on government funding. This has both benefits and costs. On the benefit side, it helps to ensure a strong link between research effort and policy needs, which serves to promote a culture of policy-relevance in social research. Against this, there is the danger that government can concentrate research funding on areas that it sees as relevant to its immediate needs, to the exclusion of curiosity-driven research that may be of greater long-term significance.

This process of specialisation can also undermine longer-term research capability by directing effort into areas that meet the current interests of funding agencies, often to the detriment of exploring new ideas or acquiring new skills and techniques that are seen as having less immediate value. One of the most important ingredients of a healthy research culture is sufficient diversity in the range of skills and interests to support a critical and open process for assessing new theories and evidence. When research becomes too closely aligned with policy, there is a danger that it will be used to justify actions already taken, rather than contributing to knowledge about the design and delivery of new policies and programs.

In order for it to be useful, research must be used and its utilisation can take many different forms. Weiss (1986) identifies seven forms of research utilisation: research as knowledge; research as a solution; research as opinion; research as ammunition; research as a tactic; research as enlightenment; and finally, research as part of the broader intellectual pursuit of society. Each perspective assumes a different role for research and adopts a different model of how research influences policy decisions. Some see research as a process of filling the 'well of knowledge' from which all may draw, while others see research as more like an irrigation system, watering particular fields of knowledge or lubricating some elements of the machinery of policy development. Others again see research as providing ammunition to be used to make a point, or to counter the claims of one's critics.

While the distinctions between alternative ways of utilising research are valuable, they do not capture two aspects of the research process that have assumed increasing importance in the context of a market economy. These relate to dissemination and funding. Because social research studies aspects of the world that surrounds us, it not only delves into the complexities of social problems, but also generates ideas and findings that resonate with people's lives. Key research findings, while generally complex and contingent, are often summarised in media accounts in ways that have a profound impact on how particular problems are perceived in the community. In this process of mass dissemination, the qualifications of the diligent researcher get lost in the search for brevity, while appropriately guarded statements or tentative hypotheses become undisputed 'facts', endorsed by the 'experts' who shape opinion and debate.

These tendencies are reinforced by the fact that a good deal of social research output is a combination of findings, interpretations and values. The statement that 'poverty has risen', for example, may be true, or it may reflect how the differing poverty trends of different groups have been combined, or it may be based on a specific judgment about where to set the poverty line. It may combine aspects of all three, yet these complex and technical issues are rarely discussed (or even mentioned) in the media reporting of the research. This provides fertile ground for those who wish to use research to support a specific point of view (even if it does not), in the process demeaning the value of the research and the professionalism of the research community.

The issue of research funding is not independent of dissemination, since the trend to increased reliance on research commissioned by the agencies of government to address specific questions generally imposes restrictions on the ability of researchers to speak openly about their findings. While often couched in terms of the need to confirm findings or protect the confidentiality of participants, these restrictions generally serve to prevent research from fulfilling its role of providing a critical (in the scientific sense) account of how the world functions. The trend towards research that is problem-solving (and away from research that is curiosity-driven) is not only changing the balance of research, but also how its findings are disseminated and added to the cumulative store of knowledge. At the same time, the pressures on researchers to protect their jobs push them towards problem-solving research, since this is increasingly where the funds are.

These pressures on social research are not all bad. Pure academic research is not free of its own criticisms. The Director of Research at the Joseph Rowntree Foundation in the United Kingdom has argued that the criteria used to judge the performance of researchers remains dominated by indicators such as publications in scholarly journals that bear no necessary relationship to meeting the needs of users (Lewis, 2000). She also notes that 'research findings, in themselves, do not change anything', drawing attention to the role of interpretation and dissemination in determining the usefulness of research findings. Research must be explained to potential users before it can be used and this may require the researcher to take ownership of the actions or changes that are justified by the research they have undertaken (Lewis, 2000, p. 369). The same point can be made about the responsibility of those who report research findings in the media, although here even the best efforts sometimes fail to prevent findings from being distorted or misrepresented.

The important point to emphasise from this discussion is that social research matters, in part because of its close association with what is happening in society and social policy, but also because it has the potential to influence public perceptions and thus shape the debate. While the former may assist in the process of short-term policy development, the latter can be more pervasive and influential over the longer-term. Increasing the impact of social policy research requires greater attention to be paid to examining the processes through which perceptions about economic and social issues are formed and modified. Only then will social research be capable of achieving its full potential to influence public opinion and shape policy development.

Overview

The chapters that follow develop the ideas sketched out above in three main areas. The next two chapters explore aspects of Australian economic and social performance over the last three decades, drawing out the main areas of success and failure and examining community attitudes to change. The statistics demonstrate that while the 1990s were a decade of substantial economic success in many areas, the failure to make substantial progress in reducing unemployment, particularly long-term unemployment, is cause for considerable concern. At the same time, there are clear signs of other unsatisfactory social outcomes relating to various forms of inequality reflecting reliance on policies that give greater emphasis to the role of market forces and others whose distributional effects have been explicit and intentional.

One theme that has guided policy development through the 1980s and 1990s is the increased reliance on economic ideas and market forces in the design and delivery of public programs (Argy, 1998). Increased reliance on market mechanisms to achieve social ends through a range of such actions as privatisation, the introduction of user charges and reliance on service brokers has led to a shift in the role of the state. This shift cannot be sustained because it fails to recognise that many social goals, as well as the means of achieving them, imply the rejection of market principles and are thus based on a fundamental contradiction. It also cannot be sustained as a political strategy because the scope for using economic means alone to achieve social goals is limited. Public opinion also has a critical role to play because it provides the legitimacy on which public policy rests in democratic societies.

Chapter 2 addresses the problems associated with measuring economic and social conditions at the level of both the individual and society, and introduces several concepts and ideas that are important for understanding the arguments developed in later chapters. Three of these that are of particular significance relate to the distinction between economic and social policy, between objective and subjective indicators and between the ends and means of policy. All three have relevance to the perpetual debate surrounding the idea that the welfare state is in crisis. The nature of this 'crisis' is examined and the role and impact of the welfare state investigated, in general and specific areas.

Chapter 3 explores the relationship between public opinion and the legitimacy of the social policies of the welfare state. It focuses on how public opinion is used to shape the debate on key social issues and the role of academic research in identifying the nature and determinants of public opinion. Understanding how public opinion affects policy involves exploring the factors that link values and beliefs to perceptions and attitudes. The normative dimension of social policy implies that values play a major role in determining public support for alternative proposals and a method for capturing different value positions about the role of state and market in a changing economic and social environment is developed.

With the welfare reform debate changing rapidly as governments struggle to adjust their policies to broader contextual changes and with little experimental evidence to guide future policy development, new ideas like mutual obligation are often tested in the waters of public opinion. However, the data collected to explore such issues can also shed light on attitudes to economic and social change and a range of related welfare issues. The *Coping with Economic and Social Change* (CESC) survey, designed and undertaken at the Social Policy Research Centre (SPRC) at the University of New South Wales, was developed with these purposes in mind. Some of the main features of the CESC survey are described in the Appendix, which may be read as a precursor to the results and analysis reported in Chapters 4 to 8. Specific attention is focused on identifying the value frameworks of different respondents on the basis of their attitudes to change, to the causes of social problems and to the role of the state in addressing them.

Chapters 4 to 7 comprise the second section of the book. Each chapter explores one aspect of the changing contemporary socioeconomic landscape using a variety of data, including results from the CESC survey. The goal is to provide an overview of those aspects of Australian society that are central to the debate over the changing role of state and market in promoting economic and social progress. The analysis draws on a range of objective (statistical) and subjective (attitudinal) indicators, highlighting the differences between the two where there is a substantial difference between the perception and the reality. The topics covered in these chapters are employment and unemployment; income and living standards; poverty and social exclusion; and inequality. These four issues reflect the factors and forces driving the welfare reform debate and the analysis attempts to bring the many changes together into a coherent account that makes sense of each of them. What is happening in each area, why and what the community regards as cause and effect are crucial ingredients in the changing policy cauldron and the CESC data are used to examine these issues.

Chapter 4 investigates the nature of labour market change and how it is affecting labour market participants in terms of the kinds of jobs they can expect to obtain, and on what basis. The nature of work has also been undergoing fundamental change. This relates to the kinds of job opportunities that are being generated in the labour market and to unpaid work performed outside the market economy (within the home or on a voluntary basis). The intricate links between work and welfare, or between the labour market and the welfare state, are explored and the dimensions of the unemployment crisis are examined. The main labour market trends are described, and the implications for individual well-being and the design of the welfare system are investigated. The chapter uses the CESC survey data to explore how well the community understands the nature of the labour market, focusing on the causes of unemployment, the policy response and attitudes towards support for the unemployed by the welfare system. Differences in attitudes are related back to the value differences introduced in Chapter 3.

Chapter 5 considers the relationship between income and the standard of living, arguing that this relationship has been changing in ways that help to explain why the increased incomes delivered by economic growth are not reflected in a corresponding rise in perceived standards of living. This raises the question of whether income as conventionally measured is the best indicator of living standards, or whether there is a need for an alternative (or extended) measure. Some possible alternatives are described and reviewed in the context of asking the central question of whether or not growth in the Australian economy has made Australians better off, as reflected in a variety of subjectively expressed indicators. The results indicate that while income does have an important impact on economic well-being, so too do many other factors, implying that a rise in income is neither sufficient nor necessary to produce an increase in the standard of living.

A vigorous debate has surrounded the measurement and trend of poverty in Australia since Prime Minister Hawke pledged during the 1987 federal election campaign to 'abolish child poverty by 1990' (Saunders and Whiteford, 1987). Researchers have disagreed on whether the existing poverty line is still appropriate and whether the notion of poverty itself remains relevant. While disputes continue to rage around the poverty statistics, more fundamental issues surrounding the meaning of poverty have been overlooked. Chapter 6 begins with a consideration of the meaning of poverty, drawing on information describing how poverty is understood in the community and what this implies for its measurement. Estimates of the extent of poverty at the end of the 1990s using both objective and subjective data are presented along with examination of the degree of overlap of the poverty populations identified using the different methods.

The discussion then focuses on the notion of social exclusion and its relationship to the narrower notion of primary (income) poverty. Social exclusion has a more causal and dynamic focus that opens up new avenues of inquiry, but it is not free of its own definitional and measurement ambiguities. Reflecting these, it is argued that social exclusion should not replace poverty as a priority for research or policy, but be used alongside it to gain better insight into the circumstances and constraints facing disadvantaged people. One of the differences between social exclusion and poverty is that the former adopts a more prescriptive view of which activities people should engage in, in order to be participants in society, whereas poverty focuses on the balance between resources and material needs. Underlying the two concepts are thus different notions of need and what is required to achieve an adequate standard of living. The kinds of items that are regarded as necessities in contemporary Australia are explored using the CESC data.

Economic inequality is addressed in Chapter 7, beginning with a discussion of the problems involved in measuring and ranking alternative forms of inequality. Inequality matters not only for its own sake, but also because it gives rise to other social problems, including poor health and, according to some research, increased rates of criminal activity. It is important to identify these effects, since they provide support for redistribution as a general strategy. The role of value judgments is an issue that has to be acknowledged and reflected in the statistical indicators used to measure inequality. Although the distribution of income is an important social indicator in its own right, the distribution of well-being is of greater significance. This again raises questions of how income is defined (discussed in Chapter 5), and the fact that what matters for welfare purposes is the distribution of income *relative to need*. A method for adjusting for differences in need is thus required before it is possible to give a welfare interpretation to the observed differences in family income.

The issue of inequality is central to the debate over the social consequences of neo-liberal economic policies. There is overwhelming evidence that Australian inequality rose sharply through the 1980s, with this trend continuing into the 1990s, placing its reputation as an egalitarian country in jeopardy. The idea that increased inequality is the price that must be paid to achieve economic growth in a modern economy is a myth – even though its proponents have managed to convince many people of its validity. The chapter presents and analyses the changes in income distribution using an approach that allows the impact of different income sources to be assessed, including the redistributive role of income taxes and social security benefits. It is argued that the 'disappearing middle' thesis, though popular in public perception, is not an accurate representation of what has been happening to Australian inequality. Data from the CESC survey are used to examine where Australians think that their own incomes place them in the overall distribution, and these results are used to explain the popularity of the 'disappearing middle' hypothesis. Finally, international comparisons of income inequality and distributional change are used to demonstrate that welfare and tax systems in different countries can produce very different outcomes, even in the face of the common economic pressures associated with globalisation.

Chapters 8 and 9 represent the third section of the book, focusing on what needs to be done to address the problems identified in earlier chapters. A key focus of the current welfare reform debate is the balance between the rights and responsibilities of welfare recipients and taxpayers, as reflected in the idea of mutual obligation. In addressing this issue, Chapter 8 returns to the earlier theme of the crisis of the welfare state, arguing that there is no crisis but that a number of forces for change require choosing between competing priorities. It is argued that the ends and means of welfare must be differentiated as part of any reform strategy and that the links between the welfare system and the labour market are crucial to the success of welfare reform.

Is mutual obligation the answer? This question is examined in the context of what mutual obligation implies for the design of the social security system and the CESC data are used to show how the community perceives and supports welfare provisions and obligation requirements on different groups of the unemployed. Attitudes to mutual obligation requirements are shown to vary with the kinds of groups affected and with the personal characteristics and circumstances of those who are questioned. They also vary systematically with people's broader frame of reference, as reflected in the values they support in relation to the relative roles of state and market in the socioeconomic framework.

Chapter 9 sets out in broad terms the other main aspects of a comprehensive strategy for addressing the many challenges facing the Australian welfare state. Welfare reform, while important, cannot be expected to address all of the issues and other changes are also required. The discussion emphasises the need to identify reform strategies that respond effectively to the actual factors driving economic and social change. Many of them currently do not pass this simple validity test. Mutual obligation has a role to play, though only where it balances (as it has since the social security system was first introduced) the rights and responsibilities of the state and its welfare clients in the light of factors such as adequacy, cost, incentives and ease of administration. It is argued that the trend towards benefit targeting and private welfare provision and delivery is not sustainable and will make the task of effective social policy development more, not less difficult. This is primarily because of the conflicts between the economic principles on which these reforms are based and the principles that underlie what social policy is designed to achieve.

Attention then focuses on identifying the main ingredients of a strategy for bringing about change in public attitudes and state commitment to social policy. Such a strategy takes equality as its central goal, with specific policies designed to achieve redistribution of the existing divisions of income and work. This will involve a combination of welfare and tax policies that are integrated with labour market programs that act specifically to moderate existing, often deeply entrenched inequalities. Ideas and argument are central to the promotion of a healthy research culture that can contribute positively to the policy debate. An attractive feature of the 'Third Way' debate in Britain is the development of Third Way politics as an integral part of the underlying intellectual framework (Giddens, 1998; 2000). The ideas and argument of social policy also need to be brought more directly onto the agendas of those responsible for social policy development in Australia.

Part I
Economic and Social Performance

2 Has the Economy Delivered?

The dominant feature of economic performance throughout the 1970s and 1980s was the emergence of mass unemployment. Increasingly, as economic policy struggled to regain full employment, the focus shifted first onto controlling inflation and then onto a set of intermediate targets that included the budget deficit, the level of taxation, interest rates and the exchange rate. Economic growth returned to previously high levels in the 1980s and 1990s, though much of the modest progress in reducing unemployment was lost during periods of deep recession when unemployment rose rapidly.

The basic intellectual message of the Keynesian revolution – that unemployment is a structural feature of capitalist economies that requires governments to manage aggregate demand – was lost as the neo-liberal agenda took control and portrayed unemployment as a consequence of disequilibrium in the labour market. The solution became focused on policies designed to 'free up' the labour market by removing the institutional barriers to competition and providing increased flexibility through greater reliance on the discipline provided by market forces. Deregulation of the economy made the arguments for state intervention increasingly difficult to sustain because intervention interfered with market forces and undermined international competitiveness. Macroeconomic policy was based on the view that there could be no growth without increased productivity and international trade, no trade without improvements in competitiveness and no hope of achieving these without dismantling the barriers to competition. In a few years, the institutional foundations of the 'Australian settlement' (Castles, 1985; Kelly, 1992; Smyth and Cass, 1998) – wage arbitration, tariff protection and strict state controls on immigration – were swept aside as policy focused on structural adjustment policies designed to set a 'level playing field' for market forces.

What was missing from the new approach was any reference to the well-being of those whose livelihoods were put at risk by the new strategy. The human suffering that accompanied the policy shift was regarded as an unfortunate but inevitable price for re-gaining the economic initiative in an increasingly integrated world economy. The people whose jobs were put at risk by the new policy paradigm were assured that increased competition would open up new opportunities as part of a more sustainable and prosperous future. In political terms, this strategy was effective because it cast those who suffered from the adjustment in terms of lost income, lost employment and lost identity against the larger numbers who would benefit from a more vibrant and competitive economy. Those who resisted economic reform were seen to be acting against the common good by preventing others from reaping the fruits that economic reform had sown across the nation.

Economic neo-liberalism became the dominant mode of thinking among the policy elite (Pusey, 1991), with the two main political parties differing only in the degree of their commitment to its basic principles. Yet many of the programs introduced as part of the economic reform agenda had little intellectual basis in any rational application of economic principles. Instead, as Argy (1998) has argued, the ideas underlying the new policy paradigm were motivated less by economic enlightenment than by a dogmatic adherence to a social philosophy and set of ethical values relating to individual responsibility, choice and self-reliance. Despite its normative philosophy and prescriptive objectives, economic neo-liberalism presented itself as the practical implementation of a project derived from neoclassical economic principles, applying 'technical' arguments in a 'scientific' way to achieve 'agreed' economic objectives such as economic growth, inflation and unemployment. The values embedded in the new economic neo-liberalism were concealed amidst a sea of logic that left no room for intellectual criticism or philosophical doubt.

What was missing from the policy debate was any serious consideration of the role that social policy could play as part of reform process. Its role was reduced to that of picking up the pieces left behind by the sweep of market forces (Saunders, 1993a). At the same time, the resources devoted to social policy were curtailed in the name of fiscal responsibility and the policies themselves were altered to allow a greater role for choice and competition at the expense of setting minimum standards and guaranteed provision. The welfare state and its escalating budget were seen as the greatest obstacles to what most politicians saw as the route to electoral success – tax cuts for the middle classes.

Underlying these policy shifts is a view about the importance of economic ideas and argument described by Bourdieu in the following terms:

> A whole set of presuppositions is being imposed as self-evident: it is taken for granted that maximum growth, and therefore productivity and competitiveness, are the ultimate and sole goal of human actions; or that economic forces cannot be resisted. Or again – a presupposition that is the basis of all the presuppositions of economics – a radical separation is made between the economic and the social, which is left to one side, abandoned to sociologists, as a kind of reject. (Bourdieu, 1998, pp. 30–1)

A basic practical problem with this separation of the economic from the social is that it does not conform to the conditions and aspirations that shape people's lives. Well-being reflects a range of intertwining objective circumstances and subjective perceptions. The separation of the economic and the social reflects traditional academic boundaries that have little relevance to the reality of living standards that depend upon economic factors but are *socially* experienced.

The result is that, in order to assess how well the economy has performed it is necessary to look beyond the economic indicators to examine how social indicators have changed. It is also important to take account of changes in both the objective conditions that affect the standard of living and subjective measures that reveal how people have reacted to the changes taking place. When both indicators are examined, a picture emerges that casts a different light on the claimed economic successes resulting from neo-liberal policies. Even in their own terms, these economic achievements have been surprisingly modest. But when set against the costs they have imposed, the overall picture becomes less obviously a success story and more a source of concern for the future. There is a sense of widespread unease with what economic reform has delivered, and at what price. The artificial separation between the economic and social spheres of which Bourdieu talks is beginning to be re-examined as the damage that economists have inflicted in the names of fiscal responsibility and sound economic management become increasingly apparent.

Assessing economic performance

One of the most fundamental and enduring changes of recent decades has been the opening up of the Australian economy to increased international competition. This has not only caused a re-shaping of the role of key institutions in domestic capital and labour markets, it has been part of a broader trend towards increased integration of national economies into a new global trading system. Critics of globalisation have argued that the ability of individual countries to pursue independent domestic economic policies has been circumscribed. However, while it is true that globalisation is associated with a closer alignment of national economic prospects in the short-term, there is still considerable scope for national policies to remain differentiated in the longer-run. A glance at any set of economic statistics covering countries belonging to the Organisation for Economic Cooperation and Development (OECD) reveals sufficient cross-country variation among even this most closely integrated set of economies to dispel the myth that there is no scope to set and seek different national priorities.

At the same time, however, the emergence of an increasingly integrated international economy has implications for how to assess domestic economic performance. It is common to hear Australian politicians proclaiming Australian economic performance to be 'the best' or 'among the best' in the world. Although these claims rarely stack up against the evidence, their significance lies in the acknowledgment that the appropriate frame of reference for evaluating domestic economic performance is against the backdrop of the world economy. For practical purposes, this is often restricted to the group of high-income, industrial countries that belong to the OECD. This is partly because there is far better coverage of comparative economic data for OECD countries, but also because the OECD includes the largest economies in terms of their impact on world trade and growth.

Macroeconomic performance

Table 2.1 compares Australian growth, inflation and labour market performance since 1983 with that of the OECD area as a whole. The comparisons cover the two seven-year periods of economic recovery 1983–90 and 1992–99 and thus exclude the recession years of the early 1980s and 1990s. The figures show that, relative to the OECD as a whole, Australia's economic performance over the last two economic upswings has been good. Economic and employment growth have both been above the OECD average and inflation fell far more sharply in the 1990s in Australia than elsewhere. The bad news is that Australia's unemployment record is not so good, and its relative performance has declined.

Table 2.1 Comparisons of Australian and OECD macroeconomic performance

	Australia		OECD	
Indicator	1983–90	1992–99	1983–90	1992–99
Economic growth[a]	3.7	4.2	3.3	2.6
Inflation[b]	7.3	1.6	7.1	4.3
Employment growth[c]	2.5	1.6	1.5	0.9
Unemployment rate[d]	7.9	9.0	7.3	7.3
'Happiness index'[e]	6.2	5.8	4.8	3.5
'Misery index'[f]	15.2	10.6	14.4	11.6
'Net misery index'[g]	9.0	4.8	9.6	8.1

Notes: (a) annual average rate of growth of real GDP; (b) annual average rate of increase in the private consumption deflator; (c) average annual average growth in total employment; (d) annual average unemployment rate (national definitions); (e) the sum of economic growth and employment growth; (f) the sum of inflation and unemployment; (g) misery index minus happiness index.

Source: *OECD Economic Outlook*, Reference Statistics, various issues.

Even so, in terms of the summary 'happiness' and 'misery' indices, Australia out-performed the OECD in both decades, particularly the 1990s. This, however, is largely attributable to the rapid decline in the inflation rate in Australia from slightly above the OECD average in the 1980s to well below it in the 1990s. This decline has been accompanied by rising unemployment in Australia, compared with the stability experienced in other countries – hardly cause for celebration. Overall, the statistics in Table 2.1 do not reflect well on economic performance during a period of significant economic reform; the market has had a greater say in all OECD economies, but thus far its voice has brought little comfort to those economies that have engineered its increasing importance.

Size of government

One area where major differences remain between OECD countries is in relation to the size of government. These differences are important because they illustrate the extent to which the state has commandeered resources to achieve social goals in the post-war period. They also provide the starting point from which to assess the impact of neo-liberal policies designed to reduce state intervention in order to make way for an increased market sector.

Statistics on the size of general government outlays and receipts relative to GDP bear this out (although these figures exclude public enterprise activity that has in many countries been declining significantly as a result of privatisation). Table 2.2 compares the relevant averages for the same periods as Table 2.1. In terms of government spending, Australia spends about 4 percentage points of GDP less than the OECD average.

Table 2.2 Comparisons of government spending and receipts in Australia and the OECD (percentages of GDP)

Indicator	Australia 1983–90	Australia 1992–99	OECD 1983–90	OECD 1992–99
Government outlays	35.2	34.5	39.3	39.1
– minimum	–	–	32.0 (Japan)	21.6 (Korea)[a]
				32.4 (USA)
– maximum	–	–	60.6 (Sweden)	61.4 (Sweden)
Current receipts	34.1	32.0	36.4	36.1
– minimum	–	–	30.4 (USA)	24.0 (Korea)[a]
				30.0 (USA)
– maximum	–	–	61.1 (Sweden)	57.1 (Denmark)

Note: (a) Korean data for the earlier period are not available.
Source: See Table 2.1.

This is a significant difference, and it would require a spending increase of over 13 per cent (in the latter period) across all programs to bring Australia up to the OECD average. In revenue terms, Australia is below the OECD average by a similar amount and the gap has been widening. In terms of individual country differences, the size of the government sector in Australia lies towards the lower end of the OECD spectrum. In 1999, only three countries (the United States, Ireland and Korea) had a lower spending ratio than Australia, while the tax burden was lower in only the same three countries, plus Japan.

Table 2.3 compares social expenditures against the background of differences in total government spending and revenues in OECD countries. Total government spending varies across OECD countries, from 22.1 per cent of GDP in Korea to 58.7 per cent in Sweden. Australia's spending ratio, at just 33.2 per cent, is well below the OECD average of 42.8 per cent and is lower in only two other countries (Korea and the United States). The last column shows that revenue levels also vary considerably across the OECD, with Australia again at the lower end. Relative to other OECD countries, the case that Australia is highly taxed (as opposed to being over-taxed) just does not stand up against the evidence. Not surprisingly, revenue tends to be lowest where spending is lowest, although there is no tendency for those who spend most to have the largest revenue shortfall.

The variation in the ratio of social expenditure to GDP is as great as it is for total spending or total revenue, with Australia again towards the lower end of the spectrum. However, there is a strong relationship between social spending and total spending which implies that the cross-country variation in the ratio of social to total government spending is much lower than for either of the two spending aggregates. The ratio of spending on social security transfers to GDP also varies considerably and tends to be lower in countries where the social spending ratio itself is lower. In broad terms therefore, total government spending is high where social spending is high, and social spending tends to be high when spending on social security transfers is high. It follows that Australia's low level of social security spending – a reflection of its targeted approach that provides means-tested benefits to cover specific contingencies – explains why social spending and total spending are both towards the bottom of the OECD spending ranking.

The comparisons in Table 2.3 show that, in 1995 social security spending in Australia was 4.3 percentage points of GDP below the OECD average. With GDP in Australia in 1995–96 equal to $508 billion (ABS, 2001a, Table 29.1), this implies that social security spending would have to increase by around *$21.8 billion* to bring it up to the OECD average. Alternatively, this can be viewed as the amount, in comparative terms,

Has the Economy Delivered? 29

Table 2.3 General government outlays, welfare state spending and taxation in OECD countries, 1997 (percentages)

Country	Total government outlays as a % of GDP	Social expenditure as a % of GDP	Social expenditure as a % of total outlays	Social security expenditure as a % of GDP(a)	Current tax and non-tax receipts as a % of GDP
Australia	33.2	18.1	54.5	8.5	32.7
Austria	50.7	25.4	50.1	14.7	48.9
Belgium	48.5	23.6	48.7	18.1	46.8
Canada	42.4	17.0	40.1	10.5	43.2
Czech Republic	40.9	19.8	48.4	11.6	38.9
Denmark	56.9	30.5	53.6	17.6	57.0
Finland	51.3	29.3	57.1	21.1	49.8
France	52.8	29.6	56.1	16.2	49.7
Germany	46.3	26.6	57.5	14.9	43.7
Greece	42.8	22.2	51.9	11.0	38.9
Iceland	33.8	18.0	53.3	8.5	33.8
Ireland	33.2	17.9	53.9	10.5	33.8
Italy	49.9	26.9	53.9	16.4	47.2
Japan	34.9	14.4	41.3	6.1	31.6
Korea	22.1	5.1	23.1	0.7	24.5
Netherlands	44.6	25.1	56.3	17.2	43.4
New Zealand	38.9	20.7	53.2	11.6	40.9
Norway	43.8	25.4	58.0	16.4	51.7
Poland	46.0	25.9	56.3	–	43.0
Portugal	43.5	18.7	43.0	8.9	41.0
Spain	40.0	20.9	52.3	13.5	36.8
Sweden	58.7	33.3	56.7	18.8	57.0
United Kingdom	40.9	21.6	52.8	15.0	38.9
United States	31.4	16.0	51.0	6.9	30.5
Average	42.8	22.2	51.0	12.8	41.8

Note: (a) These estimates are for 1995.
Source: OECD Social Expenditure Database; *OECD Economic Outlook, December 2000* Annex Tables; and Whiteford (2000, Figure 5).

that targeting and other measures have saved from the welfare budget, providing the basis for Australia's comparatively low level of taxation. But even if taxation were 4.3 percentage points of GDP higher, the overall tax burden in Australia would still be below the OECD average by more than 4 percentage points of GDP.

The figures in Table 2.3 provide no support for the argument that, in the face of globalisation, there is increased pressure for OECD countries to pursue similar economic and budgetary policies. In fact, there is no such trend apparent in these figures on the size and structure of government spending in OECD countries. If there were a relationship between the size of government and the ability to remain competitive (as some proponents of economic liberalism claim), several OECD countries would have been driven into bankruptcy some time ago. Nor is there any evidence to support the thesis that government spending and tax levels in OECD countries are converging. There has always been great variation in the size of government across the OECD region (Saunders and Klau, 1985), and Table 2.3 provides no evidence that this has changed over the last two decades.

Although the differences in tax and spending levels are open to alternative interpretation, of more importance is the fact that the living standards and well-being of individuals depend less on what has happened to tax and spending aggregates than on what has happened at the program level. Behind any downward trend in the total spending figures lie school closures, increasing class sizes, lengthening hospital waiting lists, declining standards of public services and social security cuts. While these reductions have been accompanied by lower taxes, the tax cuts have tended to benefit different groups from those who have borne the brunt of the squeeze on spending. Changes in the size and structure of government spending and taxation have important distributional effects on the employment levels, disposable incomes and overall living standards of different groups in the population, as later chapters will demonstrate. It is the impact of the cuts at this level of detail that matters for whether or not they are seen positively by the community, as opposed to those who set the policy agenda.

Income and consumption trends

The economic growth of recent decades has, not surprisingly, found its way into higher levels of household income and rising levels of consumption expenditure. Figures 2.1 and 2.2 show the trends in these two indicators since the end of the 1950s. Both series have been adjusted to reflect increases in prices and population growth. The cyclical swings in economic activity, reflected in the recessions of the early 1980s and 1990s are apparent in the disposable income data, as is the impact of periods of strong income growth in the late 1980s and after the mid-1990s (Figure 2.1). These short-run fluctuations in household income are not reflected to the same extent in household consumption (Figure 2.2). This series displays a more smoothly uninterrupted upward trend, reflecting the tendency for household savings to be used to offset income swings in order to protect living standards from temporary economic fluctuations.

Between 1979–80 and 1999–2000, household disposable income increased by more than a quarter (26.7 per cent) while household

Has the Economy Delivered? 31

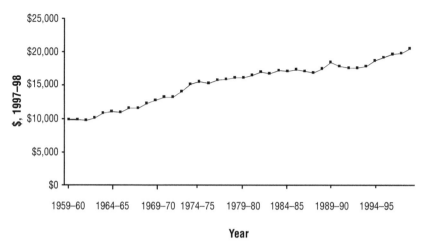

Figure 2.1 Movements in real household disposable income per capita, 1959–60 to 1998–99 ($ 1997–98 prices)

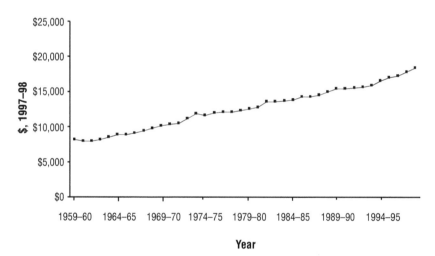

Figure 2.2 Movements in real household final consumption expenditure per capita, 1959–60 to 1998–99 ($ 1997–98 prices)

consumption rose by almost a half (49.4 per cent), even after adjusting for increased prices and population growth. Although there is some concern in the fact that consumption growth has outstripped income growth (implying a decline in household savings and thus in the ability to support future consumption), the period has clearly been marked by increased economic prosperity. Why all the fuss?

One possible reason is that average household size has been declining steadily throughout the post-war period, particularly since the 1960s (Table 2.4). Between 1966 and 1996, the number of single-person households almost quadrupled, increasing from 11.8 per cent to 22.8 per cent of all households. As average household size has fallen, the financial cost of supporting a given standard of living within households has increased. Fewer persons per household reduces the benefits from economies of scale in living costs, implying that the aggregate increases shown in Figures 2.2 and 2.3 exaggerate the increase in income and consumption benefits that economic growth has produced for individual household members.

Although the decline in household size is part of the explanation, other factors have also had a profound effect. These relate to changes in the economic and social conditions that are themselves in part a consequence of the actions taken to improve macroeconomic performance. Many of the policies introduced over the 1980s and 1990s have resulted in a more market-oriented economy that has generated increased levels of output against the background of high unemployment, growing economic insecurity and rising inequality. These developments have obvious implications for living standards, not just for those affected directly but also for those who perceive these conditions to be a potential future threat.

Unemployment

Increased unemployment hangs like a dark cloud of despair and lost opportunity over the growing material prosperity implied by the trends in Figures 2.1 and 2.2. Many of those who have experienced the increased

Table 2.4 Trends in household size, 1947–96

Year	Number of occupants per dwelling: 1	2 – 4	5 and over	Total number of dwellings	Total population in private dwellings	Average household size
1947	152,029	1,168,781	552,813	1,873,623	7,026,760	3.75
1954	213,088	1,523,238	607,095	2,343,421	8,314,362	3.55
1961	285,360	1,743,173	753,412	2,781,945	9,870,494	3.55
1966	371,861	1,958,351	821,714	3,151,926	10,930,500	3.47
1971	497,816	2,319,179	853,559	3,670,554	10,955,250	2.98
1981	839,302	3,041,213	788,396	4,668,911	13,918,445	2.98
1991	1,130,749	3,759,850	751,797	5,642,396	15,717,020	2.78
1996	1,432,820	4,122,479	726,518	6,281,817	16,751,439	2.67

Source: Census of Population and Housing, various years.

levels of income, consumption and living standards associated with a growing economy have done so (if unintentionally) on the backs of the unemployed. Economic growth has not succeeded in bringing the level of unemployment down to anything close to an acceptable level, with the result that mass unemployment has become a permanent feature of the economic landscape of the last quarter of the twentieth century.

The level of unemployment has been steadily rising throughout much of the period since 1960, although there has also been a clear pattern of cyclical variation in unemployment as the economy moves into and out of recession (Figure 2.3). After skyrocketing in the wake of the 1973 oil shock, the pattern of movements in unemployment through the 1980s and 1990s has been dominated by the recessions of 1981–83 and 1990–92. Part of the rapid increase experienced between 1981 and 1983 (when unemployment increased from 314,000 to 635,000), was offset by 1990 when strong employment growth had brought unemployment down to 420,000. Recession then sent it back up to 831,000 by 1992, after which it fell back again to 566,000 by June 2000. What is clear from these trends is that had the dramatic increases in unemployment in the early 1980s and 1990s been avoided, unemployment could by now have been far closer to a level consistent with full employment. An important lesson to emerge from recent economic experience is that the key to controlling unemployment thus lies in avoiding economic recession.

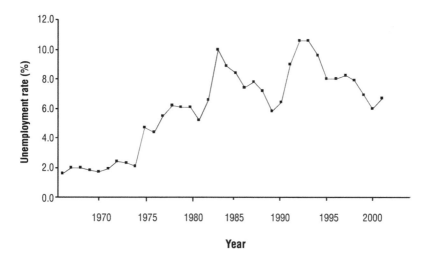

Figure 2.3 Trend in the unemployment rate, 1966–2001[a]

Note: (a) Figures refer to August in 1966, May in 1967 to 1978 and June since 1979.
Source: *The Labour Force*. ABS Catalogue No 3602, various issues.

The driving force behind movements in the overall unemployment figures is a labour market characterised by considerable short-term flows into and out of the unemployment pool. These flows have been accompanied by changes in the structure of employment, between male and female employment, as well as between part-time and full-time jobs. In broad terms, recent increases in unemployment in recession have mainly been associated with declines in the full-time male employment to population ratio, while declines in unemployment have mainly been linked with increases in the female full-time and part-time employment to population ratios (Borland and Kennedy, 1998a).

Over the two decades to 1997, the average monthly flows into and out of the unemployment pool were equivalent to between 1.3 and 1.5 per cent of the labour force, with the in-flow rising and falling with the level of unemployment and the out-flow moving in the opposite direction (Borland and Kennedy, 1998a). These patterns are reflected in movements on and off unemployment benefit for those receiving social security payments. Over the decade to 1997, between 55 per cent and 71 per cent of those coming onto benefit had moved off again by the end of the financial year (Whiteford, 2000, Table 11). Even in 1996–97, when over 61 per cent of those who joined the system had left again by the end of June 1997, almost half (48.6 per cent) of the 802,000 people receiving unemployment assistance had been doing so for more than twelve months.

Unfortunately, the changed labour market circumstances that correspond to these flows do not equally affect all of the unemployed, and a core of long-term unemployment (those unemployed for twelve months or more) has emerged. The rate of long-term unemployment tends to mirror the overall unemployment rate though lagging slightly behind it (ABS, 2000a). In April 2001, 150,000 people had been unemployed for one year or more, well down from the maximum figure of 366,000 in March 1993 (ABS, 2000a) but still far too high. Long-term unemployment is more responsive to falling employment during recession than overall unemployment, reinforcing the point that just a few recession years of low or negative economic growth 'have very significant medium-term implications for long-term unemployment' (Chapman and Kapuscinski, 2000, p. v).

More detailed examination of the characteristics of those who have been out of work for a year or more provides further insight into the nature of entrenched unemployment. Around two-thirds of the long-term unemployed are male, over half are over 35, three-fifths are not married, but over 90 per cent are seeking full-time work (Table 2.5). The fact that so few of the long-term unemployed are in the younger age categories is explained by the fact that these groups are a small proportion of the total labour force. Despite this, the rate of long-term unemployment is higher among the 15–19-year-old group (17.8 per cent) and the 20–24-year-old group (10.3 per cent) than among those aged over 25. The threat of long-term unemployment is thus particularly great among those younger people who are in the labour force, although it is also an obvious concern among older workers (who may be less able to adjust to its impact). The fact that the vast majority of those who have been without work for at least a year are still looking for full-time work illustrates the remarkable resilience of the long-term unemployed.

When the unemployment benefit system was introduced in Australia in the 1940s, it was not seen as having to provide income support for extended periods. A system that may provide an adequate safety net for a period of weeks or even months is not able to fund the purchases of new furniture, clothes and other items that inevitably arise if joblessness becomes long-term. Long-term unemployment has pernicious consequences for those affected by it including loss of self-esteem, a decline in psychological well-being and the financial stresses one would expect to face after living on a very low income for a prolonged period (Saunders and Taylor, 2002, forthcoming). Long-term unemployment also feeds on itself, particularly in a competitive labour market. Long periods of unemployment cause the skills of those affected to become obsolete or simply eroded, while employers are reluctant to take on what are often seen to be 'inferior' workers. To become long-term unemployed is thus, for many, to be condemned to remain out of work indefinitely.

Table 2.5 Selected characteristics of the long-term unemployed, April 2001

Characteristic	Males ('000)	Males (%)	Females ('000)	Females (%)	Persons ('000)	Persons (%)
AGE:						
15–19	8.5	8.7	7.4	14.3	15.9	10.6
20–24	15.1	15.4	7.4	14.3	22.5	15.0
25–34	23.1	23.5	10.9	21.1	34.0	22.7
35–54	36.6	37.3	24.0	46.4	60.0	40.1
55+	14.8	15.1	2.0	3.9	16.8	11.2
Total	**98.1**	**100.0**	**51.7**	**100.0**	**149.8**	**100.0**
MARITAL STATUS:						
Married	42.7	43.5	16.7	32.3	59.4	39.7
Not married	55.4	56.5	34.9	67.5	90.4	60.3
LOOKING FOR:						
Full-time work	90.5	92.3	38.3	74.1	128.8	86.0
Part-time work	7.6	7.7	13.4	25.9	21.0	14.0

Source: *The Labour Force, April 2001*, ABS Catalogue No. 6203.0.

Economic insecurity

Although unemployment is the most perilous of all labour market states, its underlying causes reverberate throughout the entire labour force. Increasingly, those in employment have been exposed to the fear that they too will suffer the misery associated with unemployment. It is often argued that rising unemployment is a more serious problem than high unemployment, because while those affected by the existing level of unemployment are known, everyone is potentially at risk when unemployment is rising. The number of people who are unemployed is too small in relation to the total population to have an impact on the outcome of elections. In contrast, the numbers potentially threatened by rising unemployment can make a difference, so there is a strong incentive for politicians to ensure that unemployment is falling in the run-up to an election, whatever its level.

As globalisation and trade liberalisation have made domestic companies more prone to external competition, increasing numbers of workers perceive their jobs to be under threat. At the same time, there is increased awareness that governments are less prepared to support struggling businesses than they were in the past, a reflection of the 'level playing field' approach to structural adjustment policy discussed earlier. In these circumstances, in combination with high unemployment, it is no surprise that insecurity about job prospects and the economy more generally has increased. In part, growing economic insecurity reflects an unwillingness to let go of a past in which the majority of jobs were long-term career jobs and where overall labour mobility was low. Labour market deregulation has produced a more dynamic labour market characterised by increased rates of job creation and job loss. This is a problem when the new and old jobs differ in terms of the skills they require, the hours of work attached to them and where they are located.

For the individual, changing jobs often involves having to acquire new skills, or is accompanied by more disruptive events, such as having to move house and lose contact with friends and community links. Children may have to change school, houses may have to be sold and bought (often at considerable cost), and all of the effort of establishing one's place in the community has to begin again. New relationships have to be developed, in the workplace as well as in the neighbourhood. Not surprisingly, those who support structural adjustment because of its beneficial economic effects rarely consider these social effects. These adjustment costs are associated with the increased levels of economic insecurity that detract from the benefits of rising incomes and material progress reported earlier. Increasingly, people may *be* better off, but not *feel* better off because of the costs (real and anticipated) associated with the adjustment process.

Although changes in economic insecurity have been the subject of recent intense debate in Australia, the evidence on how economic insecurity has changed is sparse and open to alternative interpretation. There are many reasons for this, most of them linked to the nature of insecurity (OECD, 1997a). For someone who has a job, the degree of insecurity will depend on the perceived likelihood of losing that job, and on the expected economic cost to be faced as a consequence. While the actual likelihood of job loss depends upon labour market conditions, beliefs and feelings about job loss will reflect subjective assessments of the expected length of joblessness and the financial cost to be borne while unemployed. Quantifying these factors involves complex calculations that depend upon projected changes in the labour market, as well as perceptions about the generosity of, and access to, unemployment benefits, and it is not surprising that clear trends in job insecurity are difficult to discern.

Reflecting these considerations, the empirical evidence on economic insecurity is mixed. While public opinion data supports the view that perceptions of job insecurity increased in Australia in the 1990s (Kelley, Evans and Dawkins, 1998), the objective labour market indicators show that actual job stability has increased (Wooden, 1998; 1999). The survey evidence reported in Chapter 4 suggests that Australians have a wide variety of views on economic insecurity, with those who express concern about losing their jobs and control over their destiny more generally outnumbered by those who do not. Other evidence reported by Pusey (1998, Figure 7) indicates that job security is an issue for 'middle Australia', yet many feel that there is little that government can do to improve things. These concerns find similar expression in the views of the 'silent majority', showing that many Australians 'feel powerless to control their lives in the face of rapid economic restructuring and social change' (Eckersley, 1999, Box 2). Despite the problems inherent in defining and measuring economic insecurity (and thus in evaluating how it has changed over time), the evidence is beginning to show that a considerable portion of the population is affected by the perception of economic insecurity.

Economic inequality

How incomes are distributed in society does not appear to be something that can affect people in quite the same way as unemployment or economic insecurity. While well-being mainly depends upon one's own income, its continuity and what it can buy, how it compares with the income of others also matters. How widely incomes are dispersed will affect the nature of the society, including the types of goods that can be purchased and the kinds of activities that can be enjoyed, and will thus affect how a given income can be translated into the pleasures associated with owning and doing things. The desire to 'keep up with the Jones's' confirms the reality that relative living standards matter, as do popular understandings of what it means to be defined as either rich or poor. Inequality can also affect living standards indirectly, through its social impacts on such things as health status, psychological well-being and criminal activity. Finally, inequality raises philosophical questions about justice and morality, opportunities and rights that affect living standards through a variety of complex channels.

Although there are many dimensions of inequality, differences in income are of particular significance in capitalist societies where income provides access to the fruits of economic progress. Largely for this reason, governments throughout the world have a long history of implementing tax and social programs designed to reduce the degree of income inequality that emerges from the processes of market production and exchange. In pursuing this objective, government is constrained by the willingness of the population to support through taxation the public programs that redistribute income (and opportunities), by community attitudes that define the acceptable limits of inequality and by the degree of income inequality that is generated by the market. These shape the ability to implement redistributive policies and how much effort is required to achieve a given distributional target in ways that may vary, over time and between countries.

One of the key pressures of recent decades has been for the distribution of market incomes to widen as increased reliance has been placed on market mechanisms to achieve economic goals. These pressures have not, however, resulted in a common pattern of distributional change because of the intervening factors mentioned above. Even so, many countries have experienced increased inequality, and this trend has given rise to community concern over the social costs of increased inequality. This issue is explored in detail in Chapter 7, where the change in Australian income inequality is investigated and compared with that experienced in other OECD countries.

Although the complex statistical indicators used to measure inequality are far removed from the everyday experience of most people, the measures reflect observable social trends that manifest themselves in the extremes of inequality – poverty and affluence. The fact that inequality has increased by so much and over such a prolonged period will have affected how people respond to the conditions that have allowed this to occur. There is evidence from public opinion surveys that the growing gap between rich and poor has been of concern to many Australians. How deep these concerns go is another matter, although the possibility that the economic prosperity of some has been built on the economic misery of others will have made many feel less content with their economic gains.

Satisfaction and financial stress

When they are asked about their economic circumstances and life satisfaction, most people respond positively. For example, when asked in 1995 about their standard of living, over 85 per cent of Australians reported that they were satisfied with it, 9 per cent had mixed feelings and only 3 per cent indicated total dissatisfaction (Eckersley, 1999, Table 2). In contrast to this subjective information, a recent analysis of the objective conditions of financial stress among Australian households in 1998–99 undertaken by the Australian Bureau of Statistics (ABS) reveals a somewhat different picture (McColl, Pietsch and Gatenby, MPG, 2001). Households were asked whether or not they had experienced each of a range of conditions associated with financial stress over the previous year. The conditions included spending more than was received as income, not being able to raise up to $2,000 in an emergency, not being able to pay bills on time, having to pawn something, going without meals and seeking assistance from a welfare or community organisation (MPG, Table 1).

The results are summarised in Table 2.6. They indicate that almost one-fifth of all households were unable to raise $2000 if they needed to within a week and a similar proportion could not afford a night out once a fortnight. Significant proportions of households had spent more than they received or could not pay their bills on time, while around one in ten had sought financial help from friends or family or could only afford second-hand clothes. Few signs of material prosperity in many of these indicators! Not surprisingly, there is a clear 'deprivation gradient' with a higher proportion exhibiting each stress indicator in the lower quintiles (or fifths) of the income distribution. Overall, around one-quarter of all households in the bottom quintile of the income distribution had experienced *five or more* of the fifteen separate financial stress indicators identified in the ABS study over the previous twelve months, while a similar proportion had experienced between two and four conditions. In contrast, very few households in the top quintile had experienced financial stress, and those that had faced fewer than four separate conditions.

These results highlight the degree of inequality that exists in the economic fortunes of Australian households (an issue examined in greater detail in Chapter 7) and show how a market economy has not benefited everyone equally – even during a period of sustained economic growth. Of greater concern is the fact that the stress indicators reflect circumstances that would be widely regarded as not acceptable by the majority

Table 2.6 Incidence of financial stress by household income quintile, 1998–99 (percentage of households reporting each indicator)

Financial stress indicator	First	2nd	3rd	4th	5th	All
Spent more money than received in last year	22	20	16	9	6	15
Unable to raise $2000 in a week if needed	36	28	15	12	5	19
Could not pay utility or telephone bills on time	26	22	15	11	6	16
Could not pay car registration or insurance on time	10	8	7	5	2	7
Pawned or sold something	9	6	3	2	1	4
Went without meals	5	5	2	1	2	3
Could not afford to heat home	5	4	1	1	—	2
Sought assistance from a welfare agency	8	6	2	1	—	3
Sought financial help from friends or family	16	12	9	8	4	10
Could not afford a night out once a fortnight	32	30	20	11	3	19
Could only afford second-hand clothes most of the time	24	20	9	4	2	12

Source: McColl, Pietsch and Gatenby, 2001, Table 1.

of Australians, including being unable to pay basic household bills or having to rely on second-hand clothes. Those who have experienced these conditions have not only missed out on economic prosperity, but have experienced what many would regard as unacceptable deprivation bordering on poverty.

The conditions portrayed in Table 2.6 suggest that economic growth has not brought everyone's standard of living up to an acceptable level. It is also possible that even those who have experienced increased incomes have had the benefits offset to some degree by other factors that have accompanied economic growth. This latter possibility is consistent with other survey evidence. For example, as noted in the previous chapter, when asked to identify critical national priorities, many Australians give less support to maintaining a high standard of living than to issues associated with the quality of education, health, the environment, the gap between rich and poor and creating work opportunities for all Australians (Eckersley, 1999).

The concerns that underlie these findings are supported in a report from the Productivity Commission, which concluded that:

> [W]hile the economic trends have been positive and strong in the 1990s, other 'quality of life' issues also concern a large section of the community. (Parham, Barnes, Roberts and Kennett, 2000, p. xv)

These findings highlight the importance attached to the social conditions that influence people's standards of living over and above the impact of economic factors such as income and material consumption. Although the economy delivered rising levels of income for most Australians over the 1990s, there are clear signs that this involved changes to the social fabric that detracted from the gains in living standards.

Economic and social policy

Discussion of the relationship between economic and social policy requires being able to distinguish between them. This is not easy. Traditionally, economic policy is defined in terms of policies aimed at achieving its goals of economic growth, unemployment, inflation and the balance of payments – with the ultimate goal being to achieve internal and external balance simultaneously. These are all macroeconomic, or economy-wide targets and attaining them involves adjusting (or announcing the decision not to adjust) policy instruments in the fields of monetary policy (interest rates), fiscal policy (the budget deficit) and trade policy (the exchange rate).

More recently, economic policy has concentrated on establishing the conditions for microeconomic reform (or structural adjustment) designed to improve productivity and increase competitiveness by promoting increased efficiency in the use of economic resources. This has involved a shift away from ultimate policy goals that translate directly into living standards onto intermediate policy goals such as the rate of productivity growth, or policy instruments such as the budget deficit that create the conditions for increased living standards but do not themselves improve living standards.

The most significant example of this shift from ultimate to intermediate policy targets and to policy instruments is in the area of fiscal policy. Here, the budget deficit (rather than the level of unemployment consistent with internal balance or full employment) has been promoted as the main policy target. This change partly reflects the attempt to divert attention away from the unemployment problem, as governments have found it easier to control the budget deficit than to reduce the unemployment rate, and 'fiscal responsibility' has become the political trademark of successful economic management. What is most disturbing about this trend is that it lacks any basis in sound economic reasoning. The size of the budget deficit itself bears no relation to how total demand affects the performance of the economy. What matters for macroeconomic purposes is how *changes* in the level of total demand are affected by *changes* in the size of the budget deficit and the goal of fiscal policy is to manipulate the budget so as to stabilise the economy at full employment.

It is true that a sequence of budget deficits will cause public debt to increase and can create economic problems in the future. Budget deficits have to be financed and this can lead to inflation (as it did in the 1970s) or involve higher interest payments on government debt (as happened in the 1980s). Government debt must eventually be reduced and this will require a combination of spending cuts and tax increases, with the budget moving into a temporary surplus. But trying to establish a budget surplus as a *permanent* feature of the fiscal landscape makes no more sense than having a *permanent* deficit. A longer-term (or structural) budget surplus means that the government is imposing more taxes or charges than is required to fund its programs and this makes no sense when unemployment is high and other social priorities are not being addressed.

A second reason to support a budget surplus is based on the view that high levels of government spending and taxation give rise to undesirable disincentive effects and otherwise distort market signals, resulting in reduced efficiency, lower levels of labour supply and productivity and lower living standards. According to this view, government must be made smaller to remove these detrimental effects on economic performance, and the best way to do this is to lower government spending and create a budget surplus, which can then be dissipated through tax cuts. The resulting budget surplus is not permanent, but a feature of the transition from big to small government. This line of argument is based on a view about the size of government and significance of the effects of government activity on the behaviour of individuals and on the economy as a whole, which has little sound evidential basis. Most studies accept that while these negative effects can exist, they are not as strong or widespread as is often presumed (Atkinson, 1995a, Chapter 6).

Market forces, market failures

As a consequence of these trends and arguments, economic policy has focused on the technical task of achieving an efficient allocation of resources and become disconnected from the actual economic circumstances of the population. This has increased reliance on the theory of perfect competition that supports the view that efficiency requires the removal of barriers that impede the free functioning of marker forces. This approach is not only naïve in its application of economic principles, but also ignores the many ways in which reality divergences from the rarefied world of the economics textbook. By setting perfect competition as the benchmark against which to assess allocative efficiency, the approach ignores market failure and the many other imperfections that are widespread features of all capitalist economies. In reality, the existence of market failure provides an in-principle case for state intervention designed to correct or adjust for its consequences.

To assess state interventions (often regarded as part of social policy) against a benchmark that effectively ignores the reason for their existence is thus not a sensible basis on which to judge their overall (social and economic) impact. Policy prescriptions derived from the market model favour market-type solutions that reflect the assumptions on which the model itself is based. Not surprisingly, social policy is seen as imposing heavy economic costs (in terms of distorted price signals and disincentive effects) because its interventions are a departure from a textbook model that assumes away the problems that social policy is addressing. This inbuilt bias against social (and other) policies undermines the claim that economic analysis of policy issues is scientific and objective. Market imperfections need to be acknowledged and reflected in the economic analysis used to assess the impact of social policy, yet this presents formidable intellectual challenges and rarely features in the policy debate.

While the focus of economic policy has been on improving material conditions (including the circumstances that produce them), social policy has traditionally been concerned with the conditions in society at large: with how the resources and opportunities generated by the economy are distributed, rather than with the efficiency with which they are used. Social security programs are designed to achieve greater equality between those with market incomes and those unable to participate in employment for reasons of old age, sickness or disability, caring responsibilities, or unemployment. Education and health services provide those with few resources greater access to key services than they could afford to buy for themselves, in the process equalising the distribution of these services among the population.

Other social programs are designed to equalise the patterns of opportunity and advantage in society by addressing equity in the treatment of specific groups in the population defined in terms of gender, age, race or ethnicity – often through regulations that limit, prevent or mandate particular courses of action. Controlling anti-social or harmful behaviour such as crime or consumption of or trafficking in illicit drugs is regarded as part of social policy because these problems are seen as symptomatic of social malaise more broadly. How these programs are funded and the role of progressive taxation also fit within this definition of social policy as redistribution.

The distinction between the concern with efficiency in resource usage and equity in the distribution of resources has often been used to contrast the more technical objective focus of economic policy with the normative and subjective basis of social policy. This is an entirely false dichotomy. Economic policy involves making choices between alternative policy goals and this cannot be done without normative judgments. There are also many aspects of social policy that can be resolved (in principle at least) by examining the empirical evidence using standard scientific techniques and methodologies. The view that economics is a 'hard science' (of the head) while social policy is much 'softer' (of the heart) is a myth because what distinguishes them is not whether each is free of value judgments, but how much effort goes into making these judgments explicit and central. Economists have been very effective at portraying themselves as technocrats, leaving it to others to determine which judgments should inform social choices, yet most economic reform proposals have major distributional implications that are rarely identified.

These considerations suggest that the conventional distinction between economic and social policy is arbitrary and lacking in rigour and logic. Endemic in much of the policy debate is confusion (already alluded to) between ends and means, which compounds the artificial separation of economic and social policy. Employment promotion, for example, is a major end of economic policy but is also one of the principal means of social policy. One of the main problems of recent Australian policy has been that the scope of social policy has been severely circumscribed by attitudes taken to fiscal prudence and incentives in the name of microeconomic reform.

The basic problem (identified in the earlier quotation from Bourdieu) is that economic and social policy decisions are seen as occurring in a linear sequence, in which it is necessary to 'get the economy right' *before* considering how to influence social conditions through social policy. While this view appeals to a simple logic in which money must be earned before it can be spent, the analogy is misleading. Although the *goals* of economic policy can be specified independently of social goals, the *means* of achieving them must take account of the consequences for society and for social policy. Economic and social policy cannot be disconnected in this way, since the economy is part of society, not the other way round.

Objective and subjective indicators

The primary motivation of policy is to improve well-being by influencing the conditions and opportunities that shape people's lives. People's overall well-being depends both on the material conditions in which they live and on their assessment of how well their needs are being met. While the former can, in principle be measured objectively the latter can only be assessed subjectively. Social scientists have long argued over the superiority of objective and subjective indicators of well-being without coming to a resolution. Economists prefer objective measures of material well-being because the theory of welfare economics provides an analytical framework for drawing inferences about well-being (or utility) from objectively observed information on income, prices and consumption patterns. These depend on the logic that an item is only purchased in the market when the willingness to pay for it exceeds its cost.

However, while this logic may explain why choices make people better off, a more important issue relates to whether and why people feel that their circumstances have improved as a consequence of economic growth. The evidence presented earlier suggests that a positive link between growth and welfare cannot be automatically assumed. Resolving some of these puzzles involves examining both objective and subjective indicators.

Income and happiness

Since access to more resources allows people to purchase more items at a given set of market prices if they want to, it follows that those who have more resources at their disposal have the freedom to purchase (and consume) more and are thus better off than those with less. This is fine in theory, but it begs the question of how 'access to resources' can be measured objectively. Income is the most commonly used measure of economic well-being, mainly because of its availability and accessibility. Conditions such as poverty, affluence and prosperity are all measured in relation to income and it is widely accepted that having a higher income is generally associated with being better off. However, the benefits that income provides depend not only on its level, but also on how it is acquired. This often involves a sacrifice of time that offsets part of the increase in well-being that income generates. Unlike unearned income that is derived from ownership of assets, earning income requires a time contribution and thus contributes less to overall well-being.

One way around this problem is to impute a monetary value for time spent outside of the market sector and add this to income generated in the market. The contribution of well-being associated with the ownership of assets can also be estimated by valuing the services they provide in terms of housing, comfort and convenience. When these items are combined into what is called 'full income' they provide a 'measure, expressed in dollars, of all the major sources of material well-being, including money income' (Travers and Richardson, 1993, p. 26). Imputing a value to non-market time and to the services derived from the ownership of assets raises a number of formidable conceptual and practical problems that detract from the use of full income as an objective indicator of well-being.

Even so, a number of studies have produced estimates of 'full income' or its components (ABS, 1996a; Johnson, Manning and Hellwig, 1995; Travers and Richardson, 1993; Yates, 1991) and explored how full income correlates with conventional income measures. In general, they find that the two measures, though fairly closely related, also differ in significant ways, in total and between different groups in the population. Which measure is used can thus affect living standard comparisons, how much measured inequality exists and where people fit in the overall distribution.

Several criticisms have been levelled at the full income approach. First, it ignores the other factors that contribute to material well-being that cannot be easily identified and valued. Examples include the value of a clean and sustainable environment, the quality of working conditions, or the kind of community in which one lives, including the quality of the social interactions that hold communities together. While some of these can be measured objectively, there is no agreed method of aggregating them into a single monetary measure that can be added to money income. The alternative is to use a multi-dimensional indicator of well-being, although this weakens the link between increases in those elements of income that can be measured and overall well-being. Furthermore, the valuation of these additional dimensions is often highly subjective, blurring the distinction between objective and subjective measures.

Aside from these measurement problems, a key question concerns the relationship between income (an objective measure of economic well-being) and happiness (a subjective evaluation of overall life satisfaction). Irrespective of precisely how income is measured, many Australian studies (like those from other countries) show that the correlation between income and happiness is positive but low (Headey and Wearing, 1992; Travers and Richardson, 1993; Saunders, 1996a; Saunders, Thomson and Evans, 2001). A higher level of income generally brings greater happiness, but not that much more. As Travers and Richardson (1993; p. 126) note, 'rich people are more likely to be happy than poor people, but only by a small margin'.

The evidence also indicates that the relationship between overall life satisfaction and income is weak enough to suggest that it is mediated by other factors (Eckersley, 1999). This is consistent with cross-country studies that show a more pronounced link between affluence (as measured by per capita income) and subjectively expressed happiness, though it is difficult to separate the effects of affluence, democracy and equality on happiness (Headey and Wearing, 1992, Chapter 7). The weak relationship between income and subjective measures of happiness and satisfaction is open to alternative interpretation. Those who favour the use of objective indicators argue that it confirms their suspicion of subjective measures, while those who favour subjective indicators see the low correlation as supporting the opposite view (Travers and Richardson, 1993, p. 124).

The main limitation of relying on subjective indicators of well-being is that over time, people adapt to their objective circumstances, which explains the small gap between the expressed happiness levels of the rich and the poor. As people adjust to the circumstances and 'accept their lot', their subjective evaluation adjusts accordingly, but this does not imply that reliance on subjective indicators of well-being should be abandoned. Happiness is, after all, one of the ultimate goals of all people and the fact that it does not correlate well with income confirms that there is more to life than income or other economic factors.

There are a number of other reasons for treating subjective information with caution. Many people find it difficult to express their subjective views and may provide an unconsidered or misleading response if asked to express them. There may be many reasons for this, including an unwillingness to admit to one's own misery, or be seen to hold unpopular or extreme views about the conditions of others. The way in which questions are worded and asked can also have a major impact on the responses received. Despite these problems, subjective information is valuable precisely because it taps directly into the views and values of those who are at the receiving end of economic and social policy. Subjective indicators are an important source of information about people's perceptions and well-being, their understanding of their own and others' circumstances and what policy can do to bring about change. Community opinion has emerged as an important determinant of whether or not policies are seen as legitimate by the electorate. Subjective information on perceptions and attitudes thus has an important role to play alongside objective economic indicators.

Attitudes and perceptions

Attitudes and perceptions play an increasingly important role in the design of social policy, particularly in the area of welfare reform. It is necessary to have a better understanding of why people appear less satisfied with their circumstances, lifestyles and material possessions, before trying to reverse these trends through new policies. Even more important is the need for social policies to attract broad community support through political action and debate aimed at securing their legitimacy. In order to understand how policies are developed in the political process, it is necessary to study how ideas are presented and refined to receive support from the public. Political packaging is part of this process, but understanding how new ideas support, challenge or seek to modify existing perceptions and attitudes is also important. Because public perceptions play such an important role in determining the legitimacy of public programs, attitudinal research is an essential part of the broader task of policy analysis.

Attitudinal research has not been a major theme in the social policy literature, even though the issue of political legitimacy has been a key focus of welfare state theorists (Ploug, 1995; Newton, 1998). This has started to change as analysts have come to appreciate the impact that attitudes can have on changing community perceptions of social programs and mobilising support for them. Politicians have long been aware of the need to tap into community opinion to explore the potential reaction to possible changes in policy. The media is also well versed in the fact that attitude studies not only boost sales, they can also affect the course of the policy debate. These issues have risen to prominence as governments have tried to tailor their social programs to meet the constraints imposed by their own fiscal policies. Cuts in social benefits and entitlements are never politically popular and those who are adversely affected sometimes have a loud enough political voice to obstruct or prevent change.

Increasingly, governments have tried to pre-empt these reactions by commissioning studies that purport to show that there is 'broad community support' for the proposed reforms and thus that the protestors are primarily seeking to promote their own interests. With politicians on all sides increasingly conscious of the need to maintain the support of public opinion, the role and impact of attitudinal studies have grown in importance. Despite this growing interest, many studies of community attitudes and opinion do not provide details of sources and methods and lack scientific rigor.

The on-going crisis of the welfare state

Although the origins of the welfare state can be traced back over one hundred years, the modern welfare state came into being in the post-war years when Western democratic governments re-established the conditions for peace and prosperity after two decades of economic depression and military turmoil. The welfare state was one of many new institutions introduced to provide a new framework for combining economic progress with social stability. Its development reflected the view that state intervention in the market economy was required to equalise the opportunities and outcomes generated by economic growth, with its distributional impact reinforced by progressive taxation.

Income transfers for those of working age unable to provide for themselves through the labour market were legislated in many countries. (Pensions for older people and widows had been introduced much earlier). Although the terms on which income support could be received and the amounts paid differed from country to country, there was widespread acceptance of the view that social transfers were an essential feature of any civilised society. Many European countries strengthened the social insurance schemes that had been in existence for decades, expanding them to cover new contingencies such as unemployment and sickness; and they expanded pension schemes as the dignity provided by adequate income replacement in old age became a major policy priority.

Australia chose to reject the social insurance approach adopted in Europe in favour of a means-tested approach that placed emphasis on *income maintenance* rather than *income replacement* and ranked poverty relief above income redistribution as a policy goal. The means-tested approach drew attention to the relationship between the transfer system and other aspects of incomes policy, particularly the wage and tax systems. Centralised wage arbitration and the award wage system were used to establish an adequate minimum wage and compress wage differentials, thereby reducing reliance on the social security system to redistribute income and increasing community acceptance of means-tested benefits in the relatively rare circumstances in which workers were expected to be out of work. From the outset, wage arbitration and full employment were integral to the success of the Australian social security system (Castles, 1985; Saunders, 1999a). While in Europe, social security eligibility was based on prior involvement in the labour market and entitlements were linked (through contributions) to previous earnings,

Australian social benefits were conditioned by current levels of need, not to replace past earnings (Whiteford, 1998).

The changing welfare context

From the outset, the scope of the welfare state extended far beyond the provision of social transfers. Governments assumed a major role in the provision, finance and regulation of basic services such as education and health. Some countries also intervened extensively into the housing market to ensure that housing needs were met equitably through a variety of measures to control the supply, quality and cost of housing. From the time of their introduction, the social programs that constituted the welfare state were expensive. Not only did many programs cover large sections of the population; they also involved the funding of labour-intensive services that experienced escalating costs driven by the combination of rising wages and an endemic tendency towards static productivity growth that is a feature of services generally (Baumol, 1967; Esping-Andersen, 1990; Saunders, 1999a).

Because the benefits of most welfare state programs were concentrated on distinct sections of the population while the costs were apportioned more broadly through the revenue system, pressure groups emerged to protect existing entitlements and argue for new ones. The 'politics of welfare' became the arena in which the conflicting interests of different groups were played out and the welfare state was the vehicle through which power interests were articulated and competed. Over time, as a result of these pressures, the welfare state grew, not only in terms of its coverage and impact but also in terms of its cost.

Throughout the 1950s and 1960s, relatively little attention was paid to the growth of the welfare state, for two reasons. First, most agreed that more effort was needed to achieve equity of outcome and opportunity for all. Second, economic performance generated the additional resources required to fund welfare expansion, while economic growth kept unemployment low and thus minimised the demands on the welfare dollar. Keynesian demand management required state spending to support private sector demand and stabilise the economy at full unemployment, and the welfare state provided an obvious way of boosting consumption demand through income redistribution. Economic and social goals could thus be achieved simultaneously through a 'Keynesian consensus' that increased government spending on the welfare state.

As welfare programs absorbed a growing proportion of national income, disquiet began to emerge over whether the process was sustainable. The formation of the OECD provided the industrial countries with a forum to discuss broad policy issues of general concern and the growth of the welfare state became a focus of attention because it was a feature common to all OECD countries. Between 1960 and 1985, government spending on social transfers, education and health increased faster than the growth of the economy, and the ratio of social expenditure to GDP crept upwards. By 1981, the average ratio of social spending to GDP was 25.6 per cent, was over 20 per cent in two-thirds of OECD countries (though not in Australia) and was projected to rise further if policy was not changed (OECD, 1985, Table 1).

These trends emerged at a time when the economic boom of the 1960s had faltered in the wake of the oil crisis and as mass unemployment became a major economic and social issue. The longer-term viability of the welfare state was brought further into question by concerns that population ageing and the disincentive effects of social programs were reinforcing the spending squeeze associated with high unemployment. The ability of the tax system to meet the longer-term demands of the welfare budget was in doubt and as taxation became an issue, the same pressures that had driven up the welfare budget were mobilised to press for tax cuts, sending the welfare state into a funding crisis.

The funding crisis of the welfare state dominated its development over the last quarter of the twentieth century. Most OECD governments agreed that the welfare budget had to be cut, in part because smaller but better designed programs were needed to reduce its disincentive effects, but also because of the perceived political need to provide tax cuts to the middle classes. As these events were unfolding, the relationship between the state, the family and the market in welfare delivery became a focus of welfare state research. The underlying paradigm shift had a profound impact on how the welfare state evolved through the 1980s and 1990s and the nature of the on-going crisis that still confronts it. The focus shifted away from the welfare state towards other welfare-enhancing institutions that support the welfare of citizens and promote the development of society. Rather than accepting the inherent desirability of all forms of state welfare, fiscal imperatives shifted the focus onto the efficiency and effectiveness of specific welfare programs. This raised questions about the role of the market-type mechanisms in promoting efficiency in the 'production of welfare' and about how best to harness the efforts of family, community and non-government agencies to produce optimal welfare outcomes.

Welfare state, welfare system

The welfare state consists of a series of rights, entitlements and obligations that are socially sanctioned and conditioned by the needs of citizens. In an evocative passage, Ignatieff (1994, p. 9) talks of a 'parable of moral relations between strangers in the welfare state' in which these needs and entitlements establish silent relations between people as resources are distributed between them. Resources flow out of the pockets of some in the form of taxation and into the pockets of others as social benefits, with these flows mediated by the bureaucratic rules and procedures of the welfare state. Through this process, the welfare state functions 'as a form of social cement, tempering the individualism of the market with a good strong dose of social altruism' (Peter Saunders, 2000, p. 5). Its popularity does not rest solely on the compassion of those whose resources fund it, but also on the knowledge that they too might one day need the support and certainty it offers.

The modern welfare state provides income and services to protect vulnerable groups, but is also an integral part of the economy providing jobs and incomes to the increasing numbers employed in welfare agencies. Accompanying the growth of welfare spending has been a substantial rise in the size of the welfare workforce. In part, this reflects de-industrialisation, but even within the service sector, employment in welfare has grown in relative terms. In the year to June 1999, for example, the health and community services and education sectors employed more than 1.4 million people or 16.5 per cent (around one in six) of the employed workforce (Saunders, 1999b, Table 3.6). With a further 4 per cent of the workforce employed in public administration and defence, many of them administering, reviewing and evaluating the functioning of welfare provision and regulation, almost one-fifth of all employed Australians work in the welfare state and earn their living from it. No analysis of the modern economy can thus ignore the economic roles and functions of the welfare state.

The welfare state's relationship with other elements of the economy and society is important. Other social institutions, including the family and charitable organisations, previously fulfilled many of the functions now performed by the welfare state. These organisations now exist alongside formal welfare state agencies, forming part of a broader welfare system. The church and other community-based organisations have traditionally played an important welfare function in Australia, which has always had a large non-government welfare sector (Lyons, 2001). The family also plays an extremely important welfare function, drawing its resources, love and expertise together when family members are in need, often turning to the welfare state only when family supports break down. Families also reinforce the redistributive activity of the welfare state by distributing resources among their members and through gifts and donations to individuals in need or to the organisations that support them.

The relationship between the welfare state and the market system has become increasingly important as the search for efficient and effective solutions to social problems has intensified. The traditional separation between the market in generating resources and the welfare state in redistributing them has become blurred along with the distinction between the scope of welfare and market activity. As the resources generated through the market rely increasingly on the existence of a large welfare state, the means of achieving welfare goals have become increasingly market-oriented. It can no longer be automatically assumed that welfare agencies are part of government or receive regular funding from government. Where such funding does exist, it is likely to be awarded after an open process of competitive tendering. Increasingly, welfare benefits are designed by government but delivered through the market, with funding split between the state (taxes), the market (user charges) and other social institutions (donations and bequests).

These changing relationships between the welfare state and the other main institutions of civil society imply that in studying the welfare state, it is important to adopt a broad framework. Equally important is the need to distinguish between the ends and means of the welfare state. Many of the changes described above reflect new ways of achieving fixed ends. Although the ends of the welfare state have also changed, much of the recent welfare revolution has surrounded the introduction of new means, particularly new ways of delivering welfare. As in the broader policy debate, it is important to differentiate between the ends and means of welfare and the relationships between them.

The ends and means of the welfare state

The welfare state is both a means and an end of social policy. As a means, it represents the institutional architecture designed to make a reality of the collective commitment to equality and the social rights of citizenship. As an end, it signifies the achievements of many decades of political struggle to protect and enhance the living conditions and opportunities of the most vulnerable groups in society. It is, however, important to separate the role of the welfare state as a means and as an end in the context of the debate surrounding the efficiency and effectiveness of social policy.

While efficiency is primarily concerned with improving means, effectiveness raises the issue of ends – what it is that is trying to be achieved and how well efforts are succeeding. Although the distinction between ends and means has analytical clarity, this neat separation has not been maintained in the policy debate. Many of the reforms that introduce market mechanisms into the design and delivery of welfare programs have consequences for what those programs are trying to achieve. They thus affect both means and ends and both effects must be addressed.

Although it is common for both sides of the reform debate to argue that they share the same ends – specifically those relating to equality – in practice there are sharp differences of view about which types of equality are important.

Those who support the neo-liberal reform agenda give emphasis to issues of individual choice and equality of opportunity and favour proposals that change the means of policy in ways that promote these ends. This is inevitable when it comes to increasing reliance on market forces, since these only function when those who drive market signals are given the choice to express their preferences. At the same time, increased emphasis on choice tends to favour self-reliance over collective responsibility and equality of opportunity over equality of outcome. In practice, many neo-liberal proposals that are advocated as a way of increasing the range of choices available to specific groups (i.e. as improved means) are in fact designed to affect choices that favour specific outcomes (i.e. to support different ends).

The debate over work incentives is a classic case of these processes in action. Although the neo-liberal rhetoric surrounding the incentives issue focuses on removing the restrictions on the choice to engage in economically important activities, neo-liberal proposals generally improve these incentives for specific groups only (generally those with higher incomes). Debate over the impact of the proposals thus becomes enmeshed not only in whether or not the new incentive structure will have its intended effects, but also whether these effects are desirable if they are achieved. The framework of philosophical beliefs that underpins neo-liberalism thus acts to extend a debate that begins by focusing on the means of policy to one that also questions the ends of policy.

This kind of reform osmosis is not only a feature of the neo-liberal policy agenda. Proponents of the welfare state have long defended its means and ends in ways that suggest confusion between the two. Proposals to improve the means of welfare were long resisted (and often still are) on the grounds that any change represents a threat to the system as a whole. This was particularly true of reform proposals that involved greater reliance on market forces, as these were seen as inconsistent with the culture of collective responsibility that was the essence of what the welfare state represents in the context of democratic capitalism. For years, many social programs provided no choices to beneficiaries and rejected any role for competition as a way of responding efficiently to people's preferences. The result was a degree of conformity in state provision that was neither efficient economically nor sustainable politically. Rigid adherence to equality as a goal of policy existed alongside evidence that the policy gave rise to unintended, undesirable and ultimately unjustifiable side effects. In displaying an unwillingness to consider new means for achieving their ends, supporters of the welfare state inadvertently paved the way for the neo-liberal revival that now dominates the policy process (Midgley, 1999).

Although the welfare state continues to be widely seen as the articulation of both the ends and means of social policy, it is more appropriate to regard it as a means of policy rather than as an end. Although the ends of policy are a matter for philosophical reflection on the nature of social justice, the means of policy will be informed by research and other evidence related to how things operate in practice and with what effects. This does not mean that researchers should only concern themselves with technical questions surrounding the means of policy. Identifying and articulating the ends of policy is a complex task that requires clear thinking, logical argument and analytical skills. While most people are in favour of 'equality', what kinds of equality they support also involves theoretical reflection and systematic study of community attitudes.

In practice, the distinction between the ends and means of policy is more complex than is implied by the above discussion. It will not always be possible to separate the two, and there will be instances where the same variable may be seen as both an end and a means. Further complications arise from the fact that the relationship between specific ends and means are often imprecise, non-linear and mediated by a range of intervening factors. The equity impact of state-sanctioned benefits for those in employment, for example, will depend upon how access to paid work is distributed among the population and any barriers to participation for particular groups. If there is discrimination in the labour market, what might in other circumstances be equitable may serve to reinforce existing inequities. The cost of attaining a particular goal may also depend on factors that have nothing to do with the policy itself. A more competitive economic environment or more information about how the tax and transfer systems operate may increase the efficiency costs of achieving greater equality in the distribution of income. This may require a new approach that places less emphasis on redistribution through the tax-transfer system and more on policies that seek to equalise primary (market) incomes directly. Reducing income inequality remains the end of policy, but the means of achieving it will change.

Unless ends are distinguished from means, the task of reforming the welfare state in response to changes in its external environment will be more difficult. Many supporters of the welfare state have not paid adequate attention to demonstrating the success of past policies when assessed against their own objectives. Too much time has been devoted to defending the ends of welfare and too little to highlighting areas where its means have not been effective. By not giving sufficient attention to the achievements of the welfare state, those welfare state critics (particularly neo-liberal, market-oriented economists) who have been critical of its adverse effects on incentives and efficiency have not had to demonstrate that the *overall balance of effects* is negative. As Atkinson (1999a, p. 5) has observed, 'much of the economic analysis concentrates on the impact of the welfare state on economic performance to the virtual neglect of the functions the welfare state is intended to perform'.

In emphasising the distinction between ends and means, the possibility that the two can find expression in a single action should also not be overlooked. Amartya Sen has argued that freedom is both the primary end and the principal means of development and that this consideration must inform the assessment of the development process (Sen, 2000, p. 36). It is tempting to argue that this is also true for equality in the context of social policy, but this presumes a narrow view of social policy and the welfare state – certainly narrower than is implied in the above discussion. While all social programs seek to alter social and market forces in some way, not all are aimed at, or actually produce, greater equality (O'Connor, Orloff and Shaver, 1999, p. 12). To judge them all against a single benchmark would thus be inappropriate and, at times, misleading. It is necessary to identify the ends to which each program is geared and judge its performance – including both positive and adverse impacts – against those ends.

Ends, means and effectiveness: 'ending' poverty

In broad terms, efficiency focuses on means (how well are things done?) while effectiveness focuses on ends (what impact do they have?). Over time, as the focus of policy has shifted more towards effectiveness, one might expect a re-orientation of attention in favour of ends of policy over its means. In fact, over time, the opposite has happened. Despite the increased prominence given to achieving explicit and demonstrable outcomes in the policy rhetoric, the reality has often seen greater emphasis placed on how things are done rather than what they are achieving.

The history of welfare reform since the mid-1980s provides a salutary example of these processes at work. The most commonly used measure of the effectiveness of social security policies relates to their poverty alleviation impact among the groups that are covered (Beckerman, 1979; Mitchell, 1991; Saunders, 1994, Chapter 4). This approach is particularly appropriate in the case of social security systems like that in Australia, which operate on a means-tested basis, providing needs-based income support on a contingent basis to those who satisfy a set of eligibility criteria. Effectiveness involves comparing pre-transfer and post-transfer poverty rates (or more complex indicators that estimate the severity of poverty) and this requires a poverty line. This has presented Australian governments with a dilemma, since no government has been willing to officially endorse a poverty line, including that developed by the Poverty Commission (King, 1991; Saunders, 1998a, 1998b) – presumably because it might be used to show policy in a bad light.

Admittedly, the poverty line developed by the Poverty Commission is not without its problems. It needs revising to reflect changes in social conditions since it was first developed and to incorporate new research and data. The reluctance to use a poverty line to estimate the impact of social security policy began when the Hawke Government pledged to 'end child poverty by 1990', and since then, the issue of poverty has gradually been removed from the reform agenda. The Howard Government went further in removing any reference to poverty from its social policy discourse. Instead, the primary aim of the social security system became to ensure that assistance is concentrated on those in greatest need (through benefit targeting) and to encourage people back into work (through a range of measures designed to 'make work pay') (Reference Group on Welfare Reform, 2000b). Ends, in other words, gave way to means, in spite of the new emphasis on policy effectiveness.

This trend is ironic because OECD research shows the Australian system, though a poor performer in terms of the (relative) level of benefits it provides, is relatively efficient in terms of targeting assistance towards those at the bottom of the income distribution (OECD, 1998a; Whiteford, 2000). At the same time, however, increased benefit targeting has contributed, over time, to higher effective marginal tax rates that trap the poor into a cycle of welfare dependency. Thus, as one set of means (targeting) replaces the appropriate focus on ends (poverty alleviation), it gives rise to a further set of problems (welfare dependency) that is addressed by changing means yet again.

Through this process, Australian social security policy has become obsessed with a debate over means rather than ends, driven by an overriding need to cut costs. The issue for successive governments has been how to justify cutting a social security budget that already lies at the bottom of the OECD generosity ranking (Table 2.3). This has been achieved by a sleight of hand, in which elements of the social security system that were previously regarded as the means of policy have been redefined as its ends. Thus, targeting has replaced poverty relief as a goal in itself, while coverage or the receipt of assistance has been equated with dependency, as something to reduce rather than promote. These changes are part of a broader strategy to shift blame away from the failure of the government to address poverty effectively onto the limitations of those who rely on the system for income support. Even the simplicity of the system, long since sacrificed on the altar of targeting to appease those in charge of the federal budget, has been re-packaged as an end in itself (Newman, 1999a, 1999b).

The disappearance of any coherent discussion of the ends that underlie these shifts has been part of a deliberate attempt to focus the welfare policy debate on technical issues of design and delivery and divert attention away from what the system should be trying to achieve. It is ironic that this process gained momentum at a time when government required other welfare agencies to justify their activity by demonstrating its effectiveness. The size of the welfare budget, how the system is designed and its effects on incentives and behaviour are all important. But they are part of the broader arithmetic that also includes the external ends of policy and how successful it is at achieving them. The first step in 'ending poverty' requires reinstating poverty alleviation as a legitimate end of welfare policy.

3 Legitimacy of the Welfare State

Although the welfare state has been changing to reflect the new emphasis on market-based solutions to public policy issues, it remains a predominantly state-run institution. The state's role is changing from that of a direct provider of benefits and services to that of regulator of private, non-government providers, and despite the growth of privately financed welfare provisions, the state still has primary responsibility for financing the welfare state. It also sets the goals of welfare, while relying increasingly on market and other non-government means to achieve them. And as shown in Chapter 2, the welfare state absorbs a large proportion of national resources that must be diverted to government through taxation and other measures before they can be allocated to welfare programs.

Many welfare programs redirect resources back to those who originally provided them, in the form of social transfers, subsidised in-kind benefits, or as the wages and salaries of those employed in the welfare sector. Neo-liberal critics of the 'income churning' this implies have argued that the net distributional impact could be achieved with far smaller state sector if the gross flows between individuals and the state could be netted out (Cox, 2001). This view is arithmetically accurate but politically naïve, because it ignores the role of broadly based programs in underpinning the support of the middle classes, without which the welfare state would founder politically. Far from being its main weakness, 'middle class welfare' (Bradbury, 1998) is the lifeblood of the welfare state. But it remains true that this massive system of income redistribution has to be justified to those whose taxes support it – even if those who pay them also benefit from some aspects of welfare state redistribution (Forma, 1999).

The viability of the welfare state thus depends upon its legitimacy, defined in general terms as 'conformity to democratic principles' (Kwon, 1998, p. 18). Legitimacy in this sense cannot be automatically assumed, but has to be established and demonstrated. Government plays an active role in this process by engaging in the politics of legitimation in which 'those in power attempt to prove their legitimacy by the use of political measures such as social policy' (Kwon, op. cit., p. 19). As an institutional expression of social policy, the welfare state is thus an instrument used by the state to assert its legitimacy that must also be judged as legitimate in its own terms.

What is the nature of legitimacy and how can it be assessed? Ringen (1987, p. 22) defines the legitimacy of collective action by the extent to which it is chosen in ways that all citizens accept as a just method of balancing conflicting individual interests. Not everyone has to agree with each particular course of action, but there should be broad support for the methods used to determine the nature of state actions designed to achieve collective goals. Defined in this way, legitimacy thus implies that the broad 'public interest' is being met, even though there will always be some who are opposed to specific actions.

Within this broad framework, theorists of the welfare state have argued that it faces an inevitable crisis of legitimacy that reflects a set of contradictory demands. Newton (1998) describes this 'legitimacy crisis' in the following terms:

> There are different forms of legitimacy crisis theory but … the modern state … must create the conditions for profitable business by investing heavily in infrastructure, while keeping taxes down. It must also legitimize itself and maintain the conditions of social order by providing welfare services. It cannot possibly meet these contradictory demands and so it increasingly alienates both its capitalists and its workers. As a result, public opinion turns against the state, and legitimacy crisis results. (Newton, 1998, p. 106)

This account of how crisis emerges is important because it draws attention to the role of public opinion in establishing and maintaining the conditions of legitimacy. This view is shared by Ringen who argues that the legitimacy of the welfare state must be judged against the attitudes of the population:

> The legitimacy of the welfare state does not depend on theoretical fashions but on the opinions and behaviour of the population. It must be investigated on the grass-roots level and not on the level of elites. Legitimacy does not come from above and it cannot be lost from above. (Ringen, 1987, p. 49)

From this it follows that it is necessary to explore the nature of public opinion in order to understand how community attitudes determine the legitimacy of the welfare state. These attitudes have profound and lasting effects on the economic, social and political choices made in society, and thus in its institutions, policies and outcomes (Bean, 1991). How the factors that underlie welfare state development influence the legitimacy question sets the context for examining how the welfare state has been challenged by the philosophies and practices of neo-liberalism.

Public opinion and legitimacy

As with other political institutions, the welfare state has evolved in response to the interplay between the factors that determine the supply of and demand for the resources on which it depends. This framework has universal applicability. In discussing these factors in the context of social security reform in China, White (1998, p. 193) identifies three main driving forces behind the dynamics of welfare reform. The first is a process of rational and pragmatic policy selection; the second, ideological contestation about the character of welfare objectives; and the third, the competing sets of interests over the benefits and costs of different welfare programs. The interaction among these three factors determines the ends and means of the welfare state – what it is trying to achieve, for whom, how and at what cost.

A central feature of this framework is the importance attached to political factors. This is clearly true of the second and third of White's three factors, since both encompass issues of ideology and power relations that are contested through political engagement. Even the first factor, although on the face of it concerned with the search for technical solutions to policy problems, must take account of how policy works *in a particular context* and thus raises issues of acceptance and willingness to comply (hence White's reference to pragmatism as well as rationality). All welfare state programs thus involve choosing between different political interests. The term 'political' refers here not just to activities undertaken by political parties in the parliamentary process, but also to the ways in which different interest groups perceive and pursue their own interests through the structures of civil society.

Most social policies involve an element of both the ideological (whose interests will be served and why are these objectives important?) and the technical (how can our goals best be achieved given existing constraints?). Many programs combine both aspects in ways that make it difficult to untangle them. Because of this, social policy debate inevitably involves politics: social policy reform must thus engage with the political process.

The view that the structures and processes of the welfare state are no longer aligned with the main strands of public opinion has emerged as an issue in the welfare reform debate in many countries, including Australia. Although the reasons for this are complex, they reflect the view that the effectiveness of social policy has been largely undermined by problems of its own making, including induced dependency, moral hazard, interest-group rivalry and bureaucratic inflexibility (Giddens, 2000). In part, these concerns have resulted in the rejection of traditional social democratic policies in favour of those that provide increased choice, greater freedom and more reliance on market-based solutions to policy problems. The uncertainties surrounding policy effectiveness have been exploited in the political process, and public opinion has been manipulated in order to manufacture support for neo-liberal policies.

Those on the left have also accepted that public opinion must be mobilised behind support for a new ('Third Way') approach that seeks to balance state and market in ways that are more appropriate to contemporary social trends and community values. For much of the post-war period through to the emergence of mass unemployment in the 1970s, the popularity of the welfare state rested on two propositions. The first reflected the need for an expansion of state protection as part of the broader project of re-building social infrastructure destroyed during the war years. The main contingencies linked with poverty (old-age, ill-health, disability, widowhood and unemployment) were identified and gradually addressed through programs that were widely supported on compassionate grounds in a context where there seemed no limits to the increased resources deriving from economic growth.

These effects were reinforced by a second set of interests. The newly emerging middle classes saw in the welfare state a form of institutional expression that could be molded to satisfy their own interests (Le Grand, 1982). This could occur in one of two ways. First, the welfare state provided free (or low-cost) access to public services such as education, health and, community services. These programs provided non-cash in-kind benefits that accompanied growing material prosperity, but also opened up new professional and semi-professional job opportunities for a rapidly expanding, educated workforce. The expansion of the welfare state thus increased the demand for the professional service providers it was designed to supply, feeding back into a further round of expansionary demands. Many welfare state services were free of charge and universal, generating a set of well-paid jobs, secure in tenure and status that absorbed the aspirations of an expanding middle class. Social security cash benefits were also designed to return a large portion of the taxes paid by the middle classes back to them in the form of universal benefits linked to age or family status.

Throughout this period, few disagreed with the need for welfare state provision and disagreements over its cost and impact were rare. It was hailed as one of the major achievements of Western society and was popular among wide sections of the population. For politicians, the main task was to identify areas of unmet need and design new programs to address them, in a context where growth and full employment continued to generate additional tax revenue, albeit accompanied by a steady increase in the overall tax burden. There was also an optimistic belief in the ability of government to devise, implement, monitor and account for policies that were capable of addressing the needs of those unable to participate in the rising prosperity produced by economic growth.

Things began to change in the 1970s, when rising unemployment simultaneously increased the demand for social transfers and reduced the revenue capacity of the tax system (OECD, 1985). Evidence that poverty still existed in many countries and that inequalities of income and health remained wide and deeply entrenched in the face of huge increases in welfare spending began to cast doubt over the effectiveness of the welfare state. A sense of disillusionment with the benefits of economic growth also began to permeate the middle classes, reflecting increasing time pressures and the realisation that the benefits associated with positional goods that had motivated their actions were, by definition, unobtainable (Hirsch, 1978). These concerns increased through the 1980s and 1990s, as economic research studies began to show that the expansion of welfare state (and tax) programs had created disincentive effects that were undermining economic growth and trapping people in a cycle of dependency and poverty. The public's confidence in the welfare state started to wane and the tide of public opinion began to turn against the welfare state.

These changing circumstances provided politicians with a range of possible responses. They could have challenged the basis of the claims of welfare state ineffectiveness, or argued that the task was more difficult than originally thought, requiring greater effort and/or more resources. They did neither. Instead, they accepted the ineffectiveness and disincentive arguments, concluding that further welfare expansion had to be halted as part of a strategy for reducing public sector debt and lowering the level of taxation. The tax tail began to wag the welfare dog. The speed and extent of the turnaround were quite remarkable. Almost overnight, responsibility for determining social policy shifted from Social Welfare Ministries, where programs were designed and delivered, to Finance Ministries responsible for raising the revenues that paid for them.

Not surprisingly, this shift saw cost-cutting emerge as a central objective of a social policy agenda obsessed with re-configuring its means in order to achieve budget savings. This occurred at the expense of any serious consideration of whether the ends of policy were in need of revision, or of how effectively the existing ends were being achieved. Beginning in the latter half of the 1970s and continuing through the 1980s and 1990s, social security policy increased the targeting of assistance through measures which removed benefits from those deemed able to look after themselves and imposed more onerous eligibility conditions on remaining recipients, particularly the unemployed. Within this OECD-inspired 'active society' framework, social security policy focused on encouraging the unemployed (and sole parents) back into work through measures that required greater involvement in job search, training and labour market programs. At the same time, social security recipients became subject to far greater administrative scrutiny and were required to provide increased evidence of their job search activity and willingness to work.

Moves to increase the surveillance of social security clients were justified on the grounds that efforts should be made to expose those involved in benefit fraud in order to protect the integrity of a system that was perceived to be lax in its administration and subject to widespread abuse. Little evidence was provided to support such claims, although increasing numbers of recipients had their benefits withdrawn after having their eligibility assessed by Review Teams set up especially for the task (Saunders, 1991). The number of cases of fraud and benefit abuse became an indicator of how tough the government was in promoting the integrity of the system and protecting the rights of taxpayers, reinforcing the artificial distinction between welfare recipients and taxpayers. As each round of benefit cancellations was announced, public confidence in the system declined, and the overall effect was to undermine, not strengthen the integrity of the system.

These trends accelerated through the 1990s, under the Howard Government when greater attention was placed on the numbers removed from benefit, and Ministerial Press Releases proclaimed the government's success in being 'tough on welfare cheats'. Welfare dependency emerged as a key issue that required a policy response and the emphasis shifted away from providing work-focused programs to those who chose to participate, towards a mandatory system that required such participation as a condition of benefit receipt. This was accompanied by a more explicit appeal to public opinion and its support for tougher policies designed to increase economic and social participation under the heading of mutual obligation. (The details of this phase of welfare reform are discussed in Chapter 8).

Public opinion was manipulated throughout this period to serve the ends of those whose primary concern was with the size of the social security budget rather than the well-being of those receiving assistance. Politicians recognised that their welfare policies had to attract popular support among an increasingly cynical electorate, and public opinion emerged as an important factor shaping the dynamics of welfare reform. Increasingly, the middle classes saw change as an enemy not as a saviour of the living standards that they had grown accustomed to. Reinforcing, but at the same time reflecting, these trends was a shift in community attitudes against economic and social changes and the policies introduced in response to them. Public opinion emerged as an important determinant of the ends and means of the welfare state.

Values, beliefs and attitudes

In order to understand the impact of public opinion on policy development, it is necessary to examine the nature of public opinion and how opinions are formed. The dictionary definition of opinion refers to 'a judgment or belief based on grounds short of proof, especially on moral questions'. Since public opinion represents the combined opinions of all members of the public, it reflects the response to two questions: first, what is the nature of individual opinion on the matter in question; and second, how are individual opinions aggregated to arrive at a summary measure?

Many questions concerning social policy and the welfare state raise moral issues and thus depend upon value judgments. These judgments reflect subjective assessments about matters that cannot be resolved by appealing to either logical argument or empirical evidence. What matters for public opinion are the attitudes that are held about the public policy issues and these depend not only on values, but also on beliefs about how the world works, or what can be called 'reality filters'. Attitudes depend upon values and beliefs and vary according to how the beliefs are formed (and change) with the processes through which people filter information and gain an understanding of the real world. If the way information is provided gives a distorted understanding of the nature of the current situation or the factors that caused it, this may result in a different set of beliefs and thus of attitudes, even among those with similar values. The reality filters that control the flow of information thus play a crucial role in shaping attitudes and public opinion, even within a given value framework.

The nature of these relationships is illustrated in Figure 3.1, which provides a simple framework that identifies and links the key variables. The lines of causation shown in Figure 3.1 indicate that the reality filter influences how values and beliefs affect attitudes. The linkages operate in both directions, so that while values may affect beliefs and the choice of reality filter, the filter itself has the potential to change not only beliefs but also values. Similarly, while the reality filter will affect attitudes, these may also influence the choice of reality filter in ways that are self-reinforcing. Very few listeners to talk-back radio shows have not already made up their minds about the issues being discussed and they listen to have these views reinforced, not to have them challenged.

All of the variables that appear in this framework can change over time. People's values and beliefs depend upon their own experiences (including their relationships with other people) and may change in the light of these, or as their perceptions of the world and what is important about it evolve. The nature of values, beliefs and attitudes and the subtle yet fluid connections between them are in a constant state of flux. Although the range of factors that can affect the key variables shown in Figure 3.1 is enormous, many of them will not change as a result of the factors that impact on the policy process and are thus of less interest in discussing policy reform. This narrows attention to those factors that can bring about change in the short-run, specifically to the flows of information that describe and explain the world that affect beliefs and serve as a reality filter.

How these factors combine to influence attitudes and public opinion is illustrated in the example shown in Figure 3.2 which shows how different attitudes to the social security treatment of the unemployed reflect differences in the values, beliefs and filters applying to each of them. Individual I has many of the classical characteristics of a social democrat, believing in pro-poor redistribution and that incentive effects are of minor significance. The main causes of unemployment are believed to rest with the failure of government (economic) policy not the individual and the onus is therefore on the government to relieve the poverty that unemployment creates for the unemployed. Individual II has values that place greater emphasis on equality of opportunity, but also believes that incentives have an important impact on behaviour. While unemployment is not initially the fault of the unemployed, the social security system can, through the creation of poverty traps, prolong unemployment once it begins. The attitudes of such an individual would thus be consistent with an unemployment benefit system that provides reasonably generous levels of support but in a manner that promotes the return to work through appropriately structured incentives. Individual III regards the unemployed as mainly responsible for their own actions and circumstances and also believes that people respond to the incentives and opportunities available to them. In this person's view, the unemployed lack motivation and have a very weak work ethic and everything possible should be done to get them back into work as quickly as possible, whatever this involves in the short-run.

The three individuals depicted in Figure 3.2 end up with different attitudes to the social security treatment of the unemployed. These vary with the values and beliefs that underlie them, and with the filter through which relevant information is acquired and interpreted. Although values are generally fixed in the short-run and will change only slowly, there are more opportunities to influence people's beliefs and the filter through which attitudes are formed. For example, the attitudes of Individual I in Figure 3.2 could move closer to those of Individual II if they were persuaded that work incentives were more important for labour market behaviour, or if unemployment could be shown to be not due solely to a lack of demand. Similarly, the attitudes of Individual III could also move towards those of Individual II if they were persuaded that incentives are

Legitimacy of the Welfare State

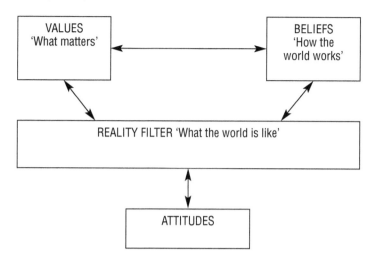

Figure 3.1 Framework linking values, beliefs and attitudes

	Individual I	**Individual II**	**Individual III**
Values:	Egalitarian – supports distribution in favour of the poor	Equal opportunity – the unemployed lack opportunity and need support	Individualist – the unemployed are responsible for their own situation
Beliefs:	Work incentive effects of social security are generally weak	People are very responsive to the incentives they face, but opportunities to work must be available	Incentives are very important; people make their own opportunities in the light of their circumstances
Reality Filter:	The causes of unemployment reflect government mis-management of the economy	Unemployment is initially due to bad luck, but social security can trap people in poverty	Unemployment results from a lack of motivation and unwillingness to work
Attitudes:	Provide adequate support for the unemployed to escape poverty with few eligibility conditions	Unemployment benefits should be modest but structured to encourage work incentives	Unemployment benefits should be lower and conditions as stringent as possible, reinforcing the work ethic

Figure 3.2 Alternative foundations of attitudes to the unemployed

less important, or that not all of the unemployed are responsible for their situation. Individual attitudes lie along a continuum, varying in response to changes in beliefs and the filters through which these affect attitudes.

Accepting that values are unlikely to change markedly in the short-run still leaves open the potential for attitudes to change in response to actions that affect beliefs or the kinds of reality filters through which information is acquired. These are the main channels through which government can seek to influence attitudes and public opinion and thus change the 'terms of the debate' in ways that suit their own purposes.

One crucial area that affects the social security reform agenda drawn out by the example in Figure 3.2 concerns the motivations of the unemployed and how they respond to incentives to work. Since there is little community support for cutting the level of unemployment benefits for its own sake, such action is generally promoted for other reasons. One such argument, put forward by writers such as Mead (1997; 2000), is that it is in the longer-run interest of the unemployed to be forced back into work by a social security regime that provides low benefits subject to very stringent eligibility conditions. Although the validity of the argument depends in part on the availability of sufficient work to absorb the increased numbers expected to seek work, it also depends on the size of the incentive effects. One reason why Mead's paternalistic ideas have become so influential is that people have been convinced that the potential incentive effects are more substantial than previously thought.

How has this come about? To answer this question, it is necessary to consider the kinds of reality filters that are used to obtain information about these and other questions that have relevance to welfare reform and other public policy issues. How do most people arrive at the beliefs and attitudes that they hold? The three main sources of information are personal observation and introspection, communicating with other people and the media. While some views reflect personal experience or observation, most views are acquired through conversation with others or are formed on the basis of what people read, hear or see in the media. The role of the media in promoting views on matters relating to public policy is thus of overwhelming significance.

The media as defined here include a large variety of avenues through which information is generated for general consumption – not only the popular press and mainstream electronic media, but also specialist media outlets and activities. Most people's beliefs reflect the stories and analyses contained in the mainstream media outlets: newspapers, radio and television. Here, one can find an abundance of material describing stereotypical 'welfare cheats' and voicing opinions based on a complete misunderstanding of how the system actually works, as well as more accurate and informative accounts of the complexities of the underlying issues.

Given their important role in shaping public opinion, the media provide obvious arenas of activity for those who wish to influence the policy debate. A good example of effective media use to promote the need for a new policy approach concerns the original research on poverty that was undertaken in the 1960s at the University of Melbourne by Ronald Henderson and his colleagues (Harper, 1967). An orchestrated release of their findings through the media enabled the research team to exert a major influence on the public's awareness of the issues that helped to mobilise support for the establishment of the Poverty Commission that went on to set a new policy agenda (Saunders, 1998c).

Researchers are not the only group capable of using the media to promote specific positions on policy reform. Others, including the media themselves, can and do exert a powerful influence. In an enlightening analysis of the role of the media in affecting popular images of poverty and welfare in Australia, Putnis (2001) concludes that:

> The media can exercise choices ... [and] ... conduct 'campaigns' for or against particular causes. In short, they are not just in the transmission business, they are major players in the 'meaning business', generating community understandings which ultimately feed back into political priorities. There is, however, nothing fixed about these understandings. The 'meaning business' is an ongoing, multi-faceted, dynamic and contested area where, potentially, crooks can be rehabilitated, fashions can come and go, the formerly marginalised can be given centre stage and, over time, new social priorities come to the fore. (Putnis, 2001, p. 100)

With such potentially far-reaching effects, it is no surprise that the media play a major role in shaping and changing public opinion, particularly in the area of social policy.

The government can (and obviously does) take advantage of this situation by releasing its own information in ways designed to influence media coverage of the issues and the factors seen as important. The government can commission studies or conduct its own research and then decide whether (and when) to release the results. It can give a high profile to comments on external studies or findings that support its own ends while ignoring those with which it disagrees. Finally, it can conduct or commission research that explores only limited aspects of key issues and it can describe problems and their context in ways that promote its own solutions. In pursuing these goals, it can exploit all of the different forms of research utilisation described in the previous chapter.

No consideration has yet been made of the second aspect of public opinion: that related to the process through which the views of individuals are combined to reflect a representative view of society as a whole. Given the variety of individual opinion that exists on almost any topic, the idea that there is any single view that is broadly representative is problematic. This does not stop politicians from claiming that they have public opinion behind them, or have a 'mandate for change' based on the outcome of an election in which it is impossible to know how much support there was for any *specific* policy. Far too often, 'the' opinion that is portrayed as representative of the public at large is that expressed most loudly (or most frequently) by those with a vested interest in promoting it.

Thus, while public opinion is an extremely powerful force for change, its nature and formation are complex. Its elusiveness does not detract from its importance, particularly for those wishing to align themselves with it. If the political legitimacy of government policy towards the welfare state depends upon its ability to attract sufficient public support to pass a basic popularity test, then it is important to understand what public opinion is, how it is formed and what can change it.

Researching public opinion

A large number of studies have explored public opinion and how it is changing. Many of these are conducted on behalf of the media by commercial survey research companies and produce results that are presented and analysed in the newspapers. These studies fall into one of two main types. The first attempts to gauge an overview of how opinion is changing by asking people to rank in order of importance a range of social and economic issues including unemployment, inflation, the budget deficit, the balance of payments, the crime rate, poverty, and so on. These rankings can then be aggregated and compared over time to provide a series of snapshots that, when linked, provide a useful barometer of how society ranks different priorities and how these are changing. But they are of limited use in explaining how opinions are formed and what causes them to change because of the lack of coverage of variables that describe the characteristics of those surveyed, including their views on other issues.

The second form of public opinion data that is commonly reported in the media concerns issues at the forefront of the policy debate. Studies of this type tend to be reported as the percentages in favour of, or against, a particular policy idea or intervention that has emerged in the political arena (sometimes with the intention of eliciting a response from the public). These surveys, often conducted within a tight time frame by telephone interview, provide a useful yardstick of community opinion on specific issues. But they are limited in the extent to which they can be used for analytical purposes because of their very specific focus and because of the lack of information collected about the respondents. The emphasis is thus again on *describing* the nature of public opinion, not on trying to understand or *explain* it.

Academic studies of public opinion – at least in the field of social policy – generally seek not only to describe public opinion but also to explore how the underlying attitudes are formed and test hypotheses about the nature of public opinion and how it varies across the population. This involves asking respondents about their opinion on social issues and questions and also about their socioeconomic circumstances. These additional questions allow the responses to be analysed in the context of the circumstances of those who provide them, giving a more sophisticated and reflective study of the nature and variety of public opinion.

The cost of conducting public opinion research can be considerable, not only in terms of the time taken to complete the questionnaire by respondents (for which they sometimes receive a modest payment), but also in terms of the cost of preparing the questionnaire and administering it. Face-to-face interviews are often ideal, since they provide an opportunity to clarify any confusion and ensure that all questions are answered, but these are very expensive to arrange and conduct. Some people may also find it harder to provide sensitive information or express controversial views directly, which militates against the interview method. Because of the high cost of personal interviews, many surveys are either conducted by telephone or mailed out to respondents who are asked to return the completed questionnaire by mail. Aside from cost, there are many other difficulties to be overcome when developing a questionnaire that is economical in the number of questions asked and unambiguous in the interpretation of responses provided. A fine balance must be struck between ensuring that respondents have sufficient information to allow them to give a meaningful response, while not providing information that might induce a specific (and hence biased) response.

Given the complexity of most social policy legislation, it is not surprising that many people know relatively little about the details of current policy. This creates further problems, since the way in which the current policy is described can influence the responses to questions about its desirability. It will be shown in Chapter 8, for example, that the community has a more sympathetic attitude towards the social security treatment of the older unemployed (those aged over 50) than to the long-term unemployed (those who have been out of work for a year or more). But these two groups overlap to a considerable degree, with many of those who have been out of work for a year or more also being over 50 years of age. How questions are framed can thus affect the responses in ways that require careful consideration when interpreting results.

Another example of this kind of effect has emerged in recent attitudinal research on the adequacy of social security provisions in Britain (Hills and Lelkes, 1999). When asked how well-off they thought a married couple on unemployment benefit were, 56 per cent of respondents replied that they were 'really poor' or 'hard up'. The remaining

37 per cent thought they had enough or more than enough to live on. However, when they were asked how well-off a couple would be on £79 a week after rent (the actual level of unemployment benefit at the time of the survey), 81 per cent thought they would be 'really poor' or 'hard up', while only 18 per cent thought that this was enough or more than enough to live on. The form in which questions are asked matters, as does who asks them, for what purpose and in what context.

There are also a number of difficulties involved in trying to elicit reliable information about people's attitudes to what are often very complex issues. Taylor-Gooby (1985) notes that the opinions expressed in surveys may reflect little understanding of the issue and be affected by extraneous and circumstantial factors, including the reaction of respondents to the immediacy of the interview situation itself. This may induce responses that are motivated by a desire to appear courteous or provoke an obstinate response that does not reflect the underlying reality. As a consequence, the views expressed in public opinion surveys may be volatile and not always a reliable guide to behaviour. Ringen (1987) is similarly cautious, adding that the opinions expressed may be artificial as respondents are not required to stand by them or test them against alternative views or counterarguments.

These problems are important but not insuperable. Modern survey and statistical techniques allow opinions to be checked for consistency and measured rigorously and with reasonable accuracy. Providing other researchers with access to the raw data can also allow independent tests of reliability to be undertaken. One problem that cannot be overcome so easily is the influence on public opinion that is exerted by government and the other agencies of civil society. These effects have the potential to distort results in ways designed to serve the interests of those in positions of power. They set the general climate of public debate at any point in time and place limits on the kinds of questions and issues that are raised and thus on the range of possible solutions that are canvassed. The impact of these effects can in principle be isolated by careful choice of questions, but this is not always easy, particularly when time and space are at a premium.

All of these factors suggest that the *individual* opinions expressed in public opinion surveys may not be totally reliable and should be treated with caution. A better picture is likely to be presented if the responses are calculated for specific *groups* in the population, since any extraneous effects that have influenced all respondents will not affect comparisons between groups. The problem of volatility can also be addressed in this way, as long as there is no systematic pattern to its causes. Finally, looking at the *trends* in public opinion provides another way of avoiding any short-run distortions, as long as the sampling methods and questions remain unchanged. In general, it is easier to identify broad changes in the shape of public opinion than to derive quantitative indicators of the strength of opinion at a particular point of time.

Legitimacy of the Australian welfare state

Although it is common to hear claims that the welfare state is in need of reform, is it in fact true that public opinion has turned against the welfare state? Evidence on this issue has generally been derived from public opinion surveys that seek to determine the degree of support for social programs by asking respondents whether they favour more or less welfare spending in specific areas. The general trend that emerges from this research is that the level of support for many (though not all) welfare state programs is high. However, since respondents are often not confronted with the fact that high levels of spending must be paid for, the implications of this finding are open to interpretation. In response to this, some studies have attempted to link expressed support for higher spending to the likelihood that taxes will also have to rise in order to assess whether this affects the degree of expressed support.

Figure 3.3 summarises trends in Australian public opinion on the levels of taxation and spending on welfare programs over the last 50 years. After a dramatic change leading up to the mid-1960s, the percentage favouring lower taxes then increased substantially, while support for higher spending on social services declined. Although there is some short-run variability in the pattern of change (which may reflect variations in survey methodology and the range of response options provided to participants), the long-term trend is clear. It is difficult to take issue with Gruen's description of the situation in the mid-1980s relative to the mid-1960s as reflecting 'a massive change in community attitudes to welfare expenditure' (Gruen, 1989, p. 35). One would have to be remarkably resistant to the evidence to conclude other than that Australian support for welfare spending fell substantially over the period. For the last decade or so, support for lower taxes has outstripped support for higher spending by a factor of more than three to one. The best that can be claimed by proponents of state welfare is that support for higher spending has remained steady since the mid-1980s and has shown a slight increase in the 1990s.

Other studies have produced somewhat different results. A study commissioned by the Economic Planning Advisory Commission asked people whether they were prepared to pay higher taxes to fund increased government spending on the condition that everyone else would also have to pay for the changes they nominated (Withers, Throsby and Johnston, 1994). The authors found that 58 per cent would be prepared

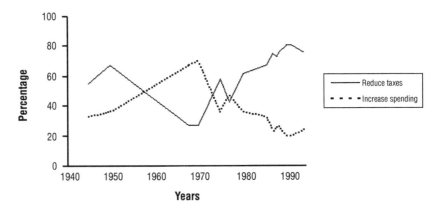

Figure 3.3 Public opinion on taxes and spending on social services.
(QUESTION: If the government had a choice between reducing taxes and spending more on social services, which do you think it should do?)

to pay 'a little more' in tax, 23 per cent were prepared to pay 'whatever was required', while only 17 per cent were 'not willing to pay more'. Respondents were then asked how much they would be willing to pay for specific government programs, having first been informed how much they were actually paying on average in taxes for each program. They were also told that if their expressed willingness to pay was above their actual payments, their tax burden would have to rise. The results showed a willingness to pay slightly more for education, about the same for health care, slightly less for family assistance and considerably less for unemployment programs (Withers, Throsby and Johnston, 1994, Table 3.3).

Results from another recent study also support the view that there is strong support for modest tax increases to fund higher levels of social spending (Baldry and Vinson, 1998). Just under 1000 people aged over 18 were asked whether they thought that increased spending accompanied by increasing income tax 'by one or two cents in the dollar' was desirable. The percentage favouring such a change was 49 per cent (in the case of spending on education), 48 per cent (spending on health and aged care), 42 per cent (spending on families in need), 39 per cent (spending on job training for the unemployed) and 37 per cent (spending on the environment). Although indicating strong support for many social programs, this evidence is somewhat flawed by the fact that the tax increase referred to in the question would in fact fund vastly different amounts of additional spending in each of the areas mentioned (Saunders, 2000a).

Although subject to qualification, Australian public opinion does appear to have moved against the welfare state – or at least against welfare expenditure – over the last three decades. Despite this, there is still strong support for many welfare programs and the situation does not represent a crisis of legitimacy. The politics of the welfare state has been an enormously significant factor in its development, despite the cynicism of economists. The ways in which governments attempt to identify, publicise, negotiate and implement their welfare reforms have an important bearing on the eventual outcomes. As Esping-Andersen (1997) notes, there are important lessons to be learnt from comparing how different governments have attempted to re-draw the welfare contract in response to changes in economic structure and community attitudes:

> A comparison of governments' policies over the past years reveals ... a very important pre-condition for reform. The average voter's "veto" is more easily overcome where governments can negotiate a broad consensus with strong, nationally encompassing, interest organisations ...[In contrast, a] policy of imposition ... is more likely to trigger massive social unrest ... [T]he ability of countries to achieve positive sum solutions under conditions of acute conflict of interest is closely related to their institutional structure of political mediation. (Esping-Andersen, 1997, p. 75)

These comments suggest that it is not so much the *nature* of policy reforms that determines their legitimacy, in terms of community acceptance or rejection of them, but rather how the reforms are *negotiated* as they move from the realm of ideas through to legislation and implementation. This process of negotiation does not take place in a vacuum. It reflects prevailing currents of thought and possibilities, both of which are intimately shaped by how public opinion enters into political debate. The potential thus exists for public opinion to exert its influence through yet another route.

Identifying and classifying Australian values

As the task of governance has become more difficult, governments have turned to public opinion to justify the very difficult policy choices that have to be made. The increased attention given to attitudinal research has been a feature of developments in the United Kingdom, where much of the research has been undertaken or commissioned by government departments (Williams, Hill and Davies, 1999). This trend has not been apparent to the same degree in Australia, although the Howard Government has promoted studies that purport to show strong community support for 'work for the dole' and its other mutual obligation policies (Tann and Sawyers, 2001; Vanstone, 2001).

In the context of the evolving policy debate over welfare reform and the role of government, a research team based at the Social Policy

Research Centre (SPRC) conducted a survey of public attitudes to changes in Australian society with an emphasis on social policy reform issues. The survey, *Coping with Economic and Social Change* (CESC) was conducted in the middle of 1999 on a random sample of the adult population (aged 18 and over) drawn from the electoral rolls (Eardley, Saunders and Evans, 2000; Saunders, Thomson and Evans, 2001). Details of the methods used to conduct the survey and an analysis of the representativeness of the sample it generated are contained in the Appendix. As is shown there, the sample of over 2,400 valid responses is a reasonably good representation of the adult population as a whole, and the results presented and analysed here and in later chapters are robust and provide a reliable guide to the views of the general population.

One of the main motivations for conducting the CESC survey was to explore community attitudes to economic and social change and to the policies that have emerged from the processes of rapid change that have been occurring in Australia. A series of questions explored whether respondents saw change as providing new and exciting opportunities or as something they just have to put up with. Responses to the three questions posed are summarised in Table 3.1. Combining the 'Strongly agree' and 'Agree' categories, it is clear that public opinion on attitudes to change is sharply divided. While almost 47 per cent find change exciting and a source of new opportunities, over 64 per cent are resigned to change and 42 per cent are openly opposed to it. Overall, however, few people express very strong views on attitudes to change, with the majority either unsure or not prepared to express a strong opinion, one way or the other.

Further examination of the results (reported in Saunders, Thomson and Evans, 2001) reveal, not surprisingly, that attitudes to economic change vary systematically with age, with older groups more opposed to change than younger people. This pattern exists across all four questions, but it is far stronger for the first of them – overall attitudes to the rate of economic and social change – than for the remaining three. Feelings of resignation to the inevitability of change are strong across all age groups, as is the view that the balance between economic and social factors has tipped undesirably in favour of the former. However, while more young people see change as opening up exciting new possibilities, so do a significant proportion of those in the older age groups. Thus while there are age patterns in the survey responses, the generational cleavages are not as sharp as is sometimes claimed.

Table 3.1 also reports the proportions of people who, whatever the nature of their attitudes to change, are concerned about the current emphasis given to the economy compared with broader social objectives. There is very strong support (almost three-quarters either agreeing or

Table 3.1 Overall attitudes to economic and social change (percentages)

Strongly agree	Agree	Neither agree or disagree	Disagree	Strongly disagree	Don't know
The rate of economic and social change is too fast and I don't like it					
12.0	30.3	32.6	19.7	2.4	3.1
Economic and social change is inevitable and I just have to put up with it					
7.2	57.0	15.9	14.6	3.6	1.6
Economic and social change is exciting and provides new opportunities and prospects					
7.6	39.3	30.7	16.5	2.4	3.5
Too much emphasis is put on improving the economy and too little on creating a better society					
33.7	41.0	14.5	7.2	1.0	2.7

Unweighted n = 2,307 to 2,331.

strongly agreeing) for the view that too much emphasis is given to economic factors, with less than 10 per cent taking the opposite view. These findings are consistent with those reported in Pusey's (1998) study of 'middle Australia', which reveals that many people feel that they have not gained from the economic changes experienced in Australia over the last fifteen years.

In addition to exploring attitudes to change, the CESC survey was also designed to provide information on a range of current social policy issues including the determinants of social problems, the role of government, welfare reform and the role of mutual obligation. A key goal of the survey was to build up a picture of alternative value frameworks to see how well these could explain the views expressed on a range of policy issues. The approach built on the responses to a series of questions relating to beliefs about the causes of social problems such as poverty and unemployment, attitudes to economic and social change and views about the role of government in addressing social and economic issues. Responses to these questions were used to classify respondents into one of three value positions that were expected to generate different views about the reform of social security (or welfare) and the role of mutual obligation.

The different value positions of the CESC respondents were classified according to the views expressed about both the ends and the means of the welfare state. In relation to its ends, the classification reflected the degree of support expressed for redistribution (or egalitarianism) as a goal of the government. In relation to means, opinions were sought on whether poverty and unemployment were seen as arising from what the previous attitudinal literature has classified as structural factors, or reflect a failing on the part of those affected, or are simply the result of bad luck (Feagin, 1972; Feather, 1974; van Oorschot and Halman, 2000). These constructed variables were combined with the responses to a series of additional questions on the respective roles of the state and the market in solving these problems.

The resulting value variables distinguished between those whose value system is broadly consistent with the egalitarian goals and collectivist ethos of the welfare state from those who support the values of choice and personal responsibility and the neo-liberal emphasis on the role of competitive markets (Argy, 1998, Chapter 5). A third value category was defined to encompass those who adopt a fatalist approach to how the forces of economic and social change interact to determine individual outcomes.

The classification of CESC respondents into one of these three value frameworks was based on responses to the series of questions shown in Table 3.2. The italicised statements in Table 3.2 are taken directly from various sections of the CESC questionnaire. Each question asked respondents to indicate which of the following options best describes their reaction to each statement: 'Strongly agree'; 'Agree'; 'Neither agree nor disagree'; 'Disagree'; 'Strongly disagree', or 'Don't know'. After excluding the (relatively few) 'Don't know' responses, the other five options were assigned scores of +2, +1, 0, –1 and –2, respectively and these were than summed to get an overall score that varies between +6 and –6 for each set of questions.

Collectivists were then defined as those whose *total score* for the first three statements was greater than or equal to +2. Individualists were defined as those having a *total score* greater than or equal to +2 for the second set of statements. Finally, fatalists were those with a *total score* greater than or equal to +2 for the third set of statements. This process allowed the value positions of 1362 CESC respondents to be identified, of which 219 were individualists, 605 were collectivists and 538 were fatalists. (The remaining 485 of the 1,847 people who answered each of the relevant questions did not achieve a total score of greater than or equal to +2 for any of the three sets of statements.)

The number of people assigned to each of the three value positions is of interest in itself. It suggests that Australia's reputation as an egalitarian nation is consistent with the collectivist views of a large proportion of the population – with almost half (44.4 per cent) of those whose value framework could be identified ending up in the collectivist camp. This is almost three times the proportion of the sample who support individualist values (16.1 per cent), but only slightly above the number of fatalists who are resigned to a world where change and unemployment are seen as inevitable and poverty the result of bad luck.

Legitimacy of the Welfare State

Table 3.2 Questions used to determine the value framework of CESC respondents

Collectivist	
	Too much emphasis is put on improving the economy and too little on creating a better society
	People are poor because other people are rich
	Solving unemployment is the Government's responsibility
Individualist	
	Economic and social change is exciting and provides new opportunities and prospects
	Most people who are poor only have themselves to blame
	People who are unemployed only have themselves to blame
Fatalist	
	Economic and social change is inevitable and I just have to put up with it
	People are poor because they have been unlucky in life
	There just aren't enough jobs for all the people who want to work

Further examination of the data reveals a degree of overlap among those falling into each of the three value positions, and these observations have been omitted from the following analysis in order to make it easier to interpret the results and to highlight the differences between those in each category. (The overlap between the fatalist group and the other two categories is not as problematic as that between the collectivists and the individualists, as it is possible to adopt a fatalist approach while also adhering to individualist or collectivist values. Further details of the number of overlapping cases for each of the three value categories are provided in the Appendix.) When the overlaps are omitted, the numbers in each value category decline to 134 individualists, 335 collectivists and 276 fatalists and it is on this further restricted sample that the following analysis has been based.

Table 3.3 compares the characteristics of those identified as individualist, collectivist and fatalist by the procedures described above. It reveals some interesting differences in the socio-demographic patterns particularly between the individualists and the collectivists. Compared with the collectivists, individualists tend to be slightly younger, more likely to be married (but less likely to have children), to be born in an overseas English-speaking country, to own or be purchasing a home, to be self-employed and to work in a white-collar occupation. In contrast, collectivists are more likely to be Australian-born, to have an on-going disability, to be separated (but have children), to be renting (private or public), to have a tertiary qualification, to not be employed, to have experienced recent unemployment in their family and to work in a blue-collar occupation. Fatalists tend to be similar to individualists in terms of their personal characteristics (though very few are born in a non-English-speaking country) but more like collectivists in terms of their labour-force status and occupation (though a large percentage have a low level of education).

The pattern of expressed political allegiances is of particular interest. It is not surprising that almost half (49.3 per cent) of individualists are Liberal voters, while two-fifths (39.7 per cent) of collectivists vote for the Australian Labor Party (ALP). But almost one-fifth of individualists are ALP voters and a similar proportion of collectivists are Liberal voters, so that traditional political alignments are by no means reflected in the value framework classification. Views on the causes of social problems and the roles of state and market sectors tend to cut across traditional party lines in the 'new politics' that now exists (Giddens, 1994 – see also Chapter 1). National Party voters are evenly split between the individualist and collectivist categories, though most are fatalists. A large proportion (close to one-fifth) of the sample describe themselves as swinging voters, further confirming the volatility of traditional allegiances in the new political ferment. This group is evenly split among the three value categories, illustrating that winning the backing of this group is crucial for electoral success.

It is clear that there are differences in the socioeconomic profiles of the three value categories, particularly in relation to age, education, labour force status and social class, although not all of them are significant statistically. While some of these differences reflect how the value variables have been constructed, it is also clear that people's experience of events like unemployment – even if only indirect, but within the family – affects the value framework they support. It also appears that younger people are more likely than older people to favour individualist values, although these differences are generally quite small.

The relationship between the value differences shown in Table 3.3 and attitudes to social issues and the welfare state is explored in later chapters. Prior to that, Table 3.4 investigates how general subjective assessments of well-being vary across the different value categories. The differences in subjective well-being between individualists and collectivists are more pronounced than the socioeconomic differences shown in Table 3.3, though again many of them are not statistically significant. In general, compared with collectivists, individualists are more satisfied with life, (slightly) happier, somewhat healthier and less worried about losing their job. Overall, the well-being scores for the fatalists are similar to those for the collectivists, except that the fatalists are slightly more satisfied with their life generally. Although some of these absolute

Table 3.3 Demographic characteristics of the value sub-samples (percentages) [a]

Characteristic	Individualist	Collectivist	Fatalist
Gender			
male	52.2	51.3	48.6
female	47.8	48.7	51.4
Age			
under 25	14.9	11.0	8.3
25–39	30.6	29.7	21.4
40–49	20.9	20.3	19.6
50–64	20.1	21.2	25.4
65+	11.2	11.3	19.2 ★
Country of birth			
Australia	66.4	77.6 ★	76.4
another English-speaking country	16.4	6.6 ★	13.0
another non-English-speaking country	17.2	15.5	10.5
Marital status			
married	73.1	69.0	73.2
separated	8.2	12.3	13.4
never married	18.7	18.5	13.4
Family status			
with children	44.8	50.4	43.5
without children	52.2	47.2	53.3
On-going disability			
yes	11.2	17.6	19.2
no	87.3	81.5	79.7
Housing status			
owner/purchaser	70.1	65.4	77.9
private renter	12.7	17.9	8.3
public renter	0.7	3.3	4.0
other	12.7	10.7	6.9
Education status			
secondary school	52.2	53.1	63.8
trade certificate	20.9	18.5	12.7 ★
degree +	17.2	20.6	18.8
other	4.5	5.4	1.8
Labour force status			
self-employed	20.9	9.0 ★	10.1 ★
employee	47.8	45.1	40.6
unemployed	–	3.6 ★	3.3
not in the labour force	29.1	39.1	44.2 ★
Unemployment history			
yes	31.3	41.8 ★	35.9
no	66.4	53.7 ★	58.7

Continued next page

Characteristic	Individualist	Collectivist	Fatalist
Occupation			
manager, professional, etc.	35.9	31.7	31.9
clerks, sales, services	29.1	23.8	26.4
tradesperson	10.4	11.9	6.6
operative, labourer etc.	10.5	15.2	14.8
other	14.2	17.3	20.3
Political allegiance [b]			
Liberal Party	49.3	18.2 *	34.1 *
Labor Party	18.7	39.7 *	34.4 *
National Party	3.0	2.4	4.7
Australian Democrats	0.7	5.1 *	2.9
swinging voter	18.7	19.7	17.4
other	3.0	7.2	1.4

Notes: (a) percentages may not add to 100 due to rounding or because of incomplete responses to some questions. (b) The question asked was: *Generally speaking, which political party do you vote for?* (c) The asterisks (*) indicate that the difference between these estimates and those for the Individualist group are statistically significant ($\rho = 0.01$).

differences are small, they become more important when judged against the low variability that exists in the scores across the sample as a whole. Seen in this light, the differences in subjective health status and concern over job security are of particularly significance.

These results set the basis for some of the discussion and analysis that is developed in the next four chapters. The approach reflects an attempt to classify community attitudes as expressed in the CESC survey in ways designed to provide insight into how attitudes differ overall and whether these differences provide a better basis for understanding the nature of community attitudes and their possible impact. Overall, the differences shown in Tables 3.3 and 3.4 suggest that individualists *do* differ from collectivists, not only in their attitudes to the causes of, and responses to social problems, but also in their objective circumstances and subjective assessments of well-being. How far these differences extend into more detailed attitudes to reform of the welfare state is an issue taken up in later chapters.

Table 3.4 Subjective well-being and value position (percentages)

Well-being Indicator	Individualist	Collectivist	Fatalist
Life satisfaction			
– very satisfied (=5)	23.1	12.2 ★	17.0
– satisfied (=4)	47.8	52.5	53.3
– neither (=3)	12.7	19.4	14.9
– dissatisfied (=2)	9.7	8.4	8.0
– very dissatisfied (=1)	2.3	4.8	3.6
Overall score[a]	*3.66*	*3.51*	*3.63*
Happiness			
– very happy (=4)	16.4	16.7	16.3
– happy (=3)	75.4	70.6	69.6
– unhappy (=2)	5.2	9.3 ★	10.9
– very unhappy (=1)	–	1.1	0.4
Overall score[a]	*3.02*	*2.98*	*2.96*
Health status			
– excellent (=4)	41.8	29.3 ★	27.2 ★
– good (=3)	45.5	50.7	54.0
– fair (=2)	11.9	15.8	14.9
– poor (=1)	0.7	3.6	3.3
Overall score[a]	*3.28*	*3.04*	*3.04*
Job security[b]			
– rarely/never worry (=3)	50.0	32.5 ★	37.0
– worry sometimes (=2)	14.9	21.5 ★	13.8
– worry all the time (=1)	1.5	5.7 ★	3.6
Overall score[a]	*1.81*	*1.46*	*1.42*

Notes: (a) The overall score is calculated by assigning the individual scores (in brackets) to the incidence of each response. (b) Job security reflects the response to a question asking how often those in employment worry about losing their job. (c) The asterisks (★) indicate that the difference between these estimates and those for the Individualist group are statistically significant ($\rho = 0.01$).

Part II
The Changing Socioeconomic Landscape

4   Employment and Unemployment

The labour market plays an integral part in people's lives, providing a source of income and social status and absorbing a major portion of people's time. Access to employment is one of the most effective guarantees against poverty and the income it generates is, for the vast majority, one of the most important determinants of economic well-being. However, the structure of the labour market and the kinds of jobs it offers is changing rapidly in response to changes in economic structure, driven by a combination of technological change and competitiveness and changing patterns of demand. These factors exert their influence through the ebbs and flows of market forces in the global economy, causing increasing uncertainty among those in work by raising the fears of job insecurity and unemployment. Attitudes to many of these changes are ambivalent on the whole, as noted in the previous chapter.

At a time when the total number of people participating in the labour market is increasing, the length of the working life is declining. Longer periods spent in formal education are delaying initial labour market entry, while early retirement is bringing forward labour market exit for many people. The total number of hours worked while in the labour market is changing, with increasing numbers working part-time and others working very long hours. The increase in casual employment is eroding the non-wage benefits associated with permanent jobs and making it more difficult for those affected to plan their lives beyond the immediate requirements of the job. Workers' entitlements are put at risk as companies are becoming increasingly vulnerable to competitive forces over which they have limited control.

The rate at which these changes in paid work are taking place exceeds the capacity of many to adjust to their implications for balancing working life within the broader tapestry of life. While there are many working part-time who would prefer to work more hours and many casual workers who want a more permanent position, there are others who find these new opportunities are better suited to their circumstances. Changes that pose a threat to traditional structures and processes by some people are seen as a source of new opportunities by others.

External market forces drive many of these trends, but their effects are experienced domestically. The logic of market competition is compelling, but the injustice of some of its effects is a potential source of social instability. Although the market may act as a spur to innovation, efficiency and productivity, its effects on inequality must be socially acceptable and endorsed. In their determination to provide an institutional environment most conducive to the operation of market forces, policy-makers have dismantled many of the social structures that were capable of moderating inequality within a framework of cooperation, consensus and conciliation, including those in the labour market. The economic success of market reforms runs the risk of self-destructing on the altar of social alienation and inequality.

Change provides new opportunities but also upsets existing patterns and the plans based on them. The labour market is at the cutting edge of structural change and the economic reforms brought about by increased competition. It is the main arena through which people's material and, increasingly, social aspirations confront the harsh reality of economic forces and the arithmetic of economic logic. This chapter explores the nature of the labour market changes that have been and are taking place, examines attitudes to what is happening and explores public understanding of the underlying causes and consequences.

Reviewing labour market change

Many studies of changing work patterns focus on what is happening in the labour market to paid work and employment. Employment plays an important role in people's lives, and the functioning and impact of the labour market has important consequences for the performance of the economy as a whole. Work encompasses more than just employment, and the labour market as an economic and social institution is central to broader trends in working patterns in contemporary society. This centrality implies that the functioning of the labour market has important consequences for, and in part reflects changes in, the separation of activities and responsibilities between state and family, as well as within the family (Borland, Gregory and Sheehan, 2001).

The changing nature of work

Economic change is giving rise to new forms of work that fit less easily into the conventional relationship between the employer and employee operating within a broad industrial relations framework that sets pay and conditions on a broad sectoral basis (Watson and Buchanan, 2001). Technological and other changes mean that it is no longer essential for paid work to be undertaken in a specially established workplace, and many highly trained professionals are able to work from home with the assistance of the internet and other computer-assisted modes of communication.

Distinctions between the worlds of paid work and unpaid domestic activity are becoming increasingly blurred. Self-employment has been growing rapidly (Eardley and Bradbury, 1997), as has the number of generally low-skilled, often female, outworkers working from home (ABS, 1995a). While the nature of work is changing to encompass a greater variety of settings and a more complex set of relationships, the overall significance that the labour market plays in the performance of the economy and the living standards of individuals continues to grow. In this regard, changes in the structure of employment have facilitated changing social trends surrounding gender equity and the changing role of women.

Structural adjustment and the labour market

Change in the labour market has been driven by structural changes in technology and how these affect productivity and cost ever since the industrial revolution heralded the switch from agriculture to manufacturing (Jones, 1990). The emergence of 'post-industrial society' has seen a further switch from the manufacturing to the service and tertiary sectors and, within the service sector, to the growth of knowledge-based and person-based services (Reich, 1993; Sheehan, 1998). These developments have had an increasingly profound impact on each new cohort of workers and are affecting the circumstances, opportunities and expectations of those already in the labour force.

The change from manufacturing to services in the structure of output has resulted in an even larger change in the structure of employment because of the labour-intensive nature of most services. Manufacturing employment grew initially from 21 per cent of total employment in 1910–11 to 33 per cent in the mid-1940s, falling back to around 25 per cent in the mid-1960s and declining to 12 per cent by 1999. Employment in services has grown steadily over this period, from 13 per cent of total employment in 1910–11 to almost 73 per cent by 1999–2000 (ABS, 2001c, pp. 230 & 244–45). Between 1966 and 1996 alone, the proportion of employed people working in service industries increased from 54 per cent to 72 per cent (ABS, 1997b, p. 94). Whereas employment in services was approximately two-thirds that of manufacturing in 1910, by the end of the century the service sector was responsible for almost six times as many jobs as manufacturing industry. A consequence of this sectoral shift from manufacturing to services has been the decline in trade union membership, from a peak of around

60 per cent of all employees in 1961 to 26 per cent in 1999 (ABS, 2001c, Figure 6.46).

Community (or welfare) services have been part of this general trend, and the community services labour force now represents a significant and growing component of the total labour force (Saunders, 1999b). The re-orientation of the labour market towards the service sector has also favoured the employment of women, who make up the bulk of employment in services (Snooks, 1994). This expansion in the provision of welfare services has increased the ability of those who use these services to engage in the labour market or other forms of work-related activity.

The shift in employment towards services generally and welfare state services in particular, reflects the labour-intensive nature of many service activities. For many services, the input of labour into production is an essential component of the output that is produced. The output of a medical practitioner or child care worker, for example, largely reflects the input of time and expertise that each puts into the task. This feature, in combination with the non-routine nature of many service jobs, implies that it is more difficult to increase labour productivity in services than in manufacturing, where many routine jobs provide opportunities to increase productivity through investment in automation and technology. Over time, these forces ensure that service sector employment will grow relative to manufacturing employment, even if output in the two sectors increases at the same rate (Baumol, 1967; Esping-Andersen, 1990, 1999).

In fact, shifts in demand have seen service output growing faster than manufacturing output, adding further to this imbalance. The demand for education and health services has increased along with growing affluence. The increasing number of dual-earner families has meant that the demand for child care and other community caring services that were formerly provided within the home by unpaid family members now has to be met by formal services provided (and paid for) by government or the private sector (Saunders, 1999b). A growing population of people with a disability has further reinforced the demand for caring services. There has also been increasing recognition of the need for labour market placement and training services to assist the increased numbers of jobless Australians (including the unemployed and sole parents) to find employment. The relative growth of welfare services has thus facilitated the increase in labour force participation that has contributed a higher income to many families over the last three decades.

While labour market change reflects structural changes in the economy, important social changes are also taking place that affect the balance between alternative forms of paid and unpaid work on both sides of the labour market. The growth in services has direct consequences for a welfare state that employs a large and growing work force providing in-person welfare services to young children, the aged, disabled and other groups with special needs. As more people participate in the labour market, their ability to meet the needs of family members (young and old) who require care, or to engage in voluntary caregiving activity declines, triggering a further increase in demand for formal care provision. The increased demand for welfare services is thus inextricably linked to the more general increase in labour supply. The nature of labour market change is reinforcing these links with the kinds of jobs provided within and funded by, the welfare state.

Recent labour market developments

Australian labour market developments since 1980 have resulted in more female workers, more part-time workers and more self-employed workers, but fewer males working full-time and fewer older workers. Full-time employment growth has been strong for women, and although there has also been rapid growth in part-time employment among men, this began from a low base. The ratio of employed men to employed women has declined from 1.74 to one in 1980 to 1.26 to one in 2001. The work force is also now more highly educated on average, has more work experience, more young people combining part-time work with education and, among those working full-time, a greater proportion working very long hours (Department of Employment, Education and Training, 1996; Norris and Wooden, 1996).

Economic and social changes have resulted in a labour market that is increasingly segmented, by gender as well as between full-time and part-time employment. Increased job segmentation has made it more difficult for the unemployed to fill the new jobs being created, increasing the probability of long-term unemployment. The trend towards segmentation is further confirmed by evidence pointing to an increased concentration of employment between neighbourhoods (Gregory and Hunter, 1995, 1996). Whereas the landscape of the Australian labour market was relatively flat in the past, it now features sharp peaks in areas of strong activity separated by deep valleys of economic decline and unemployment.

Core and peripheral components are distinguished on the basis of age and hours of work. Between 1978 and 1995, net employment growth was concentrated on 'non-standard' jobs involving less than 30 hours or more than 45 hours worked each week. The greatest increases were in the proportion of workers working less than 30 or more than 49 hours a week. Over the same period, the work force became more dominated by persons aged 25–54, and there was a decline in the earnings of younger and older workers relative to the earnings of those in the 35–44 age group. Only around one-quarter of the work force now works the conventional 'standard working week' of between 35 and 40 hours. (Sheehan, 1998, Figure 6).

The labour force is increasingly 'middle-aged' (aged between 25 and 54), reflecting the later entry of younger workers more likely to extend their education and the increased withdrawal of older workers, particularly older men. Between 1966 and 2001, the employment rates of men aged 55 to 59 and 60 to 64 declined from 89.7 per cent to 67.3 per cent, and from 78.6 per cent to 43.9 per cent, respectively. While the aggregate statistics do not show a decline in the overall labour force participation rate, there is evidence of a decline in full-time work among men aged 55 to 64 (Ingles, 1998). Many of these trends are not restricted to Australia, but have also been occurring in other OECD countries for much of the last three decades (Scherer, 1997, Table 1.3).

Factors contributing to these trends include increasing affluence and the changing values and preferences of consumers and workers, changing attitudes towards gender roles in society, changes in family structure and the ethnic composition of the population. The combination of fiscal pressure and market ideology has seen a fundamental change in the balance between state and market in the provision and finance of many public sector activities and in the overall institutional framework of the labour market. Welfare reform now gives greater emphasis to encouraging or requiring participation in some form of work or preparation for work as a condition of eligibility for the receipt of benefit. This reinforcement of the work ethic among those unable to find work can have major effects on the supply side of the labour market, thus affecting wage pressures. These issues are explored in Chapters 8 and 9.

Although labour force participation has fallen markedly for males of all ages since 1980, labour force withdrawal has been greatest for those aged under 20 (a reflection of increased participation in education) and those aged between 55 and 64 (where enforced or chosen early retirement has become common). Female labour force participation has increased across all age groups (except the very young and the very old), with the increases greatest amongst those in the 25 to 34 and 45 to 54 age ranges. The previous tendency for women's labour force participation to decline between the ages of 25 and 34 (typically due to child rearing) has virtually disappeared.

Over a quarter of employed men and almost 9 per cent of employed women were working more than 48 hours a week in March 2001 (Table 4.1). These percentages increase to 36 per cent of men and 14 per cent of women working in excess of 44 hours a week. Among OECD countries, Australia has one of the highest percentages of employed people (men and women) working long hours – defined in this case as

Table 4.1 The distribution of hours worked by employed persons, March 2001

	Males		Females		Persons	
	('000)	(%)	('000)	(%)	('000)	(%)
Weekly hours worked:						
0	231.0	4.6	183.9	4.6	415.2	4.6
1–15	355.1	7.0	750.5	18.7	1105.6	12.2
16–29	415.2	8.2	818.3	20.4	1233.5	13.6
30–34	401.2	7.9	442.8	1.0	844.0	9.3
35–39	740.7	14.7	646.0	16.1	1386.7	15.3
40	887.5	17.6	478.4	11.9	1365.9	15.1
41–44	252.8	5.0	144.6	3.6	397.4	4.4
45–48	480.0	9.5	197.2	4.9	677.1	7.5
49 and over	1291.9	25.6	347.8	8.7	1639.7	18.1
Total	**5055.7**	**100.0**	**4009.5**	**100.0**	**9065.2**	**100.0**

Source: *The Labour Force, Australia*, ABS Catalogue No. 6203.0.

over 45 hours a week (OECD, 1998b). With so many working long hours, there is obviously some potential to create additional jobs or increase the hours worked by those who are currently under-employed, another issue that is taken up later.

Unemployment, well-being and insecurity

In terms of its implications for social policy, the most important labour market trend of the past two decades has been the growing mis-match between labour supply and demand, as reflected in the increase in unemployment (Figure 2.3). In June 2001, there were over 654,000 people officially registered as unemployed in Australia, corresponding to an unemployment rate of 6.7 per cent. This is the same rate as existed in 1906 – the first year for which unemployment rate data are available (ABS, 2001a, Figure 6.44). These figures are high, both (post-war) historically and relative to the unemployment experience of other OECD countries. Over the last quarter of the twentieth century, the average unemployment rate in Australia has been closer to that of the Depression years 1925–26 to 1939–40 than to the post-war 'boom' years that ended in 1973–74 (Borland and Kennedy, 1998a, Figure 1). In February 2001, the standardised unemployment rate in Australia of 6.9 per cent was above that existing in 18 of the 29 OECD countries for which the data are available (OECD, 2001).

The official unemployment statistics cover only those who are officially defined as unemployed in the ABS labour force survey. This provides a sound basis for monitoring overall labour market trends, but obscures the full extent of the problem of inadequate demand for labour (ABS, 2001b). A more accurate indication can be obtained by including discouraged workers who are outside of the labour force but who would like to be employed and those who have only a marginal attachment to the labour force. Estimates suggest that inclusion of these categories would cause a substantial increase (by as much as 50 per cent) in the official unemployment rate (Wooden, 1996; Watts, 2000).

The unemployment rate follows a cyclical pattern, with a tendency to rise rapidly in the early years of recession and to fall more gradually as the economy improves. Since the late 1970s, unemployment has declined only modestly when the economy was growing, but rose rapidly to above its previous peak when recession struck (Chapman and Kapuscinski, 2000). This has meant that over time, the proportion of the unemployed who have been unemployed for a year or more has followed a cyclical pattern around a rising long-term trend (Norris and Wooden, 1996, Chart 7).

That the unemployment rate moves only slowly should not conceal the fact that the labour market is vibrant, with new jobs being constantly created, old jobs disappearing and people moving frequently between different labour market states. Even when long-term unemployment is rising, the flows into and out of the unemployment pool are considerable. Between mid-1993 and late 1997, for example, (when unemployment was falling slowly), the average monthly in-flow into unemployment increased the unemployment rate by 1.41 percentage points, while the average monthly outflow reduced it by 1.44 percentage points (Borland and Kennedy, 1998a, Table 3).

The emergence of mass unemployment

Although all groups have been affected by the rise in unemployment, its incidence has not been equal across different groups. In general, the young, less educated, recent migrants and those who worked in a blue-collar occupation account for a disproportionate share of total unemployment relative to their share of the labour force (Borland and Kennedy, 1998a). There have also been significant regional differences in unemployment, primarily within rather than between different States (Watts, 2000). Analysis of local area census data reveals that there has been a considerable increase in the geographical dispersion of unemployment rates between 1976 and 1991, reflecting the relative fortunes of different industries (Gregory and Hunter, 1996).

The increasing proportion of the long-term unemployed in total unemployment is one of the most significant developments, both in terms of its impact on those affected and because of the problems that entrenched unemployment presents for policy. The groups most at risk of long-term unemployment are teenage women, and men in their early 20s and late 50s, while people with a disability are also more likely to experience long-term unemployment (ABS, 2001a). Compared with other OECD countries, long-term unemployment in Australia (in 1997) was below that in many continental European countries, though similar to that in the United Kingdom. However, both the rate of long-term unemployment and its incidence among the unemployed were higher in Australia than in Canada, Japan, New Zealand or the United States (ABS, 2001a).

As the total number of unemployed people has grown, so too has the number in receipt of unemployment benefits. This has driven up expenditure on unemployment benefits and focused attention on what can be done to reverse this trend. Over time, the increase in the number of benefit recipients has outstripped the increase in the numbers unemployed, leading to a rise in the coverage ratio – the proportion of the unemployed who are receiving unemployment benefits (Saunders, 1987). In June 1999, for example, the ABS labour force survey recorded 648,500 people as officially unemployed. At the same time, administrative data from the Department of Family and Community Services (FaCS) indicate that there were just under 713,400 people receiving an income support payment in respect of unemployment (FaCS, 2001, Table 2.9).

Thus, there would appear to be more people receiving income support as a result of unemployment than were actually unemployed at the time. However, this does not imply that the difference (some 65,000 people) were receiving their unemployment benefit fraudulently. The difference can be explained by the fact that many of those receiving unemployment benefit were also working more than the one hour a week that is required for them to be classified as employed in the ABS Labour Force Survey. There is certainly no implication that these comparisons reveal anything about the extent of over-payment (or under-payment) of unemployment benefits.

Implications for the welfare state

As noted in Chapter 3, the emergence of mass unemployment has had fundamental consequences for the welfare state. Widespread unemployment has brought into question the relevance and viability of many welfare programs that were designed on the assumption of full employment. Programs intended to provide temporary assistance to a small minority of the labour force were not equipped to cope with the large numbers of people affected by unemployment, many of them long-term unemployed.

The flow-on effects of unemployment on emotional stress and health, tensions within the family, social exclusion and community decline severely complicated the task of social policy. The increase in unemployment also eroded the tax base, making it harder to raise the revenue required to deal with the escalating set of unemployment-related social problems.

As noted, unemployment hit some sections of the labour force much harder than others. Because it was not easy to change the structural conditions that caused unemployment, it was more likely that, once experienced, unemployment would be difficult to escape from. The immediate effect of unemployment is a greatly increased risk of poverty since, for those of working age, lack of employment remains the single most important determinant of poverty (as it was when the Poverty Commission reported in the 1970s). When unemployment is experienced for long periods, its negative effects cumulate for the individuals affected and for their families (Saunders and Taylor, 2002, forthcoming).

That unemployment was concentrated in specific areas also meant that its impact on communities was greater. Although Australia has not experienced the emergence of an underclass like that in the United States, some suburbs on the outer fringes of the major cities where unemployment was very high saw community life begin to disintegrate. Sustained levels of unemployment and its multiplier effects on local businesses meant that many local businesses in country towns were no longer economically viable – setting off a downward spiral that exacerbated structural unemployment. Over the longer term, the lack of jobs and the structure that regular work provides to individuals and communities created a climate in which local neighbourhoods fell into decline. As education, health, transport and social welfare services were withdrawn, so children's prospects of escaping the predicament of their parents declined.

Governments around the world have been incapable of dealing with the multiplicity of social and economic problems that can be attributed to unemployment. This is partly due to a genuine lack of ideas about what should be done, at both the economy-wide and local levels. But the two most important factors relate to ideology and lack of resources. Neo-liberal economic orthodoxy argues that the roots of unemployment can be traced to a lack of motivation among the unemployed, to labour market imperfections and to the harmful effects of the social security system on the incentive to work. Unemployment would only fall if wages declined, since this would stimulate the demand for labour and reduce supply, bringing the two into balance in a flexible labour market. Fiscal stringency meant that there were no funds available to address unemployment through state initiatives that required additional public spending. So, the unemployment problem could only be resolved through the operation of market forces.

In order for the economic policies that resulted in high unemployment to be socially acceptable, it was necessary to gain the support of those whose livelihoods were put at risk by this new market-oriented approach. This involved shifting the blame for unemployment away from the economic policies of the government onto other causes. The most obvious target was the welfare system, which imposed a 'poverty trap' on those seeking to move from welfare into work. This focused attention on the design of the welfare system and away from the need to intervene in the economy to create more jobs. By shifting the emphasis onto the purported causes of unemployment, governments were able to pursue economic policies that resulted in high unemployment while arguing that unemployment was symptomatic of misguided social policies rather than inappropriate economic policies. The welfare state has still not recovered from this attack.

While unemployment has presented formidable problems for the welfare state, so too have other labour market trends. The growth in part-time work has created a potential bridge between the worlds of welfare and work, but has also blurred the boundary between the labour market and the welfare system, creating new problems for welfare administration. Increased labour market inequalities (discussed in Chapter 7) and greater economic insecurity (discussed later in this chapter) have made it more difficult to improve the financial incentives to move from welfare into paid work. The response to these pressures has involved reforming the welfare system to reduce the attractiveness of welfare benefits relative to paid work by reducing welfare entitlements under the guise of reciprocal, then mutual, obligation (as explained in Chapter 8). Market forces and labour market deregulation have thus dominated traditional welfare goals, and welfare reform has been subsumed under broader market-promoting imperatives.

Unemployment and well-being

Although the consequences of high unemployment for lost economic production and the social security budget are important, its debilitating effects on unemployed people are of greater social significance. A number of studies have shown that unemployment has adverse effects on subjective measures of well-being, even though the dimensions of well-being affected and the strength of the statistical associations identified differ. A large body of evidence points to the adverse social consequences of unemployment. These include its effects on health, psychological well-being, youth suicide, life satisfaction, family and community life and criminal activity (Flatau, Galea and Petridis, 2000; Morrell, Page and Taylor, 2001; Harris and Morrow, 2001; Bryson and Winter, 2002; and Weatherburn, 2002).

Some of these adverse social effects are reinforced by the tendency for unemployment to be concentrated within families (Miller, 1997). Research has shown that unemployment is associated with poor psychological functioning as a consequence of the loss of income and sense of purpose and structure in the lives of the unemployed (Feather, 1990; 1997). A range of Australian studies show that unemployment is causally linked to poor health, criminal activity and reduced life satisfaction (Borland and Kennedy, 1998a).

A recent study using data from the first wave of the European Community Household Panel, shows that unemployment has a powerful effect on life satisfaction across twelve EU countries, even though there is some cross-country variation in the strength of this association (Whelan and McGinnity, 1999). Using data from the British Household Panel Study, Clark and Oswald (1994) found that the unemployed had much lower levels of 'mental well-being' than those in work. This is consistent with Australian findings reported by Headey and Wearing (1992) who conclude that unemployment has a greater impact on psychological stress than on well-being, with the unemployed showing more symptoms of emotional strain than those who were employed (Headey and Wearing, 1992, p. 82).

There is thus a considerable body of evidence showing that unemployment has adverse effects on many dimensions of well-being. This issue is explored using the CESC data in Table 4.2, which compares the circumstances of the unemployed and the employed across a range of indicators of well-being. The indicators are grouped into those that include conventional measures such as life satisfaction, happiness and health status; those measuring the extent of alienation; and those that reflect beliefs about the causes of unemployment.

The results in the upper section of Table 4.2 indicate that unemployment has a negative impact on well-being. Although the differences are not numerically large (aside from the percentage reporting difficulty managing on their income), they are all statistically significant. Relative to those in employment, the unemployed are less satisfied with life, less happy, in poorer health and less able to manage financially. Results in the middle section of Table 4.2 indicate that the unemployed feel more alienated, in the sense that they are more likely to feel that they have lost control of their economic future and are more resigned to economic change. They are also more likely to agree that too much emphasis is given to economic as opposed to social factors and that machines have displaced people from employment. However, there is an equally strong

Employment and Unemployment

sense of resignation to the inevitability of economic and social change among both the unemployed and the employed.

Not surprisingly, there is strong disagreement among the unemployed with the statement that the unemployed only have themselves to blame, although many of the employed also disagree with this statement. The unemployed are also strongly of the view that unemployment reflects demand rather than supply factors; many of them agree that there aren't enough jobs for all those who want to work, but there is less agreement that fewer people want to work these days. Those in employment, in contrast, appear to support neither a simple demand nor supply side

Table 4.2 Subjective well-being, attitudes and employment status

Indicator	Specification	Employed	Unemployed
WELL-BEING			
Life satisfaction	Five-point scale; very satisfied = 5 to very dissatisfied = 1	3.73	2.73
Happiness	Four-point scale; very happy = 4 to very unhappy = 1	3.05	2.77
Health status	Four-point scale; excellent = 4 to poor = 1	3.25	3.05
Managing on income	Percentage who cannot get by on their income	3.8%	42.9%
ALIENATION [a]			
Lost control	I have lost control of my economic future	−0.25	0.11
Resignation	Change is inevitable and I just have to put up with it	0.47 *	0.36 *
Wrong balance	Too much emphasis on economy	0.94	1.22
Machines take jobs	Machines do more of the work	0.80	1.23
VIEWS ON UNEMPLOYMENT [a]			
Blame unemployed	The unemployed only have themselves to blame	−0.58	−1.17
Not enough jobs	There are not enough jobs for all who want to work	0.01	0.74
Always be some unemployment	We will never get back to full employment	0.81 *	0.88 *
Fewer people want to work	Fewer people want to work these days	0.15	−0.65

Mean score shown for Employed and Unemployed columns.

Notes: (a) These variables are measured on a five-point scale from strongly agree (= +2), agree (= +1), neither agree nor disagree (= 0), disagree (= −1) to strongly disagree (= −2). * Indicates that the differences are NOT statistically different. Unweighted sample size (n) = 1,096 consisting of 1,032 employed and 64 unemployed.

explanation of unemployment. Both the employed and unemployed are equally pessimistic about the prospects for getting back to full employment. Overall, the results in Table 4.2 confirm that unemployment has profound and debilitating effects, not only on the subjective well-being of the unemployed, but also on their attitudes to the forces of change in society generally.

Job insecurity

It has been argued that the combination of high levels of unemployment and increased inequality of earnings has produced greater insecurity among the work force. Economic insecurity reflects 'the anxiety produced by a lack of economic safety, i.e. by an inability to obtain protection against subjectively significant potential economic losses' (Osberg, 1998, p. 23). Changes in economic insecurity have been the subject of intense debate in Australia. The question of increasing insecurity of *employment* has emerged as an issue in a number of OECD countries, although the evidence does not provide strong and unambiguous support for the view that job insecurity is increasing (OECD, 1997a).

Labour market research has unearthed an apparent contradiction between objective labour market indicators such as job mobility and employment duration – which suggest that *employment instability* is declining (Wooden, 1998; 1999) – and public opinion data which show that *job insecurity* increased in Australia in the 1990s (Kelley, Evans and Dawkins, 1998). Research by Borland (2001) shows that perceptions of job security are influenced by changes in unemployment and this can explain the different trends in job security and job stability.

It is also important to note however, that what matters for changes in insecurity is not just the *objective conditions* that determine the probability of losing a job and of being able to find a new one, and expectations about income in the interim, but the nature of *subjective perceptions* about these factors. Higher (or rising) levels of unemployment will cause more of those who have a job to worry about the prospect of losing it, while what is happening to earnings will affect expectations about likely earnings in any new job. Overall, it seems plausible that the changes in objective labour market conditions described earlier may have fostered an increased level of job insecurity amongst Australian workers.

The CESC survey included two questions on economic insecurity. The first concerned overall loss of economic control and was designed to obtain a broad indication of the extent of the problem. The question asked whether control has been *lost*, and thus presupposed that some degree of control has been present in the past. The second question refers specifically to those in employment and asks about whether or not they worry about losing their job. The responses to both questions are summarised in Table 4.3. In overall terms, over 31 per cent agreed with the proposition that they had lost control over their economic future, while almost one-third (32.0 per cent) indicated that they worry about losing their job. Against this, 42.2 per cent of respondents did not feel that they had lost control over their economic future, while a substantial proportion (59.7 per cent) of those in employment rarely or never worry about losing their job. Opinion thus appears evenly divided on the issue of economic insecurity; while there is evidence that many people feel insecure and worry about losing their job, there are more that do not.

Table 4.4 explores whether there are systematic differences in the incidence of job insecurity between demographic groups. These results show that concern about job prospects among those in employment is greater among men than women and increases with age; very few workers below the age of 25 worry about losing their job, whereas this is quite common among workers aged over 40. Those born in Australia worry less about losing their jobs than those born overseas, particularly those born in non-English-speaking countries and there is a clear tendency for job insecurity to be greatest among those with fewer educational qualifications. These patterns in job insecurity reflect different underlying vulnerabilities in the work force as a whole, with those who (for good reason) feel less able to compete for new jobs more likely to worry about losing their current ones.

Community Understanding of Unemployment: Causes and Cures

One of the main factors behind the increased acceptance of high levels of unemployment has been the change in community understanding of the causes of unemployment and what can be done to reduce it. This change is reflected in economic and attitudinal imperatives. With the increased

Table 4.3 Indicators of economic insecurity (percentages) [a]

Strongly agree	Agree	Neither agree nor disagree	Disagree	Strongly disagree	Don't know
I feel I have lost control over my economic future					
9.1	22.3	23.4	35.6	6.6	3.1
IF YOU HAVE A JOB, how secure or insecure do you feel about it?					
Worry all the time	Worry sometimes	Rarely or never worry	Don't know	Missing	
5.4	26.6	59.7	3.0	5.3	

Note: (a) Full sample: n = 2,319; employed sample: n = 999 (includes those aged between 18 and 64 only)

influence of economic neo-liberalism have come a stronger emphasis on market solutions to communal problems and a renewed emphasis on the importance of incentives and individual motivation as factors contributing to unemployment.

Within the philosophical and analytical framework provided by these ideas, governments have tried to convince people that the major cause of unemployment is the structure of welfare support for the unemployed rather than the failure of economic policies. Under this new paradigm, the main responsibility of government is to re-structure welfare provision so that it discourages passivity among those receiving it in favour of active job search and employment participation. Intervention should thus focus on facilitating engagement with a deregulated labour market left to follow the imperatives of market forces.

Extent and nature of unemployment

The strength of opinion about alternative responses to unemployment is likely to depend upon perceptions of the severity of the problem. In order

Table 4.4 Incidence of job insecurity by socioeconomic characteristics (percentages)

Characteristic	Worry all the time	Worry sometimes	Rarely or never worry	Don't know	Missing
Gender					
male	6.6	29.1	54.6	3.3	6.4
female	4.0	23.6	65.8	2.7	4.0
Age range					
18-24	1.2	13.3	79.5	4.8	1.2
25-39	3.2	28.0	63.1	2.9	2.9
40-64	7.6	27.7	54.2	2.8	7.6
Country of birth					
Australia	4.8	24.6	62.2	3.0	5.4
overseas (ESC)	6.6	32.0	51.6	3.3	6.6
overseas (NESC)	8.9	35.6	49.5	3.0	3.0
Education					
less than secondary school	6.7	27.6	51.4	6.2	8.1
secondary school/ trade certificate	6.4	27.0	59.7	2.7	4.2
degree plus	3.2	25.0	65.9	0.8	5.2
other/missing	1.8	26.8	62.5	3.6	5.4

Note: The question is shown in Table 4.3. Sample size = 999.

to gain insight into how well informed people are about the scale of unemployment, the CESC survey asked respondents to indicate what they thought the official unemployment rate was at the time of the survey and what proportion of those officially unemployed had been out of work for one year or more. Although respondents were provided with a limited range of possible answers from which to choose, the difficulty of these two questions should not be under-estimated. It is not surprising that around 5 per cent did not respond to these two questions, and a significant proportion of those who did respond indicated that they did not know the answer.

Of those who did respond, Table 4.5 shows that just over half of those who replied correctly assessed the official unemployment as being in the 7–9 per cent range (it was approximately 7.5 per cent in June 1999). Almost one-third thought it was higher than this and very few thought it was below 7 per cent. There was thus a general tendency to over-estimate the unemployment rate, although there are also some interesting differences within the sample. In general, men, Liberal Party voters, higher income groups, home owners and those with higher educational qualifications were less likely to overestimate the severity of unemployment (Eardley, Saunders, Evans and Matheson, 2000, Appendix B).

When it comes to knowledge about long-term unemployment, a substantial proportion again over-estimated the extent of the problem, which stood at about one-third of total unemployment at the time of the survey (Table 4.6). Just under 40 per cent of responses were in the correct range, but over 30 per cent thought the figure was much higher than it was and around one-fifth said they did not know what proportion of the unemployed were long-term unemployed. It is difficult to know whether these estimates indicate that many people are poorly informed about the unemployment figures, or whether there is a distrust of the official statistics and a sense that unemployment is more severe than presented. As noted earlier in this chapter, there is evidence that the official statistics under-estimate the full extent of unemployment.

Table 4.5 Estimates of the current unemployment rate (percentages)

Question	Less than 3%	3–6%	7–9%	10–12%	More than 12%	Don't know
What do you think the current official unemployment rate is in Australia?	0.2	3.9	53.5	20.6	11.5	10.3

Unweighted n = 2,275.

Table 4.6 Estimates of the level of long-term unemployment (percentages)

Question	Less than a quarter	Between a quarter and a half	More than half	Don't know
What proportion of people who are officially unemployed do you think have been out of work for one year or more?	10.7	38.1	31.5	19.7

Unweighted n = 2,272.

Causes of unemployment

In order to gauge perceptions of the causes of unemployment, respondents were asked to indicate the strength of their agreement or disagreement with a set of alternative explanations of unemployment. The statements of explanation and the responses they generated are shown in Table 4.7. The proposed explanations have been arranged so that the first two refer to *aggregate demand explanations*, the next three to *demand switching explanations*, the next two to *supply-side explanations* and the final two to *job-imbalance explanations* of unemployment. The results indicate that people are more likely to agree with the various propositions put to them than to disagree. This effect is frequently found in attitudinal surveys, but it may also reflect a realistic understanding of the multiple causes of unemployment. Despite this pattern, there is still noticeable variation in the strength of views on the different causal explanations.

Looking at broad agreement as a whole (by combining the 'Strongly agree' and 'Agree' responses), there is over 70 per cent support for the view that unemployment is caused by technology and over 60 per cent for the view that it is caused by cheap imports. Around 50 per cent agree that a range of demand-side and supply-side factors contribute to unemployment, including a shortage of jobs, ease of access to social security, lack of skills among the work force and long working hours. There is about 40 per cent support for the role of fewer people wanting to work, and around 30 per cent support for government economic mismanagement of the economy and the impact of trade unions. The lowest level of support (26.5 per cent) is for the view that migrants are taking the jobs of Australian-born workers.

Opinion is most polarised about the role of government mismanagement of the economy and of excessive wage demands by trade unions, where around one-third were in overall agreement and a similar proportion in overall disagreement. However, these statements also attracted the highest levels of 'agnosticism', with 28.7 per cent neither agreeing nor

Table 4.7 Explanations for high unemployment (percentages)

	There just aren't enough jobs for all the people who want to work	There aren't enough jobs because the Government isn't managing the economy properly	Nowadays machines do more of the work and that means there are fewer jobs	Trade unions demand wages that are too high, so employers can't afford to take on more workers	Cheap imports from overseas have destroyed Australian jobs	Fewer people want to work these days	It's easier to get social security these days	Migrants are taking the jobs of Australian-born workers	Some people aren't skilled enough to fill the jobs that are available now	People who have jobs are working longer hours, so employers don't have to take on more workers
Strongly agree	12.0	10.8	22.8	9.4	20.8	9.8	21.2	9.2	7.9	13.2
Agree	36.9	22.3	53.6	23.8	43.1	34.3	34.6	17.3	46.1	37.6
Neither agree nor disagree	14.0	28.7	8.3	20.4	14.6	16.2	13.8	19.7	15.0	17.7
Disagree	25.9	23.8	8.2	26.5	11.5	25.6	16.0	32.8	20.0	19.3
Strongly disagree	4.0	3.8	1.1	9.1	1.5	6.4	4.1	12.8	2.8	1.8
Total agree minus disagree	**19.0**	**5.5**	**67.1**	**-2.4**	**50.9**	**12.1**	**35.7**	**-19.1**	**31.2**	**29.7**
Don't know	1.5	5.0	0.6	5.3	2.9	1.8	4.5	2.7	2.4	4.8
Missing	5.6	5.6	5.4	5.5	5.5	5.8	5.9	5.7	5.7	5.5
Total	100.0	100.0	100.0	100.0	100.0	100.0	100.0	100.0	100.0	100.0

Unweighted n = 2,403.

disagreeing that unemployment is caused by the government's management of the economy, and 20.4 per cent unwilling to offer a view on the role of trade unions. Two other statements that attracted a similar pattern of responses were that there are not enough jobs for those who want to work, and that fewer people want to work.

Overall, the results in Table 4.7 indicate that there is considerable diversity in public opinion about the causes of unemployment in Australia, with many people acknowledging (correctly) that there are many contributing factors. Overall, there is more support for the demand-side explanations of unemployment than for supply-side explanations, with considerable support for the view that unemployment reflects imbalances in the skills needed and in hours worked (too few of the former and too many of the latter). More than half (50.8 per cent) agreed that current employees working long hours has contributed to unemployment by eliminating the need for employers to take on more workers.

In terms of the overall difference between agreement and disagreement, the two most popular explanations of unemployment are technological change and overseas competition, with the ease of access to social security ranked third. That there is no consensus among Australians regarding the causes of unemployment suggests that opinion is also likely to differ about who is responsible and what should be done about it. These issues are now considered.

Solutions to unemployment

Community views on who should be held responsible for solving the unemployment problem reveal widespread pessimism about the prospects for returning to full employment (however respondents conceived of this). Table 4.8 indicates that over three-quarters (75.8 per cent) agree that 'some people will always be unemployed'. Close to one-third (29.4 per cent) thought that there was enough work available but that it needs to be shared more evenly. Opinion is now seen to be more evenly divided on the issue of work sharing. There is a similar pattern of support for the role of government and business in solving unemployment. However, the requirement on business to create more jobs would presumably have to come from government, implying that most people regard some form of action from government as necessary to solve unemployment.

Very few people blame the unemployed themselves for unemployment, with less than 14 per cent agreeing with this diagnosis and almost 58 per cent disagreeing. Thus, despite the earlier finding (Table 4.7) that approaching half (44.1 per cent) thought that a reluctance to work was contributing to unemployment, 'blaming the victim' is not a widespread reaction to the plight of the unemployed.

Table 4.8 Views on the responsibility for solving the unemployment problem (percentages)

	People who are unemployed only have themselves to blame	Businesses should be required to create more jobs	Solving unemployment is the Government's responsibility	Some people will always be unemployed – we will never get back to full-employment	There's enough work available now – we just have to share it around more evenly
Strongly agree	3.9	8.9	13.0	17.7	4.8
Agree	9.6	34.9	34.2	58.1	24.6
Neither agree nor disagree	23.9	26.3	23.4	8.7	25.3
Disagree	44.4	22.6	22.3	7.6	33.1
Strongly disagree	13.4	1.9	2.3	2.0	4.5
Total agree minus disagree	**−44.3**	**19.3**	**22.6**	**66.2**	**−8.2**
Don't know	1.5	1.9	1.7	3.0	4.7
Missing	3.4	3.6	3.2	3.0	3.1
Total	100.0	100.0	100.0	100.0	100.0

Unweighted n = 2403.

Although Table 4.8 implies that many people see a role for government in solving the unemployment problem, there is no indication of what form this might take. In order to explore this issue in more detail, respondents were provided with a list of thirteen possible actions that the government could take to solve unemployment, and asked to indicate which *three* they thought were the most important. The options provided can be classified as falling into one of three broad responses:

1. Those which clearly involve more government intervention.
2. Those which imply support for a restructuring of existing intervention, without necessarily supporting more or less state intervention overall.
3. Those which suggest support for either less state intervention and/or increased reliance on market-based solutions to unemployment.

The precise options are listed under each of these three categories in the upper, middle and lower panels of Table 4.9, respectively, along with the responses produced. One further alternative – to keep economic growth as high as possible – is presented separately, as it does not easily fit into this tripartite classification.

It is important to emphasise that the options were not listed in the CESC questionnaire in the order in which the responses are shown in Table 4.9. The numbers shown in brackets after each option in Table 4.9 indicate the order in which they appeared in the questionnaire itself. The number of responses for each option are shown for the total sample of

Table 4.9 The role of government in solving unemployment

	Percentage of responses			
Listed below are a number of things the Government might do to solve unemployment. Which THREE (3) do you think are most important?	All respondents (n = 2299)	Individual (n = 134)	Collectivists (n = 335)	Fatalists (n = 276)
1. Increased Intervention				
Create more public sector jobs (2)	5.1	2.6	5.9	5.6
Give employers subsidies to take on unemployed people (4)	11.1	9.2	12.0	10.5
Provide more training to unemployed people (6)	12.1	9.5	12.9	12.1
Expand regional employment policies (8)	4.4	1.5	4.8	4.8
Spend more on labour market programs (9)	1.9	0.0	2.7	2.1
Give more help to small business (11)	13.7	11.5	14.7	14.1
2. Restructured Intervention				
Reform the tax system (3)	9.1	11.8	8.6	9.4
Improve work incentives in the tax and social security systems (7)	10.6	12.0	9.7	13.4
Make it easier for people to combine work and family responsibilities (13)	11.2	10.2	13.8	7.4
3. Reduced Intervention/Market-based Strategies				
Freeze pay awards (5)	1.3	1.3	1.0	1.5
Make it harder to get unemployment benefits (10)	8.2	17.6	4.2	6.1
Deregulate the labour market further (12)	1.0	2.6	0.9	1.0
4. Neutral with respect to Intervention				
Keep economic growth as high as possible (1)	10.3	10.0	8.6	11.9
5. Total	100.0	100.0	100.0	100.0

respondents as well as for those individuals who have been classified into each of the three value positions – individualist, collectivist and fatalist – described in Chapter 3.

Looking first at the overall pattern of responses, three of the four most popular responses (provide more help to small business; provide more training for the unemployed; and give employers subsidies to take on the unemployed) all involve increased intervention by government. The third, fifth and seventh most popular options (make it easier for people to combine work and family; improve the incentive structure; and tax reform) are examples of policies that involve restructuring existing intervention with no clear implications for the overall level of intervention. Very few people think that the government should freeze award wages or further deregulate the labour market, which involve less state intervention in order to reduce unemployment. However, over 8 per cent thought that it should be more difficult to get unemployment benefits, while over 10 per cent were in favour of addressing unemployment through strategies designed to keep economic growth at a maximum.

When the responses of those who support different value frameworks are separately identified, several patterns emerge. The most popular response to unemployment among individualists is to make it harder to get unemployment benefits – a finding that is consistent with an incentive-induced supply-side explanation of unemployment that sees individuals as primarily responsible for what happens to them. Individualists are also in favour of restructuring the tax-transfer system in ways that improve incentive structures and of programs directed at employers and small business (even though these options might involve increased government spending).

Collectivists are strongly supportive of programs that make it easier to combine work and family, while fatalists (like individualists) are strong supporters of improving the incentives in the tax and social security systems. Collectivists and fatalists favour programs that involve increased or restructured intervention, with the emphasis on providing assistance to small business, employer subsidies and increased training. Support among both groups for the more traditional state-centred responses to unemployment, such as public sector job creation, regional employment policies and labour market programs is much higher than among individualists, but still rather low in absolute terms. Increased spending on labour market programs receives a very low level of overall support, only slightly more than deregulating the labour market and freezing award wages. Support for labour market programs is consistently low, attracting less than 3 per cent support even among collectivists.

Table 4.9 suggests that the great majority of Australians support the need for government to both increase its level of intervention, and to restructure existing policies, in order to help reduce unemployment. In combination with earlier results (Table 4.8), people not only think that the government should do something to help reduce unemployment, they also have views as to what should be done. It is less clear whether or not people think that increased intervention should also involve extra government spending, (although this is implied in the way many of the survey questions were phrased). There are important differences of opinion within the population concerning the kinds of actions that should be taken to address unemployment. But it is clear that, overall, there is strong support for the view that *something* should be done, with both government and business expected to play a role in reducing unemployment.

Support for the unemployed

Evidence from previous survey research suggests that support for extra spending on the unemployed in Australia is low by international standards (Eardley and Matheson, 1999). What is the nature of community opinion regarding the level of support provided to unemployed people? In considering this issue, it is important to recognise that many people may have little idea of what the current level of support provided to the unemployed (and other groups) actually is. Support for a reduction in the level of support provided to the unemployed may thus be based on the mistaken perception that they receive a lot more support than they actually do, and vice versa. If respondents were provided with 'the facts' their responses might well be different, but to do so risks inducing a bias in the responses, as noted in Chapter 3. Nevertheless, the fact that between 15 per cent and 30 per cent replied 'Don't know' to this question (a good deal higher than in most other questions) suggests that many people were unaware of the support provided to different groups of the unemployed.

The question asked about the level of support for the unemployed, and the responses it generated are shown in Table 4.10. The question was asked for each of six separate categories of the unemployed so that variations in the nature of attitudes according to the circumstances of the unemployed could be examined. It needs to be recognised, however, that some of the categories specified in the question are rather vague (e.g. 'people constantly in and out of work'), while others overlap each other (e.g. many of the long-term unemployed have young children or are aged over 50). However, the reason for specifying the different categories was to explore which of the characteristics of the unemployed affect community attitudes to the level of support they should receive, and the categories are adequate for this purpose.

Table 4.10 Views on levels of government support for unemployed people (percentages)

	Young single unemployed (under 25)	Older unemployed (over 50)	Long-term unemployed	People constantly in and out of work	Unemployed people with young children (under 5)	Unemployed migrants
Too much	25.7	1.6	24.2	26.0	13.6	28.1
About right	39.1	25.8	26.4	33.8	34.5	27.1
Not enough	21.5	57.9	31.6	15.8	32.1	13.4
Don't know	13.7	14.6	17.8	24.5	9.7	31.4
Total	100.0	100.0	100.0	100.0	100.0	100.0

What do you think about the overall level of support the Government provides for the following groups of unemployed people at the moment?

Unweighted n = 2,331 to 2,359.

The results indicate that public opinion is divided on the adequacy of current levels of support for the unemployed, although there is a widespread view that older unemployed people do not receive enough support, and very few people thought that they receive too much support. About a quarter of CESC respondents thought that other groups of the unemployed, apart from those with young children, receive too much support, while nearly one-third thought that both the long-term unemployed and people with young children did not get enough. There seems to be a distinction in people's minds between treatment of the older unemployed and the long-term unemployed, many of whom are one and the same. This may be a result of the way the question was posed (as noted above), but it also suggests that many people may be unaware of long-term unemployment being a particular problem for older people.

In spite of the limited understanding of how much support is provided to the unemployed, there is no evidence in Table 4.10 that public opinion is in favour of large-scale cutbacks in the level of support. Indeed, the variation in attitudes to support for the different groups of unemployed reveals a refined understanding of the different needs and claims of different groups among the unemployed. In general terms, the views are consistent with those identified in recent studies of attitudes to the deservingness of different groups to social support in the United States, the United Kingdom and the Netherlands (van Oorschot, 2000).

Community attitudes towards the support provided for different groups of the unemployed vary systematically across the three value groupings (Table 4.11). All three value groups rank the older unemployed first in terms of the need to provide additional support and all three rank the young unemployed, along with those who are constantly in and out of work and unemployed migrants, last. The precise rankings between these extremes vary, but the overall pattern is similar to that existing for the population as a whole (Table 4.10). But there are also some marked differences among the three groups. For example, the percentage of individualists who agree that there is too much support for the long-term unemployed (50.0 per cent) is more than three times higher than for fatalists (15 per cent) and almost three times as much as collectivists (17.9 per cent). Across all six categories, the attitudes of individualists are consistently tougher than those of either collectivists or fatalists.

The extent of variation between the value group differentials is highlighted by comparing attitudes to support for the two groups that attract most (the older unemployed) and least (people moving constantly in and out of work) overall sympathy. The (very similar) attitudes of collectivists and fatalists to those with a marginal attachment to work is closer to the individualists' views on support for the older unemployed than to individualist attitudes to those who move in and out of work. But even so,

Table 4.11 Views on levels of government support for unemployed people among different value groupings (percentages)

What do you think about the overall level of support the Government provides for the following groups of unemployed people at the moment?

	Young single unemployed (under 25)	Older unemployed (over 50)	Long-term unemployed	People constantly in and out of work	Unemployed people with young children (under 5)	Unemployed migrants
Individualists (n = 116)						
Too much	45.7	5.2	50.0	43.1	30.2	43.1
About right	35.3	31.9	22.4	35.3	40.5	23.3
Not enough	10.3	49.1	15.5	6.9	17.2	12.1
Don't know	8.6	13.8	12.1	14.7	12.1	21.6
Collectivists (n = 274)						
Too much	18.2	0.7	17.9	20.1	12.0	24.1
About right	31.8	19.0	20.1	33.2	32.1	23.4
Not enough	36.1	70.1	43.8	25.2	39.1	23.0
Don't know	13.9	10.2	18.2	21.5	16.8	29.6
Fatalists (n = 206)						
Too much	21.8	0.5	15.0	19.9	7.8	23.3
About right	45.6	24.3	33.5	39.3	39.3	29.1
Not enough	21.4	59.2	35.0	14.1	34.5	15.0
Don't know	11.2	16.0	16.5	26.7	18.4	32.5

almost half (49.1 per cent) of individualists think that existing support for the older unemployed is not enough. There is considerable ambivalence about the treatment of unemployed migrants, with many people unsure of how they are currently treated and thus unable to decide whether or not it is appropriate.

Community attitudes to the treatment of the unemployed vary according to the characteristics of the unemployed and with the respondents' views on social issues generally. These differences reflect the nature of unemployment itself, its causes and the range of factors that can play a part in its solution. Many of these attitudinal differences relate systematically to the values and beliefs of those who hold them, as well as to the characteristics of the unemployed themselves. Some of these latter characteristics, such as commitment to the work force and being young (under 25) or older (over 50) probably reflect deep-seated views about deservingness and responsibility for one's circumstances (as the work of van Orschot, 2000, for example, suggests). Whatever the explanations, it is clear from the diversity in attitudes to the unemployed that no single position can hope to capture community opinion on the topic.

There is strong community agreement that something should be done about unemployment, with most solutions requiring more from government and business. The differences in attitudes suggest that finding solutions to the unemployment problem that attract broad community support will be extremely difficult. But it does not follow that the task is impossible. There is strong support for doing more to reduce the level of unemployment and providing additional support to some of the unemployed. These views provide the platform for mobilising community support behind a sustained attack on unemployment.

5 Income and Living Standards

Economic transactions in a market economy reflect the exchange of goods and services and the incomes that are generated. For individuals and households, the income received from participating in market activity provides the means to purchase the goods and services that contribute to economic well-being or material living standards. Income is a natural starting point for investigating the average standard of living in an economy, or comparing how standards of living have changed over time, or vary between different regions or groups in society. Income provides the means by which individuals interact as consumers and producers in the market place; it can be used to support current consumption or be put aside to support future consumption. An increase in income is thus generally presumed to correspond to an increase in the standard of living, since it provides the means to increase the level of consumption now and/or in the future.

The relationship between income and the standard of living is, however, more complex than implied in this simple account of the underlying economic arithmetic (Sen, 1987). This complexity applies at the level of both the household in which individuals live and society as a whole, and although the main emphasis here is on the standard of living of households, there are lessons from studying the problems involved in measuring well-being at an aggregate level. Although most empirical studies of household income adopt a cash income measure, this reflects only one component of the standard of living. Households with the same cash income need not have the same standard of living, while the same standard of living may be associated with different levels of household income.

This divergence between cash income and the standard of living reflects two important factors. First, some forms of income are derived from activities undertaken outside the market sector that are not captured in conventional measures of cash income. Examples include the income derived from unpaid domestic work, from owning one's home, or from engaging in do-it-yourself activity that improves the value of assets owned. Second, the form in which income is received may have implications for its impact on the standard of living. Income received as charity or as a government benefit paid only after undergoing a (possibly demeaning) examination of circumstances and motivations may be less valued than untied transfer payments, or income that has to be earned in the market. The ability to translate a given level of income into a specific standard of living is also conditioned by several intervening variables, including the size and the composition of the household, what has to be sacrificed to generate the income, and the ownership of wealth.

To further complicate matters, the relationship between income and the standard of living is conditioned by changes in society and social policy that affect how income is generated, received and valued by those who receive it. The introduction of occupational superannuation in Australia, for example, has had the effect of lowering the *current* incomes of many wage and salary earners while increasing their claims to a *future* income stream. Its effect on lifetime income differs from its effect on current income and, to the extent that the standard of living reflects the former, a gap is opened up between current income and the standard of living. These considerations caution against adopting a simplified approach to income measurement in the context of living standards. This is also true when studying economic inequality (as explained in Chapter 7), where an inappropriate income measure may provide an inaccurate and misleading guide to the degree of inequality. In order to understand the factors involved and how social change is influencing them, it is useful to begin by discussing how income is defined and manipulated when studying living standards.

The economic and social dimensions of income

Income represents a flow of resources that can be used to finance consumption. Under its conventional economic definition, income is defined as the maximum level of consumption that can be supported in any period without causing any change in net wealth. Not all income is necessarily spent on consumption items, but any income that is not spent is, by definition, saved and increases the stock of wealth. Income is thus equal to the sum of *actual* consumption and the change in net wealth, or saving. Two households with the same level of income may experience very different levels of consumption, depending on how the stock of wealth that each owns is changing. A young family on a modest income, for example, may struggle to make ends meet while they are saving the deposit for their first home. In contrast, an older couple on the same modest income may enjoy a higher standard of living as they run down their accumulated savings during retirement.

In general, those who own more wealth at a particular point in time have a greater opportunity to sustain a higher level of consumption from a given income (or do so for longer) and are thus better off. However, the level of income often changes as people move through the life cycle, as do their wealth and their needs, leading to a standard of living profile that differs from that of income. Because the life cycle profile of income is often predictable (at least in general terms, though not for particular individuals), economists have argued that permanent income is a better indicator of economic well-being than actual current income. Permanent income measures the average expected income over the entire lifetime and thus evens out the year-to-year fluctuations in actual income that inevitably occur. Consumption is more closely related to permanent income (Friedman, 1957; Slesnick, 1993, 2001, Chapter 2) and consumption thus follows a smoother path over time, with saving and dissaving used to insulate living standards from transitory movements in actual income (see Figures 2.1 and 2.2).

Defining income

Although income is an important theoretical concept, it is also a statistical construct. Money income is received in exchange for participating in the production process, or as interest income on previously acquired assets. These are equal to income from labour and capital, respectively. The former includes wage and salary income and income from self-employment, while the latter includes income in the form of rent, interest and dividends – depending on which kinds of assets make up total wealth. In principle, these components of income are readily quantified as they enter into routine commercial calculations (of the cost of production, for example) or are included within the scope of income as defined for tax purposes. This is an example of how public policy (in this case income tax policy) affects the collection of income data and thus the reliability of the available statistics.

There are formidable problems surrounding the measurement of some forms of cash income. One example is self-employment income, where the whole question of tax deductibility of legitimate business costs casts doubt on the reliability of reported income data. As a consequence, it is likely that the incomes of the self-employed will provide a less accurate guide to their standard of living than is the case for employees. This is borne out by evidence which indicates that while the median weekly income of the self-employed in 1988–89 was 20 per cent below that of employees, median expenditure was 6 per cent higher for the self-employed. Assuming a stable relationship between income and expenditure across the two groups suggests that the incomes of the self-employed may be understated relative to employees by as much as one-quarter (Eardley and Bradbury, 1997).

Another area where the measurement problems are formidable is capital gains. Here, the basic problem reflects the inherent difficulty of defining capital gains conceptually and distinguishing between nominal and real (inflation-adjusted) gains. The associated practical limitations mean that such gains (or losses) are rarely captured in the income statistics. Again, these aspects depend partly on the tax system; the introduction of a comprehensive tax on capital gains would require their more accurate measurement, and the quality of official (and survey) statistics would improve.

Income that is derived in exchange for the sale of labour or investment of capital in the market is referred to as *primary income*. Another important source of income is transfer payments received from others, including from other individuals (private transfers) or from government in the form of social security or other cash benefits (public transfers). Adding private transfers to primary income gives *market income*. Adding in public transfers gives *gross income*, from which direct taxes are deducted to arrive at *disposable income*. Disposable income corresponds to the income available after the receipt of transfers and payment of taxes and is the basis of most studies of living standards and income distribution.

The above income framework is widely used in studies of household income and its distribution (Atkinson, Rainwater and Smeeding, 1995; ABS, 1995b; Harding, 1997; Saunders, 2001a; Saunders and Hobbes, 1988). It has the advantage that it highlights the role and impact of the market and the state in the formation and distribution of income and thus allows these effects to be separately identified and their impact estimated. This involves comparing the level and distribution of pre-transfer, pre-tax market income with that of post-transfer, pre-tax gross income, and with post-transfer, post-tax disposable income, with the differences attributed to the impact of the public transfer and tax systems, respectively.

Income or consumption?

Given the difficulty involved in using income as a proxy for the standard of living, it has been argued that it would be preferable to use an alternative indicator. The most obvious such measure is total consumption, as this more directly captures the material standard of living actually experienced. It also more closely reflects permanent income that, as noted above, reflects the average (anticipated) income level over the life cycle. Although many economists have argued that consumption is a superior measure, there are a number of conceptual and practical problems associated with using consumption to measure the standard of living.

The superiority of consumption over income has been argued on the grounds that, 'generally, income is not valued for its own sake but for the ability it provides to buy goods and services. It is thus more satisfactory to measure directly the level of goods and services bought' (Travers and Richardson, 1993, p. 24). Others see the choice between income and consumption as being less clear-cut. Atkinson (1989, Chapter 1), for example, argues that the choice between income and consumption depends in part on the framework within which living standards are conceived. Whereas a *standard of living* approach suggests the use of a consumption-oriented measure, a *minimum rights to resources* approach favours an income-based measure, since income provides the opportunity to consume resources, but leaves the final decision to the individual.

Although this line of argument suggests that consumption is preferable to income as an indicator of the standard of living, a low level of income constrains the choices available. In general, what determines the standard of living of the rich as well as the poor is the level of resources available for consumption, irrespective of how much is actually consumed at any point in time. It is also important to note in this context that while a low level of consumption may reflect the choice to live a frugal life, income is also the result of choices relating to decisions to work and invest. A low level of income may indicate an unwillingness to work, just as a low level of consumption may indicate an unwillingness to spend. The conceptual basis for preferring income over consumption is thus not as strong as is sometimes claimed.

There are compelling practical reasons against the use of consumption (or permanent income) to measure living standards. Consumption is extremely difficult (and hence expensive) to measure, and the measures that are available – produced in surveys of household expenditure – relate to *consumption expenditure* rather than *actual consumption* itself. These differ because not all of what is spent on consumption goods in any period is used to support consumption in that period. Many of the most expensive consumer items, including the family home, motor vehicles and consumer durables such as a washing machine, refrigerator or home computer, provide a flow of services that last over many years. What these items contribute to the standard of living is the services they provide – the flow of housing services, increased ease of transport, the ability to wash clothes and the information associated with using a computer – rather than the amount actually spent on purchasing them. If it were actual spending that mattered, the standard of living would increase dramatically in the week that a new car was bought, but then fall equally dramatically the following week.

Although it is possible to estimate the service flows associated with the ownership of durable goods, this gives rise to many problems that detract from the advantages of using consumption in the first place. One way round this problem is to ignore consumer durables altogether and to focus on non-durable expenditure as Barrett, Crossley and Worswick (2000a; 2000b) have done in studying trends in inequality. However, this approach provides an incomplete and distorted picture, particularly when comparing groups with differing expenditures on durables such as households at different stages of the life cycle. Removing expenditure on durables is consistent with the use of household consumption as an indicator of the standard of living proposed by the ABS (1995b). However, the ABS approach treats the ownership of durables as generating an income (thus contributing to living standards) through the stream of the services that they provide. To exclude consumer durables altogether is thus to omit an important source of well-being.

Aside from the complications surrounding the treatment of consumer durables, another major problem with the use of consumption data is that expenditure surveys are prone to serious under-reporting of expenditure on such items as alcohol, tobacco and gambling. Although expenditure on alcohol and tobacco alone amounted on average to only $38 a week, or less than 5 per cent of total expenditure in 1998–99 (ABS, 2000b), there is substantial variation across household types that distorts comparisons of expenditure-based measures of well-being and distribution. There are also problems surrounding the inclusion of taxation into a consumption-based standard of living framework. Unlike the income framework spelt out earlier, the level of consumption expenditure is influenced by indirect taxes (which affect the relative price of different items) as well as by income tax (which affects the affordability of all items). Accounting for the impact of government taxes and transfers in a consumption framework is thus considerably more complicated than using income as a proxy for the standard of living.

Non-cash income

Measurement problems arise when income is received in the form of in-kind or non-cash income rather than as a direct cash payment. These sources of income have potentially important effects on living standards that should be identified and, where possible, quantified. Two areas where non-cash income is most important are imputed rental income from home ownership and unpaid domestic production. Homeowners receive an implicit income from owning their home that corresponds to the income they would receive from owning any other asset. Although this income is not observable, it still represents an implicit payment for the rental services provided by the home to its owner, in just the same way that the rental income received by the landlord on his/her property is part of his/her income. Because it is not observable, the value of the rental income must be estimated (or imputed) indirectly. This can introduce measurement errors, but is still preferable to omitting the item altogether.

Another important form of in-kind income is the value of time spent in various forms of non-market activity including leisure, looking after one's children and unpaid domestic work, including cooking, cleaning and home maintenance and repairs. Child care and domestic production are activities that can be purchased in the market and undertaken by someone else in exchange for a wage. If they were, they would generate an income and be included in national income (and in the incomes of those who performed the tasks). The fact that these activities are performed by individuals for themselves (or for their families) and are thus not paid for makes no difference in principle to the income they generate, although in this case the income is 'received' by the household itself rather than paid to an external agent. Once again, there are difficult problems surrounding the estimation of these incomes, although there are methods for imputing them and some studies have done so, with varying degrees of sophistication (Ironmonger, 1994, 1996; Travers and Richardson, 1993).

Leisure is another activity that generates an implicit income for those who engage in it. The issue here is not that the activity could be performed by someone else and paid for, since it is not meaningful to pay someone else to read a novel, watch a play or listen to some music for you. Rather, leisure is an important source of income because time is valuable in its own right and leisure time thus contributes directly to the standard of living of those who participate in it. In addition, because leisure generally has to be sacrificed in order to derive other income, particularly earnings, the net impact of paid work on the standard of living is less than the gross earnings received, since leisure time is reduced and so is the implied value of leisure income. Thus, an increase in income that results from working more hours contributes less to the standard of living than an increase in income that results from receiving a higher hourly wage for working a fixed number of hours. Unless leisure time is included as part of income, these effects will not be captured.

One method for doing this, pioneered by Garfinkel and Haveman (1977) and developed subsequently by Haveman and Buron (1993) and Saunders, O'Connor and Smeeding (1998), involves estimating 'earnings capacity'. Earnings capacity draws on the theory of human capital and is defined as equal to the amount of earnings that each individual could generate if they were to engage in paid market work on a full-time basis. This involves estimating each individual's potential earnings on the basis of observed information on their human capital (level of education, skills and work experience), combined with other characteristics that affect labour market outcomes such as age and gender. In effect, the approach includes as income an estimate of the value of hours spent not in paid work that is based on the (actual or estimated) hourly wage rate received while in paid work. The key feature of the earnings capacity approach is that it assumes that all individuals work for the same number of hours in paid market work and thus everyone has access to the same number of unpaid, non-market hours.

Another important example of in-kind income reflects the benefits that are provided to households by the government in the form of free or subsidised 'social wage' services, including education and health services that are financed through the tax system. Since the taxes paid for these services are reflected (in part) in the calculation of disposable income, consistency requires that the benefits derived from the services funded by those taxes should also be included as income. Once again, however, there are difficult problems involved in trying to attribute a value to non-cash government benefits, particularly when there is no private market to guide the valuation process. What is the market value of a year of primary school education, or a life-saving surgical procedure performed free of charge in a public hospital? In the absence of information on which to answer these questions, the benefits are often equated with the cost of provision and then allocated across groups in the population according to service utilisation rates (ABS, 1996; Saunders, 1994; Johnson, 1998). This approach is likely to lead to serious error in some cases, but is again preferable to excluding these items altogether (which effectively assigns a zero value to them).

Recognition of imputed rent, domestic production, leisure and social wage benefits as legitimate forms of income raises questions about the use of conventional cash income to measure the standard of living and how it varies over time and between groups in the population. These problems are likely to be particularly serious where the balance between cash and non-cash income is changing over time, or varies systematically between sub-groups in the population in accordance with socioeconomic characteristics such as age, household composition or household wealth. All three possibilities are likely. Households of different ages not only tend to have different levels of wealth, they also tend to have different structures that make domestic production more or less likely. Single adults and couples without children are less pressed for time than families with children (particularly sole parents) and thus have more opportunity (though perhaps less proclivity) to benefit from domestic production. Many new dual-earner couples will have experienced an increase in market (cash) income that is largely offset by a decline in the implicit value of (non-cash) domestic production and this may explain part of the paradox of affluence discussed in Chapter 1.

The patterns of behaviour that determine the extent of cash and non-cash income do not arise in a vacuum. Many factors influence the decision to purchase a home as opposed to renting, including movements in house prices and the tax treatment of non-cash housing-related income, such as imputed rent and capital gains. Similar effects also apply in the case of cash income. Individuals are influenced by a range of economic and social factors when deciding whether to participate in the labour market and what form of employment to look for. Some will choose to work part-time or on a casual basis because this better suits their family circumstances or the constraints and opportunities they face. The rules and conditions of the tax and transfer systems will exert an influence over such decisions. The fact that income from domestic production, for example, is not liable to income tax in the same way as other sources of income may induce a bias towards this form of income compared with the alternatives.

The influence of these external conditions on income choices is reinforced by the social significance of different forms of income and the patterns of behaviour that underlie them. Income provides not only a means of fulfilling material needs but is also a source of status in societies where ownership of resources is an increasingly important determinant of identity, prestige and power. Earned income signals one's place in the occupational hierarchy, while asset income is a sign of wealth that carries its own status-oriented connotations. The social significance of these relationships implies that different forms of income are associated with status effects in addition to their direct effects on economic well-being and living standards.

The opposite may apply in the case of transfer income, particularly where there is a degree of stigma attached to the receipt of public transfers for groups like the unemployed and sole parents. The tightening of benefit eligibility under policies of targeting and mutual obligation (discussed in Chapter 8) has reduced the immediate contribution of these incomes to material standards of living and may have lowered their value for those who still receive them. And where governments raise the spectre of benefit abuse and fraud in order to promote the conditions for welfare reform, these negative effects become more pronounced and pernicious. Extending the income definition to include in-kind income adds further to these complexities. Does an extra dollar of cash income in the form of higher wages have the same effect as an extra dollar of non-cash education benefits resulting from increased government spending on teachers' salaries? To include both in the final income of families with teacher parents and school-age children involves an element of double counting, but this is the logic of the full income approach.

The net effect of these arguments is to cast doubt on the validity of the standard economics assumption that 'a dollar is a dollar' irrespective of its source. Instead, the factors that shape the social conditions surrounding the receipt of income and the social status accorded to the different components of income suggest that it may be better to consider the role and impact of the different income sources separately. The contribution an extra dollar of income makes to the standard of living depends on how that increment to income came about. Whether or not it resulted from an increase in wages, higher interest rates, or involved some sacrifice of time, or a bureaucratic assessment of entitlement to a social benefit, or resulted from an episode of ill-health requiring medical treatment clearly makes a difference. That methods have been developed that allow each of these incomes to be valued in monetary terms should not conceal the underlying differences in their contribution to living standards.

Accounting for differing needs

Although the focus of well-being should be on the individual, the role that income plays must be seen in the context that most individuals live together in families and/or households and most share their incomes and other resources for the good of the family/household unit as a whole. The fact that most children have no income does not mean that they are deprived in terms of their standard of living. This depends on the combined income of their parents and how much of it is devoted to the children, but it will also vary according to the number of children in the family. The degree of income sharing within families is thus a crucial determinant of individual living standards, but how widespread is such sharing and what is its impact? These are difficult questions to answer without inquiring into the minutiae of family finances to a degree that would, for most people, be regarded as unacceptably intrusive.

A choice has to be made about the appropriate unit of analysis within which incomes are shared before the relationship between incomes and living standards can be thoroughly investigated. Most studies use the household, or some variant thereof that more closely resembles the nuclear family, on the grounds that this represents the basic unit within which economic decisions are made and their consequences experienced. Differences in the incomes of individuals living in the unit are then ignored and it is assumed that income is pooled and shared equally among all members of the unit. Despite its widespread use, the equal-sharing condition is an assumption that many have questioned. Detailed studies of household decision-making suggest that although it is a reasonable approximation in many cases, equal sharing within nuclear families is not universally practised and its use will thus give rise to misleading results (Jenkins, 1991a; Johnson, 1998; Redmond, 1999).

Once the unit of analysis has been determined, a further problem arises in adjusting for the fact that the standard of living associated with a given level of income depends upon the needs and hence the size and composition of the unit. An income sufficient to generate a comfortable standard of living for a single person living alone may be totally inadequate to meet the needs of a couple family with four children. Some basis is required for placing the incomes relative to the needs of differently structured income units onto a common metric that allows them to be compared. The device used to achieve this is an equivalence scale that reflects the *relative* needs of different types of unit (Saunders, 1994; Slesnick, 2001).

Equivalence scales are generally expressed in terms of the number of equivalent adults in the unit. The first adult is assigned a scale value of 1.0 and other members given an equivalence score that reflects the additional needs associated with their membership of the unit relative to that of the first member. Thus, the equivalence score for the second adult is generally less than 1.0, reflecting the fact that two adults living together can share many costs of living and thus require less than twice the resources of the first adult alone. The potential benefits from economies of scale increase with the size of the unit, so that needs per person within each unit decline as the size of the unit increases. In addition, the needs of children are lower than those of adults (at least up until they are well into their teenage years), which implies that they should have a lower equivalence score. Once the equivalence points for each member of the unit is determined, they are added to give the total number of equivalent adults and used to calculate the *equivalent income* of the unit by dividing its total income by the number of equivalence points (or equivalent adults).

Because equivalent income reflects both the income and the needs of the unit, it is a key indicator of the standard of living of the unit as a whole and of its individual members (who are assumed to attain the same standard of living under the equal-sharing condition). But how is the equivalence scale determined? There is no single method for deriving an equivalence scale, although most methods use theoretical models of consumer demand that are estimated from the expenditure patterns of households of differing size and composition (Deaton and Muellbauer, 1980). Different models and methods tend to produce different results and these will in turn affect comparisons of living standards based on equivalent income.

In addition, most equivalence scales are strictly relevant to cash income only, and may not be appropriate for adjusting non-cash income, particularly those components that reflect the social wage benefits associated with meeting specific health and educational needs (Radner, 1997). Furthermore, as in the case of the choice of unit of analysis, a different equivalence scale may produce different results – sometimes sufficiently different to exert a substantial impact on the conclusions drawn from results (Atkinson, Gardiner, Lechene and Sutherland, 1998). Different units of analysis and different equivalence scales thus further add to the complexity involved in studying the relationship between income and the standard of living.

In summary, while the standard framework for analysing income (and its distribution) has many strengths, it also suffers from a number of limitations as the basis for comparing standards of living over time and between different family types. Problems arise in defining some income components and in identifying and measuring others. But one of the most important limitations of the standard approach is its inability to take account of the impact of social factors on the meaning of different forms of income and their contribution to the well-being of those who receive them. Significant advances have been made in the quality of income statistics and in the sophistication of the methods used to analyse them. At the same time, however, the social factors that link income in its various forms to the standard of living are often overlooked, leaving their meaning and interpretation unclear.

Examining aggregate income trends

The relative importance of the different components of cash income has changed over time in line with broader changes in society. The main trend has been the increasing importance of transfer income and in the share of tax in household income (Table 5.1). Whereas in 1960, households kept almost all of the income they received from market participation, forty years later, state transfers and taxes played a major role in the overall structure of household income and in its distribution between households. The share of labour income in total income has remained broadly unchanged at between 55 per cent and 60 per cent, although it accounted for an increasing proportion of household income throughout the 1960s and early 1970s before declining through the 1980s and then increasing again in the 1990s. Property income increased in importance between 1960 and 1990 but has declined since then. This is the most variable component of household income, being sensitive to changes in interest rates, house prices and the performance of the stock market.

The rather stable longer-term structure of household income conceals profound, sometimes offsetting, differences at the household level. Accompanying the recent growth in labour income (the result of economic growth and rising employment in the 1990s) has been a widening disparity in the employment and income positions of different households (see Chapter 7). The proportion of workless households has also been increasing (Gregory, 1999) and a division has emerged between multiple-earner ('job rich') and no-earner ('job poor') households

Table 5.1 The changing composition of household income, 1959–60 to 1999–2000 (percentages of gross income)

Income Source	\multicolumn{9}{c}{Financial year ending 30 June}
	1960	1965	1970	1975	1980	1985	1990	1995	2000
Compensation of employees	57.0	57.7	59.7	61.8	55.9	54.4	51.8	54.2	55.2
Property income	7.4	7.9	8.7	9.4	9.6	12.2	15.5	10.4	9.5
Other primary income	28.6	26.8	24.0	18.8	22.5	19.3	21.0	19.9	20.1
Market income	93.0	92.4	92.4	90.0	88.0	85.9	88.3	84.5	84.8
Social assistance benefits	4.9	5.0	4.7	5.8	7.5	8.2	7.0	9.7	9.6
Gross income	**100.0**	**100.0**	**100.0**	**100.0**	**100.0**	**100.0**	**100.0**	**100.0**	**100.0**
Income tax payable	7.0	8.7	10.1	12.5	12.9	14.2	14.1	13.1	14.7
Other income payable	4.9	5.3	5.9	7.6	8.8	9.8	12.6	9.3	9.3
Disposable income	88.3	86.0	84.0	79.9	78.3	76.0	73.4	77.3	75.7

Source: Saunders (2001a)

(Borland, Gregory and Sheehan, 2001), with the incomes of the former predominantly made up of earnings and those of the latter mainly social security benefits (Dawkins, 1996).

Both groups have experienced some negative consequences associated with these changes. Households in work have increased their hours of work (both at the level of the individual and of the household) leading to a squeezing of the time left to perform household tasks and leisure (Bittman, 1998). Households unable to participate in the labour market have experienced a tightening of social benefit conditions and eligibility requirements, adding to the stigma associated with the receipt of social security income. In conjunction with increases in economic insecurity and inequality in employment patterns (Chapter 4), these trends imply that the link between changes in money income and living standards has become more tenuous.

There have also been important changes in the structure of employment remuneration that have seen a decline in the significance of the direct cash component of wages or salaries. The growth in work-related fringe benefits was halted by the introduction of the fringe benefits tax, but other public policies have worked in the opposite direction. The expansion of superannuation has seen a switch from current to deferred income that is not adequately captured in income statistics at the household level (ABS, 1999a). Although the main impact of the superannuation reforms is on the life cycle *profile* of household income, the immediate effect of contributions has been to drive a wedge between current cash income (as opposed to its average level over the life cycle) and the standard of living. For those higher up the salary scale, share options have become an increasing source of income that is again poorly covered in the official statistics. Executive packages are now commonplace and few top executives rely solely on the standard salary component of their earnings – even though this has been a source of growing earnings inequality (see Chapter 7).

Fundamental changes have also been occurring in the balance between cash and non-cash income. As already observed, the increase in employment participation has, for some, been offset by a decline in the time available for leisure and other activities that generate in-kind income. As these time constraints have become tighter, their (negative) impact on full income has increased, leading to increased 'outsourcing' of domestic tasks that imposes an additional burden on the (cash) budget of the household (Bittman, Meagher and Matheson, 1998). The expanded role of the welfare state (see Table 5.1) has also resulted in an increased contribution of non-cash social wage income (see Table 5.2 below).

The pattern of home ownership that affects in-kind income in the form of imputed rent has also been changing. At the aggregate level, home ownership has declined slightly since it reached its peak in the 1960s (ABS, 2001a, Figure 8.9), possibly as a result of increased employment insecurity and marital instability. The emergence of these trends cautions against committing large proportions of one's wealth to a single asset that is difficult to divide up and expensive to divest. Housing affordability is a barrier to many new potential home-owners, who are unable to enter this part of the housing market. At the same time, average household size is declining (Table 2.4) and the total number of households is rising, so that the number of dwellings is continuing to increase, even as the ownership rate has fallen.

Implications for living standards and inequality

The relative size of different components of household income and the relationship between income and the standard of living have been examined in a number of studies. These have had to overcome a number of formidable conceptual problems and data limitations in order to produce a broad picture of how the economists' conventional (cash) income measure is related to living standards and inequality. The existing Australian research is fragmented, with most studies focusing on only specific aspects, making it difficult to ascertain whether the effects identified have an offsetting or reinforcing impact when combined.

Living standards research

Australian studies fall into one of two types. The first, epitomised in the work of Travers and Richardson (1993) and the Australian Institute of Family Studies (McDonald and Brownlee, 1994), focuses on the impact of broadening the income measure on the measurement of living standards and patterns of inequality. The second strand of research has focused more specifically on how government cash and non-cash social wage benefits affect household incomes and inequality. Not surprisingly, this latter strand of research has become enmeshed in political debate over the impact of government on living standards, making it difficult to reach an independent conclusion about the merits of alternative studies. Many of these latter studies have thus been undertaken by official government agencies (ABS, 1996a; Office of EPAC, 1987), or been commissioned by government (Johnston, Manning and Hellwig, 1995), although there are also a number independent contributions (Saunders, 1994; Harding, 1995; Johnson, 1998).

The study by Travers and Richardson (1993) begins with an examination of the relationship between economic measures of material affluence and philosophical ideas of freedom and moral values. This is important because it highlights the fact that underlying different approaches to the measurement of well-being are philosophical differences related to the role of the state and the freedom of the individual. The authors then develop a measure of full income that includes, in addition to (equivalent disposable) cash income, estimates of the value of imputed rent, non-employed time (including leisure and domestic production) and the income from ownership of (selected) consumer durables.

Using data collected in a national survey of over 1200 Australian households conducted in 1987, they show that there is a relatively low correlation between cash income and the other components of full income. From this, they conclude that the inclusion of these additional income sources has important effects on the relative living standards of different groups. Furthermore, since the inequalities in the different dimensions of well-being tend to offset each other, inequality of full income is considerably less than cash income inequality, with inequality of cash income contributing only just over half (52 per cent) to overall inequality of full income.

Similar findings emerge from research undertaken by the Australian Institute of Family Studies (AIFS) on the living standards of families with children reported by McDonald and Brownlee (1994). The results presented by McDonald and Brownlee compare families at the bottom and top of the (equivalised cash) household income distribution against a broad range of direct measures of deprivation, financial stress and subjective well-being. Although these direct measures tend to vary with the income position, the patterns of variation are sensitive to the direct measures employed. While those at the bottom of the income distribution were just over two times more likely than those at the top to have difficulty meeting health costs, they were seven times more likely not to have enough money for school outings and eighteen times more likely not to own a car.

Although the influence of personal preferences and choice are likely to enter into the determination of some of these comparisons, the stability of the overall patterns is indicative of more fundamental relationships that capture the impact of resource constraints rather than individual preferences. Against this, the AIFS research provides support for the view that income performs rather well as a single summary measure of living standards. Composite measures have the potential to provide more information on changes in living standards. But as the Productivity Commission has emphasised, there are problems with interpreting what may be an inconsistent pattern given the multidimensional nature of the standard of living and the number of factors that influence it (Parham, Barnes, Roberts and Kennett, 2000). Income may not be ideal, but none of the alternatives offer a way around its limitations without introducing additional complexities.

The social wage

One aspect of non-cash income that has received considerable attention is the impact of the social wage – government cash and non-cash provisions that provide directly identifiable benefits to households. The impact of government social wage benefits and taxes on household income has been the subject of a series of studies undertaken by the ABS (1992, 1996). Although the methods used in these studies vary somewhat, the same methodology has been used to derive the comparisons summarised in Table 5.2. These estimates reveal that government tax and spending programs have significant effects on the incomes of households. In round terms, cash and non-cash benefits increase household income on average by about 30 per cent (rising to over 33 per cent in 1993–94), while income and indirect taxes absorb between 27 per cent and 30 per cent of household income. (The slight differences between the estimates in Table 5.1 and those in Table 5.2 reflect definitional differences in data coverage).

In both 1984 and 1988–89, government benefits and taxes almost cancel each other out in aggregate, whereas their net impact on households was positive in 1993–94 – as indicated by comparing the figures for market and final income. This implies that although the gross flows of transfers and taxes between the household and state sectors are large, the net flows are, on average, much smaller and tend to be considerably more

Table 5.2 The effects of government benefits and taxes on household income, 1984–94

	1984		1988–89		1993–94	
	$/week	% of gross income	$/week	% of gross income	$/week	% of gross income
Market income	401.4	88.5	576.2	90.0	637.0	86.8
Plus: Cash transfers	52.2	11.5	64.0	10.0	96.8	13.2
Equals: Gross income	**453.6**	**100.0**	**640.2**	**100.0**	**733.8**	**100.0**
Minus: Direct tax	91.6	20.2	129.3	20.2	137.0	18.7
Equals: Disposable income	362.0	79.8	510.9	79.8	596.8	81.3
Plus: Non-cash benefits	82.8	18.3	127.3	19.9	146.4	20.0
Equals: Extended income	444.8	98.1	638.2	99.7	743.2	101.3
Minus: Indirect taxes	37.7	8.2	66.4	10.4	62.6	8.5
Equals: Final income	407.1	89.7	571.9	89.3	680.6	92.8

Source: ABS, 1996, Tables 33, 34 and 35.

stable. However, although the *net effects* are small, it is still possible that the *gross effects* may give rise to other effects (e.g. on incentives) that may be large. Furthermore, although the net effects of government benefits and taxes are small *on average*, there are substantial differences once the figures are broken down into different classes of households. There are many ways in which these breakdowns can be undertaken, and Table 5.3 compares the distribution of benefits and taxes of households ranked according to the level of their (gross) income.

On average in 1993–94, government benefits contributed $231.80 a week to household income, of which $96.80 (41.8 per cent) was in the form of direct (cash) benefits and the remaining $135.00 in the form of indirect (non-cash) benefits. Clearly, any account of the impact of government on household living standards that ignores the non-cash contribution will be of limited value. Not too much significance should be attached to the fact that the average weekly tax bill of $199.60 (of which $137.00 or 69.4 per cent was income tax) is less than the average value of benefits, since the estimates do not include all aspects of government activity. There is certainly no implication that since the balance of allocated benefits and taxes is negative, that this is also true of the overall contribution of government activity to households.

The average value of benefits and taxes across all households conceals the variation in each – and, by implication, in their net value – for different households. Table 5.3 shows the pattern of these latter differences

Table 5.3 Social wage benefits and taxes, by household gross income quintile, 1993-94 (average weekly $ value)

Income, benefits and taxes	Lowest 20%	Second quintile	Third quintile	Fourth quintile	Top 20%	All households
Private income	13.5	168.0	503.5	860.0	1586.2	626.4
Direct benefits	138.2	185.9	88.8	49.1	22.6	96.8
Gross income	151.7	353.9	592.3	909.1	1608.8	723.2
Direct tax	2.1	18.0	80.3	171.2	412.9	137.0
Disposable income	149.6	335.9	511.9	737.9	1195.9	586.2
Indirect benefits						
education	17.1	42.8	62.7	67.4	71.2	52.2
health	56.6	71.9	58.6	55.3	55.4	59.5
housing	8.8	6.6	2.7	1.0	0.3	3.9
welfare	30.0	35.5	16.7	10.1	4.7	19.4
Extended income	262.1	492.7	652.6	871.6	1327.4	721.2
Indirect taxes	28.9	43.2	59.0	73.8	96.6	60.3
Final income	233.2	449.5	593.6	797.8	1230.8	660.9

Source: ABS, 1996, Table 1.

as they relate to the gross income of households. The distributional effect can be most clearly seen in the fact that the ratio of incomes in the top and bottom quintiles changes from over 117 to one in the case of private income, to just over 5 to one in the case of final income. This massive distributional shift occurs largely as a result of the impact of direct (cash) transfers and taxes. The indirect (non-cash) components of income tend to be spread evenly across the income quintiles, or to increase modestly in absolute size (though not proportionately) with income.

Further analysis of the data summarised in Table 5.3 (which can be found in the ABS report cited in the table) suggests many other dimensions in which the impact of benefits and taxes can be analysed, including by age, household type and principal source of income. Each reveals a different aspect of the impact of government programs and how they are financed on the levels and distribution of household incomes. A few words of caution must apply to all of these estimates. First, they take no account of differences in household need (by using an equivalence scale) and thus provide no clear indication of the effectiveness of government programs in meeting household needs (other than those that are used to allocate the non-cash benefits). Second, because they refer to 1993–94, they pre-date the introduction of the GST, which is likely to have had a major impact on the overall pattern of effects.

Income perceptions and subjective well-being

Thus far, the argument has been that even though insufficient attention is often paid to the social significance of different income sources and how this has changed over time, income is still the best single, readily available quantitative indicator of the standard of living of households. The fact that, as shown in Figures 2.1 and 2.2, household income and consumption have both increased significantly over the last forty years even, after allowing for price increases and population growth (Saunders, 2001a) thus suggests that living standards have improved considerably. That is what the quantitative evidence indicates about the change in objective conditions. But to what extent is the undeniable increase in objective economic conditions reflected in subjective perceptions of well-being and living standards?

Recent research

Unfortunately, the subjective evidence reveals a somewhat different picture from that implied by the objective statistics. A recent review of the evidence on alternative indicators of progress in Australia concluded that although most of the economic indicators show an upward trend, there are a number of offsetting influences on the quality of life and ecologically sustainability (Eckersley, 1998; 2000). As a result, when they are asked about their subjective assessment of how their quality of life is changing, the number of Australians reporting an overall decline far outnumbers (by a factor of about four to one) the numbers who think that it is improving. The conclusion arrived at on the basis of this evidence is that material progress is now associated with diminishing benefits and escalating costs. The overall social cost–benefit arithmetic is turning against those obsessed with material prosperity and economic growth.

Research on the beliefs and attitudes of 'middle Australia' reveals a similar sense of disillusionment with the benefits of economic growth. People's own experience and judgments lead them to a different assessment of progress and improvements in the quality of life from that implied by the economic statistics (Pusey, 1998, p. 196). Understanding what lies behind these judgments is an important but elusive task. Pusey suggests this is partly because recent distributional changes have favoured the rich at the expense of those in the middle and income from capital at the expense of wage and salary income. However, when his survey respondents were asked where their anger or resentment was mainly directed, only two of the four most cited targets – 'big business' and 'the economic system' – are primarily economic in origin. Equally important were 'the education system', 'the media' and 'politicians' – which suggests that community anger is directed as much at those who shape the terms of public debate and influence social choices as it is at the economy and its institutions, including those of the state.

A similar message emerges from other recent public opinion research. As was noted in Chapter 1, when they were asked in May 1999 whether the quality of life was getting better, only one-quarter (24 per cent) of Australians thought that it was; 36 per cent thought it was getting worse and 38 per cent were undecided (Eckersley, 1999, p. 3). A similar survey conducted in 2000 by Newspoll for *The Australian* produced very similar overall findings, with a large majority (70 per cent) in favour of reducing inequality rather than seeking to maximise the rate of economic growth (Kelly, 2000).

These figures need to be treated with some caution, in part because of the short-run volatility of the data. As noted in Chapter 3, questions about overall attitudes can be sensitive to how the questions are worded, as well as to what is happening at the time they are asked, and this will reduce their ability to capture longer-run trends. The opinions expressed in public surveys also do not have to be defended by those who express them, nor does actual behaviour have to be consistent with the views expressed to pollsters. It is all too easy for busy people to use the opportunity to 'let off steam' when asked to respond to a survey, even though a more considered and reflective response might be different. However, the fact that these polls were conducted in the midst of a long economic upswing that had already produced several years of rising average incomes indicates that economic factors alone cannot explain public perceptions of the quality of life.

Satisfaction, happiness and health

The CESC survey explored several aspects of the quality of life. Participants were asked at the beginning of the questionnaire a series of questions about their well-being and standard of living. Table 5.4 summarises the responses to two questions concerning how the standard of living had changed in the past and was expected to change in the future. The overall pattern of expected future changes in living standards over the next five years is very similar to those reported for the past five years, although a much larger percentage (almost 10 per cent) indicated that they did not know in which direction their living standards were heading.

The fact that the overall percentages of people who expect their future living standard to move in a certain direction are similar to what is reported about the past could be taken to imply that people extrapolate past experience when asked to predict the future. However, the cross-tabulations do not support this simplified explanation. For example, only slightly over one-half of those reporting increased living standards in the past expect this to continue into the future, while only around 40 per cent of those who report that their living standards have fallen expect this trend to continue.

However, the most important point to emphasise about these results is that they reflect the response to a question asked after a period in which

Table 5.4 Past and future changes in standards of living (percentages)

	Do you think your standard of living will be higher, lower or about the same in five years time?				
Is your standard of living, higher, lower or about the same as five years ago?	Higher	About the same	Lower	Don't know	Total
Higher	15.0	10.1	1.9	1.7	28.6
About the same	9.2	26.4	7.4	4.4	47.4
Lower	3.8	6.3	10.0	3.2	23.4
Don't know	0.2	0.1	0.0	0.3	0.6
Total	28.2	42.9	19.2	9.7	100.0

Unweighted n = 2,345.

the economy had been growing strongly for at least five years. Thus, *real incomes had actually, on average and for the majority of the population, been rising*, and yet, over 70 per cent reported that their standard of living had either not changed or had declined over the period. The tenuous link between real incomes and living standards emphasised in the earlier discussion is thus given empirical confirmation in these results.

The same broad pattern of perceptions of how living standards have changed to that shown in Table 5.4 is reflected in recent ABS research on financial stress within households (McColl, Pietsch and Gatenby, 2001, Table 9 – see also Chapter 2). When asked how their standard of living in 1998–99 compared with its level two years before, 28.2 per cent said it had improved, 42.6 per cent reported no change and 26.1 per cent said it had deteriorated. (The remaining 3 per cent of households had changed composition over the period). These figures are remarkably close to those in Table 5.4, reinforcing their validity. The ABS study also found that the proportion reporting that living standards had fallen was greater among households at the bottom of the income distribution than at the top. The incidence of financial stress was also greater (at both ends of the distribution) for those reporting a decline in their standard of living. Yet this was a period in which average real incomes were increasing, suggesting that many people were missing out on the prosperity associated with economic growth or that increased income was not sufficient to offset other negative impacts on living standards.

Table 5.5 compares responses to CESC questions concerned with satisfaction with overall living standard and happiness. They indicate that while the majority of Australians (over two-thirds) were satisfied with their overall standard of living, almost one-fifth were not able to decide whether or not they are satisfied, and 13 per cent (around one in seven) were clearly dissatisfied. The proportions expressing happiness with their situation are uniformly higher, although again a significant minority (around one in seven) reported being either unhappy or very unhappy.

Not surprisingly, those who were satisfied with their standard of living were generally also happy, although the overlap between the two categories is by no means exact. For example, of the 87.6 per cent who were either happy or very happy, a total of 6.4 per cent (around one in thirteen) were either fairly or very dissatisfied with their standard of living. Although the numbers reporting themselves to be very or fairly satisfied with their standard of living but either unhappy or very unhappy are lower, there are still some people in this category. Since the survey question about satisfaction referred explicitly to people's *material* standard of living while that relating to happiness did not, these results once again suggest that for many Australians, material prosperity does not guarantee happiness.

Table 5.5 Standard of living and happiness (percentages of total)

The things people buy and do – their housing, food, cars, recreation and travel – make up their material standard of living and determine how well off they are. How satisfied or dissatisfied do you feel about your overall standard of living at present?	\multicolumn{5}{c}{*Overall, in terms of how you feel generally, would you say you are:*}
	Very happy	Happy	Unhappy	Very unhappy	Total
Very satisfied	7.0	7.6	0.1	0.0	14.8
Fairly satisfied	6.8	44.8	2.3	0.0	53.9
Neither	0.6	14.6	3.1	0.1	18.4
Fairly dissatisfied	0.2	5.0	3.7	0.1	9.0
Very dissatisfied	0.2	1.0	2.0	0.9	4.0
Total	14.8	72.8	11.2	1.2	100.0

Unweighted n = 2,305.

The overall trends in satisfaction and happiness since Australia embarked on its deregulatory market-oriented economic reforms in 1983 are summarised in Table 5.6. These results are taken from a series of surveys that asked somewhat different questions and provided a different menu of possible responses and thus need to be interpreted carefully. However, the overall trends are clear. The percentage of respondents indicating both satisfaction and happiness declined steadily over the period (although the decline in satisfaction since 1995 is probably exaggerated by the smaller number of response options provided in the 1999 survey). What is most striking about these results is the sharp increase in dissatisfaction and unhappiness between 1995 and 1999 – a period in which economic growth was delivering rising real incomes to most Australians.

One possible explanation of the results in Table 5.6 is that they reflect the fact that the unemployed are less satisfied and more unhappy than those in employment, as was shown in Table 4.2. However, unemployment was lower in 1999 than in 1995 and substantially lower than in 1983 (see Chapter 4), so that changes in unemployment cannot explain the decline in satisfaction and happiness. It follows by implication that there is increased dissatisfaction and unhappiness even among those who have shared in the increased prosperity associated with employment and income growth during the 1990s.

Another possible cause of unhappiness is ill-health. This relationship can operate in both directions, with poor health not only contributing to

Table 5.6 Trends in satisfaction and happiness, 1983–1999 (percentages)

	Response category	1983	1995	1999
Satisfaction with standard of living [a]	Total satisfied	89.0	84.9	68.7
	Mixed feelings	7.4	9.2	18.4
	Total dissatisfied	3.7	3.4	13.0
Overall happiness [b]	Very happy	35.5	43.0	14.8
	(Quite) Happy	60.0	51.6	72.8
	Total happy	95.5	94.6	87.6
	Unhappy/Very unhappy	4.5	5.4	12.4

Notes: (a) Responses in 1983 and 1995 are to an 8/9-point scale, from delighted to terrible. Responses to the CESC survey in 1999 are to a 5-point scale (see Table 5.5). (b) Responses in 1983 and 1995 are to a 4-point scale, from very happy to not at all happy. Responses to the CESC survey in 1999 are to a 4-point scale, from very happy to very unhappy (see Table 5.5).

Source: Eckersley, 1999, Table 2 and CESC survey as reported in Saunders, Thomson and Evans (2001).

unhappiness but also deriving from it. For this reason, it is dangerous to assign causation to the observed statistical correlation between poor health and unhappiness. The CESC survey included a question on subjective health status and the relationship between self-assessed happiness and subjective health status is shown in Table 5.7. These results indicate that good health does not guarantee happiness, any more than poor health necessarily prevents it. Although very few of the 87.2 per cent of respondents who reported themselves to be either very happy or happy indicated that they were in poor health, more than half of the 2.8 per cent

Table 5.7 Self-assessments of happiness and subjective health status (percentages of total)

Subjective health status	Very happy	Happy	Unhappy	Very unhappy	Total
Excellent	8.2	19.9	1.6	0.4	30.2
Good	5.8	39.3	5.2	0.4	50.8
Fair	0.7	11.8	3.6	0.2	16.3
Poor	0.1	1.4	1.1	0.2	2.8
Total	14.7	72.5	11.6	1.2	100.0

Unweighted n = 2,294.

who reported their health as poor said that they were either very happy or happy. At the same time, one in fifteen of those reporting themselves to be in excellent health were either unhappy or very unhappy.

The role of income

The above analysis has explored the relationships between happiness, health and satisfaction with the material dimensions of living standards. The issue now addressed is the extent to which these variations reflect differences in reported income. In considering this issue, it is necessary to recall the limitations of the CESC income data mentioned in Chapter 3 and the Appendix, including the fact that income is only available in a number of ranges. This creates potential problems where the underlying relationships are non-linear at the extremes of the income distribution and also complicate the task of determining equivalent income accurately.

One of the key points to emerge from the earlier discussion of income as a proxy for the standard of living was the need to take account of the needs of the household or receiving unit in determining the adequacy of income in supporting a particular standard of living. Table 5.8 indicates that the relationship between reported income and its perceived adequacy is positive though weak, a finding that is consistent with the failure to take account of the impact of family size on the adequacy of a given level of income. This may explain why well over one-quarter of those in the lowest income bracket say that they have more than enough to get

Table 5.8 Income levels and income adequacy (percentages)

What is your income (before tax from all sources), of your FAMILY?	I/We haven't enough to get by on	I/We have just enough to get by on	I/We have enough to get by on and for a few extras	I/We have much more than I/We need	Total
Less than $400 per week	4.6	16.3	8.8	0.2	29.9
$400–$699 per week	1.7	12.4	9.4	0.5	24.0
$700–$1,249 per week	0.8	8.8	14.2	0.6	24.5
Over $1,250 per week	0.3	3.1	16.6	1.5	21.6
Total	7.5	40.7	49.1	2.8	100.0

Thinking of your present situation which of the following statements best describes how you are managing on your family income?

Unweighted n = 2,128.

by, whereas around two-fifths of those with incomes between $700 and $1,250 a week indicated that they are only just able to get by. However, if income adjusted for family need (or equivalent income) is a superior measure of the standard of living than unadjusted income, then there should be a stronger association between income and independent indicators of living standards after the equivalence adjustment has been incorporated. This observation provides the basis for assessing the validity of the superiority of equivalent over unadjusted income.

In undertaking this analysis, the fact that income is only reported in brackets in the CESC survey imposes restrictions on the sophistication of the tests that can be conducted. Some of the income ranges provided in the CESC questionnaire span a large section of the income distribution, and the inaccuracy involved in setting income at the mid-point of the range provided may, in some instances, be substantial. There are also questions surrounding where to set the income limits for analytical purposes and what equivalence scale to use when making the equivalence adjustment. The income categories used in Table 5.8 each contain approximately one-quarter of the sample, and the equivalent income figures (Table 5.9) have been similarly divided into (approximate) quintiles, each containing a similar number of families. The equivalence scale used is equal to the square root of family size. (Although more sophisticated equivalence scales are available for Australia, the simple one used is better suited to the quality of the CESC income data).

The above procedures for adjusting family income were applied to the CESC data, and the comparisons in Table 5.8 were repeated after replacing actual by equivalent income. As Table 5.9 indicates, the equivalence adjustment makes relatively little difference to the results, which still show that same pattern as Table 5.8. (The only major difference is that the equivalence adjustment reduces the higher incomes because of the positive relationship between family income and family size). This is also true for the results presented in Tables 5.10, 5.11 and 5.12, and for this reason, only those that use actual income are presented, thus avoiding the complications and additional uncertainties surrounding the equivalence adjustment.

The relationship between family income and life satisfaction, happiness and subjective health status are examined in Tables 5.10, 5.11 and 5.12, respectively. The main findings are straightforward and easily summarised. In terms of overall life satisfaction, while family income and satisfaction are positively related, the relation between them is weak and tends to show up more clearly in dissatisfaction rather than in satisfaction (Table 5.10). Thus, total satisfaction ('Very satisfied' and 'Fairly satisfied' combined) is 18.9 per cent in the top income range, compared to 17.7 per cent in the lowest income range. In contrast, while there are few (less

Table 5.9 Relationship between equivalent income and income adequacy (percentages)

	Thinking of your present situation which of the following statements best describes how you are managing on your family income?				
What is the (weekly) income (before tax from all sources), of your FAMILY?	I/We haven't enough to get by on	I/We have just enough to get by on	I/We have enough to get by on and for a few extras	I/We have much more than I/We need	Total
Less than $250 per week	4.5	16.4	8.0	0.1	29.0
$250–$449 per week	2.1	12.2	9.8	0.4	24.5
$450–$699 per week	0.5	8.9	13.1	0.6	23.0
Over $700 per week	0.4	3.2	18.1	1.75	23.4
Total	8.0	40.5	48.9	2.7	100.0

Unweighted n = 2,128.

than one per cent) dissatisfied high income respondents, 6 per cent of those with lowest incomes expressed a degree of dissatisfaction.

The relationship between family income and happiness is similarly rather weak (Table 5.11). In fact, those in the lowest income range report a slightly *higher* level of happiness than those in the highest income range (23.8 per cent compared to 21.0 per cent). The story is rather different,

Table 5.10 Income levels and satisfaction with standard of living (percentages)

	How satisfied or dissatisfied do you feel about your overall standard of living at present?					
What is the (weekly) income (before tax from all sources), of your FAMILY?	Very satisfied	Fairly satisfied	Neither satisfied nor dissatisfied	Fairly dis-satisfied	Very dis-satisfied	Total
Less than $400	3.2	14.5	6.1	3.9	2.1	29.8
$400–$699	2.9	12.2	4.9	3.3	0.8	24.0
$700–$1,249	4.0	14.3	4.2	1.4	0.5	24.4
Over $1,250	5.4	13.5	2.0	0.7	0.2	21.7
Total	15.5	54.5	17.3	9.2	3.6	100.0

Unweighted n = 2,103.

Income and Living Standards

Table 5.11 Income levels and overall happiness (percentages)

What is the (weekly) income (before tax from all sources), of your FAMILY?	Very happy	Happy	Unhappy	Very unhappy	Total
Less than $400 per week	3.1	20.7	5.2	0.9	29.9
$400–$699 per week	3.1	17.5	3.3	0.2	24.1
$700–$1,249 per week	3.7	18.3	2.2	0.1	24.3
Over $1,250 per week	5.0	16.0	0.6	0.1	21.8
Total	14.9	72.5	11.3	1.3	100.0

Unweighted n = 2,119.

however, when it comes to unhappiness, where there is a much larger incidence of unhappiness among low-income families. Thus it seems that while more money does not guarantee more happiness, it does lead to a marked decline in unhappiness. There is certainly no support for the view that high income is associated with a less happy life, or that the poor are as happy with their lot as the rich. Money cannot buy happiness, but it helps to avoid unhappiness.

The relationship between income and self-assessed health is positive and stronger than the impact of income on either life satisfaction or happiness (Table 5.12). The possibility of reverse causation (low income resulting from poor health) should be borne in mind as a qualification to these findings. Nevertheless, taken at face value, the percentage of those in the highest income range who report their health to be excellent is

Table 5.12 Income levels and self-assessed health status (percentages)

What is the (weekly) income (before tax from all sources), of your FAMILY?	Excellent	Good	Fair	Poor	Total
Less than $400 per week	5.3	14.9	7.6	1.9	29.8
$400–$699 per week	6.5	12.7	43.3	0.8	24.4
$700–$1,249 per week	8.7	12.8	2.6	0.3	24.4
Over $1,250 per week	9.4	10.6	1.5	0.0	21.5
Total	29.9	51.0	16.0	3.1	100.0

Unweighted n = 2,131.

almost twice as high as for those with the lowest incomes. In contrast, poor health is much more prevalent among those on a low income and is virtually non-existent among the high income group.

In summary, those with higher incomes tend to report greater life satisfaction, are happier and have better self-assessed health than those with lower incomes. All of these relationships are, however, rather weak and may reflect the influence of intervening variables or moderating factors. It seems that increased income brings with it many of the characteristics associated with a 'better life' but the effects are weak enough to suggest that life satisfaction is dependent on factors other than just monetary income. The rising incomes produced by economic growth may result in a somewhat more satisfied population, but other factors are also important determinants of well-being. Material prosperity alone will not satisfy all human needs, however much it increases.

6   Poverty and Exclusion

Because of its significance as an indicator of the impact of social security and other policies, the measurement of poverty has been the focus of intensive research (Ravallion, 1996). The findings of poverty studies are widely reported in the media and used by welfare advocates to criticise government policy and argue the case for more funding or new policies. This is borne out by the recent highly publicised controversy between The National Centre for Social and Economic Modelling (NATSEM) and The Centre for Independent Studies over how poverty should be conceptualised and measured (Harding, Lloyd and Greenwell, 2001; Tsumori, Saunders and Hughes, 2002; Saunders, 2002b). Yet, there is little evidence that poverty research has any impact on the views of government or on the thinking of those responsible for developing social policy. The official response to poverty research has been to ignore it, to deny the existence of poverty or to argue that the measurement ambiguities make estimates of poverty arbitrary and thus of no use for policy.

In part, this situation has arisen because too much has been asked of poverty research. It has been expected to produce estimates of the extent and nature of poverty, but also to provide a basis for developing political action designed to alleviate poverty. Because poverty research provides ammunition for those wishing to criticise existing policies, its findings have come under attack from politicians and policy makers, with the poverty line itself in the firing line (Abel-Smith, 1984). These developments have occurred against a background of rising unemployment, increased family breakdown and inequality – all of which add to the risk of poverty.

Currently, the *need* for poverty research is thus increasing at the same time as its *impact* is declining. While the Commonwealth Government refuses to acknowledge poverty as an issue worthy of serious research, State Governments have conducted their own inquiries into the topic (ACT Poverty Task Group, 2000; Western Australian Poverty Taskforce, 1998). And while welfare agencies continue to commission or undertake their own studies of the nature and impact of poverty (St Vincent de Paul Society, 1999; 2001; Harding and Szukalska, 2000a; Johnson and Taylor, 2000), the term does not receive a mention in official policy documents.

Poverty, it seems, appears frequently in the hearts of the population but rarely enters the minds of (federal) politicians.

This situation does not augur well for the future of poverty research or for the prospects of the poor in a country, which is still widely regarded as a leader in the design and implementation of cost-effective poverty alleviation policies. The current gulf between poverty research and poverty policy stands in stark contrast to situation that existed in the 1970s. Then, the Poverty Commission was widely expected to 'provide a catalyst for informed discussion as well as assist welfare organisations and all levels of Government in determining measures required to alleviate poverty in the Australian community' (Stanton, 1973, p. 32).

While mindful of its limitations, Australian poverty research has continued to use the poverty line adopted by the Poverty Commission because this has been the closest to an official poverty measure (Saunders, 1998a). The great advantage of a poverty measure that is officially endorsed by government is that it prevents those in positions of power from criticising the methods used to measure poverty in order to escape the policy implications of rising poverty. As United States poverty expert Robert Haveman has argued, one of the most significant contributions of the 1960s War on Poverty in the United States was the establishment of an official national poverty line (Haveman, 2000). Despite the many problems with the United States poverty line, its use in countless poverty studies has focused attention on trends in poverty and their policy implications. The United States poor have in general been well served by their poverty line – if not always by the policies designed to assist them!

There is an urgent need to develop a consensus on the concept and measurement of poverty that is relevant to the conditions prevailing in contemporary Australia. This will require a substantial input from the research community, since research is needed to provide the expert input required in a complex area of study. This does not mean that the poverty measure should be divorced from the views and priorities of the community. That input is also critical to the development of a measure that conforms to prevailing judgments about the nature and definition of poverty.

The fact that a poverty measure involves value judgments does not prevent poverty research from striving for the highest academic standards. Recent experience in Ireland illustrates how well-conceived and professional poverty research can put poverty onto the policy agenda and set in train community pressures to address the problem (Nolan, 2000). However, it may be too much to expect the poverty measure to be endorsed by those responsible for political actions concerned with the adequacy of social assistance programs (Veit-Wilson, 1998). If the poverty measure can attract strong community support, it will have persuasive effects in the political arena without constraining the freedom of political actors to also take account of other factors and arguments.

The meaning and measurement of poverty

Ever since serious investigation of the extent and nature of poverty began over a century ago with Seebohm Rowntree's study of poverty in York, England (Rowntree, 1901), poverty research has had a descriptive and a policy dimension (Sen, 1995). In the first of these, the primary aim has been to *describe the nature* of poverty, with any policy conclusions being derivative. In the second, the primary purpose has been to identify the *focus of public action*, with descriptions of poverty serving only a derivative purpose (Sen, 1995, p. 107). The goals of these two forms of research require different measures against which to assess what is happening. While a technical poverty line is required to inform and guide descriptive research, an adequacy standard that has an explicit political dimension is more appropriate as an instrument to guide policy (Veit-Wilson, 1998). The discussion that follows is based on this division and focuses on poverty in the descriptive sense, on the grounds that from a research perspective, diagnosis precedes policy choice.

Statistics and values

As already noted, politicians have become acutely aware of the powerful effect that poverty statistics can have on community perceptions of the impact of policy. They have responded by denying the existence of 'real' or 'genuine' poverty, which the statistics imply, and emphasising the judgments embedded in them. This has not opened up a debate over the nature and relevance of those judgments. Instead, attention has focused on the limitations of the methods used to estimate poverty, including weaknesses in how the poverty line is set and adjusted over time (Whiteford, 1997). At the same time, disagreement among the 'experts' on these issues has played into the hands of those who wish to see poverty removed from the policy agenda (Manning and de Jonge, 1996).

Without an active dialogue over the nature and meaning of poverty, there is little prospect of promoting action designed to alleviate it. In part, this involves responding to the criticisms of the available poverty measures by making them better suited to contemporary conditions. More fundamentally, it also involves asking basic questions about the nature of poverty in order to provide information that can be reflected in how it is conceived and measured.

Choice and resources

A key aspect of poverty is that it restricts the range of *choice* available to those affected by it (Saunders, 1997a). To be poor is to be denied the chance to enjoy the consumption of goods, or the ability to achieve and maintain good health, or to participate in social activities or other aspects of community life. Those who have the resources to enjoy these options but choose not to are not poor, even though they may appear so in terms of their actual consumption patterns. Unlike the person who chooses to fast, someone forced into starvation through lack of resources is poor, even though both end up inadequately nourished (Sen, 1995, p. 112).

It is the *opportunity to consume* that determines whether one is poor or not rather than actual consumption. However, while it is reasonably easy to observe people's consumption patterns, it is not possible to observe their consumption opportunities. Income is an obvious proxy for potential consumption, while actual consumption is an alternative. Both measures have been used in poverty research, though each suffers from a series of conceptual and practical limitations, as discussed in Chapter 4, and both have a role to play, in providing information that enriches the understanding of the circumstances associated with poverty (Saunders, Bradshaw and Hirst, 2002).

The Poverty Commission, drawing on an earlier study of poverty in Melbourne (Henderson, Harcourt and Harper, 1970), focused its attention on measuring the extent of primary poverty or poverty due to inadequate income relative to need. Although it was acknowledged that there are other forms of poverty, primary poverty was regarded as its most fundamental and easily measurable dimension. The Poverty Commission's focus on primary poverty led it to recommend the provision of adequate income as the key to eliminating poverty, on the grounds that 'an adequate income is fundamental to a person's security, well-being and independence ... [and] ... contributes greatly to personal freedom and the extent of opportunities available' (Commission of Inquiry into Poverty, 1975, p. 2).

This perspective leads naturally onto strategies for improving incomes through employment creation (combined with an adequate minimum wage) and the provision of social security benefits for those unable to work. The main focus of policy is thus on establishing an income safety net that allows a minimum level of basic needs to be met in all situations. Poverty is something 'out there' that happens to people and the immediate task is to protect those affected, not to inquire into what caused the situation or to assign responsibility for it.

Deciding which measure to use as an indicator of living standards still leaves open the question of where to set the poverty line. How much income is deemed to be adequate to avoid poverty and on what basis is this to be determined? If a consumption approach is chosen, which items or activities (or functionings in the terminology introduced by Sen, 1985) are seen as sufficiently important that their absence (or capability failure to quote Sen again) is indicative of poverty? These issues cannot be determined independently of prevailing social conditions, including the ways in which various types of hardship are perceived and measured.

Poverty is thus relative in the sense that the *resources* required to avoid hardship will depend upon social conditions, but this can still be consistent with a measure of deprivation that is absolute in relation to *capabilities*. Being able to achieve an adequate level of nutrition is an absolute requirement, but what this means in terms of an actual diet and the resources required to purchase the food that makes up that diet will vary with social custom and food prices (Sen, 1995, p. 116).

Poverty is also relative in another sense, although this is often neglected when poverty is defined relative to the overall standard of living. In a famous quotation from *The Wealth of Nations* (for many the book on which the tenets of neo-liberalism rest), Adam Smith equates poverty with a lack of necessities where these are defined as 'whatever the custom renders it indecent for creditable people, even of the lowest order, to be without' (Smith [1776], 1976, p. 351). One of the modern pioneers of poverty research, Peter Townsend, similarly refers to people as being poor when they lack whatever is 'customary, or at least widely encouraged or approved, in the societies to which they belong' (Townsend, 1979, p. 31). In both cases, it is clear that custom implies a degree of conformity with social conditions and expectations that extend beyond material resources. What this means in practice is difficult to discern with precision without enquiring into the perceptions of poverty that are widespread in specific communities at specific times. Embedded in the notion of relative poverty is the idea that community perceptions can help to identify the customs that shape the definition of poverty.

Although it will always be difficult to define poverty precisely, the definition proposed by Mack and Lansley (1985) as *an enforced lack of socially perceived necessities* captures three of the most important aspects of poverty. First, it emphasises that poverty is an enforced state that involves restrictions on choice beyond what is required to obtain the basic necessities of life; second, that poverty can only be meaningfully defined relative to a particular social environment; and third, that the definition must be endorsed in some way by the community living within that environment. While the role of (lack of) choice has already been mentioned, identifying necessities and the nature and role of social perceptions raises new issues. How broadly should necessities be defined, and can the lack of necessities be captured in a single income poverty line? How are community perceptions to be measured, whose perceptions matter and what impact should they have on where the poverty line is set? These issues are now considered.

Understanding the nature of poverty

The most obvious and direct way to find out what people mean when they think about poverty is to ask them. This is not as simple a task as it might appear. First, it is necessary to decide *whom* to ask and then to determine precisely *what* to ask them. Since the rationale for asking about the perception of poverty is to ascertain whether there are any commonly held views about its nature and definition, it is obviously desirable to sample a broad cross-section of the population. Given that the wording of these sorts of questions can affect the responses received (as noted in Chapter 3), it is important not to pre-judge the issue when framing the questions. Furthermore, in light of the nature of poverty and the possible diversity of opinion surrounding it, the questions can only be rather broad, with any inferences for where to set the poverty line left aside. This introduces two new factors into the equation. The first is the method used to aggregate the responses into a summary indicator. The second concerns how to set a poverty line that reflects community perceptions of poverty.

The CESC survey contains a series of questions in which respondents were asked about their understanding of the nature of poverty and its causes. As far as possible, the questions replicate those used in previous research, thus providing a basis for comparison of the results with other studies. Three specific issues were addressed in the questionnaire. The first relates to people's understanding of what poverty means, in a definitional sense. The second is concerned with perceptions of the causes of poverty and, in a limited way, people's views on what should be done about it. The third relates to people's perceptions of their own poverty status, as implied by their response to questions about their ability to make ends meet.

The meaning of poverty

There are two distinct ways in which to reflect on the meaning of poverty (Saunders, 1997b). The first concerns what poverty means to those who *study* it; the second emphasises what poverty means to those who *experience* it. The first approach has dominated the poverty literature and has focused on how to set a poverty line. The second approach to poverty, though neglected, is also very important because it addresses the impact of poverty on the poor themselves and is thus inextricably linked with the immediate and longer-term consequences of poverty (Saunders, 1998a; 2000b). While not producing specific guidance on how to measure poverty or where to set the poverty line, it offers a framework for thinking about the nature of poverty that is grounded in experience in ways that enrich understanding and add to the legitimacy of this second approach.

Turning first to people's understanding of poverty in a narrow, definitional sense, the CESC survey asked respondents to indicate how strongly they agreed with each of six different statements about what poverty means. The statements proposed and responses received are summarised in Table 6.1. People obviously had little difficulty answering the question, as can be seen from the tiny percentage of 'Don't know' responses. A far larger number were unable to decide whether they agreed or disagreed with each option, particularly those based on generalised conceptions of poverty that emphasise notions of 'decency', 'what most take for granted' or 'the good things in life'. Aside from the last option ('not able to afford the good things in life') there is strong agreement with *all* of the proposed meanings of poverty, although support is strongest for those that describe poverty in subsistence terms. Over 85 per cent agree that poverty involves not being able to make ends meet, while well over 90 per cent agree that poverty involves having to struggle constantly and not having enough to buy basic items. The average scores shown in the final row confirm that these are the most popular perceptions of what poverty means.

The strong degree of community support for subsistence notions of poverty does not imply that people regard poverty in absolute terms. Although there are some who still argue that poverty can be defined absolutely (in the sense that the poverty line is independent of social conditions), most poverty experts agree that this is not possible. Social conditions matter because they determine how basic needs are identified and defined and thus affect the level of resources required to purchase the items that satisfy basic needs. Proponents of absolute poverty favour a poverty line that is adjusted to reflect only price movements not increases in real community incomes and their main argument with the relativists is thus about where to set the line when real incomes are growing. This has obvious implications for the generosity of the social benefits required to alleviate poverty. Most Australians support a definition of poverty that means not being able to buy the goods that meet basic needs for food, clothing and shelter. But this does not preclude them from agreeing that the levels of consumption of these goods should be defined relative to consumption patterns in society generally.

Table 6.1 also indicates that there is much less agreement with notions of poverty that are explicitly relative. Few people see poverty as missing out on what others take for granted, not having enough to live decently, or being unable to afford the good things in life. These definitions embody a degree of relativism that differs from the subsistence notions described above, in that they tie poverty explicitly and directly to the living standards of those who are not poor. In contrast, a relativist interpretation of the subsistence approach emphasises the ability of the poor to meet basic needs, leaving open the question of how closely these needs depend upon general social conditions or standards of living.

Table 6.1 Community perceptions of the meaning of poverty (percentages)

	Not having enough money to make ends meet	Not having enough to buy what most take for granted	Not having enough to buy basics like food, housing and clothing	Having to struggle to survive each and every day	Not having enough to be able to live decently	Not being able to afford any of the good things in life
			Being in poverty means ...			
Strongly agree	42.3	24.7	64.4	63.2	35.6	16.9
Agree	43.5	38.6	31.6	30.4	40.8	28.5
Neither agree nor disagree	6.4	13.2	1.9	3.4	12.6	18.2
Disagree	6.6	21.0	1.0	2.1	8.7	28.3
Strongly disagree	0.7	1.5	0.4	0.3	0.9	7.0
Don't know [a]	0.5	1.1	0.7	0.6	1.5	1.1
Average score [b]	**1.21**	**0.65**	**1.60**	**1.55**	**1.03**	**0.20**

Notes: (a) Includes the (very small number) of multiple responses. (b) Mean score calculated from a five-point scale, Strongly agree = +2 to Strongly disagree = -2.
Unweighted n = 2,325 to 2,335.

Having asked people how strongly they agreed with a number of alternative views of poverty, the survey then asked them to indicate which view best describes what poverty means to them. This produced the responses shown in Table 6.2, which also shows the patterns elicited when a similar question was asked of a sample of clients of the (then) Department of Social Security as part of a survey conducted in 1995 (Saunders, 1995). It is important to emphasise that the two surveys were not only undertaken at different times, but also for different purposes. Unlike the CESC survey, the main objective of the earlier survey was to explore how the wives of unemployed men responded to the social security reforms introduced in 1995. The question on perceptions of poverty was included in order to establish whether it could be answered and, if so, what kinds of responses it produced.

In light of these differences, the similarity in the response patterns shown in Table 6.2 is remarkable. Both produce an identical ranking of the alternative views on the meaning of poverty and the degree of support for each alternative is also very similar across the two surveys. The 1995 survey suggests that those on low incomes and at the margins of poverty had rather modest expectations of what they needed to escape poverty – enough money to buy basic items without having to face a constant struggle to make ends meet. By 1999, support for these modest subsistence notions of poverty had strengthened, at least among the general

Table 6.2 Overall descriptions of poverty (percentages)

QUESTION: *Overall which of these statements BEST describes what being in poverty means to you*	Sample of Adult Australians (1999)	Sample of DSS Clients (1995)
Not having enough to buy basics like food, housing and clothing	43.8	41.9
Having to struggle to survive each and every day	32.2	26.4
Not having enough money to make ends meet	10.5	12.3
Not having enough to be able to live decently	6.5	8.6
Not having enough to buy what most others take for granted	2.7	–
Having a lot less than everyone else	–	1.8
Not being able to afford any of the good things in life	2.0	6.7
Don't know/multiple response	2.5	2.5
Sample size	2,269	1,146

population. In addition to providing a valuable insight into how Australians view poverty in the 1990s, the most important aspect of these results is their overall stability. This is significant because it affirms the potential value of trying to base a definition of poverty on community perceptions of what poverty means.

Causes of poverty

Studies of the causes of poverty traditionally distinguish between external factors and those that are a feature of the poor themselves. Writing almost thirty years ago, Feather (1974) distinguished between causes of poverty that were *individualistic* (a reflection of the behaviour of the poor themselves), *structural* (the result of external forces such as lack of education or low wages), or *fatalistic* (the result of factors such as illness or bad luck). In a similar vein, Haveman (2000), citing the work of Lampman (1965), has described economists' views about the causes of poverty in the 1960s as also consisting of a constellation of three factors. The first is events that are *external* to individuals, the second relates to *social barriers* in the form of caste, class or custom, and the third the *limited ability* of the poor to earn their way out of poverty.

Drawing on an earlier American survey, Feather asked just over 300 Adelaide households how importantly they rated a number of possible causes of poverty. The results, summarised in Table 6.3, provide a fascinating insight into what Australians saw as the causes of poverty at a time when the long post-war economic boom was coming to an end. The two most commonly cited explanations for poverty were lack of thrift and money management, and sickness and physical handicaps. At the other extreme, few people saw bad luck or being taken advantage of by the rich as factors causing poverty. Most people thought that poverty was the result of a combination of individual, structural and fatalist factors, although Australians were less likely than Americans to blame poverty on the personal characteristics of the poor and more likely to see fate and structural factors as important. Although many Australians saw low wages as a cause of poverty, few thought that lack of jobs was an important factor – not surprisingly, given the low level of unemployment that existed at the time of the survey.

Attitudes to the causes of poverty and to the poor themselves are likely to change along with economic conditions and community values, as reflected in public debate over 'the moral climate of society'. This appears to have changed attitudes to poverty in the United States, where economic experience and changes in American society have seen less support for external factors as the primary cause of their poverty and more support for the motivations of the poor themselves. These changes

Poverty and Exclusion

Table 6.3 Perceptions of the causes of Australian poverty in 1973 (Adelaide survey)

	Per cent endorsement		
Reason	Very important	Somewhat important	Not important
1 Prejudice and discrimination against the poor (S)	28	37	35
2 Lack of jobs provided by industry (S)	25	39	36
3 Lack of thrift and money management (I)	58	33	9
4 Low wages (S)	43	42	15
5 Failure of society to provide good schools (S)	35	40	25
6 Just bad luck (F)	9	26	65
7 Lack of effort by the poor themselves (I)	41	48	11
8 Sickness and physical handicaps (F)	57	38	5
9 Being taken advantage of by rich people (S)	28	29	44
10 Lack of ability or talent (F)	40	42	19
11 Loose morals and drunkenness (I)	38	38	25

Note: S = structural explanation; I = individualist explanation; F = fatalist explanation (see text).
Source: Feather, 1974, Table 3.

are reflected in United States poverty policy, which now focuses on encouraging self-reliance and reducing welfare dependency among the poor (Haveman, 2001).

Has a similar change in attitudes to the causes of poverty taken place in Australia? Table 6.4 provides part of the answer. It summarises the responses to a CESC question asking whether or not people agreed with a series of statements about the causes of poverty. The three factors that most agree are causally related to poverty are joblessness, low wages and lack of opportunity. The first two (and possibly also the third) reflect structural conditions in the labour market, and all three are external to the individual in the sense described earlier. While each of these factors received majority support, almost half disagree that bad luck is a cause of poverty, while over 60 per cent do not support the view that poverty is a direct reflection of the wealth of others. The strength of opinion against this last causal factor is almost matched by the extent of disagreement with the view that the poor only have themselves to blame for their situation.

Differences in views on the causes of poverty are highlighted in the average scores shown in the final row of Table 6.4. The new social conservatism that emphasises self-reliance and sees the cause of poverty as

Table 6.4 Community views on the causes of poverty (percentages)

	They have been unlucky in life (F)	They have not had the opportunities that other people have (S)	(Mostly) because they only have themselves to blame (I)	They do not have a job (S)	Their wages are too low (S)	Other people are rich (S)
Strongly agree	4.3	9.5	3.1	9.8	12.1	5.9
Agree	20.8	41.8	10.4	44.1	39.5	10.8
Neither agree nor disagree	26.7	19.2	23.9	19.1	23.1	18.3
Disagree	36.0	24.5	43.2	22.9	21.0	40.6
Strongly disagree	10.4	3.9	17.6	2.8	2.9	21.6
Don't know [a]	1.8	1.2	1.8	1.3	1.2	2.8
Average score [b]	**−0.28**	**0.29**	**−0.63**	**0.36**	**0.37**	**−0.63**

People are poor because ...

Notes: F = Fatalist explanation; S = Structural explanation; I = Individualist explanation.
(a) Includes those who gave a multiple response; (b) Mean score on a five-point scale, Strongly agree = +2 to Strongly disagree = −2.
Unweighted n = 2,242 to 2,261.

internal to the individual receives little support among the Australian community, whatever its support among Cabinet Ministers. After more than a decade of labour market deregulation, most Australians are still far more likely to blame poverty on the weak performance of the labour market than on any aberrant or dysfunctional behaviour on the part of individuals.

A comparison of Tables 6.4 and 6.3 provides an insight into how Australian views on the causes of poverty have changed since the 1970s. To facilitate this comparison, the causes shown in Table 6.4 have been classified into the three sets of factors (individualist, structural and fatalist) identified in Feather's earlier work (as shown in Table 6.3). It is clear that there has been a major shift in public opinion over the last 25 years, with less support now for individualist explanations of poverty and far more support for structural explanations, particularly those relating to the role of the labour market as a cause of poverty. In contrast, the low level of support for the role of fate identified in the early 1970s still existed at the end of the 1990s. Compared with the earlier results, support for low wages as a cause of poverty has increased from 43 per cent to 52 per cent, while support for lack of jobs has more than doubled, from 25 per cent to 54 per cent. These trends are not surprising given the massive increase in unemployment and the trend to low wages associated with the emergence of a new class of 'working poor' (Eardley, 2000).

A natural question to ask of these results is whether views about the causes of poverty bear any relation to the circumstances of those who hold them. Are those who perceive themselves to be poor or on the margins of poverty more likely to agree that the causes of poverty are external, with those well above the poverty line more likely to blame the poor themselves for their poverty? The short answer appears to be no. Table 6.5 suggests that agreement with the different causes of poverty bears no apparent relation to respondents' subjective assessment of the adequacy of their own incomes.

The subjective adequacy variable shown in Table 6.5 was based on the reported answers to the following question:

Thinking of your present situation, which of the following BEST describes how you are managing on your family income?
1 I/We haven't enough to get by on
2 I/We have just enough to get by on
3 I/We have enough to get by on and for a few extras
4 I/We have much more than I/We we need

These four categories are shown in Table 6.5 as 'Not enough'. 'Just enough', 'More than enough' and 'Much more than enough', respectively

Table 6.5 Reasons for poverty by adequacy of family income (percentages in each managing categoty who strongly agree or agree)

Ability to manage on family income:	They have been unlucky in life (F)	They have not had the opportunities that other people have (S)	(Mostly) because they only have themselves to blame (I)	They do not have a job (S)	Their wages are too low (S)	Other people are rich (S)
			People are poor because ...			
Haven't enough	30.0	60.1	14.1	60.2	74.7	25.2
Just enough	28.2	54.4	15.2	57.4	59.0	18.3
More than enough	23.4	47.3	13.9	54.0	44.7	14.4
Much more than enough	18.5	50.9	16.1	53.6	33.9	13.5

Note: See Notes to Table 6.4.

and the percentage agreeing with each statement about the causes of poverty question is shown for each adequacy category.

While the same broad pattern of responses is evident across all four subjective income adequacy categories, the strength of opinion on the causes of poverty varies systematically (and, in a statistical sense, significantly) with each respondent's subjective assessments of the adequacy of their own income relative to need. The strength of support for the external causes of poverty is greatest among those in the 'Not enough' and 'Just enough' categories, while agreement with the 'bad luck' and 'wealth of others' explanations is much weaker among those whose incomes can buy more than they need. These results demonstrate how the views people hold about the causes of poverty depend on their own circumstances and experience. Attitudes to social problems and conditions like poverty are not independent of people's own exposure to them.

Primary poverty

Primary poverty is determined according to whether or not income is above or below a poverty line that reflects what is required to meet needs. Despite the reservations surrounding how and where to set the poverty line, the method is based on an objective assessment of income in relation to need. It thus avoids many of the problems involved in interpreting subjective responses like those just considered, but introduces new problems surrounding where to set the poverty line. The poverty line most often used to estimate poverty in Australia is the Henderson poverty line (HPL) established by the Poverty Commission and modified subsequently to adjust for some minor imperfections (Manning, 1982).

It is now almost forty years since the elements of the HPL were first developed and while a strong case can be made for revising it, there are also good reasons for not doing so. The most useful role of a poverty line is to estimate poverty and make comparisons of poverty – how it has changed over time, how it varies between different groups and how the changes relate to what is happening in the economy and to society and its institutions. These comparisons provide important insights into the forces being propagated by economic and social change and allow the effectiveness of social security and other policies to be determined.

The value of these estimates is reduced whenever the poverty measure is changed. The United States experience is salutary in this regard. As a measure of poverty, the United States poverty line suffers from at least as many limitations as the Henderson line. Not only is it older; the methods used to construct it have been subjected to extensive criticism from United States poverty researchers (Ruggles, 1990; Citro and Michael, 1995). Yet, the original line continues to be used in almost all studies of

United States poverty, and the results of this research have at times had a powerful impact on thinking about the causes of poverty and the impact of poverty alleviation programs (Danziger and Weinberg, 1986; Glennerster, 2000; Haveman, 2000). Although the official status of the United States poverty line can partly explain its popularity and impact, the fact that it has not been revised has allowed the longer-term trend in poverty and the impact of policy and other factors to be identified.

It does not follow from the United States experience that criticism of the HPL should be ignored in order to avoid having to change how poverty is measured in Australia. There will come a time when any poverty line becomes so out of date that poverty estimates based on it lose all credibility. But even in these circumstances, there is a need to be certain that a better poverty measure is available before abandoning the one that already exists. The most vocal critics of the HPL have been silent when it comes to proposing an alternative (Sullivan, 2000). That no alternative poverty measure yet exists that has the familiarity and legitimacy of the Henderson measure suggests there are good reasons to stick with the HPL, recognise its limitations but be prepared to defend its strengths as a research and policy tool.

This approach makes even more sense if researchers assess the sensitivity of estimates of poverty to variations in where the poverty line is set. This also overcomes some of the limitations of measuring the extent of poverty by the percentage below the poverty line – an approach that ignores the severity of poverty among the poor. This approach is now commonly used in Australian poverty studies (e.g. Saunders, 1996c, 1998b; Harding and Szukalska, 2000a, 2000b; Whiteford and Bond, 2000) and it allows changes in the rate and severity of poverty to be assessed against the HPL without necessarily endorsing all of its components.

Although most attention has focused on the role of the poverty line in affecting estimates of poverty, the quality of the income data used to estimate poverty can also create problems. The income data used to estimate primary poverty are collected by the ABS in its surveys of household income. The first nation-wide study of income distribution was conducted in 1969, with subsequent surveys undertaken about every four or five years between then and 1990. The method used to conduct the income survey was changed in 1994–95, when the previous method of conducting a special survey over a two-month period was replaced by a survey undertaken continuously throughout the year (ABS, 1999a, p. 45). A consequence of this change is that the data for the years prior to 1995 are not consistent with those for the years after the new survey was introduced, making it difficult to estimate how poverty has changed over time.

Table 6.6 reveals a rising overall poverty trend between 1989–90 and 1996–97, but there are also a number of specific instances where poverty has fallen over the period. In particular, there is a marked decline in poverty among sole parent units, from almost 60 per cent in 1989–90 to less than 37 per cent in 1996–97. After rising rapidly up until 1994–95, poverty among aged couples without children also fell over the next two years. Estimates of poverty are most volatile among the aged, where the sharp swings reflect the fact that the pension is close to the poverty line so that a small change in income can shift thousands of pensioners just above or just below the line.

Some will argue that the upward trend in poverty reflects an upward bias in how the poverty line has been adjusted over time. The poverty line is adjusted in line with movements in household disposable income per capita, which increased markedly in real terms over the period (Figure 2.1). However, while this suggests that there may be some truth in this, it cannot explain the different trajectories experienced by different income unit types. Here, the patterns of movement provide more convincing evidence of the relative poverty risks facing different groups and the adequacy of government support for each group. The sharp rise in poverty

Table 6.6 Estimates of income poverty in Australia, 1989–90 to 1996–97 [a]

Income unit type	Poverty rate (%) 1989–90	1994–95	1996–97
Single person[b]			
non-aged	19.8	19.4	25.5
aged	27.9	31.1	31.7
All single people	20.4	22.3	26.9
Couples without children[b]			
non-aged	6.3	7.1	9.1
aged	6.7	19.8	13.9
All couples without children	6.4	11.7	10.6
Couples with children	10.5	11.4	14.2
Sole parent unit	58.0	39.8	36.9
All income units	**16.7**	**18.3**	**20.7**

Notes: (a) The estimates are based on annual income in each financial year and have been derived from the detailed Henderson poverty lines that vary with the age, gender and labour force status of each person and the living arrangements of the family as a whole. (b) Aged income units include single males aged 65 and over, single females aged 60 and over and couples where the male is aged 65 and over.

Sources: Saunders, 1994, Table 9.2 and ABS unit record data from later surveys.

among non-aged single people since the mid-1990s is of particular concern, since it suggests that many in this group have missed out on the increased incomes that economic growth has produced for others.

Perceptions of poverty

Reaching agreement on how to allow for the statistical complexities and value judgments built into any poverty line is very difficult if not impossible. This suggests that it may be valuable to determine whether or not people are in primary poverty by asking them. Two methods of determining poverty by using people's perceptions of it have been suggested. The first ('subjective poverty') involves asking people directly about their subjective assessment of their own poverty status. The second ('consensual poverty') involves using people's perceptions about the income required to meet basic needs as the basis for setting a poverty line, then determining poverty objectively by comparing income with it. The two methods differ in their use of information about community perceptions of poverty. The 'subjective poverty' method asks people about their own poverty status and cannot be used to determine the poverty status of others; the 'consensual poverty' method can, but only after the different responses have been used to develop a poverty line.

There is no guarantee that the two methods will produce consistent results and they may in fact produce contradictory findings (see below). These inconsistencies reflect the complex and multi-dimensional nature of poverty and the inaccuracies involved in identifying poverty perceptions, but they also undermine the usefulness of the approach to some degree. Against this, the fact that the understanding and measurement of poverty are derived from community perceptions addresses the criticism that the estimates are arbitrary and lack legitimacy. Perceptions of poverty thus provide new insights into the nature of poverty, but do not resolve all of the problems faced when identifying and measuring it.

Poverty perceptions also raise difficulties of measurement and interpretation. People adjust to the circumstances they face, and perceptions are thus not independent of the conditions actually experienced. Even the very poorest may become so inured to their deprivation that, when asked, they may deny that they are poor. Others may be ashamed to acknowledge their poverty, while some of those with higher incomes may have unmet needs that lead them to claim that they are, in some respects, poor. These factors greatly complicate the task of identifying who is poor on the basis of information about who is prepared to admit it.

A further set of problems associated with asking people about their own poverty status is that subjective perceptions of poverty are inconsistent with the notion of a single poverty line that can be used to determine each person's poverty status objectively. While providing increased income to those who perceive themselves to be poor may reduce the extent of their perceived poverty, there is nothing in their expressed deprivation that indicates how much income is needed to remove them from poverty. Should greater assistance be provided to those whose perceived poverty is greatest irrespective of their objective circumstances? This would contradict most accepted tenets of social justice and create all kinds of perverse incentives that would undermine the community acceptability of such arrangements.

Although there is value in exploring differences in how poverty is perceived among different groups in the community, these differences weaken the usefulness of the approach for policy formulation. There is little sense in linking income support to the severity with which poverty is perceived by those who claim to be poor. The practical application of the perceptions of poverty approach needs to reflect these concerns, and it is difficult to argue that a poverty line based on expressed perceptions of poverty should vary for those in the same objective circumstances.

Consensual poverty

One of the strongest arguments in support of the consensual approach is that a poverty line derived from community perceptions of poverty may attract greater support and increased legitimacy in the community; so too, for the degree of identified poverty and for policies to alleviate it. The term 'consensual poverty' is used to signify the determination of poverty with reference to a poverty line derived from community perceptions of poverty. To avoid confusion, it should be acknowledged that there is in fact little consensus in the community about where to set an income poverty line (Saunders and Matheson, 1992).

A vast literature has developed which attempts to derive a consensual poverty line from public perceptions of minimum income (Hagenaars, 1986; Walker, 1987). The most influential strand of this literature is associated with the work of researchers based at Leyden University in the Netherlands. The method developed by the Leyden group derives a poverty line from responses to a question asking people how much money they need to make ends meet (Goedhart et al., 1977: see also Saunders, 1994 and Saunders, Hallerod and Matheson, 1994). The question is referred to as the minimum income question (MIQ) and it takes the following form:

> *In your opinion, what would be the very lowest net weekly income that your family would need each week just to make ends meet?*

The response to the MIQ question has been shown to vary systematically with actual family income, reflecting the fact that people become accustomed to the income they receive. It also varies with the circumstances of the family, since these determine the 'ends' that have to be met from the income available. This information can be used to determine the income level at which, on average, people would indicate that their current income level is equal to the lowest amount required to make ends meet.

If family circumstances are represented by the variable (C), then the following relationship is assumed to exist between the MIQ response (Y^m), actual income (Y) and family circumstances (C):

$$Y^m = F(Y, C) \qquad (6.1)$$

Statistical methods are used to estimate equation (6.1) and then to calculate the income level at which people would say that their current income level is equal to the lowest amount required to make ends meet. This income level is equal to the consensual poverty line (Y^p), which is derived from the following equation:

$$Y^p = F(Y^p, C) \qquad (6.2)$$

The method produces a single poverty line (given family circumstances) from the variety of responses that the MIQ generates that has a straightforward and intuitive explanation. Against this, the consensual poverty line is sensitive to the precise formulation of equation (6.1) and thus represents only one of many possible ways of combining the reported MIQ responses into a poverty line. The approach also ignores the uncertainty regarding how people interpret the relationship between poverty and what is involved in being able to 'make ends meet'.

There is no guarantee under the MIQ approach to consensus poverty that those whose actual income is below that nominated in their response to the MIQ will be defined as in poverty, even though this is implied by their response to the MIQ. Thus, it is possible for the method to produce an estimate of Y^p such that $Y < Y^m$ and $Y > Y^p$ or where $Y > Y^m$ and $Y < Y^p$. Consensual poverty is not the same as subjective poverty. The former is based on the relationship between Y and Y^p while the latter is based on the relationship between Y and Y^m.

In order to illustrate the method and highlight some of its limitations, equation (6.1) has been assumed to take the following log-linear form:

$$\log(Y^m) = \alpha + \beta \log(Y) + \delta \, FS \qquad (6.3)$$

Where Y = actual reported family income and FS = family size. (This formulation has been shown in earlier research by Saunders and Matheson, 1992 to be a good representation of the data.) Estimates of equation (6.3) derived from the CESC data and the corresponding consensual poverty rates are presented in Table 6.7, along with the estimates using 1988 data reported by Saunders and Matheson (1992,

Table 4.1). The estimated parameters of equation (6.1) shown in the upper half of Table 6.7 are statistically robust and appear to be stable over the two years. However, this stability is misleading when the estimates are used to estimate the consensual poverty lines, as can be seen by comparing the relativities between the poverty lines for different family types (which represent the implied equivalence scale, discussed in Chapter 5).

In broad terms, an increase in family size beyond two, which represents the costs of children, adds about $16 a week to the poverty line in 1988, but closer to $50 a week in 1999. When expressed relative to the poverty line for a two-person family, the relative costs of each child are estimated at around 6 per cent of the cost of an adult couple in 1988, but more than double that, at around 12 per cent in 1999.

The estimated 1999 poverty line for a family of four (two adults and two children) of $482 a week is virtually identical to the Henderson poverty line for that family of $483. However, this remarkable similarity is mainly coincidental and does not apply to other family types, because the relativities shown in Table 6.7 differ markedly from those implicit in the Henderson line. The final two columns convert the 1999 poverty lines into 1988 dollars to facilitate comparison with the estimates for the earlier year. The real increase in the poverty lines is greater where there are more children, whereas the increase for a single person is less than 5 per cent.

Community perceptions of poverty as reflected in these measures thus suggest that poverty level incomes increase over time in real terms, but also vary with family size in ways that change inexplicably over time. These variations cast considerable doubt on the ability of the entire consensual poverty line methodology to produce a consistent set of poverty benchmarks across family types or over time.

The fact that the consensual poverty lines in Table 6.7 are so high – particularly for single people and large families – implies that poverty rates for these families will also be high. This is borne out by the estimates of consensual poverty shown in the first column of Table 6.9 (below) that are based on the family income data reported in the CESC. The overall poverty rate in 1999 is estimated to be over 42 per cent – more than double the Henderson poverty rate for 1996–97 shown in Table 6.6 and well above the rate of 22.6 per cent estimated by Harding and Szukalska (2000a, Table 9) to apply in 1999. Even more alarming are the estimated rates of consensual poverty among the aged of over 82 per cent (for single people) and 75% (for couples), which are implausibly high. So too are the estimates of poverty among sole parents, which other measures suggest have been declining through the 1990s and are now much lower than those shown in Table 6.9. Comparisons

Table 6.7 Consensual poverty lines (CPL) and consensual poverty, 1988 and 1999

Log-linear formulation of (6.1): $\log(Y^m) = \alpha + \beta \log(Y) + \delta FS$

	1988			1999			CPL for 1999 in 1988 prices [a]	Real increase in CPL 1988–99

Parameter estimates [b]

	1988	1999
α	3.79 **	3.55 **
β	0.30 **	0.38 **
δ	0.04 **	0.07 **

Consensual poverty lines

	$ per week	Relativity	$ per week	Relativity	$ per week	Increase (%)
FS = 1	237.8	0.94	343.3	0.89	248.8	4.6
FS = 2	251.8	1.00	384.4	1.00	278.2	10.5
FS = 3	266.6	1.06	430.3	1.12	311.4	16.8
FS = 4	282.3	1.12	481.7	1.25	348.6	23.5
FS = 5	298.9	1.19	538.3	1.40	390.3	30.6
FS = 6	316.4	1.26	603.8	1.57	436.9	38.1

Notes: (a) Adjusted using the consumer price index. (b) ** indicates that all estimated parameters are statistically significant at the 1 per cent level.

Poverty and Exclusion 165

of consensual poverty rates with these other estimates thus cast further doubt on the reliability of the approach.

Subjective poverty

It does not follow from the above discussion that community perceptions of poverty have no role to play in how poverty is defined and measured. Alternative ways of using community perceptions of poverty are needed. One of these, mentioned earlier, involves exploring directly people's perceptions of their own poverty status rather than inferring this indirectly from their response to the minimum income question, as is done in the consensual approach. This approach can be explored using the CESC data by comparing actual reported family income (Y) with the response to the minimum income question (Y^m). This avoids the statistical and other complexities surrounding the specification and estimation of equation (6.1) and is a more transparent and explicit method of determining whether or not people think they are poor.

However, it is possible to explore the nature of subjective poverty even more directly by examining responses to the perceived income adequacy question described earlier. It is possible to use the 'income managing' question to define those who respond in each of the four managing categories shown in Table 6.5 as 'poor', 'on the margins of poverty', 'modestly well-off' and ' comfortably off', respectively. This approach to subjective poverty avoids many of the complexities introduced by data limitations and statistical methodology, but this comes at a cost. In particular, this version of the subjective approach does not generate an estimate of the poverty line that can be compared with other estimates and validated against other measures. This makes it difficult to determine how useful the approach is, even if it produces plausible estimates of the extent of poverty.

Notwithstanding these qualifications, Table 6.8 uses the CESC data to examine the responses to the 'income managing' question by family type. Looking first at the overall figures, less than one in twelve (7.9 per cent) indicated that they did not have enough to get by on and were thus in subjective poverty in the sense defined above. Although this is quite a small proportion of the sample, a further two-fifths (41 per cent) indicated that they had just enough to get by on and were thus on the margins of poverty. Very few people (less than 3 per cent) were prepared to admit that they had much more than they needed. The fact that so few people place themselves in this category (the true percentage must be far higher) illustrates that the question itself is problematic and this casts some doubt on its usefulness for estimating poverty. The fact that the numbers in the fourth response category are under-estimated implies

Table 6.8 Perceptions of income adequacy (percentages)

Thinking about your present situation, which of the following statements BEST describes how you are managing on your family income?	Single person	Couple without children	Couple with children	Sole parent	Other[a]	Total
I/We haven't enough to get by on	12.6	4.2	6.7	24.7	8.9	7.9
I/We have just enough to get by on	46.3	38.4	41.6	50.9	37.3	41.0
I/We have enough to get by on and for a few extras	37.6	55.3	49.3	24.4	50.0	48.4
I/We have much more than I/We need	3.5	2.1	2.4	0.0	3.8	2.7

Note: (a) Other includes multiple family types living together.
Unweighted n = 2,348.

that the numbers in at least one of the other three categories are biased upwards. This bias seems most likely to be concentrated in the middle two categories, suggesting that the number in the lowest (subjective poverty) category may also be an under-estimate.

When the estimates are broken down by family type, clear differences emerge in the perceived adequacy of the incomes of different families, as reflected in their ability to manage. Sole parent families are in the worse situation, followed by single people and multiple family households. Families with two adults have less trouble getting by than single-adult families, reflecting the possibility that they may have two incomes on which to draw. Within couple families, there is a tendency for those with children to have more trouble getting by, although the differences according to whether or not there are children present are not great. The tendency for responses to bunch into the two middle options is repeated across all family types, with at least three-quarters of all respondents placing themselves in one of these two categories.

The most striking feature of the subjective poverty estimates in Table 6.8 is how much they differ from those using the consensual poverty lines shown in Table 6.6. The consensual poverty rate, at 42.2 per cent (Table 6.9), is more than five times higher than the subjective poverty rate of 7.9 per cent (though the gap narrows considerably if those on the margins of poverty are included as poor under the subjective method). Though not shown in Table 6.8, the differences between the two sets of estimates are greatest for the aged (single and couples) and younger single people. For the aged, the consensual method implies that more than three-quarters are in poverty, whereas only around 5 per cent of older Australians indicate that their incomes are not enough for them to make ends meet. Among the non-aged population, both methods produce a similar pattern of poverty rates, although the levels of poverty differ substantially. Both methods suggest that poverty is highest among sole parent families, followed by single people and then couples with children (where poverty rises with the number of children). Similar patterns emerge when poverty is measured objectively (Table 6.6) suggesting that, in this respect at least, poverty perceptions reflect the underlying reality.

Having explored the differences between consensual and subjective poverty, Table 6.9 examines the overlap between them. Only 14 per cent of families identified as being in consensual poverty indicated that their incomes were not enough for them to make ends meet. The degree of overlap is greatest for sole parent families, single people and couples with children, reinforcing the earlier conclusion that these are the groups at greatest risk of poverty. But the fact that the overlap is so low illustrates how different forms of perceived poverty can be used to reach very different conclusions about the extent of poverty. Trying to interpret

Table 6.9 Comparing consensual and subjective poverty rates, 1999 (percentages)

Family type	Consensual poverty rate	Subjective poverty rate	In consensual poverty and: In subjective poverty also	In consensual poverty and: Not in subjective poverty	Adjusted consensual poverty rate [a]
Single non-aged adult	51.5	12.8	21.7	78.3	11.3
Single aged adult	82.6	7.3	9.0	91.0	7.3
Non-aged couple	26.6	3.9	10.0	90.0	2.7
Aged couple	75.4	4.0	5.4	94.6	4.1
Couple + 1 child	25.3	6.1	15.9	84.1	4.0
Couple + 2 children	33.7	7.8	18.3	81.7	6.1
Couple + 3 children	31.4	7.4	18.4	81.6	5.8
Couple + 4 children	41.7	8.3	12.0	88.0	5.0
Sole parent + 1 child	72.0	20.0	29.4	70.6	20.8
Sole parent + 2 children	65.7	23.7	26.1	73.9	17.1
Sole parent + 3 children	81.8	30.8	44.4	55.6	36.4
All families	42.2	7.3	14.1	85.9	5.9
(sample size)	(1582)	(1692)	(654)	(654)	(1555)

Note: (a) The adjusted poverty rate includes those defined as in both consensual and subjective poverty.

perceptions of what poverty means is thus as difficult as trying to measure poverty objectively using an external poverty standard.

The final column of Table 6.9 shows what the poverty profile would look like if people are only regarded as poor if they are below the consensual poverty line *and* indicate that their income is not enough to get by on. On this basis, the poverty rate is 5.9 per cent, well below that implied by all of the other methods. The two groups with the greatest risk of income poverty are sole parent families and single people (aged and non-aged) with couples with children now experiencing below-average poverty rates. Together with the evidence presented earlier, it appears that adults who live alone or have sole responsibility for caring for children have a greater exposure to poverty than adults who live with another adult. This pattern consistently emerges from both the objective and subjective poverty estimates, and although the latter produce many peculiarities, they tell the same broad story about the relative risks of poverty among Australians as the objective measures.

Beyond income poverty

Estimates of primary poverty, whether objectively or subjectively determined, capture only that aspect of poverty that is due to inadequate income relative to need. Although income remains a very important determinant of well-being, it was argued in Chapter 5 that the social meaning of income is changing in ways that weaken its links with the standard of living. This has lead to criticism of the concept of primary poverty on the grounds that income no longer provides a sound basis for determining how well needs are being met. Other factors must also be taken into account, including other determinants of material well-being, the ability to sustain living standards over time and the structural conditions that shape people's lives.

The relevance of these arguments is particularly compelling when measuring the economic status of Indigenous Australians. Several studies have used the Henderson methodology to estimate poverty among the Aboriginal population (Ross and Whiteford, 1992; Ross and Mikalauskas, 1996; Altman and Hunter, 1998; Hunter, 2001). But it is widely acknowledged that measuring Indigenous poverty must go beyond a narrow income framework to incorporate measures of direct deprivation and structural disadvantage. This involves recognising the diversity of Indigenous circumstances and the alternative values and choices of Indigenous Australians. Although the Henderson poverty line provides a useful starting point from which to consider the issue of Indigenous poverty, a more relevant approach involves combining several social indicators of well-being rather than a single income-based measure (Altman and Hunter, 1998, p. 256).

The limitations of income

Reflecting on the nature of Indigenous poverty highlights the fact that while income is important, so too are the many other factors that determine the options available to people and influence the choices they make. As was recognised in the Report of the Poverty Commission three decades ago, unless the structural conditions and inequalities that produce poverty are addressed, income redistribution will achieve only limited goals (Commission of Inquiry into Poverty, 1975, p. viii). Reflecting this view, the narrowness of an income poverty line was criticised at the time on the grounds that it mistakenly equated the causes of poverty with its manifestation, producing a 'solution' that involved increased incomes for the poor within an unchanged social structure (Bryson, 1977).

The importance of the source of income is reflected in the new approach to welfare reform (considered in more detail in Chapter 8), which emphasises that income provision does not address the underlying causes of poverty, and may exacerbate them. The argument is that uncontingent income assistance may induce those who receive it to become dependent on the state and less able to achieve financial independence through their own efforts. Economic reasoning suggests that a dollar of state benefits is preferable to a dollar that has to be earned in the labour market (because the latter involves a sacrifice of time that has a positive value, as noted in Chapter 5). However, earnings are preferable on social grounds because they avoid dependence on state-funded benefits, reflect active economic participation and convey status and prestige. Thus, while the manifestation of poverty is low income (by definition), in order to understand the *causes* of poverty it is necessary to ask why income is low and address those factors directly. By focusing on technical aspects of poverty measurement, conventional poverty research has diverted attention away from the causes of poverty.

Poverty dynamics

One way of paying greater attention to the causes of poverty is to investigate the *processes* that contribute to low income and increase the risk of exposure to poverty. This requires longitudinal data that track the economic fortunes of people through time, including the extent of income variability and the factors that cause it. The study of poverty dynamics not only distinguishes between temporary and permanent poverty – each of which may require a different policy response – but also highlights the role of contextual factors such as family, job and neighbourhood (Walker, 1994). Income alone, particularly when measured in static terms, cannot encapsulate the complex and multi-dimensional nature of poverty, defined to include access to private and public consumption, ownership of assets, personal dignity and autonomy (Walker and Park, 1998).

In relation to income dynamics, longitudinal data provide a basis for exploring income trajectories through time as a way of identifying the events that trigger an increased poverty risk (Jarvis and Jenkins, 1995, 1997; Hills, 1998). Through such examination, it may be possible to identify the key factors, processes and opportunities that serve to prevent poverty and thus assist in the design of interventions designed to reinforce these patterns. Research based on the early waves of the British Household Panel Survey (BHPS) reported by Hills (1998) and Jarvis and Jenkins (1997) indicates that most poverty in Britain is not permanent. Over the first four waves of the BHPS in the early 1990s, almost 36 per cent of the British population experienced low income (i.e. were located in the bottom fifth of the income distribution) in at least one year, but only 6.9 per cent were poor in all four years (Hills, 1998, Table 5).

The data reveal a complex series of mobility patterns, with some experiencing relatively flat income trajectories, others following a steadily rising (or falling) trend and others again experiencing 'blips' (short-run variations from a basically flat trajectory) that can take people unexpectedly into (or out of) poverty. These complex dynamic patterns highlight the fact that income alone does not tell the whole story of what causes poverty, even when poverty is measured in terms of income. There are important inter-relationships connecting income with family, labour market, health status, psychological well-being, self-esteem and spatial processes reflected in the nature of the local community that affect attitudes to employment. These are transmissible across generations. Income has to be understood within this broader constellation of factors if we are to uncover the causes of poverty.

We must focus not only on the incomes that people experience, but also on how these reflect the opportunities available to them. This involves examining the kinds of jobs available to people and the nature of the workplaces where those jobs are located. It also requires an understanding of the factors that determine population mobility, and why some communities are able to adjust to changing economic circumstances more easily than others. The role of government is crucial, as is the way in which government intervention is supported or subverted in the public discourse surrounding poverty and disadvantage (Fincher and Saunders, 2001, Chapter 1). Some have argued that the notion of poverty no longer provides a useful framework for thinking about the role and impact of a nexus of social relations and processes that can result in exclusion.

Social exclusion

Provision of an adequate income is necessary for complete social integration, but will not guarantee it if other integrative mechanisms have broken down. Inadequate income thus results in primary poverty as a static outcome, which produces a dynamic process leading to impoverishment, just as relative deprivation (Townsend, 1987) can start a dynamic process that results in social exclusion. Social exclusion reflects much more than a lack of economic resources and will not be avoided by social transfers that favour the excluded. However, exclusion necessarily involves some form of differentiation and is thus related to the notion of inequality.

The concept of social exclusion

Although the term 'social exclusion' only appeared in the language of social policy relatively recently, its impact on thinking and policy has been pervasive and profound. The term was originally used in France in the 1970s, where it gave rise to the need for social integration policies 'composed of economic, professional, cultural and social fields of action, aimed at enabling individuals to regain their independence and position within society' (Whiteford, 2001, p. 52). There are links between social exclusion and Sen's idea of capability, since both acknowledge the intrinsic importance of being able to 'take part in the life of the community' (Sen, 2000, p. 89). Although the need to take part (or be included) is absolute and applies to all communities, its achievement may require resources, opportunities and motivations that differ according to the standard of living and customs applying in specific societies.

Social exclusion and poverty are related but distinct concepts. Whereas the main focus of poverty is on *distributional issues*, social exclusion emphasises the importance of *relational issues* (Room, 1995; Berghmann, 1997). Unlike poverty, social exclusion is an intrinsically dynamic concept that is the outcome of processes through which some individuals or groups are excluded by the actions (or inaction) of others (Atkinson, 1998a). Thus Donnison argues that:

> Poverty arises when needs cannot be met. But needs change as society evolves ... That's fine for those who share in the country's generally rising living standards, but those who get left behind suffer new forms of poverty which inflict real hardships ... The process goes further. A neighbourhood in which most people are poor is not an attractive place for shops, banks, building societies, bus companies and other enterprises to do business. That's why there are so few of them there. Its political clout is likely to be weaker than that of a community in which everyone has telephones and is used to demanding helpful responses from public officials. So poorer people's needs ... are less likely to be met than are those of richer people living in more comfortable neighbourhoods. Unmet need, and therefore poverty, excludes people from the mainstream of their own society. (Donnison, 1998, p. 19)

In his analysis of social exclusion, Atkinson (1998a) identifies three recurring themes. The first is the idea of *relativity* – the notion that exclusion can only be identified and measured in a particular place at a particular time. The second theme is that of *agency* – the idea that exclusion involves actions taken by people, either by excluding themselves, or by excluding others. This is the crux of the concept according to Donnison, because it asks the right kinds of questions:

1. Who are excluded and by whom?
2. What factors exclude people and how can they be overcome?
3. What are the 'mainstream' communities from which people are excluded and what are the routes back to integration?

The third aspect of exclusion is its emphasis on the operation and outcomes of *dynamic processes*. To understand these, it is necessary to study behaviour through time (using longitudinal data as described earlier) and to juxtapose what actually happens with prior expectations and aspirations. Long-term poverty among families can affect the prospects of poor children and cause poverty to be transmitted across generations and transformed into social exclusion.

The Economic and Social Research Council (ESRC) in the United Kingdom has defined social exclusion as involving 'the processes by which individuals and their communities become polarized, socially differentiated and unequal' (ESRC, 1997; quoted in Barry, 1998). Giddens goes further, equating exclusion with inequality and equality with inclusion, where:

> Inclusion refers in its broadest sense to citizenship, to the civil and political rights and obligations that all members of society should have, not just formally, but as a reality of their lives. It also refers to opportunities and to involvement in public space. In a society where work remains central to self-esteem and standard of living, access to work is one main context of opportunity. Education is another, and would be even if it weren't so important for the employment possibilities to which it is relevant. (Giddens, 1998, p. 103)

Social exclusion exists wherever processes or actions deny people inclusion in this sense. Such exclusion may be either enforced (as it is for those at the bottom of society), or voluntary (for those at the top), the latter involving the affluent elite withdrawing from social interaction and removing themselves from the public sphere, including public education and health systems.

Some concern has been expressed over how exclusion can be combated through programs that encourage participation, and the notion itself remains somewhat obscure and contested (Jones and Smyth, 1999).

However, its strategic significance has been seized on, and social exclusion has an obvious attraction to policy-makers who view the concept of poverty with suspicion because of its powerful combination of normative judgment and moral authority. For them, poverty is too complex to estimate, too simple to respond to, too expensive to ameliorate and too likely to become entrenched in response to untied social transfers. In any case, low income is a symptom rather than a cause and policy needs to address causes if it is to have a lasting impact. One advantage of replacing poverty by social exclusion is thus that it allows researchers to engage with the policy dialogue on what needs to be done. Government spokesmen are thus able to 'talk about exclusion despite being required by their masters to deny that their countries have any poverty' (Donnison, 1998, p. 4).

Indicators of exclusion

A recent British study of social exclusion highlighted its complexity by developing a list of 46 separate indicators. The list includes, in addition to income, measures of employment insecurity, anxiety among older people, vulnerability to crime, overcrowding, the youth suicide rate and the number of children in offenders' institutions (Howarth et al., 1999 – see also Gordon and Pantazis, 1997). In Australia, the development of indicators of social exclusion has been promoted by research on the measurement of social capital (Onyx and Bullen 2000; Stone and Hughes, 2000; Winter, 2000).

In earlier work Travers (1986) and Travers and Robertson (1996) constructed a measure of deprivation that included several indicators of exclusion. A small sample of clients of the (then) Department of Social Security (DSS) were shown a list of possible items and asked to indicate how necessary they thought each item was, using a four-point scale from 1 (not necessary) to 4 (very necessary). A broadly similar list of items was shown to CESC respondents, who were asked to indicate whether they thought that each item was necessary for achieving an acceptable standard of living. There is considerable overlap between the specific items included in the two surveys, and it is therefore possible to compare the results, as is done in Table 6.10.

Of the 24 items included in the CESC survey, ten are related to aspects of social exclusion and these are shown in italics in Table 6.10. They can be broken down into two groups. The first includes aspects of actual participation such as celebrations on special occasions and regular social contact with others. The second covers items such as owning a car and telephone, having decent clothes and having secure locks on doors and windows (a necessary condition for leaving the home unattended)

Table 6.10 Identification of necessities and indicators of social exclusion

Standard-of-living items in rank order	Percentage of cases who consider item necessary (rank), CESC sample	Mean score from Travers and Robertson study (ranked across comparable items)
Warm clothes and bedding in winter, if it's cold	99.4 (1)	2.94–2.97 (2/3)
Access to affordable medical treatment and medicine, if needed	98.7 (2)	2.99 (1)
A substantial meal at least once a day	97.6 (3)	2.93 (4)
Access to affordable dental treatment if needed*	96.6 (4)	2.70 (9)
A washing machine	94.1 (5)	2.82 (6)
Heating in at least one room of the house, if it's cold	91.5 (6)	2.90 (5)
A telephone	91.1 (7)	2.51 (10)
Secure locks on doors and windows	89.8 (8)	2.80 (7)
Up to $500 in savings for use in an emergency	85.7 (9)	NA
Insurance on contents of home	85.2 (10)	2.48 (11)
Regular social contact with others*	84.2 (11)	2.21 (17)
A car	78.6 (12)	2.38 (16)
Presents for friends or family at least once a year	66.0 (13)	2.40 (15)
Celebrations on special occasions, like birthdays	62.0 (14)	2.43 (12)
A 'best outfit' for special occasions	57.2 (15)	2.41 (14)
A holiday away from home for at least one week a year	54.1 (16)	1.80 (18)
Up to $2,000 in savings for use in an emergency	54.0 (17)	NA
A separate bedroom for all children aged 10 and over*	48.2 (18)	2.42 (13)
New, not second-hand, clothes	43.7 (19)	2.74 (8)
A microwave oven	34.3 (20)	0.82 (20)
A night out once a fortnight	31.9 (21)	1.38 (19)
A video cassette recorder	25.4 (22)	0.58 (21)
A clothes dryer	18.1 (23)	NA
A home computer	17.1 (24)	NA
Sample size	2,342	110

Notes: (a) Three of the items (indicated with an asterisk, *) used in the CESC survey were worded slightly differently than in the Travers and Robertson study: 'Examination of teeth by a dentist once a year.' 'Friends/family for a meal once a month.' 'Not more than two persons in each room'. (b) NA: These items were not identified in the Travers and Robertson study.

that facilitate participation but also serve other objectives. When the items are ranked according to how much support they receive as being necessary for an acceptable standard of living, the participation-related items achieve high scores, though not the highest. They tend to attract lower levels of support from DSS clients than from the general population –

a possible indicator of acceptance by low-income people of a lack of their own participation and hence exclusion.

The rankings produced by the two surveys are similar and the rank order correlation coefficient between them is equal to 0.84 and highly significant. While these results only touch on a few limited examples of participation, they suggest that Australians regard regular social participation as essential and the items that facilitate such activity as necessary. Not being able to afford these items or the activities themselves would thus represent one form of social exclusion in the minds of most people.

Exclusion, poverty and inequality

The strong links between social exclusion and poverty also exist between social exclusion and inequality in the distribution of income (the subject of the next chapter). This point has been emphasised by Barry (1998), who notes that the relationship between the two depends upon how institutions are set up. Where there is an extensive array of public services in fields such as education, health, recreational facilities and transport, people will be more likely to share a common fate and thus be less susceptible to exclusion. In contrast, where the scope of the public sphere is more restrictive, the potential for some individuals or groups to be excluded will be greater.

A high level of good-quality public provision will make it less likely that the rich will wish to opt out in favour of private suppliers and make this less affordable because of the high taxes associated with extensive public provision. In contrast, where there is considerable inequality in the income distribution, the rich will be able to opt out (or voluntarily exclude themselves), and a flourishing private sector will pose a threat to the exclusion of others. It follows that while public provision can moderate the impact of a given degree of inequality on social exclusion, in situations where goods and services provided publicly can also be bought privately, there is an inextricable link between the extent of income inequality and social exclusion.

This link is reinforced by the relationship between inequality of income and inequality of opportunity. The traditional neo-liberal idea of equality of opportunity, though influential, is self-contradictory in a world characterised by inequality in the distribution of actual income when viewed from a cross-generational perspective. The reason is that those with high incomes will bequeath some of their economic advantage onto their children, thereby disturbing the conditions of equality of opportunity in the next generation. It is not only the conditions of deprivation and disadvantage that are transmitted across generations. As the privileges resulting from prior inequalities cumulate, social and economic divisions will widen, posing a potential threat to social stability and promoting the emergence of social exclusion. Unless the situation is kept in check through policies that redistribute income and offset the financial advantages of inheritance, social exclusion will emerge automatically as wealth is transferred across the generations.

It follows that policies aimed at addressing social exclusion must also give consideration to the issues of primary poverty and income distribution, however uncomfortable this conclusion is for those responsible for formulating policy. Social exclusion is a characteristic of modern society in which (to paraphrase Galbraith) private affluence has provided some with the means to escape from the public squalor that has been forced onto others. These two phenomena – private affluence and public squalor – have resulted from spending cutbacks and declining standards in public sector services introduced to provide tax cuts to those in the middle and top parts of the income distribution. This has given the rich the increased disposable income needed to purchase private services, thus avoiding the decline in public services that are a direct consequence of the tax cuts they have enjoyed. At the same time, those at the bottom have had to contend with the increasingly poor public services that are a feature of social exclusion, with neither the economic nor political power to reverse this process of cumulative decline.

It is probably true that social exclusion has focused attention on these issues in a way that poverty and income distribution alone could not. The emphasis in the social exclusion literature on identifying and understanding the main processes that determine observable outcomes has been important. In combination with the insights provided by longitudinal data, social exclusion has not only provided a new perspective on issues of deprivation and inequality, but has also breathed new life into traditional approaches to the relative nature of these issues.

7 Inequality

Research on income distribution fuels public debate over how much inequality has changed, why it has changed and whether or not change represents an improvement. Underlying these public accounts of distributional change are complex issues surrounding the collection and reliability of the data and the choices and assumptions that have to be made to measure inequality. These details are generally lost in the clamour to convey the stylised 'facts' of distributional change, but they have important implications for what the results imply about how much has changed and for what reasons.

Inequality is a more complex and multi-dimensional phenomenon than poverty because it relates to the whole distribution, not just to one section of it. Its measurement thus raises a number of important issues:

Which particular economic variable(s) should be used?

Is the issue one of inequality among individuals, or, since people live together in families, is it family inequality that matters?

How can the millions of observations of the variable(s) selected for study be combined into a single index of inequality?

How sensitive is the inequality index to changes in the value of the variable(s) that underlie it, and does a given change in the index always reflect the same underlying change?

If the rich get richer and the poor get richer at the same time, does this signify increased inequality or does it depend on the magnitude of the changes, or on other things also?

These are complicated questions and there is no single answer to any of them. So, in examining the extent and nature of inequality and how it has changed, it is necessary to be precise about what is being studied and acknowledge that it may not always be possible to summarise change in a simple unqualified description. Given its nature and normative significance, the study of inequality is beset by complexity, and ambiguity is commonplace. It is difficult to decide whether inequality has changed or not, and the interpretations placed by different people on the changes that do occur reflect differences in data and measurement that can conceal deep philosophical differences. These circumstances do not augur well for agreement on the nature of observed inequality, but the topic is sufficiently important to warrant the most careful and open-minded analysis.

Why inequality matters

The study of economic inequality is important, not only in its own terms, but also because of its economic and social consequences. Societies are often judged by the degree of inequality that they are prepared to tolerate. The existence and size of many of the consequences of inequality are strongly contested and even where there is agreement that they exist, there are still likely to be differences of view surrounding their significance. While there is widespread support for the principle of equality, there is disagreement about what equality means in practice and how much equality is desirable. As Sen (1992, p. 12) has put it, 'every normative theory of social arrangement that has at all stood the test of time seems to demand equality of *something*' – but exactly what that something is remains the subject of intense debate.

Inequality of what?

Within economics, most discussions of equality concentrate on measures of economic resources, including income, consumption and the ownership of wealth. The extent of inequality in the distribution of income is the main focus of this chapter. Wealth is not discussed explicitly, in large part because so little is known about the distribution of wealth in Australia. Most social scientists and many economists agree that there is a need to reduce the degree of income inequality that results from the operation of market forces. This has traditionally been achieved through a combination of progressive income taxation and a social security system, with the actual design left to normative judgments about inequality as expressed through the political process.

Those who have argued against the introduction of policies designed specifically to reduce inequality have generally used one of two arguments. The first rests on the premise that what matters from a social justice perspective is not *equality of outcome* (as reflected in income, consumption or wealth) but *equality of opportunity*. Liberals, who see market competition (supported by state laws that protect and enforce property rights) providing the framework that guarantees equality of economic opportunity, often argue this. The market is open to all and its rewards are distributed in accordance with performance (as reflected in effort and skill) in ways that are widely endorsed within capitalist societies. According to this view, the fact that some finish ahead of others in terms of economic outcomes does not imply that the process that produced these outcomes is unjust, any more than the fact that some athletes finish ahead of others is proof of an unfair race.

The notion of 'equality of life chances' is widely regarded as a fundamental goal of any decent and compassionate society, but trying to define what it means in practical terms is exceedingly difficult. Part of the problem arises because whether or not life chances have been equalised can only be ascertained for groups in society, not for individuals (Thurow, 1980). The reason is that how well any individual fares is dependent upon a large number of variables. Those that can be observed, such as level of education, age, gender, job experience explain only a small proportion of individual differences in earnings, with the remainder reflecting factors such as good luck or motivation that cannot be observed. This means that one can never be certain whether the earnings of particular individuals reflect discrimination or inequality of opportunity, or the effect of one or more of these unobservable factors.

Because issues of discrimination or unequal opportunity can only be identified at the level of the group, the fact that women earn less than men, or that poverty among Indigenous Australians is far above that of the rest of the population, even after adjusting for variations in age and education, would be indicative of discrimination against these groups. Establishing this requires reliable data on the circumstances of different groups that are often not available. However, the more important point is that because discrimination can only be identified at the level of the group, it can also only be remedied at the level of the group. Thus, even though it may be widely agreed that no individual should be discriminated against, in practice it is not possible to create a society in which all individuals (as opposed to all groups) are treated equally, at least in terms of objective conditions or observable outcomes. Yet much of the neoliberal criticism of the welfare state is founded upon the idea that the focus should be on its impact on individuals not on groups, with groups seen as serving minority interests that have captured welfare state benefits at the expense of the population as a whole.

This does not imply that equality of opportunity should no longer be a goal of policy, since without equal opportunity and an end to discrimination, any achievements in equalising actual outcomes will be only temporary. The significance of these group effects lies in the implied difficulties for assessing the impact of the welfare state. Unlike equality of outcome, which can be measured and monitored at the level of the individual (or family), equality of opportunity does not lend itself to this kind of assessment. Those who favour equality of opportunity as a goal need to indicate what they think this means in practice and provide indicators (other than outcomes themselves) against which progress can be assessed.

Some have argued that it is possible to assess the extent to which equality of opportunity has been achieved by studying labour mobility over time. Individual movements into and out of specific income ranges, for example, indicate that even if there is discrimination, it is not strong enough to prevent people from improving their incomes. Income mobility is thus an indication that discrimination is being overcome, and that some degree of equality of opportunity is being achieved in practice. Income mobility is desirable and where mobility is high, there should be less concern over the degree of inequality that exists at a point in time. (Similar arguments apply to occupational mobility). The fact that my income is low today is of less concern (to me and to the society in which I live) if there is a reasonable prospect that my income will rise tomorrow.

These arguments should be treated with suspicion. Although many would agree that greater income mobility is desirable, this does not have to be paid for by an increase in the degree of income inequality that exists at a point in time. There is no reason why high mobility and low inequality cannot co-exist. The two are not substitutes for each other. Indeed, it can be argued that the latter will, by compressing income differentials, make it easier to achieve the former: low income inequality promotes high income mobility. Against this, neo-liberals have argued that the greater the dispersion of incomes, the greater the financial incentive to improve one's position in the income distribution, implying that high income inequality promotes income mobility.

One problem with these arguments is that not all forms of mobility are possible. While it is possible to change one's effort or motivation, or occupation, or industry of employment, or place of residence, it is not possible to change one's ethnicity, race or gender. Mobility can thus break down the income differences between some groups, but not others. This suggests that when discrimination applies to groups where mobility is low or impossible – such as those defined on the basis of race or gender – its removal should receive particular attention. There are other instances where low levels of income and income mobility may fade automatically over time. For example, the incomes of recently arrived immigrants in Australia, particularly those from non English-speaking countries tend to congregate at the bottom of the income distribution. Over time, however, as immigrants adjust to local conditions, they are assimilated into the general population so that their relative incomes improve to the point where they do not differ from those of people who were born in Australia (Saunders and King, 1994).

A further problem with the equality of opportunity or life chances perspective is that it takes no account of past injustices, nor of the potential for creating injustice as the patterns of current outcomes are passed across the generations. Where there is evidence of past inequity, then it is not sufficient to provide everyone with the same chance to compete in today's market place. Some individuals or groups may need help to get to the starting line, or may need a head start to offset the disadvantages associated with past injustice. In addition, as noted in Chapter 6, equality of opportunity will produce unequal outcomes, and if those who succeed today pass on the fruits of their economic success to their children through inheritance, equal opportunity will not be guaranteed tomorrow. One generation's inequality of outcome becomes the next generation's inequality of opportunity (Tobin, 1999), and it becomes necessary to ensure that the conditions of equal opportunity, once established, are maintained.

Another opposition to economic equality rests on the alleged costs of policies designed to reduce market-generated inequalities. Many neo-liberals argue that, however well meaning their intention, redistributive policies distort market signals and impose efficiency costs that reduce initiative and productivity growth and thus result in lower living standards for everyone. The cake is more evenly divided, but all end up with a smaller slice. The key issue here is the size of the efficiency costs, and this has generated an enormous literature without reaching any definitive conclusions as to their size or significance (Atkinson and Mogensen, 1993). It is now widely accepted that social programs often give rise to disincentive effects that are harmful to economic growth. Gone are the days when a social program could be analysed purely in terms of 'winners and losers' at the point of its introduction without considering its effects on incentives, disincentives and income trajectories over time.

This whole approach is epitomised in the idea that there is a trade-off between equity and efficiency and that seeking greater equality necessarily involves some sacrifice in terms of efficiency. The American economist Arthur Okun (1975) introduced the 'leaky bucket' experiment in which the transfer of resources between groups takes place through a bucket that leaks due to the efficiency costs associated with the programs introduced to achieve the transfer. Because the redistributive bucket leaks, not all of the resources earmarked for redistribution end up with the groups for whom they were intended. It is thus important to identify the source of the leaks, determine how large they are and try to fill the bucket in ways that minimise leakage (Okun, 1975, pp. 96–106). The equality/efficiency trade-off has been of enormous significance to economists who have argued that, in terms of efficiency losses, the costs of equality have been, or have become, too high.

Some have argued that priority should be given to fixing up the leaks in the bucket or building a bigger bucket, even if this involves distributing fewer resources in the short term. This is an example of the 'trickle down' theory, which asserts that the best way to help the disadvantaged is by promoting strong economic growth that generates more resources for everyone. The cake must be allowed to grow larger before it can be divided up. This may involve giving tax cuts that benefit those who are most likely to make a contribution to increased economic growth – often presumed to be those who already have the highest incomes and the largest potential to invest additional resources. Inequality may thus rise in the short run, but the interests of those at the bottom will be improved in the longer run. To paraphrase Galbraith (again!), 'in order to make the poor richer, it is first necessary to make the rich richer'.

Although the equity/efficiency trade-off notion retains its influence among many economists, the evidence to support it has always been rather weak. This is not to deny that there have been vast numbers of micro-studies in which the efficiency costs associated with tax, transfer and regulatory interventions have been identified and shown, in some instances, to be substantial. But there have also been many studies reporting effects that are either non-existent or too small to be of any practical or policy significance. Macroeconomic or economy-wide studies provide even less evidence to support the view that economic equality and economic performance are inversely related. Far from being a 'leaky bucket', government intervention has been described as more like an 'irrigation system' providing nutrition to the soils in which the market can flourish (Korpi, 1985).

If equality and efficiency were inversely related, one would expect this to show up in international comparisons, particularly after controlling for the impact of other factors. However, many cross-national studies reveal a *positive* relationship between equality and economic growth, casting serious doubt on the trade-off hypothesis (Persson and Tabellini, 1994). Reflecting this evidence, new developments in the theory of economic growth suggest that inequality reduces economic growth, while redistribution may increase it. These new arguments relate to the impact of inequality on incentives to invest in human capital, particularly in developing countries. Where there is considerable inequality, families with low wealth may not be able to borrow the funds required to finance the education of their children if capital markets are imperfect. This results in a lower level of investment in education which in turn means that human capital is lower than otherwise and this results in a reduced level of economic growth (Osberg, 1995).

Additional support for the existence of these effects is provided by political economy arguments emphasising that unequal societies face constant political pressures for redistributive policies that absorb resources (time and effort) and are harmful to growth. In summary, the conventional view that equality can only be bought by sacrificing economic growth has been turned on its head; redistribution is good for growth, and inequality matters because it reduces economic growth, not the other way round. The empirical evidence in support of the predictions of the new growth theory is strong. A comprehensive review of the literature concludes that 'the view that inequality is growth-enhancing has been ... challenged by a number of empirical studies, often based on cross-country regressions of GDP growth on income inequality. They all find a negative correlation between the average rate of growth and a number of measures of inequality' (Aghion, Caroli and Garcia-Peñalosa, 1999, p. 1615).

Research on the social effects of inequality reinforces the idea that, in addition to its adverse economic consequences, inequality can be detrimental to the well-being of individuals and affect them indirectly through the social conditions they face. These adverse social effects include the effects of inequality on social stability and cohesiveness, psychological well-being, mental and physical health and crime. An enormous volume of research effort has been devoted to identifying and measuring the adverse social effects of inequality. While much of this evidence is in dispute, there is a solid body of empirical evidence supporting the view that inequality gives rise to *some* negative social effects. Almost nobody has claimed that inequality has positive social effects, and those who favour more inequality base their arguments on the positive economic consequences resulting from the stronger incentives structure associated with greater diversity in economic outcomes. It follows that if there are negative social effects associated with increased economic inequality, the positive economic effects need to be even larger to offset them.

Measuring trends in economic inequality

In relation to economic inequality, the distribution of income is the area in which official statistics are most readily available and where most research has focused. Interest in the topic among academic economists is relatively new, with Atkinson (1997) citing Professor Hugh Dalton's assertion in 1920 that the study of income distribution was an area 'which professors of economic theory were content to leave to lesser men' (quoted in Atkinson, 1997, p. 297). Income distribution is now one of the most dynamic areas of economics, reflecting the changes that have occurred and the ability of economists to monitor and analyse them.

Income has the advantage that its different elements are all measured in the same (monetary) units, and this is important since, as indicated in Chapter 5, there are a number of different income measures and the relationship between them provides important information about the structure of income and its distribution. At the same time, as emphasised earlier, not all aspects of well-being are captured by money income, which implies that the distribution of income provides an incomplete account of the overall distribution of economic inequality or standard of living.

The key issue here is how those items other than income that influence the standard of living are correlated with income itself (Richardson, 1998). If these correlations are positive, then income inequality will tend to understate overall inequality; whereas, if the correlation is negative, the opposite will be the case. If there is no relationship between income and these other determinants of well-being, then it may not be possible to draw any conclusions from the shape of the income distribution about the overall inequality profile. In practice, it is true that income tends to be associated with other aspects of economic power and privilege that reinforce its effect on inequality. The income-rich tend to own more assets and live in bigger houses in better suburbs than the income-poor, who live in poorly-serviced areas, are often forced to send their children to lower quality schools and experience many of the forms of exclusion described in the previous chapter. Income statistics can never capture these effects, and the limitations of focusing solely on income need to be acknowledged.

The significance attached to income has also been criticised by Sen (1992) on the grounds that income bears only an indirect relationship with well-being as reflected in the opportunities that people have to realise their capabilities. From a capability perspective:

> The extent of real inequality of opportunities that people face cannot be readily deduced from the magnitude of inequality of *incomes*, since what we can or cannot do, can or cannot achieve, do not depend upon our incomes, but also on the variety of physical and social characteristics that affect our lives and make us what we are. (Sen, 1992, p. 28; italics in the original)

The problem with using income to proxy well-being, according to Sen, is not just that income represents only one among many means for achieving real ends, but also that the precise relationship between means and ends varies between people.

Against this, the arguments for using income are pragmatic and practical. The primary means through which public policy seeks to influence the distribution of well-being is through programs such as progressive taxation and social security, which redistribute income. In light of this, it is important to assess the success of such initiatives by investigating how the distribution of income changes when account is taken of the impact of tax and transfer arrangements, as is done in Table 7.2 below (and in Table 5.2 in Chapter 5).

A key determinant of the distribution of income is the unit of analysis to which income is attributed (Atkinson, 1996a). The standard assumption made in most income distribution studies is that the unit of analysis is the nuclear family consisting of parents and children living together. Children are defined for this purpose as dependent children who rely on their parents for financial and other forms of support that meet their needs. As children get older, the assumption that they are dependent on their parents becomes more tenuous and at some point, they are treated as adult members of a separate independent unit. This is often taken to occur when they leave the education system and start working, although their degree of independence may be reduced if they remain living in the parental home.

Once the unit has been defined, it is assumed that income is pooled and used for the equal benefit of all individual members of the unit (as explained in Chapter 5). In effect, the assumption of 'equal sharing' within the unit ignores any inequality of income *within* the unit of analysis, focusing only on the income differences *between* different units. It is important to recognise that this is an assumption, the relevance of which will depend upon how the unit itself is defined. It is possible to define the unit to include all family members who live together (including those related by *de facto* marriages), in which case young adults living at home would be included, as would any other family members in the household (e.g. aunts or uncles or adult siblings). One could go further and define the household as the unit of analysis, although some households clearly function as independent economic units, for example, where there are boarders present or in the case of group households. The choice of the unit of analysis will have an obvious impact on the total number of units in the population and, because inequality within each unit is ignored, will also influence the degree of measured inequality (Atkinson, 1989, 1995a; Redmond, 1999).

Where there are economies of scale in living costs, household structure will influence the ability of a given level of total income to generate well-being amongst its members. As explained in Chapter 5, an equivalence scale is used to adjust income to reflect these effects. In aggregate, the larger the average size of the unit, the greater will be the level of well-being that a given level of total income can sustain. If everyone lived alone, there would be no potential for economies of scale, so that total need would be at a maximum and the well-being supported by a given level of national income would be at a minimum. From this it follows that the decline in average household size shown in Table 2.4 will have had a depressing effect on the level of economic well-being associated with a given level of national income. This does not mean that the population may not be enjoying a higher level of *overall* well-being. Since most of the factors underlying the trend to smaller households reflect the deliberate choices of individuals, it seems likely that those involved are indeed better off, whatever the trend in equivalent incomes.

Having decided on a definition of income, the unit of analysis and the equivalence adjustment, it is necessary to select a measure of inequality that describes how incomes are distributed among the relevant population. This is not straightforward, because there are a large number of alternative inequality measures from which to choose, each with its own specific characteristics and properties. These can affect the conclusions drawn about the extent and nature of inequality. Most inequality indicators reflect differences in relative incomes, although the extent to which they are sensitive to changes at different points in the distribution varies according to the measure selected (Amiel and Cowell, 1999; Jenkins, 1991b). Thus, some people may regard a change in income distribution that favours both the rich and the poor at the expense of those in the middle as an increase in inequality, but others may regard it as a decrease. These differences reflect differing judgments about the desirability of inequality at different points in the income distribution, and these judgments need to be made explicit.

Most inequality measures are derived by dividing the distribution into equal-sized tenths (or deciles) of individuals, families or households, after ranking these units according to the level of their income. The degree of inequality can then be represented by the income share of each decile, or by the ratio of the incomes of those who fall at specific points in the income ranking. Thus, inequality can be measured by the income shares of the lowest (S1) or highest (S10) deciles, or by the ratio of the incomes of people whose incomes place them at specific percentiles of the overall income ranking. Examples include the ratio of the tenth (P10) to the fiftieth (P50) percentile, P10/P50, or the ratio of the ninetieth (P90) to the fiftieth (P50) percentile, P90/P50, which indicate the extent of inequality at the bottom and top of the distribution, respectively.

Another commonly used summary measure is the Gini coefficient, a statistic that varies between zero (when all incomes are equal) and one (when one person or family has all of the income). The Gini coefficient is related directly to the area between the Lorenz curve and an upward sloping 45 degree line that indicates complete equality, where the Lorenz curve is obtained by plotting the cumulative share of income against the cumulative proportion of the population of income units. In general, the closer the Gini coefficient is to one, the more inequality there is. However, this statement is not necessarily true when the Lorenz curves intersect, since the interpretation of changes in the Gini coefficient then depends upon the weight given to changes at different points of the distribution (Atkinson, 1970).

Exploring distributional change

The central issue of whether consumption is a better measure than income of economic well-being has been discussed in Chapter 5. While there is some truth in the view that part of the observed inequality of income reflects transitory income fluctuations, it does not follow that income inequality is of any less concern. Considerations of justice may dictate the need to dampen temporary income fluctuations, particularly at the bottom end, in order to establish a minimum income floor below which no one should be expected to fall – even temporarily. As noted earlier, income and consumption indicators are both relevant to issues of inequality and poverty. There is no need to abandon income-based measures in a world where income provides access to consumption items and is widely used as an indicator of economic status.

The distributions of income and consumption spending

The measurement of income distribution requires detailed statistics on the incomes of a large representative sample of the general population. Such data are very expensive to collect and are susceptible to reporting errors that can distort the true inequality picture. In a country where privacy is protected, the reluctance that many people have to providing details of their income makes it difficult to assemble reliable data on income distribution – particularly if the reluctance to disclose information is greatest for those with very low or very high incomes. As noted in Chapter 5, official nation-wide surveys of income distribution have only been conducted since 1969 (Commonwealth Bureau of Census and Statistics, 1973). Data from the surveys conducted since 1982 have been released in a form that enables researchers to construct their own measures of income distribution while protecting the confidentiality of respondents. However, results from the earlier surveys are only available in published form, so that it is not always possible to replicate these published estimates using the data for later years.

The ability to examine longer-run distributional trends using official data is thus constrained, although several studies have explored other data sets in an attempt to piece together the longer-run story (Jones, 1975, McClean and Richardson, 1986; Saunders, 1993b). The estimates shown in Table 7.1 cover the longest period that is possible using the official (ABS) income statistics. They compare the distributions of gross income among *families* in 1968–69 and 1999–2000, this being the only form in which the data for the earlier year were published using a conventional distributional measure. The estimates exclude 'non-family individuals' (single people living alone) who were analysed separately in the earlier survey – an omission that is potentially significant given the increased incidence of single person households referred to earlier (Table 2.4).

Over the period, the relative income position of families at the bottom of the income distribution declined, while the relative incomes of those at the top increased. Although the results imply that family incomes rose faster than prices over the period (as indicated by the increase in the decile cut-off levels, which have been adjusted for price increases), the extent of this increase varies across the income distribution. While a family at the boundary of the top decile of the distribution (P90) experienced real income growth of over $38,600 a year (in 1999–2000 prices) over the 31-year period (or around $740 a week in 1999–2000), a family at the upper end of the bottom decile experienced an increase of just over $2,500 (or less than $49 a week). This fifteen-fold differential in income gains is another way of capturing the increase in inequality over the period.

In terms of the overall distributional change, there was an income transfer away from families in the bottom five deciles towards families in the top four deciles, with those in the top two deciles gaining most from this shift. Overall inequality in the distribution of income among families increased between 1968–69 and 1999–2000, with the Gini coefficient rising by more than 15 per cent. The Lorenz curve for this section of the population moved further away from the line of complete equality, implying that inequality increased unambiguously, and by a considerable margin.

A more detailed exploration of changes in income distribution is restricted to the period since 1981–82, when the ABS income surveys were regularised and data stored electronically. There have, however, been some changes to the survey methodology over this period, as noted in Chapter 5, most notably the change to a continuous survey introduced in 1994–95. An attempt has been made to minimise the impact of these changes in deriving the estimates that follow.

Table 7.2 summarises changes in the income distribution for selected years between 1986 (the first year for which consistent data on disposable income are available) and 1999–2000 (ABS, 2001c). In order to shed light on the factors underlying the observed distributional profile in each year, several different distributions are shown. The distribution of wage and salary income among full-time workers has significance because wage income is the most important source of income – in aggregate and for the majority of households who have an employed member (see Table 5.1). It also allows the degree of inequality that exists among the 'core' (full-time) labour force to be assessed. The distributions of market income, gross income and disposable income, correspond to successive steps in the income framework introduced in Chapter 5. The final

Table 7.1 Changes in income distribution among families, 1968–69 to 1999–2000

Income deciles	1968–69 Income share (%)	1968–69 Upper bound ($1999–2000)(a)	1999—2000 Income share (%)	1999—2000 Upper bound ($1999–2000)(a)	Change, 1968–69 to 1999–2000 Income share (% points)	Change, 1968–69 to 1999–2000 Upper bound ($1999–2000)(a)
First	2.2	13,370	1.8	15,910	−0.4	+2,540
Second	4.6	20,500	3.3	21,200	−1.3	+700
Third	6.0	24,800	4.6	26,970	−1.4	+2,170
Fourth	6.9	28,960	6.2	38,500	−0.7	+9,540
Fifth	8.5	33,270	7.7	47,850	−0.8	+14,580
Sixth	9.3	37,730	9.4	57,000	+0.1	+19,270
Seventh	10.6	43,070	11.2	68,040	+0.6	+24,970
Eighth	12.2	50,350	13.4	82,000	+0.8	+31,650
Ninth	14.9	63,570	16.3	102,200	+1.4	+38,630
Tenth	24.8	–	26.3	–	+1.5	–
P10/P50[b]	–	0.402	–	0.333	–	−0.069
P90/P50[b]	–	1.911	–	2.136	–	+0.225
P90/P10[b]	–	4.756	–	6.423	–	+1.667
Gini coefficient	0.33	–	0.38	–	15.5%	–

Notes: (a) Incomes have been inflated to 1999–2000 in line with movements in the prices of private final consumption expenditure items; (b) The percentile ratios (P10/P50, etc.) show the ratio of the upper bound income of the first decile (P10) to the fifth decile, or median (P50), and so on.

Sources: Saunders, 2001a, Table 3.

distribution adjusts disposable income using the 'OECD equivalence scale' (OECD, 1982) in which the first adult in each income unit is assigned an equivalence value of 1.0, the second adult a value of 0.7, and each child a value of 0.5.

The anatomy of inequality, as indicated by how inequality changes when moving from full-time wage and salary income to market income, gross income, disposable income and equivalent disposable income displays a consistent pattern in each year. The degree of inequality in the distribution of wage and salary income among full-time workers is considerably less than that for total market income. The operation of market forces may thus generate overall inequality, but centralised wage determination and the emphasis given to achieving 'comparative wage justice' in Australia have moderated inequality among the full-time labour force. Despite this, there are signs of increased wage dispersion in the 1990s, as the wages of low-paid workers have fallen relative to the median while wages growth at the top of the distribution outstripped that at the median. Both social security transfers and income tax reduce inequality, with social security having the largest effect. In 1999–2000, social transfers reduced market income inequality (as measured by the Gini coefficient) by 22.2 per cent, while income taxes reduced it by an additional 12.1 per cent. In that year, the two main distributive instruments of the welfare state – progressive income taxation and social security transfers – thus combined to reduce market income inequality by almost one-third.

The effect of adjusting for differences in need using the OECD equivalence scale further reduces the extent of inequality considerably – approximately equal in magnitude in most years to that produced by the personal income tax system (i.e. by around 12 per cent). This effect reflects the positive association between income unit size and the level of total income received by the unit. This association implies that when the equivalence scale adjustment is made, the incomes of those with low and high incomes both move closer to the middle of the distribution, causing the degree of inequality to decline.

Trends over time in inequality within each of the income measures shown in Table 7.2 show that there has been some instability in the distributions of the different income measures over the period, although most show an increase in inequality. In general, the increase in inequality was greatest between 1986 and 1994–95, after which there is little overall distributional change. However, this apparent overall stability conceals an on-going process of change, with both the tenth and ninetieth percentiles gaining relative to the median since the mid-1990s. One exception to the general pattern occurs in the case of full-time wage and salary income, where inequality fell up until 1990, then rose sharply up to 1994–95, before stabilising. Inequality in the distribution of equivalent disposable income fell in the latter half of the 1980s but has been rising steadily since 1990, although the overall change shows a slight decline. Over the period as a whole, Gini inequality increased by 15.5 per cent in the case of full-time wage income, 7.5 per cent (market income), 6.7 per cent (gross income) and 7.4 per cent (disposable income). In contrast, inequality in the distribution of equivalent disposable income decreased by 1.7 per cent. (This latter finding is somewhat puzzling because it is out of line with the others and may reflect an unidentified peculiarity in the data that, along with the treatment of income tax in 1986 caused an upward bias in measured inequality in that year.)

These overall differences, as well as those that have taken place within the period for each measure illustrate how economic conditions as well as public policies have affected the income inequality profile. The general pattern of distributional change is consistent with the view that deregulation of the economy and the increasing role of market forces has produced an increase in market income inequality that has been moderated, but not eliminated, by the operation of the social security and income tax systems (Pappas, 2001).

A clear trend implied by all of the distributions in Table 7.2 (aside from the equivalised measure during the late 1980s) is for the relative income position of those at the top of the distribution to improve markedly. This differs from the 'disappearing middle' story of distributional change in which the increased share of those at the top has been accompanied by an increased share of those at the bottom and a hollowing out of the middle of the distribution (Harding, 1997). The 'disappearing middle' description of distributional change is consistent with changes in the structure of full-time jobs towards those paying wages that are high and low relative to the median (Gregory, 1993). However, much of the change in the structure of jobs occurred after the mid-1970s and there is no reason why a change in the distribution of the earnings of full-time jobs available to *individuals* should be reflected in a change in the distribution of income among *family income units*. The income distribution estimates presented here suggest that the change since the 1980s, while significant, is not characterised by a 'disappearing middle' but rather by increases in the income share of those at the top at the expense of falling shares for everyone else.

Several recent Australian studies have examined changes in inequality of consumption expenditure, arguing that this is a better measure of economic inequality. This is because, as noted in Chapter 5, consumption reflects permanent or underlying patterns, whereas income is subject to short-run transitory changes that can be smoothed out by borrowing and saving. The implication is that income inequality, measured at a point in time exaggerates the variation in the distribution of economic welfare that is better reflected in inequality of consumption. This argument is borne out by ABS household expenditure data, which show that the Gini for (non-durable) consumption is more than 20 per cent lower than that for income and increased by around half as much between 1975–76 and 1993–94 (Barrett, Crossley and Worswick, 2000a; 2000b). This study

Table 7.2 Changes in the distribution of weekly income, 1985–86 to 1999–2000

	Wage and salary income[a]	Market income[b]	Gross income[b]	Disposable income[b]	Equivalent disposable income[b]
1986 [c]					
Gini coefficient	0.238	0.532	0.417	0.364	0.352
P10/P50	0.603	0.000	0.318	0.373	0.453
P90/P50	1.711	2.632	2.517	2.289	2.193
P90/P10	2.838	–	7.922	6.137	4.841
1990					
Gini coefficient	0.224	0.543	0.427	0.375	0.330
P10/P50	0.607	0.000	0.337	0.386	0.494
P90/P50	1.721	2.806	2.677	2.315	2.081
P90/P10	2.833	–	7.937	6.000	4.215
1994–95					
Gini coefficient	0.271	0.570	0.436	0.385	0.338
P10/P50	0.645	0.000	0.344	0.392	0.501
P90/P50	1.775	2.963	2.721	2.415	2.129
P90/P10	2.913	–	7.916	6.157	4.251
1997–98					
Gini coefficient	0.272	0.582	0.443	0.390	0.343
P10/P50	0.600	0.000	0.326	0.377	0.502
P90/P50	1.833	3.163	2.736	2.408	2.172
P90/P10	3.056	–	8.393	6.377	4.326
1999–2000					
Gini coefficient	0.275	0.572	0.445	0.391	0.346
P10/P50	0.597	0.000	0.333	0.384	0.498
P90/P50	1.832	3.085	2.839	2.448	2.129
P90/P10	3.069	–	8.517	6.369	4.278

Notes:
(a) Includes full-time workers only. Includes wage and salary income from first and second jobs. (b) Includes all income units. (c) Income tax for 1986 was imputed from annual income and converted to a weekly figure.

Sources: ABS unit record file data for each year, as reported in Saunders, 2001a, Table 5 and Saunders, 2001b, Table C5.7.

Inequality   193

also found little change in the share of the middle section of the income distribution, even though overall inequality increased by 17 per cent (but fell slightly between 1984 and 1988), with most of the change occurring at the top of the distribution.

Some of these findings have been confirmed in another study of consumption inequality, although inequality is estimated to have fallen between 1975–76 and 1993–94 if expenditure on consumer durables is included (Blacklow and Ray, 2000). Income inequality increases by more than 10 per cent over the period, although this study also casts doubt on the 'disappearing middle' thesis, arguing that the change in inequality is dominated by income disparities at the extremes of the distribution.

Earnings inequality

Because earnings represent the main source of income for the majority of families, contributing around 70 per cent to average family income (Saunders, 1996d), widening earnings disparities have important consequences for changes in the income distribution as a whole. There is clear evidence of growing earnings inequality in Australia since the mid-1970s, particularly among employees aged 25–54 years and males generally (Borland, 1998; Borland and Wilkins, 1996; Borland and Kennedy, 1998b, Sheehan, 2001). Between 1982 and 1994–95, earnings inequality among full-time employees increased by 12.9 per cent (Borland and Kennedy, 1998b, Table 1). Between 1975 and 1994, the ratio of the highest to the lowest decile of full-time, non-managerial adult male earnings rose from 1.86 to 2.57, or by 38 per cent (Norris and Wooden, 1996, Table 3; Borland and Norris, 1996, Chart 9).

Movements in earnings at different points of the earnings distribution disaggregated by gender and sector are shown in Table 7.3. The figures cover full-time adult employees only and thus abstract from earnings variations that reflect differences in hours worked or those arising from changes in youth wages and employment patterns. Earnings dispersion is measured by the percentile ratios described earlier, specifically by the ratios of earnings at the tenth (P10), fiftieth (P50, or median), ninetieth (P90) and ninety-ninth (P99) percentiles, as these ratios summarise earnings disparities at different points of the distribution.

Beginning with the entire distribution, summarised in the bottom panel of Table 7.3, it is clear that, in line with the research cited above, earnings inequality increased between 1985 and 1998. Workers at the bottom of the distribution experienced slower earnings growth than those at the median, while the opposite occurred for those at the top of the distribution – particularly those at the very top. Earnings inequality thus increased, particularly for men. By 1998, the top 1 per cent of

Table 7.3 Earnings distribution ratios for full-time adult employees, 1985–98

	1985	1987	1989	1991	1993	1994	1995	1996	1998	Change, 1985–98
Males										
P10/P50	0.70	0.69	0.66	0.67	0.65	0.65	0.65	0.64	0.62	−0.08
P90/P50	1.62	1.62	1.63	1.66	1.69	1.67	1.69	1.70	1.75	+0.13
P99/P50	2.57	2.61	2.73	2.79	2.93	3.02	3.15	3.10	3.20	+0.63
Females										
P10/P50	0.78	0.75	0.73	0.74	0.73	0.73	0.72	0.71	0.70	−0.08
P90/P50	1.50	1.50	1.51	1.54	1.55	1.54	1.54	1.53	1.55	+0.05
P99/P50	2.09	2.07	2.20	2.14	2.20	2.35	2.38	2.41	2.62	+0.53
Private sector										
P10/P50	0.73	0.71	0.69	0.70	0.69	0.70	0.69	0.67	0.66	−0.07
P90/P50	1.64	1.68	1.70	1.79	1.75	1.72	1.79	1.79	1.83	+0.19
P99/P50	2.63	2.82	2.94	3.02	3.12	3.17	3.42	3.28	3.46	+0.83
Public sector										
P10/P50	0.70	0.70	0.69	0.70	0.67	0.67	0.67	0.66	0.66	−0.04
P90/P50	1.55	1.54	1.51	1.50	1.49	1.49	1.47	1.48	1.45	−0.10
P99/P50	2.46	2.32	2.20	2.14	2.20	2.35	2.38	2.41	2.62	+0.16
Persons										
P10/P50	0.72	0.70	0.68	0.69	0.68	0.68	0.68	0.66	0.65	−0.07
P90/P50	1.63	1.63	1.62	1.68	1.66	1.65	1.67	1.68	1.72	+0.09
P99/P50	2.58	2.63	2.73	2.80	2.85	2.95	3.07	3.05	3.17	+0.59

Source: *Survey of Employee Earnings and Hours*, ABS Catalogue 6306.0, unpublished data, as summarised in Saunders (2000b).

full-time earners were earning almost 4.9 times the earnings of someone at the tenth percentile, implying that they were earning in around a day what a worker at the tenth percentile of the distribution earned in a week.

The decline of earnings at the tenth percentile relative to the median was experienced by both men and women employees and by those employed in the private and public sectors, although the decline was smallest for those employed in the public sector. In contrast, changes at the top of the distribution were more varied, with men experiencing larger increases than women, and with very different trajectories in the public and private sectors. Public sector employees were also the only group that did not experience a growing gap between those at the ninetieth percentile and the median over the period. This was a very different outcome to that experienced in the private sector, where the increase in relative earnings for high-earning private sector employees was substantial and for those at the very top, it was spectacular.

These changes in relative earnings reflect movements in both the earnings associated with given jobs and in the numbers of jobs paying different earnings. If, for example, the number of low-paid jobs declines (perhaps because these jobs 'move off-shore') this will result in an *increase* in the ratio of the tenth percentile to the median, indicating that earnings inequality has *fallen*. If there is a transfer of low-paid jobs from the public sector to the private sector, possibly as a consequence of the contracting-out of basic services such as cleaning and routine plant maintenance to private contractors, then earnings inequality among public sector employees will fall while earnings inequality in the private sector may rise. Changes in the numbers of jobs paying different earnings, and in the sectors in which they are located can thus exert effects on the earnings distribution and estimates of distributional change need to be treated with caution, particularly when the labour market is undergoing rapid structural change (see Chapter 4).

Other research indicates that the rise in earnings inequality since the early 1980s has mainly occurred within groups of employees with the same levels of education and labour market experience, although some dimensions of inequality between different education and experience groups have fallen slightly (Borland, 1998; Nevile and Saunders, 1998). The increase in earnings inequality among full-time employees has been concentrated in a sub-set of industry sectors – primarily in manufacturing, construction, transport and storage, wholesale and retail trade and finance, property and business, and community services (Borland and Kennedy, 1998b, Table 9).

The fact that increased earnings inequality has been greatest among groups of employees with the same levels of education and work experience suggests that the cause of increasing inequality lies with unobserved variables such as the ability to work with computers, or changes in labour market institutions such as the role of trade unions (Borland and Kennedy, 1998b, p. 29). In the Australian context, changes to centralised wage bargaining and the arbitration system may also have played a role.

Table 7.4 examines the extent to which recent changes in the distribution of earnings have affected Australia's position in the international ranking of earnings inequality. The first two columns report OECD data on the P10/P50 and P90/P50 percentile ratios for full-time workers in years close to 1995. They show that in 1995, both low-paid and high-paid workers in Australia ranked closer to the median (implying less overall inequality) than their counterparts in a number of other OECD countries. On both measures, Australia lies around the middle of the overall inequality ranking, similar to France, Japan and Portugal at the lower end and closest to Austria and New Zealand at the top end.

However, when it comes to executive salaries relative to the average earnings of a manufacturing worker, Australia's relative position is closest to that in the United Kingdom and exceeded only by the United States in terms of the size of the differential. With a CEO/average manufacturing worker earnings ratio of 19.0, it is difficult on the basis of these figures to sustain the view that, at the very top of the earnings hierarchy, Australia can lay claim to its egalitarian reputation. And it should be borne in mind that the data in Table 7.4 pre-date the major shift to enterprise bargaining that has further widened earnings differentials (Table 7.3) – although it is possible that a similar trend has also been occurring in other OECD countries. Indeed, there is evidence that many other OECD countries experienced increased earnings inequality during the 1980s (OECD, 1993) though fewer experienced these trends in the first half of the 1990s (OECD, 1997b). These developments left Australia's relative earnings inequality ranking broadly unchanged – at least up until the early 1990s (Whiteford, 2000).

The distribution of work among families

Accompanying the overall increase in employment identified in Chapter 4 has been a growing division in the distribution of work. Paid work provides the main source of income for most people, and so a large part of the income differences that make up the income distribution can be attributed to how work is distributed. Work has become more unequally distributed in several dimensions, including between families with and without employed members and between those employed for short and long hours (Burbidge and Sheehan, 2001). The overall result of these changes has been that 'a smaller proportion of individuals and

Table 7.4 International comparisons of earnings differentials (percentile ratios)

Country	P10/P50 ratio [a]	P90/P50 ratio [a]	CEO salary ratio [b]
Australia	**0.61**	**1.77**	**19.0**
Austria	0.50	1.82	n/a
Belgium	0.70	1.57	13.0
Canada	0.44	1.84	13.0
Finland	0.71	1.70	n/a
France	0.61	1.99	15.0
(West) Germany	0.69	1.61	11.0
Italy	0.57	1.60	16.0
Japan	0.61	1.85	10.0
Netherlands	0.64	1.66	14.0
New Zealand	0.58	1.76	n/a
Portugal	0.61	2.47	n/a
Sweden	0.75	1.59	11.0
Switzerland	0.63	1.71	10.0
United Kingdom	0.55	1.87	18.0
United States	0.48	2.10	24.0

Notes: (a) These estimates refer to full-time workers and are for years between 1993 and 1995; (b) These estimates reflect the ratio of the average Chief Executive Officer salary to the average earnings of a manufacturing worker in 1997.

Sources: For the earnings ratios, OECD (1997b, Table 3.1) and for the CEO ratio, Mishel, Bernstein and Schmitt (1999, Table 3.52).

households have become responsible for larger proportions of paid work' (Dawkins, 1996, p. 282). This trend, in combination with the increased inequality in the earnings of those in work has contributed to the increase in income inequality between individuals and, more significantly, between families and households.

The unemployed and the over-worked experience the immediate financial and psychological effects of an enforced lack of paid work and of excessive working hours, respectively. However, these effects spill over onto other family members and are reinforced by the fact that there is a tendency within couples where one partner is unemployed for the other partner to also be out of work (Bradbury, 1993; Miller, 1997). This is illustrated in Table 7.5, which compares the labour force status of husbands and wives in couple families in June 2000. The unemployment rate of husbands is far greater if the wife is also unemployed than if she is employed (full-time or part-time), the differential being in the order of ten to one. Looked at from the perspective of the wife, a similar pattern emerges, with the unemployment rate of wives around ten times higher

Table 7.5 Labour force status of husband and wife in married couple families aged 15 and over, June 2000 (numbers in thousands and percentage distribution in brackets)

		Wife					
		Employed full-time	Employed part-time	Unemployed	Not in the labour force	All labour force states	Wife's unemployment rate
Husband	Employed full-time	1104.2 (38.6)	926.6 (32.4)	64.7 (2.3)	765.3 (26.8)	2860.7 (100.0)	3.1
	Employed part-time	58.5 (24.2)	84.0 (34.7)	8.3 (3.4)	90.9 (37.6)	241.8 (100.0)	5.5
	Unemployed	17.5 (14.3)	20.8 (17.0)	17.5 (14.3)	66.3 (54.3)	122.1 (100.0)	31.4
	Not in the labour force	64.8 (6.2)	67.6 (6.5)	9.6 (0.9)	898.2 (86.3)	1040.4 (100.0)	6.8
	All labour force states	1245.0 (29.2)	1099.2 (25.8)	100.1 (2.3)	1820.7 (42.7)	4265.0 (100.0)	4.1
	Husband's unemployment rate	1.5	2.0	19.3	7.2	3.8	

Source: *Labour Force Status and other Characteristics of Families, June 2000*, ABS Catalogue No. 6224.0.

(31.4 per cent) if the husband is also unemployed than if the husband is employed full-time (3.1 per cent).

One summary measure of the extent to which the burden of unemployment falls on families is the percentage of total unemployment among couple families that occurs where both husband and wife are unemployed (Miller, 1997). If there were no instances in which both partners are unemployed the percentage would be zero, whereas in the other extreme case where all unemployment affected both husband and wife in the same family, the percentage would be 100. In general, therefore, the higher the percentage, the more concentrated unemployment is among members of the same family.

Between 1974 and 1994, the concentration of unemployment among families rose as the above percentage increased almost three-fold, from 8.6 per cent to 23.8 per cent (Miller, 1997, Table 1). However, the social security income test that contributed to this problem was changed in 1995 when a separate income test was applied to each member of the couple (at least over certain income ranges) thus lowering the effective tax penalty on the second earner (Saunders, 1995). The result, as Figure 7.1 indicates, is that the upward trend in unemployment concentration of earlier years has been reversed since 1995. By 2000, the measure of unemployment concentration had fallen to 15.7 per cent – almost back to its level in the mid-1980s.

Despite this decline, unemployment is still concentrated within couple families, leading to a magnified effect on family income and exacerbating the social problems associated with unemployment. Between 1980 and 2000, the number of 'work-poor' (no job) and 'work-rich' (two job) families increased at the expense of those with one adult employed (Burbidge and Sheehan, 2001, Table 7.5). Further, while most of the increase in the number of work-rich families occurred before 1990, the main growth in work-poor families occurred after 1990 (Gregory, 1999, Table 1). In the first period, employment was growing and the polarisation of work reflected how employment was distributed among families, rather than a lack of jobs. In contrast, increased polarisation during the latter period reflected a lack of jobs and the growth of jobless families.

Reflecting these changes in the distribution of work among adult family members has been a rise in the proportion of dependent children living in jobless families (Gregory, 1999). Between 1979 and 1998, the proportion of families with children (married couple and sole parent families) where no parent was employed increased from 11 per cent to 18 per cent, with the percentage rising sharply during each recession and declining much more modestly thereafter. By 1998, almost one in five Australian children were living in families where no adult was employed.

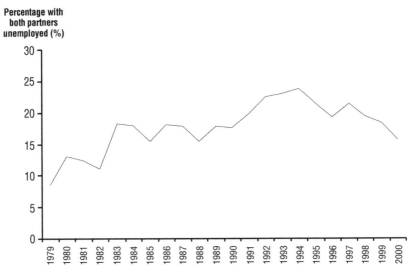

Figure 7.1 The burden of unemployment on family units aged 15 and over, 1979–2000

The fact that joblessness is highly concentrated within specific families implies that many children will have spent a considerable portion of their childhood years growing up in a jobless family (Gregory, 1999, p. 12). These children will have had access to far fewer resources than those living in 'job-rich' families and are likely to face the prospect of diminished life chances associated with prolonged periods of joblessness. Labour market inequalities can have powerful effects that lead to entrenched deprivation and exclusion that rarely show up in the statistics on income and earnings distribution.

The regional distribution of work

Unequal access to employment among families and changes in how jobs are distributed among families raises the question of where jobs are located geographically. As noted in Chapter 4, the Australian economy has been undergoing a structural shift away from primary and manufacturing industry, as jobs growth has been concentrated in the service sector. A consequence of this shift has been a decline in employment opportunities in areas whose economic prosperity was built on the existence of local manufacturing industries. The resulting multiplier effects have spilled over into the local economy, sending it into a downward spiral of business closures, declining demand and reduced job opportunities. While the loss in employment has been partially offset by the growth of new service industries, these have often not been located in the areas where manufacturing employment fell most dramatically.

The consequence of these processes of technical change and structural adjustment has been a growing geographical divide in employment growth and labour market prospects. Attention was drawn to this development by Gregory and Hunter (1995) who analysed changes in the distribution of income and employment across Australian neighbourhoods using census data for the period 1976–91. They explored changes across census collector districts (CDs) ranked according to their socioeconomic status (SES), as reflected in family income, education, occupation and housing size in each CD.

They found evidence of growing neighbourhood disparity over the period in mean household income and employment participation by men and women. In terms of income, the gap between the first percentile CD and the median doubled (in 1995 prices) from $116 in 1976 to $230 in 1991. At the same time, the income gap between the top percentile and the median also almost doubled from $442 to $854 (Gregory and Hunter, 1995, Table 1). The main factor underlying these changes was changes in male and female employment to population ratios across CDs. For men, employment participation fell in all neighbourhoods, but by much more (42 per cent) in the lowest 5 per cent of CDs than in the top 5 per cent (where the decline was 20 per cent). For women, the changes across neighbourhoods were even more differentiated: the proportion of women employed in the top half of neighbourhoods increased by around 10 per cent; whereas, it fell by 40 per cent in the bottom half.

Underlying these geographical changes in employment participation is the decline in manufacturing industry (Hunter, 1995), coupled with the collapse of full employment (Gregory and Sheehan, 1998). As manufacturing companies have gone out of business, they have vacated areas, leaving behind high levels of unemployment and a labour market in which those out of work face intense competition for few jobs. At the same time, the unemployed lack access to a job network that can link them back into the labour market because everyone else is in the same situation. Lack of an adequate transport system acts as a further barrier, entrenching the spatial mismatch between labour supply and demand, reinforcing inflexibility in the labour market (Gregory and Sheehan, 1998).

The developments described above – growing inequalities between work-rich and work-poor families and across neighbourhoods – remain concealed within the income distribution statistics presented earlier. At the same time, they provide insight into the processes underlying distributional change and sound warnings about the potential adverse social effects of growing inequality. These include the decline in life chances among children who spend much of their early life in jobless families and the serious consequences of spatial inequality for neighbourhoods and communities where employment is becoming the exception rather than the rule. These structural labour market shifts affect the risks of poverty and, as earlier results indicate (Table 6.4), these effects are well understood in the community.

Attitudes to inequality

Australia is widely acknowledged as an egalitarian society, and most Australians are proud of this egalitarian tradition. The 'fair go' ideal is central to what it means to be an Australian, now and as it has been historically. Political scientist Elaine Thompson (1994) has argued that:

> Australia has had strong egalitarian impulses throughout most of the last 200 years, which have made it distinctive. Indeed the nature of Australian democracy and Australians' attitudes to the role of the state cannot be explained without reference to egalitarianism [which] has shaped our democratic institutions, our definition of democracy and our definition of ourselves. (Thompson, 1994, p. 250)

Yet, Thompson goes on to argue that this traditional notion was built around the *central egalitarian idea of sameness*, as reflected in a social and cultural homogeneity that found expression in exclusionary trends such as the White Australia policy and the disenfranchisement of Indigenous Australians. It was not until the late 1960s that this notion began to be challenged by the idea of inclusive egalitarianism founded on fair shares for all in a diverse and multicultural society. However, this conversion came at a time when economic performance began to decline and as the ideological foundations of egalitarianism were coming under attack from the neo-liberal arguments of the New Right (Thompson, 1994, pp. 252–3).

Although egalitarianism is a multi-dimensional concept, its expression in Australia has generally been identified as including economic equality, specifically as it applies to the distributions of individual earnings and family incomes. This reputation was in part based on early studies showing that, among industrial countries, Australia fared well in terms of equality in the distribution of earnings (Lydall, 1968) and income (Sawyer, 1976). The first of these studies is now well out of date, while the second was based on data that have been the subject of extensive criticism. More reliable cross-country comparative data (discussed later in this chapter) cast doubt on the validity of Australia's claim to lie at the upper end of the international income equality league table.

Aside from the statistical trends in income distribution, public attitudes to inequality may help to explain why Australians believe that they live in an egalitarian country and shed light on what it means to be egalitarian. Such evidence may indicate whether the increase in inequality documented earlier in this chapter has taken place against the wishes of the community, or with its support. Australians may continue to hold egalitarian attitudes, even though the interactions between market and state are delivering less equal outcomes. This issue raises problems concerning how to define an 'egalitarian attitude'. The only meaningful interpretation of egalitarian is a relative one, but what is the benchmark against which to make comparisons? There are two obvious candidates: the first involves comparisons with past experience; the second is to compare oneself with others.

Exploring how perceptions of inequality have changed over time is limited by a lack of data, although there is evidence that Australian attitudes are becoming somewhat less egalitarian. Data from the 1995 National Social Science Survey indicate that the percentage of people who think that most people are at the bottom of the distributional ladder has declined over the last forty years, but is expected to increase again over the next thirty years (Eckersley, 1999, Table 4). There is also evidence suggesting that Australians became more accepting of inequality between 1987 and 1994 (Kelley and Zagorski, 1999). Analysis of international public opinion data indicates that in 1985–86, Australians were less supportive of government attempts to redistribute income and wealth between rich and poor than were several European countries (Bean, 1991). Although this could be interpreted as indicating greater satisfaction with the current distribution (including the impact of past redistributive efforts), inequality in Australia in the mid-1980s was not low by international standards (Atkinson, Rainwater and Smeeding, 1995, Chapter 4). At best, this evidence therefore suggests that Australian attitudes to inequality were based on a misperception of how much inequality existed at the time. People took comfort from a misplaced faith in the egalitarian nature of their society and thus saw no need for additional redistribution.

An alternative way of describing perceptions of inequality involves asking people not what they think about the extent and desirability of inequality, but to ask them where they think they themselves fit in the bigger distributional picture (Saunders, 1999a). If, for example, the common perception is that there is considerable income equality, one should expect to find that many people locate themselves towards the middle of the distribution. In contrast, if the perception were one of considerable inequality, fewer people would be likely to think that they fall in the middle and more would expect to fall towards one or other extreme. The CESC data are again relevant to this issue, as they include respondents' perceptions of where they thought their current income placed them relative to other Australians.

The results, summarised in Figure 7.2, show that the vast majority believe that their incomes place them in the middle section of the income distribution. Around three-quarters of all respondents (76.5 per cent) thought that they were in one of the four middle deciles (4 through 7) whereas this can, by definition, only contain 40 per cent of the population. Very few people (5.9 per cent) thought they were in the bottom two deciles and almost nobody (0.8 per cent) thought they were in the top two deciles. The fact that most people think that they fall around the middle of the overall income ranking may help to explain why the perception of income equality is so pervasive. It may also go some way towards explaining the popularity of the 'disappearing middle hypothesis' that claims that distributional change has impacted most adversely on those who are in the middle of the distribution.

How do the perceptions shown in Figure 7.2 vary with the actual distributional position of those who hold them? This is examined in Table 7.6, which classifies people's perceived income ranking with where their actual income as reported in the CESC survey places them in the distribution. In order to keep the comparisons manageable, the data are shown by quintile rather than decile (where each quintile contains two deciles). The actual distributional quintiles have been constructed by updating ABS income data for 1996–97 to 1999 after adjusting for differences between the ABS and CESC income definitions.

The figures in Table 7.6 show that it is primarily in the top 40 per cent (two quintiles) of the distribution that people have the least accurate idea of their true position (or where people are less prepared to express their views honestly in a survey like the CESC survey). Only 2 per cent of those who are actually in the top income quintile think that they are,

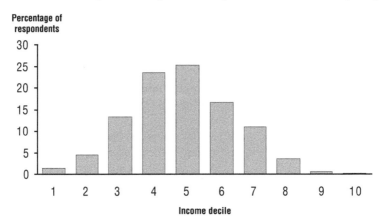

Figure 7.2 Where Australians think their incomes place them relative to the incomes of others.

Table 7.6 Comparison of perceived and actual distributional ranking (row percentages)

		Perceived quintile: First	Second	Third	Fourth	Fifth	Total
	First	**23.7**	48.2	25.3	2.8	0.0	12.2
	Second	13.3	**58.2**	26.6	1.9	0.0	17.5
Actual	Third	2.1	50.7	**39.9**	7.4	0.0	23.9
quintile:	Fourth	0.5	33.1	56.6	**8.9**	0.9	6.0
	Fifth	0.4	11.2	51.2	35.1	**2.1**	30.5
	Total	5.9	36.8	41.9	14.5	0.8	100.0

Source: CESC survey and updated ABS income survey data for 1996–97; see text.

whereas over 86 per cent of those in this quintile believe themselves to be one or two quintiles lower. In contrast, almost one-quarter of those in the lowest quintile think they are there and another 48 per cent think they are only one quintile higher. This tendency for those at the bottom to over-estimate their position and those at the top to under-estimate it explains the extreme bunching of perceptions around the middle of the distribution shown in Figure 7.2.

The figures in the final column and row of Table 7.6 show the overall percentages in each quintile of the perceived and actual distributions. If the survey were a true representation of the total population and survey respondents were able to gauge accurately into which quintile their incomes fell, these figures would all be equal to 20 per cent. The bunching of the perceptions has already been discussed, while the non-representative nature of the CESC income data has been commented on in the Appendix (see Table A.4). Taken in conjunction with Figure 7.2, these data show how poorly informed many Australians are about how their own incomes compare with those of others. Media accounts of middle Australia 'doing it tough' thus provide a misleading picture of how the income distribution has actually been changing to many who mistakenly think that the account applies to them. It is no surprise that rational discussion of distributional change and its implications is difficult given this sea of confusion.

How Australia fares comparatively

Australia is not unique in having experienced an increase in economic inequality over the last three decades. Other countries have faced an increasingly deregulated policy environment, de-industrialisation, technological change, population ageing, the trend to smaller government and the changing economic role of women. Against this background of rapid economic and social change, many (though not all) countries have experienced a widening of their income distribution. This trend to increasing inequality has been described as 'one of the most important issues facing our societies and the world as a whole' (Atkinson, 1999b, p. 1). How far the tendency for market incomes to become more widely dispersed translates into greater overall income disparity depends upon the design and functioning of the tax and transfer systems.

To some degree, these traditional instruments of redistribution have also been under pressure for producing an inappropriate set of economic incentives. The extent to which this has caused a reversal of the state's role in income redistribution has an important bearing on how much inequality has been allowed to increase. Are there similar patterns across countries, or have some used their tax and transfer systems more actively to offset part of the market-driven trend to inequality? How does the increase in inequality in Australia compare with that of other countries, and is Australia's reputation as an egalitarian nation warranted?

In order to answer these questions, it is necessary to compare income distributions across countries and to rank them in terms of inequality. Such an exercise provides the basis for thinking more systematically about how the causes of income inequality relate internationally to national differences in institutional structures and policies.

Early comparisons

As noted earlier, a series of international studies of income distribution in the 1970s suggested that Australia was characterised by relative equality in its income distribution. The most famous of these studies, undertaken by the OECD secretariat, used published data on income distribution to compare inequality in ten OECD countries, including Australia (Sawyer, 1976). Using a range of different income measures (before-tax and after-tax, original and per capita household income), the study concluded that Australia, along with Japan and Sweden, had the lowest degree of inequality in its post-tax income distribution. At the other extreme were France and the United States, both of which consistently showed up as having most inequality. The study was, however, severely limited by the available data, which restricted the scope for any adjustments that could improve cross-country comparability. Despite this, the view of Australia as an egalitarian country, already firmly embedded in the national psyche, was confirmed by the results, and the 'myth of Australian egalitarianism' was reinforced.

Many of the problems of data and definitional difference from which the OECD study suffered are deep-rooted. How much priority is attached to the collection and release of income distribution data depends upon the significance attached to research generally, and to inequality research in particular. The ways in which families and income are defined also reflect aspects of national culture and historical experience. In Australia, for example, the collection of income data using an income unit consisting of parents and, if present, dependent children was originally chosen to align with the unit of eligibility for social security benefits (Saunders, 1998c). This definition was of less relevance in countries where social benefits were linked to the previous contributions of individuals, where a conventional nuclear family or household definition was more appropriate. Older (or adult) children living with their parents and couples living together who are not legally married also received different treatment in different countries. Of greater significance was the fact that results were published in ways that reflected national concerns and priorities and could not be manipulated to conform to a common set of specifications.

To resolve this latter difficulty, researchers needed to have access to the raw data so that they could impose a common framework of concepts and definitions across all countries. Only after this has been achieved is it possible to determine whether the observed differences in income distribution reflect different statistical concepts and definitions rather than real differences in the underlying inequality profile of each country. This became potentially feasible as more and more countries released income distribution data at the family level (adjusted to protect the confidentiality of respondents). Eventually, the possibility of imposing a common definitional framework became a practical reality with the establishment in 1983 of the Luxembourg Income Study (LIS).

The Luxembourg income study

The aim of the LIS project is to gather, in one central location, sophisticated microdata sets containing comprehensive measures of income and economic well-being for a group of industrialised countries in order to allow researchers to measure economic inequality and test ideas about its extent and causes. The LIS project originally began with seven countries, to which Australia had been added (along with the Netherlands and Switzerland) by 1989. Since then, membership of LIS has gradually expanded and the project now covers twenty-one countries with three waves of data, covering years around the mid-1980s (Wave I), around 1990 (Wave II) and the mid-1990s (Wave III). (The fourth wave of data, covering the mid-1990s is being added in 2001 and 2002.)

Although development of the LIS database has been an important vehicle for documenting, comparing and analysing income distribution in different countries, it is still limited by the original data on which it is based. Sometimes, it is simply not possible to derive fully comparable data for different countries (or for different time periods in the same country) because of the way the data were originally collected. The scope and definition of income varies across time and space, as does the treatment of dependent children and multi-generation households, for example. Different countries also adopt different methods for protecting confidentiality by suppressing data on very low and/or very high incomes, and this can influence measured inequality. Finally, differences in social income, imputed rent or in-kind subsidies that are linked to the consumption of specific items (e.g. housing subsidies) mean that comparisons based on cash income alone may be imperfect. For these reasons, in terms of comparability, the LIS data are not ideal, but they are without doubt the best that can be generated given existing data limitations and constraints.

The LIS data have been used to examine how income distributions compare and have changed and also form the basis of the most comprehensive comparative study of income distribution yet undertaken, commissioned and published by the OECD (Atkinson, Rainwater and Smeeding, 1995). The framework developed in that study has been applied to the third wave of LIS data by LIS Research Director Professor Timothy Smeeding (Smeeding, 2000), whose results are summarised in Table 7.7. (The estimates for Japan in Table 7.7 were generated within that country to conform to the LIS framework, because Japan is not yet a member of LIS.) The income measure used is disposable (after-tax) at the household level, adjusted for need using an equivalence scale equal to the square root of household size. The distributions refer to individuals, where each individual is assigned the equivalent income of the household in which they are living, and inequality is summarised using the Gini coefficient and percentile ratios described earlier.

The countries have been ranked in Table 7.7 by the value of their Gini coefficient, which allows the overall degree of inequality to be compared, while the percentile ratios allow inequality at the lower (P10/P50) and upper (P90/P50) ends of the distribution to be compared. The overall variation in inequality is substantial. The Gini coefficient in the lowest ranking country (the United States) is 69 per cent higher than that in Sweden, which has the most equal distribution. Australia ranks sixteenth out of the twenty-one countries included – hardly justifying its claim to be an egalitarian nation, at least in terms of its income distribution. In terms of its Gini coefficient, inequality in Australia is about 43 per cent greater than in Sweden and 15 per cent less than in the United States. It

Table 7.7 Income distribution in selected countries around 1995

Country/Year	Gini coefficient	P10/P50	P90/P50	P90/P10
Sweden (1995)	0.222	0.603	1.562	2.589
Finland (1995)	0.226	0.594	1.591	2.677
Belgium (1992)	0.230	0.588	1.625	2.764
Luxembourg (1994)	0.235	0.591	1.726	2.919
Denmark (1992)	0.240	0.545	1.546	2.840
Norway (1995)	0.242	0.556	1.570	2.825
Austria (1987)	–	0.562	1.623	2.888
Taiwan (1995)	0.277	0.560	1.880	3.357
Netherlands (1994)	0.282	0.555	1.712	3.085
Canada (1994)	0.286	0.473	1.844	3.898
France (1994)	0.290	0.539	1.790	3.321
Germany (1994)(a)	0.300	0.545	1.735	3.185
Israel (1992)	0.305	0.497	2.049	4.121
Spain (1990)	0.306	0.499	1.974	3.958
Japan (1992)	0.315	0.460	1.920	4.174
Australia (1994)	**0.317**	**0.455**	**1.919**	**4.222**
Switzerland (1982)	0.323	0.545	1.847	3.390
Ireland (1987)	0.330	0.498	2.091	4.196
Italy (1995)	0.346	0.430	2.013	4.685
United Kingdom (1995)	0.346	0.463	2.089	4.515
United States (1997)	0.375	0.380	2.142	5.637
Average	**0.290**	**0.521**	**1.821**	**3.583**

Note: (a) Refers to West Germany only.
Source: Smeeding, 2000; data provided by the author.

lies about mid-way between Canada and the United Kingdom, with around 10 per cent more inequality than Canada, but 10 per cent less than the United Kingdom. Overall, the income distribution in Australia is very similar to that in Japan.

The percentile ratios provide insight into the factors contributing to inequality in each country. At the lower end of the distribution, the P10/P50 ratio largely reflects the relative generosity of social benefits in each country compared with median income. In Scandinavia and many other parts of Europe, a combination of generous social security benefits and access to wages among low-income groups provides a safety net set at about 60 per cent of median income. In Australia, Canada, the United Kingdom and Japan the ratio is closer to 45 per cent, while in the United States it is below 40 per cent. At the top of the distribution, the percentile ratios reveal the impact of income taxes and (the lack of) institutional controls on high wages. Again, the differences are stark, with the P90/P50 ratio varying from just over 1.5 in parts of Europe to 2.1 in Ireland, the United Kingdom and the United States. In terms of Australia's low overall inequality ranking, it is apparent that it is inequality at the bottom of the distribution rather than at the top that is mainly responsible. This suggests that social security benefits (which are the main source of income for those around the tenth percentile) are low (relative to the median) in Australia compared with most of the other countries in Table 7.7.

Changes in income inequality over the first three waves of LIS are summarised in Table 7.8 using the Gini coefficient and the P90/P10 percentile ratio. Countries are ranked in this case according to the change in Gini inequality over the period. Inequality has increased in most countries, although there are exceptions, with three countries showing declining inequality and a further three a very modest increase. Both measures show that inequality increased in Australia between 1986 and 1995, confirming what the national statistics showed earlier (Table 7.2).

Table 7.8 Differences in income distribution changes between countries, 1980s–1990s

Country (time period in brackets)	Gini coefficient (G) G_1	G_2	Percentage change	Percentile ratio (P90/P10) (P) P_1	P_2	Percentage change
Austria (1987–95)	0.227	0.277	22.0	2.89	3.73	29.1
Poland (1986–95)	0.271	0.318	17.3	3.51	4.04	15.1
Belgium (1985–96)	0.227	0.260	14.5	2.73	3.20	17.2
United Kingdom (1986–95)	0.303	0.344	13.5	3.79	4.57	20.6
Italy (1986–95)	0.306	0.342	11.8	4.05	4.77	17.8
United States (1986–97)	0.335	0.372	11.0	5.71	5.57	–2.5
Israel (1986–97)	0.308	0.336	9.1	4.29	4.86	13.3
Finland (1987–95)	0.209	0.226	8.1	2.59	2.69	3.9
Australia (1986–95)	**0.292**	**0.311**	**6.5**	**3.97**	**4.33**	**9.1**
(West) Germany (1984–94)	0.249	0.261	4.8	3.01	3.18	5.6
Taiwan (1986–95)	0.267	0.277	3.7	3.21	3.38	5.3
Canada (1987–97)	0.283	0.291	2.8	3.89	4.01	3.1
Norway (1986–95)	0.233	0.238	2.1	2.92	2.83	–3.1
Sweden (1987–95)	0.218	0.221	1.4	2.71	2.61	–3.7
Luxembourg (1985–94)	0.237	0.235	–0.8	2.95	2.92	–1.0
Netherlands (1987–94)	0.256	0.253	–1.2	2.94	3.15	7.1
France (1984–94)	0.292	0.288	–1.4	3.46	3.54	2.3

Source: Luxembourg Income Study.

Although there is considerable variation in the change in inequality between countries, the magnitude of these changes is small compared with the cross-country inequality differences shown in Table 7.7. For example, the increase in (Gini) inequality Australia of 6.5 per cent is equivalent to an annual rate of growth of around 0.7 per cent a year. If inequality were to continue to increase at this rate, it would take almost 26 years before Australia reached the United States Gini of 0.372 (assuming that it remained unchanged).

In summary, Table 7.8 illustrates that increasing inequality has not been inevitable over this period of increased deregulation and globalisation of financial, capital and product markets. Globalisation and market forces may produce disequalising tendencies, but they do not find common expression across countries, even among those with similar economic structures and experiences. Some countries have managed to resist the increase in inequality by the operation of their tax and transfer policies, though it is noticeable that nowhere has inequality declined to any noticeable degree. The important point to emphasise is the value of comparisons like those shown in Tables 7.7 and 7.8, not only in describing how income distribution varies in different countries, but also in raising important questions about why the differences arise and what can be done about them. The LIS project has contributed to the analysis of income distribution by providing a sound statistical basis for making cross-country comparisons and raising awareness that the income distributions of different countries *are* different.

Part III
Reform Directions and Strategies

8 Welfare Reform

The effects of the welfare system run like a thread linking all of the topics discussed in the previous four chapters. The benefits provided by the welfare system, the purposes they serve, the ways in which they are structured and the taxes that fund them have important effects on living standards, poverty and inequality, both directly and indirectly through their labour market effects. The potential magnitude of these effects can be gauged by the fact that, in 1999–2000, total spending on income support payments amounted to more than $42.9 billion (ABS, 2001a, Table 7.5), equivalent to 6.8 per cent the nation's total economic output, or GDP.

Yet, these huge monetary totals cannot convey the important role that the social security system plays in the lives of many Australians. Some of these effects have already been identified, particularly those relating to the contribution of social benefits to family income and living standards and their role in protecting people from poverty. These provide the background for the discussion in this chapter, which focuses on the design of the welfare system and the public's understanding of, and attitudes to, a system in the midst of rapid change.

Discussion of the social security system (or the welfare system as it has come to be called when referring solely to provisions for those of working age) cannot be isolated from wider economic and social trends. These influence the system's goals and how it goes about trying to achieve them. How the system is designed also reflects the assumptions that underlie policy, specifically assumptions about the motivations of people and how their behaviour is likely to change in response to social support. Far too little is known about these issues – a reflection of the inadequate resources put into social security research over many decades. Although this is beginning to change, the welfare reform debate (even the term itself) is driven as much by ideology and wishful thinking as by informed reflection, impartial analysis and the possibility of practical implementation.

The larger the number of unknown effects and impacts, the greater the scope to propose reforms that are not grounded in knowledge of the limitations of the current system, but in perceptions of what might work, if only the world were as it is imagined to be. Welfare reform is an inherently normative and thus controversial topic, but many of the underlying issues are technical and enduring. Passionate disagreement over the shape of welfare reform often reflects differences in the ordering of priorities or the interpretation of the evidence. These have different implications, since the former reflect a specific set of philosophical principles, while the assumptions that drive the latter may or may not be valid.

Setting the welfare reform agenda

As noted in Chapter 2, the welfare state has been in crisis since the economic downturn that hit the industrial world following the stagflation that emerged in response to the oil shocks of the 1970s. Underlying this crisis is an economic perspective – more narrowly, a budgetary perspective – in which a key question for policy has been: 'Can we afford a welfare state characterised by a spiralling social security budget?' Mindful of the longer-run cost pressures, successive Australian governments have introduced reforms designed to improve targeting and cut costs (or at least the growth in costs) by narrowing the categories eligible to receive support. This has been seen as preferable to the alternative of reducing the level of support provided within categories because of its implied political risks.

The budgetary imperative

Much of the discussion has proceeded as if the welfare system must be tailored to fit within what the public purse can afford. This metaphor is inappropriate because it treats the issue as essentially financial and thus ignores the institutional and political factors that define the parameters of the welfare state, how they can be changed, at what rate and with what effects. In any case, despite their political rhetoric about the lack of affordability of the welfare state, governments have generally been unwilling to translate these words into action. The ratio of social expenditure to GDP continued to increase between 1984 and 1997 in all nineteen countries included in the OECD Social Expenditure database (OECD, 2000a).

Running alongside the debate over the budgetary cost of welfare has been a debate over the extent to which the escalating cost of welfare provision has been a consequence of welfare programs themselves. There is concern that economic costs arise from incentive structures that distort choices in labour and capital markets in ways that are detrimental to economic growth, thus undermining future living standards. Such concerns have been particularly acute in countries like Australia, where the social security system operates on a means-tested basis, and support is withdrawn as private income rises. This has created a complex array of 'poverty traps' that targeted systems have been unable to remove without extending the scope of welfare benefits (and their cost) well into the income ranges occupied by middle Australian families.

The political costs of welfare provide governments with little room to manoeuvre if they want to appease middle class demands for tax cuts without prompting a backlash by cutting welfare benefits. Advocacy groups for those accorded favourable treatment under the welfare system have impeded the cutting of welfare. Drawing on public sympathy for welfare clients, these groups have opposed moves to re-configure existing entitlements, imposing considerable political costs on reformist governments. At the same time, it has been possible to portray them as protecting the privileges of small minorities at the expense of the 'common good' – a tactic that governments of all persuasions have been all too ready to exploit.

Disincentive effects

Despite opposition, the welfare system has come under sustained attack from right-wing academics and commentators who have seized the intellectual initiative and dominated the policy agenda. Many of these attacks originated in the United States, where the structure of the welfare system and the social problems it seeks to address differ markedly from those found in Australia. Even so, the American influence on much of the thinking underlying policy development has become increasingly important, drawing on a common theme relating to the role of incentives in creating patterns of behaviour that worsen the problems that the welfare system is trying to address. This was most clearly evident in Charles Murray's critique of American post-war social policy (Murray, 1984). But there are also similarities in the work of the 'new paternalists', who argue that the responses to perverse incentive structures have become so embedded that they can only be overcome through coercive measures (Mead, 1997; 2000).

It is important to emphasise that taking account of the incentive structures created by the welfare system is not a defining feature of the neo-liberal approach. All welfare proponents must recognise that disincentives can undermine policies by diluting or even reversing their intended effects. To take account of the responses to new incentive structures is an essential part of the task of building a sustainable welfare policy. What is unique about the neo-liberal approach is the emphasis given to reducing disincentive effects as both an end of policy and as a principle that should have an over-riding influence on its means. It is this lack of balance that must be challenged, not the importance of the incentive effects themselves.

While its adverse effect on incentives has been one focus of attack on the welfare system, a second area of disenchantment relates to the moral basis for, and consequences of, welfare provision by the state. Here, the critics have argued that far from promoting social cohesion and solidarity, the welfare system has encouraged individual self-interest among those who were dependent on its benefits, at a cost to taxpayers who have been required to underwrite an escalating welfare budget (Peter Saunders, 2000, pp. 7–8). In raising the issue of personal responsibility, this line of attack opened up a debate over the moral basis of the welfare system and the balance between rights and responsibilities in its design and funding. Implicit in this argument is the view that the interests of those who benefit from welfare provision are in conflict with those of the people who fund it.

This simplified account of the politics of welfare is founded on a misleading dichotomy between 'welfare beneficiaries' and 'taxpayers' that has become even less relevant since the introduction of the GST, which taxes the spending of all consumers equally. But the alleged conflict between welfare beneficiaries and taxpayer interests has become sharper as the targeting of universal benefits away from the middle classes has undermined the broad consensus on which the past legitimacy of the welfare system had rested. Benefit targeting may save money in the short run, but it opens up cleavages between beneficiaries and taxpayers that reinforce and perpetuate the fiscal crisis of welfare in the longer run, as noted in Chapter 3.

The focus on the moral dimensions and (dis)incentive effects of the welfare system has occurred against a background of growing disparities in the economic fortunes of different groups (Chapter 7). Although economists emphasise the benefits of competition as a spur to profitability and efficiency, there are also losers from the process of competition, and as more people are exposed to competitive forces, it is inevitable that insecurity and vulnerability will increase. How serious these factors are, in political as well as social terms, depends on how widely the misfortunes are shared and whether their impact is permanent or transitory. As Esping-Andersen has argued:

> Popular discourse has already recognised the arrival of a new class of losers. Witness labels such as the 'A-team' and 'B-team', or the new underclass. Behind such labels lurks the idea that there is a class of marginals trapped in lifelong underprivilege. But whether this is true or not remains an open question. It is undeniable that bad jobs, low pay, unemployment and poverty afflict more and more people. Yet if people's experience of marginality and

want is only temporary, life-chances will probably not be seriously impaired
... We face a real crisis of social polarisation only if the losers of today are
losers for life, and if they pass their underprivilege on to the next generation.
(Esping-Andersen, 1997, p. 64)

Avoiding entrenched and unacceptable polarisation is one of the main contemporary challenges facing the welfare system. Yet as observed in Chapter 6, public service cutbacks and privatisation have contributed to some of the processes that have given rise to voluntary and involuntary social exclusion and (as Chapter 7 shows) have been accompanied by growing inequality. The key issue is how to avoid increased polarisation, given increased global competition that is producing a more complex set of working arrangements and given rapidly changing household structures. These circumstances demand welfare programs that offset income falls and facilitate integration back into the labour market, but income support alone cannot achieve both, as demonstrated by the poverty trap quandary. At the same time, the interventionist sentiment that underlies such initiatives is at odds with the neo-liberal market philosophy that gives rise to the need for them in the first place. Throughout the industrial world, the welfare system has been squeezed between these contradictory forces.

An important lesson of recent historical experience is that welfare programs can give rise to behavioural changes that may distort or subvert their effectiveness. Although the bulk of the empirical evidence indicates that the behavioural responses to tax and transfer programs are generally not large, the evidence also suggests that such effects can be *large enough to matter*. Accounting for such distortions thus has to be part of the reform process. However, it is important to emphasise that rather little is known about the size of such effects in Australia. This is all the more surprising given that our social security system is widely recognised – and actively promoted – as being one of the most highly targeted among OECD nations. One might have thought that the designers of the extremely complex social security system that we now have would have put considerable effort into identifying the size of these disincentive effects so as to minimise their impact. Not so. Australian research on the disincentive effects of tax and social security provisions has been virtually non-existent, and much of the policy debate still relies on United States empirical evidence that is of doubtful relevance to Australia.

Disincentive effects are important, but they are not inevitable, even where poverty traps exist. To be *encouraged* to reduce one's labour supply is one thing, to *actually do so* is quite another, given the complexities and uncertainties surrounding the labour market and the employment prospects it offers. Much more is known about what the system encourages or discourages in terms of behavioural response than about its actual effects, yet we need to know about actual effects to decide what to do about the system. The resulting vacuum provides ample scope for uninformed or ideological views to hold sway.

Missing from this debate is any consideration of the role of unemployment and the lack of jobs in creating the conditions of welfare crisis. A large part of the increase in the welfare budget reflects the direct and indirect effects of higher unemployment on unmet need and thus on the numbers dependent on welfare benefits. Despite evidence (e.g. on the extent of involuntary under-employment, or on the high ratio of unemployment to vacancy rates) that the demand for labour is not adequate to generate full employment, the attention of policy-makers remains focused on the supply side of the labour market and how it is affected by the disincentive effects of the benefit system. In these circumstances, it is difficult to believe that increasing the intensity of job search activity among those receiving welfare benefits can have anything other than limited effects on the level of unemployment, whatever its success in specific instances. Without also creating more jobs, attempts to make welfare recipients look harder for work will only exacerbate the imbalance that already exists in the labour market.

Thus, while there are good grounds for regarding the welfare system as beset with problems, many of these have been manufactured by government in order to create the conditions for reform. Furthermore, the main purpose of at least some of the proposed reforms is to reduce the welfare rolls and the welfare budget, irrespective of their effect on the welfare of recipients (Goodin, 2001). This is not to deny that there is a need to ensure that the system is compatible with the environment within which it is situated and to take advantage of reform opportunities as they arise. Welfare reform has been driven by the goals of cutting costs and expanding the role of market forces. These are important factors that shape the context within which the welfare system functions, but they will never provide the basis for a system whose primary purpose is to protect the living standards of those denied the opportunity to achieve this for themselves.

Principles of income support

The traditional goal of the welfare system is to provide income support to those unable to earn enough in the labour market to meet their own needs. This includes those of working age who are prevented from working due to sickness, disability, caring responsibilities or unemployment. Support can be provided either directly in the form of an income transfer, or indirectly in the form of services that assist people to gain access to employment and generate an income for themselves. Where income is provided directly, the amount may be designed to maintain previous standards of living, or to set an income floor to protect people from poverty. The provision of earnings-related benefits under social insurance schemes serves an income maintenance role, whereas the means-tested transfers provided under social assistance schemes are designed with poverty alleviation in mind.

Reform strategies

In providing income support in the form of entitlements to those unable to earn, the welfare system reduces the financial rewards for working relative to receiving a welfare benefit. Under a means-tested system of benefits, the disincentive effect operates through two channels. First, the benefit provides an income floor below the wage system (the benefit replacement rate) that may discourage some from seeking work. Second, paying benefits according to means (generally assessed according to any non-benefit income) provides a disincentive to earn an income by working because this causes a reduction in the benefit received and thus in the net income from working (the poverty trap).

In responding to these undesirable disincentive effects, social assistance schemes have pursued a combination of three strategies. The first (categoricalism) relates to the way in which the categories within which support is provided are defined and administered. The second (conditionality) involves linking the payment of benefits directly to participation in paid work or other activities likely to increase the probability of finding work. The third (income contingency) attempts to alter the structure of the income (or earnings) component of the means test. All three approaches have been used to minimise the disincentives associated with social assistance and Australia has pioneered the targeted approach to social security provision (Saunders, 1991; 1999).

All social assistance schemes must define the categories that are eligible to receive support in ways that prevent potential claimants from re-arranging their affairs in order to qualify for assistance. In practice, it is difficult to achieve the right balance between discouraging illegitimate claims from those who are not eligible whilst ensuring that those who are eligible are treated with respect and provided with their due entitlements. The more that the administration of the system is geared towards minimising fraudulent claims, the more it runs the risk of discouraging those who are eligible under the rules from claiming benefit (Goodin, 2001). Although it has not received much attention in Australia until relatively recently, the administration of the welfare system has an important effect on its ability to function effectively in delivering support where and when it is needed and in preventing it where it is not (Saunders, 2001c, 2001d).

The emphasis given to each of the three responses to the incentive problems that arise under the social assistance model provides an insight into the importance attached to other goals of the welfare system. Categoricalism represents an attempt to limit the scope of the system to what can be afforded by establishing a hierarchy of legitimacy within and between the broad categories of eligibility such as the unemployed, sole parents and those with a disability. Conditionality involves tailoring how elegibility categories are defined and policed in order to reinforce other goals of the system, including cost containment and encouraging participation. Contingency reflects a more explicit attempt to link the welfare system to the labour market and is likely to involve the provision of services to complement income transfers if it is to be successful. Here, the medium-term emphasis is on the value of work and financial independence as ends in themselves, whatever the immediate implications for income. Compulsion may be justified if past policies have so entrenched patterns of benefit dependency that beneficiaries become increasingly unlikely (and unable) to choose to re-engage with the labour market. Income contingency attempts to create a smooth transition from welfare to work, while leaving the final decision to the individuals themselves – the system seeks to encourage those on welfare into work, but does not require it.

The politics of welfare

The above discussion focuses on two of the main goals of welfare, to provide an adequate system of income support where it is needed and to promote the incentive to achieve financial independence through paid work. How these two goals are balanced against each other has implications for the complexity of the system and the ease and transparency of its administration. These three goals – adequacy, efficiency and simplicity – provide a framework for assessing the overall quality of the welfare system (and the tax system, where similar principles and trade-offs exist). They provide a basis for evaluating the technical economic merits of the system in terms of its ability to meet its stated objectives with minimal adverse effects.

However, to fully understand the welfare system, it is necessary to go beyond these effects and consider its longer-term social and political functions and consequences. In social terms, it has long been argued that an important function of the welfare system is to promote social stability and cohesion. This is achieved by sharing the risks associated with joblessness and ill-health through a system that provides contingent income transfers, financed by contributions or taxes. By offering such protection, the system promotes community willingness to allow economic fortunes to be determined by the impersonal calculus of market forces. Whether social protection is achieved through an insurance-type model that imitates private sector risk-protection provision (commercial insurance) or by a means-tested approach where redistributive goals and methods are a more explicit feature of tax and transfer arrangements, the intended impact on social cohesion is the same.

This assumes that the specific provisions of the system attract community support for the principles on which assistance is provided, the scope of the groups who are eligible to receive support and the penalties imposed on those who break the rules. Acknowledgement of the importance of community support for the welfare system leads to a consideration of its underlying political purposes. Because the welfare system provides benefits to specific groups in the community, it is inevitable that political interests coalesce around particular programs and processes, including the schemes that fund welfare. The interests that these groups represent often conflict and these tensions must be resolved in the political domain. Thus, the welfare state is an instrument of political action and an arena for political struggle.

In Australia, this has taken the form of political support for the establishment and protection of the welfare system coming predominantly from the labour movement, whose interests have been served by the role of welfare benefits in supplementing wage incomes under a 'wage earner's welfare state' (Castles, 1985; 1994; Ramia, 1998). The interests of capital have been protected in part by allowing some backward shifting of social benefits onto wages (thus maintaining profitability), but also by a strictly enforced targeting regime that has kept costs, and thus the level of taxation, to a minimum.

Over the longer-run, a key ingredient of the success of the welfare system is that it is economically and politically sustainable. The former (economic sustainability) relates to the ability to fund current and projected welfare benefits through the budget without imposing unacceptable financing requirements on those expected to pay. In achieving this goal, account must be taken of the interdependence that exists between the structure of benefits and the willingness of taxpayers to pay the taxes that fund them. This line of argument has been used to support the case for broadly based (universal) benefits that provide some protection or support for the entire population (Titmuss, 1958). It is the taxes of the middle classes that ultimately provide most of the revenue on which the welfare system depends, and it is therefore necessary to give the middle class a stake in the welfare system by extending its benefits to them.

This occurs automatically under social insurance arrangements because middle class contributions provide the gateway to social benefits set well above minimalist safety net levels. Under social assistance, these considerations constrain the extent to which middle class benefits can be means-tested away without alienating their support, thereby eroding the tax base on which the entire structure rests. Targeting that removes too many middle class benefits may thus end up being counter-productive if the willingness to pay taxes declines at a faster rate than the welfare budget itself.

It is also necessary for the welfare system to remain politically sustainable over the longer-run. This depends upon the degree to which both the ends and the means of welfare attract support in the community. While this will depend in part on the coverage of welfare benefits, it will also vary with the degree of public support for how eligibility categories are defined and the conditions on which support is provided. There is an element of truth in the proposition that the success of the welfare system depends on the popularity of both its ends and its means. This was recognised by British Prime Minister Tony Blair who began his 1999 Beveridge Lecture with the following words:

> Today I want to talk to you about a great challenge: how we make the welfare state popular again. How we restore public trust and confidence in a welfare state that 50 years ago was acclaimed but today has so many wanting to bury it. (Blair, 1999, p. 7)

His emphasis on the popularity of the welfare state was significant because it drew attention to the interaction between public opinion and political legitimacy, two factors crucial to the sustainability of welfare policy. As in Australia, welfare reform in Britain had been characterised by rapid social change on the one hand, and by policy failure on the other (Atkinson, 1999c). The British welfare state had lost touch with the realities of British life, as reflected in changes in the labour market, in family structures and in attitudes generally, and no longer enjoyed the support of the British public who were expected to pay for it. In order to make the system sustainable, it was necessary to understand why support had declined and identify what needed to be done to restore it.

The idea that the tide of public opinion has turned against the welfare system is not restricted to Britain. Similar views have been expressed in Australia by successive Ministers of Social Security, who have claimed that the system has lost its integrity in the face of mounting evidence of fraud and abuse. Not surprisingly, these claims have persuaded many people that the welfare system is close to collapse under the weight of massive abuse of its provisions and have thus further undermined public support for it. At the same time, however, changes in jobs, family structures and social attitudes have raised questions about the welfare system's ability to deal with contemporary problems. This has set in train the need for reforms that reflect current conditions and attitudes. In combination with the intellectual attacks on its goals and methods, community support for welfare reform has emerged as an issue driving the policy agenda.

Targeting, dependency and obligation

The central feature of any welfare system is the establishment (through formal legislation) of a set of entitlements (or rights) to certain sections of the population. These entitlements are conditional. Conditionality clauses have applied in all welfare systems, although they differ according to the nature of the system and the kinds of benefits and coverage it provides. Conditionality clauses represent the responsibilities that beneficiaries must fulfil in order to access their rights or entitlements. Other eligibility conditions linked to residence requirements ensure that beneficiary responsibilities to pay domestic taxes are also enforced. How the favoured categories are defined, how benefit levels are established and maintained and the nature of the means test determine the impact of the system and reflect its underlying philosophy, principles and objectives.

Welfare conditionality

In terms of these broad features, the Australian social security system provides means-tested assistance to those who satisfy a set of conditions that define them as eligible for support (Whiteford, 1998). Since its inception, the system has required claimants to satisfy various conditions in order to establish their eligibility and to provide the information required to apply the means test. These conditions have generally been accepted as a necessary feature of any targeted system and have not met with strong resistance in the community. Although the role of means-tested versus flat-rate, universal or earnings-related benefits has emerged as an issue from time to time, a strong political and community consensus in favour of means-testing has been maintained. At the same time, paying benefits subject to income and assets tests has not resulted (at least not yet), as it has in the United Kingdom and elsewhere, in benefits being seen as stigmatising for those who claim them. The means test has been widely seen as bestowing legitimacy on those who receive welfare benefits 'the Australian way'.

The same degree of acceptance does not apply to the setting of benefit levels, nor to the ways in which eligibility categories have been defined. The criteria used to determine where to set benefits reflect the system's adequacy objectives. It is traditional to judge means-tested social security systems against an income adequacy benchmark such as a poverty line.

However, as noted in Chapter 6, Australia has never endorsed an official poverty line that can serve this purpose, and the prospects of this happening look extremely bleak. Instead, benefit levels have tended to be set on a discretionary basis by government according to their priorities, the resources available and the political pressures they face. The extent of discretion has been reduced since the introduction of automatic indexation of benefits in the 1970s, but it is still possible to provide increases outside of indexation, or to vary the indexation rules to favour (or penalise) specific groups of beneficiaries.

However, it is how the favoured categories are defined that has dominated the Australian welfare reform agenda over the past two decades. It is not difficult to understand why. There are three broad options for cutting the welfare budget, or for slowing its rate of increase. The first and most obvious involves cutting benefits. This has proved to be very difficult politically and governments have generally avoided this option because of the obvious risks. A second option, tightening the means test within a fixed structure of benefit categories, has also proved to be unpalatable, because a tighter means test worsens the poverty trap and exacerbates disincentive effects. The general trend has in fact been to reduce the severity of the income test component of the means test in order to ease the poverty trap and encourage the transition from welfare to work. (The introduction of the assets test was aimed primarily at the aged and has had almost no impact on the vast majority of working age recipients whose assets are well below the exemption level.)

This leaves the third option, redefining the favoured categories in order to reduce the numbers who are eligible for support, as the principal method for reducing the pressures on welfare spending. This has been a feature of those welfare reforms that have involved changing the conditions of welfare eligibility in order to narrow their scope and promote the change to a more 'active society' approach to welfare eligibility (Kalisch, 1991). Subsequent reforms have built on these by further tightening the administrative surveillance of welfare recipients and by placing additional eligibility requirements linked more closely to the aim of getting them back into work. Some of these latter reforms have replaced the choice regarding whether or not to participate in work-orientated programs such as work for the dole with compulsion to participate in approved activities, or forfeit benefit eligibility.

Welfare to work

Two factors underlie the emphasis on compulsion that has become a central feature of the welfare reform agenda. The first is the increase in 'welfare dependency' that so alarmed Family and Community

Services Minister Jocelyn Newman and prompted the establishment of a Reference Group to review and develop proposals for welfare reform (Newman, 1999a; Reference Group on Welfare Reform, 2000a). What the Minister failed to recognise was that a substantial portion of the increase in the proportion of the working-age population receiving social security assistance was a direct reflection of past policy reforms that had extended the coverage of benefits by changing eligibility rules and easing the income test (Henman, 1999; 2000).

The term 'dependency' not only has negative moral connotations, it also implies that compulsion may be necessary to break the cycle of inactivity that is claimed to describe the reality of many welfare recipients. As the leading United States advocate of this position, Lawrence Mead has argued:

> [T]he most dramatic breakthrough has come in requiring work with welfare. In America, welfare reform mostly means work enforcement. ... [M]andatory work programs are a lot less punitive than they seem on the surface. Their philosophy is not to hold the poor personally culpable for their failures. Rather, it is to hold them at least partially responsible for their futures. The notion is that government will make special efforts to support work, through child care and other services. But in return, welfare adults must make serious efforts to work. Through shared effort, society and the individual can together overcome dependency and poverty. (Mead, 2000, pp. 51–3)

The new emphasis on work as an end in itself rather than as a means to an end (financial independence through earnings) is a radical change that has dominated the welfare reform agenda not only in the United States, but also increasingly in the United Kingdom and Australia. It represents a fundamental shift in the foundations of welfare policy, away from issues associated with people's overall economic circumstances (as reflected in their income) towards their labour market circumstances (as measured by their participation in paid work or other forms of approved activity such as caring or volunteering).

Rather than work being seen as a means to an end – a step towards financial independence – work is now regarded as an end in itself, at times irrespective of its effect on income. The discipline, self-respect and positive messages that the world of work brings to those engaged in it (and to their families) are seen as sufficient to justify the use of whatever actions are required to achieve this outcome. This includes the element of compulsion required to overcome the understandable but nonetheless debilitating resistance of those who have come to accept that the security and stability of welfare income are preferable to the risks and uncertainties associated with entering the labour market. Poverty traps are only a problem for those able to exercise choice over whether to accept a job that may have little impact on their total income. The solution rests not in another round of complex adjustments designed to ease the poverty trap, but in replacing choice by compulsion based on the assumption that work is desirable on virtually any terms, at least in the longer-term.

The relationship between the welfare system and the labour market is crucial to the success of this strategy, and this varies across countries with differing historical and institutional backgrounds. Comparisons among Australia, the United States, and the United Kingdom are instructive in this regard as they shed light on how this crucial relationship has evolved and how it needs to change (Perry, 2000). In the United States, where the labour market is deregulated and minimum wages are very low, most welfare recipients have little trouble finding work when the economy is performing strongly. This in part reflects additional welfare to work measures, including the earned income tax credit described by Ellwood (1999; 2001). However, the wages of many United States workers have not been high enough to provide an escape from poverty, despite the low level at which the United States poverty line is set (Mishel, Bernstein and Schmitt, 1999, Figure 6I). Thus, the United States welfare reform experience has resulted in fewer welfare recipients, a decline in welfare spending on cash transfers (offset by increased spending on work-related information and support services), but little evidence that those who have accepted work are financially better off or less likely to be poor.

In the United Kingdom, the introduction of a new minimum wage has been central to the Blair Government's version of welfare to work. This, in combination with labour market programs, increased requirements on the unemployed to seek paid work and a range of other supportive measures, has been described as providing a New Deal for the unemployed in the United Kingdom. There is some evidence of success in moving sole parents off the income support system, although the improvements are modest – as were the schemes themselves (Millar, 2001). Overall, however, the 'jury is still out' on whether or not welfare to work has been successful (Giddens, 2000), although it is clear that the strong performance of the United Kingdom (and United States) economies in the 1990s has made the welfare to work transition more feasible for many. One clear message to emerge from the experience of both countries is that the impact of welfare to work reforms depends crucially on labour market conditions. Promoting paid work among those on welfare increases labour supply at the lower end of the labour market. If this is not to result in lower wages (as has happened in the United States), labour market interventions are necessary to prevent this from happening, as with the minimum wage and other United Kingdom interventions (Saunders, 2001c).

In Australia, welfare to work remains more of an idea than a concrete reality, although there have been moves to impose compulsory requirements on welfare recipients under the principle of mutual obligation. Before discussing these, the broad context for welfare to work needs to be set against the background of the historical relationship between the labour market and the welfare system. As writers such as Castles (1985, 1994, 1996) and Watts (1999) have noted, the centralised wage determination system and the setting of wages according to the needs of workers have been a central feature of the Australian welfare system. Throughout the 1950s and 1960s, in combination with the full employment that prevailed through the period, work was guaranteed for all that wanted it, and the arbitration system ensured that wages were sufficient to avoid poverty. In this period of the Australian welfare state, the term 'working poor' was a contradiction in terms and the success of income support policy was founded primarily on the fact that no one needed it.

These conditions no longer apply. Wages are increasingly determined at the enterprise level and are linked to productivity growth, and the unemployment rate is at a level that was unthinkable prior to 1973. Wage dispersion has increased markedly (see Chapter 7), and the working poor are emerging as a labour market reality (see Chapter 6). In these circumstances, requiring welfare recipients to accept work can no longer provide the automatic security and income adequacy that it once did.

The conditions for United States-style welfare reform have been gradually put in place in Australia over the last decade. Labour market deregulation and the erosion of centralised wage determination have exposed the labour market to market forces to a degree not previously experienced. This, in combination with changes in the structure of industry, employment and jobs (Chapter 4) represents a marked change in the nature of the labour market. These changes cannot be ignored when considering the welfare system, particularly given the delicate balance that exists between the labour market and the welfare system in the context of a wage earner's welfare state.

A deregulated labour market changes the relationship between work and welfare in ways that have fundamental implications for how the welfare system is structured. The main lesson of United States experience is surely that the logic of a deregulated labour market eats away at the foundations of the welfare system and makes the provision of an extensive array of state-provided welfare benefits to those of working age problematic and, in the limit, not sustainable. How can this logic find expression in public policy in a country where there is a strong tradition of egalitarianism and widespread community support for the idea of a 'fair go'?

Mutual obligation

The answer provided by the Howard Government has been to use mutual obligation to re-define the boundaries of welfare and re-assert the importance of work over welfare, and of market over state in the provision of income and in the move from dependency to self-reliance. The basic principle underlying mutual obligation is 'the simple yet compelling premise that responsibility between the community and the individual flows both ways' (Newman, 1999a, p. 4). Or as Prime Minister Howard argued in his 1999 Federation Address, mutual obligation involves 'asking people to give back something to the community in return for assistance in time of need' (Howard, 1999). As this latter statement makes clear, there are in fact three separate aspects of mutual obligation: to whom should it apply; what should they be asked to 'give back' in return for receiving support; and, on what terms should such 'giving back' be based?

In the debate over mutual obligation that has resulted from the analysis and reform proposals of the Reference Group on Welfare Reform (RGWR, 2000a; 2000b), the answers to these questions have been shaped by the new paternalism views outlined earlier. In particular, mutual obligation has been seen as a vehicle for reducing welfare dependency by encouraging welfare recipients back into work. Its coverage has thus been restricted to those on welfare that have a realistic prospect of finding work – the unemployed, jobless people with a disability and certain categories of sole parents. Although there is no reason in principle why mutual obligation might not also be applied to those receiving assistance in the form of age or service pensions, the focus on work as an alternative to welfare has (so far) excluded these groups from the debate.

The second two aspects of 'giving back' – what to give back, and on what terms – have also both been interpreted with the aim of increasing the move from welfare to work. Thus, what is asked of welfare recipients is that they undertake paid (or unpaid) work, or demonstrate their willingness to do so by actively engaging in job search, education and training programs. The United States has gone further, focusing on providing programs designed to divert welfare claimants into the labour market at the point of entry into the welfare system, or to deny them benefits, not encourage the transition to work: 'work not welfare' as opposed to 'welfare to work'. Further, since work is seen as a far more effective strategy for reducing welfare dependence than education, training or labour market programs, many States in the United States have made work a compulsory requirement for those on welfare (Wolfe, 2001).

The issue of whether or not mutual obligation should be compulsory has generated a lively debate in Australia, with many critics arguing against compulsion on the grounds that it is a distortion of the principle of reciprocity that underlies the welfare contract (Goodin, 2001) or that it erodes welfare rights and diminishes welfare entitlements (Yeatman, 2000). While the RGWR was sympathetic to the idea that obligations should reflect broad community expectations, it also endorsed the view that 'some form of requirement is necessary' (RGWR, 2000b, p. 5).

It is clear that mutual obligation has raised a number of issues related to the philosophical basis for social security provision and the ends and means of the welfare system. Most of them are not new, but have featured in past debates, albeit under different guises. Imposing compulsory requirements on welfare recipients, for example, has as long a history as the system itself, stretching back to the introduction of unemployment benefit in 1942, since which time applicants have always been required to satisfy some form of work or activity test or be denied benefits. Similarly, the linking of eligibility to those prepared to conform to certain forms of moral behaviour has existed since the age pension introduced in 1909 did not cover those who were deemed to lack a 'good moral character' (Thompson, 1994, p. 167).

To object to mutual obligation on the grounds that it represents a change from past practice is to deny the need for the welfare system to adjust to broader social and economic changes. Issues of fairness and compulsion are important and need to be debated, but they are not the only determinants of the success or popularity of the welfare system. Equally important are questions relating to the practical implementation of mutual obligation and its effects on those who fail to comply with its requirements. Any scheme designed to toughen up on those who use welfare to avoid having to work will have the effect of removing benefits from some who genuinely want to work but are incapable of dealing with the scheme's bureaucratic complexities.

There is also the bigger question of whether Australia can import from the United States a scheme whose success is by no means guaranteed in the very different welfare and labour market structures that exist in Australia. To what extent can the success of the post-1996 United States welfare reforms be attributed to the flexibility of the United States labour market, and is this a necessary ingredient of success? If so, there are major implications for the future of the Australian labour market that warrant very serious investigation. How far did the booming United States economy of 1996–2001 contribute to the success of its welfare reforms and what happens when the economy turns down and jobs become scarce? Will the public continue to support a system that requires work as a condition of welfare when there are no jobs available? Are Australians prepared to accept the social consequences (so strikingly visible in the United States) that are associated with denying welfare benefits to those unable to meet the mutual obligation requirements in a context of high and/or rising unemployment?

These questions focus on the impact of mutual obligation on the work behaviour of welfare recipients rather than on the nature of the welfare system itself. They also raise the whole issue of the integrity of welfare, as reflected in community perceptions about the fairness and impact of its provisions. The impact of mutual obligation on the transition from welfare to work is an important project for the longer term. It will require detailed empirical study of the nature of changes in work and welfare receipt and the factors contributing to them. This project goes beyond the scope of this book and is left to others. The extent to which community perceptions endorse the principles and practical application of mutual obligation is, however, a topic that is central to the issues addressed here.

Attitudes to welfare and mutual obligation

Four separate aspects of the relationship between the welfare system, unemployment and the treatment of the unemployed (including sole parents) were addressed in the CESC survey. The role of the welfare system in contributing to unemployment and what can be done to improve things through reform have been discussed in Chapter 4. The results indicate that there is considerable support for the view that ease of access to social security has contributed to the rise in unemployment (Table 4.7) and that many people think that social security reform has a role to play in solving unemployment (Table 4.9). Community attitudes towards the levels of support for different groups of the unemployed were also considered in Chapter 4, where clear differences emerged in these attitudes, which also varied systematically according to people's beliefs and values (Tables 4.10 and 4.11).

Attention now focuses on exploring attitudes to the kind of support provided for the unemployed, the nature of mutual obligation requirements and the penalties for those who fail to meet them. Although many of the CESC questions were framed to elicit attitudes to unemployment and the unemployed generally, the questions on mutual obligation distinguish among different groups of the unemployed. This provides the basis for examining whether and how attitudes to mutual obligation vary according to the characteristics of those to whom they apply and of those who hold them.

The nature of support

It is useful to begin by reporting on attitudes to the nature of the support that the welfare system should provide in general. Such support is

Welfare Reform

predominantly provided in the form of cash transfers, on the grounds that this maximises the freedom that recipients have to decide how to use the support provided. However, as noted earlier, many proponents of the work-oriented welfare reform agenda regard untied cash grants as inappropriate because they do not reinforce the idea that there are responsibilities attached to welfare rights and thus encourage dependency. They prefer support that is either conditioned by participation in approved forms of work-focused activity, or that is provided in the form of services that assist people to get back into work rather than cash.

The provision of services has the added advantage that greater control is exercised over how the resources provided to the unemployed are used. While this latter feature is counter to neo-liberal notions of freedom of choice, it may make taxpayers more willing to fund support through taxation, and also resonates with the paternalistic views that underlie mutual obligation.

Community attitudes to the different forms of 'support' provided by the welfare system can be examined using the CESC data, which includes responses to the following question:

There are different ways of providing assistance to the poor. Please indicate whether you agree or disagree with the following options.
a) Poor people should be given enough money to make ends meet.
b) Giving poor people money alone is not enough. They also need advice on how to spend it wisely.
c) Wherever possible, poor people should be given free access to services (like Medicare and public transport) as well as *enough money to make ends meet.*
d) Wherever possible, poor people should be given free access to services (like Medicare and public transport) rather than *money.*

The responses generated by this question are summarised in Table 8.1.

It is important to note that the question refers explicitly to the nature of public support *for poor people only*, so no conclusions can be drawn about attitudes to the structure of welfare (or other) support more generally. The question also refers to specific services (Medicare and public transport) because of their familiarity and community acceptance of their importance, particularly for low-income people. Reference to these particular examples may have deflected respondents' thoughts away from other services such as child care, or disability support that are also important in the wider debate over the nature of welfare provision. It should also be noted that since the final two options included in the question are alternatives, consistency dictates that those who agreed with one should disagree with the other. In spite of this, close to half of the CESC sample provided apparently inconsistent responses to these two questions (either agreeing or disagreeing with both) although no attempt has been made to adjust for this.

The results in Table 8.1 indicate that while only around one-half of respondents agreed that poor people should be given enough money to 'make ends meet', there is stronger support for also providing budgeting advice on how to spend money wisely. Opinion was similarly split on the last two options canvassed – whether access to services should be in addition to, or in place of, provision of cash assistance to the poor. In both instances, the level of support was around 50 per cent, with around 20 per cent opposed, with a slight preference for providing access to services *rather than* cash. Overall, these results suggest that there is strong community support for providing the poor with an adequate level of cash support, but even stronger support for also providing budgeting advice and ensuring that the poor have access to services that meet their needs directly.

Mutual obligation requirements for the unemployed

As noted earlier, the imposition of requirements on the unemployed as a condition of benefit receipt has been a feature of the social security system since its inception. What is new about mutual obligation requirements (MOR) is that the requirements are linked to participation in a set of approved activities expected to increase the probability of finding work. MOR are also intended to ensure that the unemployed are genuinely and actively seeking work and, most importantly, generally involve an element of compulsion. This latter aspect is important, not because compulsion itself is new – it isn't – but because in order for compulsion to be effective in practice, the MOR must be accompanied by a series of penalties on those who fail to satisfy them. This raises difficult questions about the severity of penalties and how far society is prepared to go to enforce them.

Table 8.1 Community views on the nature of welfare support (percentages)

Option proposed	Strongly agree	Agree	Neither agree nor disagree	Disagree	Strongly disagree
Enough money to make ends meet	11.8	38.9	19.1	19.1	2.7
Cash and budgeting advice	35.5	47.1	6.5	3.2	1.1
Services as well as cash	14.5	35.2	19.6	20.4	2.6
Services rather than cash	17.9	39.3	14.7	17.3	3.0

Unweighted n = 2,201 to 2,243.

In order to assess the nature and strength of community attitudes to mutual obligation requirements linked to activity testing, questions were asked about which of a series of activities people might be required to do in order to receive unemployment benefits. The options did not relate to specific legislative requirements, but included the kinds of activities and expectations proposed under the rubric of mutual obligation. Distinctions were made among different groups of the unemployed and different types of requirement and the responses generated are summarised in Table 8.2.

Over half (24 out of 45) of the mutual obligation requirements attracted majority support, although the degree of support varied according to the nature of the requirement and the characteristics of the groups among the unemployed to which they would apply. The requirements with most overall support were training or re-training, looking for work, undertaking useful community work and improving reading and writing skills. Those MOR that are less closely linked to labour market success, such as work for the dole and completing a dole diary, received considerably less support, as did the more personally intrusive measures such as having to change appearance, accept any job offer, or move to another town or city.

Among groups of the unemployed, it is clear that there is much greater support for imposing MOR on the young unemployed and the long-term unemployed than on the older unemployed, those looking after young children and those with a disability. One of the most striking features of the results in Table 8.2 is that the variation in the responses is much greater across the rows than down the columns. This suggests that while there is support for some forms of MOR, people are able to make a distinction between how they should be applied to different groups according to their circumstances or characteristics. While support for the kinds of requirements listed in Table 8.2 clearly does exist, especially as applied to young unemployed people, it cannot be seen as wholehearted or applicable to all of the unemployed (Eardley, Saunders and Evans, 2000).

Young people are the group most people feel should face the greatest number of requirements. Yet while nearly everyone agrees that they should have to look for work, the idea that they should have to move in order to find work does not even receive majority support. This suggests that people prefer policies designed to bring jobs to where people live, rather than forcing them to move to where jobs are available. It is also striking that nearly half the respondents thought that neither the older unemployed nor those with young children should even have to look for work, even though this has been a requirement ever since unemployment benefit was introduced in the 1940s. Support for making the dole diary,

Table 8.2 Levels of support for activity test requirements (percentages)

Requirements	Young unemployed (under 25)	Older unemployed (50+)	Long-term unemployed (of any age)	Unemployed people with young children (under 5)	People affected by a disability	Mean level of support
Look for work	92.8	53.7	81.2	51.6	33.5	62.6
Complete a 'dole diary' detailing efforts to find work	79.9	40.9	71.1	42.7	25.7	52.1
Take part in a 'work for the dole' scheme	82.5	38.2	72.3	35.6	24.6	50.6
Undergo a training or re-training program	81.8	61.5	80.5	55.5	51.8	66.2
Undertake useful work in the community	78.4	62.8	77.0	47.7	46.3	62.4
Accept any paid job offered	64.9	32.8	64.5	29.7	18.1	42.0
Move to another town or city to find work	49.1	9.4	40.8	11.0	5.3	23.1
Change appearance (eg. get a haircut)	71.2	33.8	57.6	34.5	25.4	44.5
Improve reading and writing skills	83.9	51.1	74.9	53.7	45.4	61.8
Mean level of support	76.1	42.7	68.9	40.2	30.7	–

Unweighted n = 2373.

training, useful community work and remedial literacy obligatory is only between two-fifths and two-thirds. This suggests that once people begin to view unemployed people as facing circumstances that might conflict with a strong employment focus such as having to care for young children, they tend to soften their attitudes to the scope of MOR. This is particularly the case when it comes to 'people affected by a disability', where there is only minority support for extending most aspects of the mutual obligation principle.

Table 8.3 examines how attitudes to MOR vary with the different value positions of the CESC respondents, as specified in Chapter 3. These results show the average number of MOR that those who fall within each of the three value categories – individualist, collectivist and fatalist – thought should be required of the different groups of unemployed people. For each of the five categories of unemployed people, the maximum number of requirements is nine, implying that the total number of requirements across all categories is forty-five. The pattern of support for applying MOR to each group of the unemployed is similar across all three of the value groups to that for the entire sample (Table 8.2). Attitudes to MOR are again much tougher for the young and long-term unemployed than for the older unemployed, those with young children and those with a disability. These findings are robust, with the relationship between value position and attitudes to mutual obligation remaining statistically significant after controlling for the effect of other variables (Saunders, 2002a).

Similar patterns also exist *within* each of the separate value categories, although there are substantial differences in the level of support for MOR *between* the three value framework groups. In general, the mean level of support for applying MOR to a specific group of the unemployed is greater among individualists than among collectivists by between 1 and 1.5 points (out of a maximum of 9), with the mean MOR score for fatalists falling in between. Attitudes to mutual obligation thus vary systematically with people's attitudes to economic and social change, their beliefs and values about the causes of social problems and the role of government.

The severity of penalties

To maintain credibility, any set of requirements must be accompanied by a system of penalties for those who break the rules. Those caught committing social security fraud are generally denied further benefits and are often prosecuted under the provisions of the *Social Security Act*. The penalties for failing to comply with activity test or other mutual obligation requirements are more lenient and apply only temporarily. There

Table 8.3 Support for mutual obligation across different value categories (mean values)

Value position	Young unemployed (under 25)	Older unemployed (over 50)	Long-term unemployed	Unemployed with young children (under 5)	Unemployed with a disability	All categories
Individualist	7.6	4.9	7.4	4.7	3.6	28.2
Collectivist	6.3	3.5	6.0	3.4	2.6	21.7
Fatalist	7.3	4.2	6.4	4.1	3.1	25.0
All [a]	7.0	4.0	6.5	3.8	2.9	24.2

Note: (a) Includes those who could not be classified into one of the three value categories.
Unweighted n = 1,827.

are two main reasons for this. First, the community would not tolerate a situation in which people were denied assistance entirely if the offence is relatively minor and possibly the result of a misunderstanding or unforeseen event. Second, denying people social security benefits also prevents them from having access to programs that may assist them back into work and out of their dependence on state transfers.

But are the penalties that apply to those caught breaking the benefit eligibility requirements too lenient? The CESC survey asked whether or not people felt that the penalties for breaching activity test requirements were reasonable. At the time of the survey these penalties were such that the first breach could lead to a loss of up to 18 per cent of the basic payment for 26 weeks, while two breaches in a two-year period could result in a 24 per cent reduction in their benefit. Three breaches in two years could lead to a loss of the entire basic payment for 8 weeks (Eardley, Saunders and Evans, 2000). The penalty system is complex and few people can be expected to be aware of its details. In light of this, it was decided that, in formulating the CESC question on attitudes to penalties, providing some information about the current situation was likely to produce more reliable responses. The earlier comments on the dangers of doing this should be borne in mind when assessing the implications of the results.

The two questions asked about penalties were:

At the moment, if unemployed people fail to meet their requirements under Social Security regulations they could lose up to 24 per cent of their basic payment for 26 weeks. How does this penalty seem to you?

and

At the moment, if unemployed people fail to meet their requirements under Social Security regulations three times in two years they could lose their payment altogether for 8 weeks. How does this penalty seem to you?

Figure 8.1 indicates that just over half (between 52 per cent and 54 per cent) thought that both levels of penalties were 'About right', with most of the rest fairly evenly divided between those who thought they were 'Too harsh' and those who thought they were 'Too lenient'. About 12 per cent could not say. The pattern of responses to both questions is very similar, which suggests that there was not strong support for adopting a tougher line for 'repeat offenders' than already existed. It is worth noting, however, that the questionnaire did not indicate the dollar value of the potential fines or invite respondents to consider the impact they might have on recipients who already have very low incomes. It is possible that if this had been done, the responses might have been somewhat different.

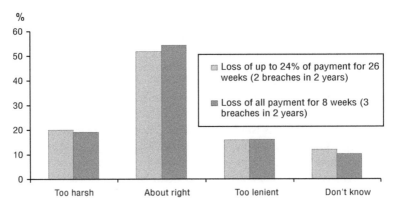

Figure 8.1 Views on penalties for not meeting social security requirements.

Table 8.4 investigates how attitudes to MOR penalties vary across the three value categories described earlier. It has been argued above that the details of the penalties are a more significant feature of the new approach to MOR than the nature of the requirements themselves. This is borne out by the results in Table 8.4, which show very large differences in attitudes to penalties between those classified as individualists, collectivists and fatalists.

The differences between individualists and collectivists are particularly striking, with collectivists being around 6 and 7 times more likely to regard the respective penalties as too harsh and individualists around 3 times more likely to regard them as too lenient. Close to half of both groups think that the penalties are about right, suggesting that the wording of the question may have produced a bias in favour of this response.

Table 8.4 Attitudes to social security penalties by value position (percentages)

	'Too harsh'	'About right'	'Too lenient'	'Don't know'
	Loss of up to 24% of payments for 26 weeks (2 breaches in 2 years)			
Individualists	5.4	53.9	35.4	5.4
Collectivists	30.6	46.3	11.1	12.0
Fatalists	18.0	59.3	13.9	8.8
	Loss of all payments for 8 weeks (3 breaches in 2 years)			
Individualists	3.8	55.0	36.6	4.6
Collectivists	28.2	48.4	11.7	11.7
Fatalists	19.5	61.4	13.9	7.9

Unweighted n = 1,847.

Overall, the responses from the fatalists again fall between those of the individualists and the collectivists, with more fatalists also regarding the penalties as 'About right'.

The above results (and those in Chapter 4 relating to attitudes to the level of support for the unemployed) describe community attitudes to how the welfare system treats different groups of beneficiaries in terms of the support provided, the conditions on which support is provided and the penalties for breaking the rules. Despite the complexity of the issues of fairness, incentives and compulsion underlying these questions, the results reveal a finely grained understanding of the issues at stake, the extent to which the goals of the system are currently being achieved and the limits on future reform proposals. Overall, community attitudes show strong support for many existing provisions, but there is also evidence of a willingness to accept change in some areas, and for some groups.

Among the unemployed, community support is strongest for the older unemployed and for those with young children or with a disability. Generally, the community considers these groups deserve additional support and should be required to comply with no more, and possibly fewer requirements in order to receive it. The opposite applies to the young unemployed and the long-term unemployed, both of whom should be required to satisfy numerous mutual obligation requirements designed to get them back into work.

Are community attitudes consistent with the view that the parameters of the welfare system need to be changed? Overall, probably not. The results suggest that most Australians have confidence in how the welfare system treats the unemployed and few appear to support radical change to its structure and purpose. At the same time, there is a willingness to consider reform proposals on their merit and there is support for taking a harder line in some instances, but a softer line in others. There is a diversity of opinion as one would expect, but most Australians, when they are asked to reflect upon it, have little trouble identifying the strengths of the current system and areas where it could be improved. In this sense, community attitudes to welfare can be mobilised behind change, but only if the changes are seen as fair and consistent with broader social trends and expectations.

9   Re-mapping the Contours of Welfare

The welfare system discussed in previous chapters is an integral and important component of the welfare state. It embodies many of the assumptions on which other welfare programs are founded and its ends and means have broad applicability and relevance. The welfare system sits at the interface between state and market and must adjust to all of the complexities and contradictions that this implies. Above all, increased unemployment has affected the welfare system more than other welfare programs because of the nature of its purpose and structure. With reduced state intervention now a cornerstone of the economic reform agenda, the role of the welfare system in promoting social justice and offsetting the adverse social consequences of economic change has come under increased criticism.

The claims that the welfare system has produced adverse economic and, according to some, social effects have been based on weak evidence, much of it imported from the United States where the welfare system and the structures and values that support it differ greatly from those in Australia. This has resulted in welfare reform being increasingly subverted to economic reform, compromising its ends and distorting its means. The contours of the welfare system must conform to changing priorities about objectives, the body of evidence about what works best and the undeniable reality that resources are limited. While its economic effects must, in the end, form part of the assessment of the welfare state, economic theory is the wrong place from which to start considering the role of the welfare system. It is necessary to begin by asking what is expected from the welfare state and how best to go about getting it – the ends and means of welfare.

Studying community attitudes to the ends, means and effects of the welfare system is important for restoring balance to a debate that has far-reaching consequences for the future development of Australian society. Although public opinion is only one of many factors driving change, its nature and effects have not been given sufficient attention in the reform agenda. Politicians who make the decisions on which reform is based understand that public opinion must be understood before it can be influenced to support their own ideas and ideologies. The media understands the power of public opinion to affect perceptions about key issues, but its interest is generally short-term and instrumental. Politicians and the media generate and manipulate public opinion in order to achieve specific ends and neither has much intrinsic interest in understanding how and why beliefs and attitudes differ.

One of the main motivations for undertaking this study of community attitudes was to examine public opinion on economic and social change and welfare reform systematically. The *Coping with Economic and Social Change* survey was designed to identify community attitudes to the broad contextual changes and specific policy proposals that shape the welfare reform agenda. The results are frozen in time and a similar survey conducted now might discover that opinions have changed, as new ideas, perspectives and challenges have emerged. But in democratic systems, the scope for welfare policy to stray too far outside of the boundaries of public acceptability is limited. If it does, support for the welfare system will decline, leading to a crisis of legitimacy that poses a major threat to its sustainability.

It is thus important to study the nature of public opinion, what affects it and how it is changing, in order to provide an insight into the political forces that support or oppose change. This information can supplement the economic and financial imperatives for reform that have come to dominate the debate. In thinking about the directions that welfare reform might take, it is important to balance the financial arithmetic of the budget bottom line with the democratic accountability reflected in community attitudes and public opinion. The welfare state was designed to achieve economic as well as social and political goals, and its programs represent more than a transfer of resources between social classes. It represents the institutional expression of social justice and social solidarity. That these ideas cannot be easily codified as entries in the national accounts or as line items in government budgets does not make them any less important.

The changing welfare policy context

Although the evidence to support the idea of a welfare crisis is limited, there is concern over some of its effects in aspects of public opinion. The fact that community attitudes have not turned against the welfare state, as some have claimed, does not mean that the system can avoid responding to past failings, current priorities and emerging goals. Given the changes taking place in its economic and social context, the nature of its competing and contradictory goals and the mixed research evidence on its effects, welfare reform will always be high on the policy agenda.

This is particularly true in situations where ideological imperatives seek to shift the boundaries between state, market and family in the provision of welfare. Trying to improve the design and delivery of welfare in response to changing conditions and circumstances is an on-going project whose course will be determined in part by community attitudes.

Why attitudes matter

Since all welfare programs involve an element of redistribution, their viability depends upon the support of those who are made worse off by the resource transfers involved. For this reason, public opinion and community attitudes have an important role to play in securing and maintaining the legitimacy of the welfare system. In achieving this, it is a self-evident truth that, at some level, the system must balance the altruistic ideals of those who pay for it against the need to promote self-reliance among those who benefit from its programs.

The American Nobel Prize winning economist Robert Solow has expressed this idea in the following words:

> ... [M]ost voters are prepared to sacrifice some private economic advantage so that those with the very lowest earning power should not have to live at the impoverished standard that their own wages could support. That motive is surely not constant; common observation suggests that it may be weakened by the observation that many people seem to violate the norm of self-reliance, or by the perception that the welfare benefit is relatively high compared with the earning power of many working citizens. It is easy to see how a politics of welfare can emerge and develop. (Solow, 1998, p. 20)

Although a somewhat simplified account of the factors underpinning the welfare system, the essential point is that there is a *political* dimension to the welfare system and its legitimacy cannot be assumed to automatically exist.

The legitimacy of the welfare system will be threatened if its provisions are perceived as contravening the idea (fundamental to all capitalist systems) that self-reliance is best achieved through paid work. There is some evidence that public opinion may have turned against the Australian welfare state (see Figure 3.3), although attitudinal evidence also suggests that community support is stronger for the age pension, education and health programs than for programs that support specific groups like the unemployed and sole parents. Against this, the CESC data show that when they are asked about their views *on specific proposals*, most Australians reveal a sophisticated understanding of the needs of different unemployed welfare recipients and an appreciation of the complexity involved in achieving adequacy while promoting the work ethic. There is little support in these data for the view that the values of 'middle Australia' diverge markedly from those that the welfare system is seen to be encouraging – a factor that has been driving welfare reform in the United States (Solow, 1998; Haveman, 2001).

Change and continuity

Much has been written about the need for the welfare system to adjust to changes in the labour market, in patterns of family formation and dissolution, in economic structure, in governance and administrative capability and in social norms and community values. But insufficient attention has been paid to the role of the welfare system in protecting vulnerable groups from the adverse effects of these changes. One of the main goals of the welfare state is to insulate people from the decline in living standards that they would otherwise experience as a result of economic and social change. In order to serve this function (and thus promote the social acceptance of economic change), a degree of stability in the pattern of welfare provision must be balanced against the imperatives for change.

Social security provision for those of working age is designed to share the social risks associated with unexpected disruption of earnings due to ill-health, unemployment or other barriers to workforce participation (Esping-Andersen, 1999, Chapter 8). Market failure prevents these risks from being covered adequately through the provision of commercial insurance. By maintaining living standards during these periods, social security provides workers with an assurance that living standards will not fall below certain prescribed levels, thus encouraging them to accept the financial risks associated with the functioning of market forces. Income redistribution brought about by social security and other programs also eases the resource constraints on parents, allowing them to invest in their children's education, thus increasing overall investment in human capital and contributing to economic growth (Scarth, 2000). The welfare settlement also provides a political solution to conflicts over how income is distributed that could otherwise have had disruptive consequences for political stability and economic growth (Osberg, 1995).

In order to satisfy its diverse goals, the welfare system must maintain a reasonable degree of stability over the time horizons for which people make major decisions about such matters as their children's education and whether or not to accept a new job. Social insurance guaranteed such stability through its system of defined benefits and/or contributions, but no such explicit guarantees are provided under social assistance schemes of the Australian kind. However, the fact that they are not made explicit does not mean that they do not exist. Legislation establishing eligibility for social benefits in contingent circumstances such as unemployment, sickness or disability and the maintenance of benefit levels through indexation were designed to make concrete these implicit guarantees. The establishment of these entitlements created community support for the welfare system, since everyone was exposed to the risks that were being covered and all were thus covered by the contingent benefits it provided.

Social assistance schemes were not able to guarantee the same level of protection as social insurance, but they had greater flexibility to vary the conditions and level of benefits in line with changes in external conditions. However, there is a limit to how far the ability to vary the conditions of welfare benefits can be exploited without undermining the implicit contract on which the system is based. The flexibility to respond to change must thus be balanced against the need to maintain a degree of stability commensurate with risk-protection. From this perspective, the pace of welfare reform can undermine its ability to provide income stability in the face of rapid economic and social change. Welfare reform is thus not just a response to a broader crisis, but is also in part a determinant of it.

Reform fatigue

The last thirty years have seen a number of comprehensive examinations of the Australian welfare system. They began in with the pioneering work of the Henderson Commission of Inquiry into Poverty (1975), which recommended a series of sweeping changes designed to increase the adequacy and coverage of the system while simplifying its basic structure. The changes were intended to ease the way towards the introduction of a guaranteed minimum income (GMI) scheme that would replace the existing plethora of benefits categories with a flat-rate universal payment for all citizens.

The Commission proposed a two-tier GMI system funded by an income tax system that would claw back the benefits paid to those on higher incomes (Saunders, 1976). Its primary goal was to alleviate poverty in the simplest way possible, with relatively little attention paid to what this would cost. The assumption that economic growth would generate the resources to fund the scheme seemed reasonable given the economic conditions and expectations that existed at the time, but these conditions were about to change at the very time that the Commission's recommendations assumed their continuation (Manning, 1998).

A similar approach to reform was recommended by the Taxation Review Committee, which also supported a simplification of the social security system through the introduction of a negative income tax (Taxation

Review Committee, 1975). In contrast, an alternative reform strategy was developed in separate inquiries into national superannuation and workers' compensation that recommended the introduction of earnings-related benefits and contributions, along traditional social insurance lines (Manning and Saunders, 1978). The emphasis was again on how to improve the coverage and increase the assistance provided by systems that were seen as unnecessarily complex and not adequately meeting the needs of workers.

The alternative reform blueprints developed in these official inquiries had little impact. The system continued to develop through a series of incremental reforms and welfare programs have been under constant budgetary scrutiny to identify areas where costs could be cut through measures such as targeting, combined with selective reductions in benefits or postponement of indexation increases. In the late 1980s, the Social Security Review set in train a series of reforms designed around the principle of the 'active society' while also heralding major reforms of family assistance and retirement incomes policy (Cass, 1986). A further series of welfare reforms was introduced in 1995 as part of the Working Nation package (Commonwealth of Australia, 1994), although many of them were abandoned by the Howard Government, which embarked upon its own welfare reform agenda, guided by the Reference Group on Welfare Reform (see Chapter 8).

The main themes running throughout the reform agenda of this period have been conditioned by the need to control welfare spending by increasing the efficiency of service delivery and reducing the growth in the numbers receiving social support. Benefit targeting, welfare privatisation and mutual obligation have all been directed at achieving the same underlying objectives, albeit by different means. Many of the reforms introduced in this period have been innovative and, in their own terms valuable, but none have addressed the structural failings of a system unable to cope with the consequences of mass unemployment. The last three decades have seen an unrelenting struggle to design a welfare system capable of coming to terms with the entrenched unemployment that was left in the wake of the economic crises of the 1970s.

Shaping the reform agenda

One of the most important obstacles preventing the welfare system from responding to the pressures it now faces is lack of resources. More than two decades of targeting and shifting responsibility away from the state through privatisation has resulted in a system that is starved of resources. It is not reasonable to expect more from public services without higher taxes, but increased taxation is not an issue that figures high on the agenda of most politicians. The major political parties agree that the key to electoral success lies in pursuing 'sound economic management' through the kinds of fiscal policies that are a barrier to increased public expenditure spending. The first stage in the welfare reform process involves convincing voters that higher taxes will be necessary to finance the additional demands placed upon an improved welfare system.

This will not be easy, but it is not impossible. There is evidence that the public is prepared to accept some increases in taxation, although they also have strong views on how the money should be spent. Programs that provide broad community benefits receive more support than those whose benefits are focused on specific groups (Withers, Throsby and Johnston, 1994). The irony is that benefit targeting has removed many from the benefits of spending programs (not only in the welfare field), thus causing community support to follow spending levels in a downward spiral without resolving the underlying financing problems.

Attitudes and resources

Results from the CESC survey reveal considerable ambivalence in community attitudes to economic and social change, though by no means everyone is opposed to change and many see it as providing new and exciting opportunities (Table 3.1). The CESC data also suggest that widespread acceptance that full employment is no longer an achievable goal has focused people's minds on the inevitability of unemployment and engendered sympathy for those unfortunate enough to become unemployed. But there is also little support for providing untied benefits, with most favouring a system that encourages or requires involvement in work-related programs as a condition of benefit receipt for many welfare recipients.

Taxpayers are understandably keen to ensure that their valuable tax dollars are put to good use, through programs that have clear goals and are efficiently administered. Yet while much has been done to clarify welfare goals and improve benefit administration and delivery, these changes are rarely given prominence in a political debate that focuses on the numbers caught abusing the system, bureaucratic bungling and other inefficiencies. In these circumstances, there is little prospect that the community will support more welfare spending unless it is accompanied by changes in how it is spent.

Bringing about this kind of attitudinal change requires a new welfare discourse that emphasises its positive contributions to social justice, risk management and economic efficiency. The changes required to bring this about must emerge from within the political process. Economic management is important, but it is increasingly apparent that people's life satisfaction is not inextricably linked to economic performance, which provides the means to increased prosperity, but does not guarantee it.

The standard of living also depends on the social context within which the economy functions and the policy and institutional architecture through which its fruits are generated, distributed and redistributed. Until this is recognised and reflected in economic decision-making, perceived living standards will remain disconnected from the official statistics on real incomes and household consumption.

Ideas and arguments

New and enriched notions of prosperity and inequality are beginning to emerge in the literature on social capital and in the juxtaposition of participation and exclusion as central ideas in the modern analysis of the welfare state. In Britain, social exclusion is providing a new framework for thinking about contemporary social problems, although the conventional notion of income poverty continues to attract wide interest and attention (Centre for the Analysis of Social Exclusion, 2001). Social exclusion has become a key component of 'Third Way' politics because it directs attention to the 'social mechanisms that produce or sustain deprivation', shifting attention away from the *relativity of resources* that defines poverty towards the *relationality of processes* that gives rise to exclusion (Giddens, 1998; 2000).

Giddens identifies several strands in the Third Way approach to welfare reform that fit within the framework of relational processes that characterise social exclusion. They include balancing the competing interests and power of government, the economy and civil society to achieve egalitarian goals within a diversified society, promoting the idea of 'no rights without responsibilities' and ensuring that the supply-side effects of the welfare state do not impede economic growth. The welfare system has its own internal inconsistencies and contradictions, and while these must be addressed, globalisation has made traditional left–right conflicts between state and market outdated and irrelevant as a framework (Giddens, 2000, pp. 103–5).

Others have argued that the reasons welfare reform is needed, and the principles that should guide it, reflect the same basic conflicts that the welfare state has been grappling with since its inception in the post-war years. In the Australian context, for example, Watts (1999) argues that many of the Third Way ideas promoted by Labor politician Mark Latham (1998) were part of the reform agenda of the 1980s. That the ideas are not new is not, of itself, a reason to reject them. What is new about the Third Way is its attempt to re-capture the *intellectual basis* on which welfare policy is debated from the economic neo-liberals that have dominated it for the last two decades.

While it is true that Third Way reforms have been implemented in countries such as Australia, the United States, Canada and New Zealand, this has not been accompanied by the strong intellectual underpinnings that exist in Britain, where:

> Third way politics ... isn't an ephemeral set of ideas. It will continue to have its dissenters and critics. But it will be at the core of political dialogues in the years to come, much as neo-liberalism was until recently and old-style social democracy was before that. Third way politics will be the point of view with which others will have to engage. (Giddens, 2000, p. vii)

The Third Way approach to welfare reform attempts to replace the neo-liberal notions of individual freedom, choice and market hegemony with a renewed commitment to equality (albeit under the banner of inclusion) as the centrepiece of the welfare state debate. Not since Beveridge was at the peak of his influence in the 1940s (Beveridge, 1955), has such a strong alliance been forged between ideas and politics in the welfare field. The resulting intellectual vacuum has been exploited by neo-liberals, as welfare state supporters have been unable to mount a coherent intellectual defence of its institutions or achievements (Midgley, 1999). In creating a forum in which progressive ideas can influence policy directly, the Third Way offers an alternative approach to the *cul de sac* into which welfare policy has been heading.

There is no shortage of ideas concerning how the welfare system needs to be reformulated in light of contemporary challenges and constraints. What is lacking is a broad political agenda that recognises the value of the welfare system and is not afraid to commit additional resources to achieving welfare goals. The neo-liberal agenda of targeting, privatisation and mutual obligation is a recipe for the eventual demise of state welfare. The logic of market competition leaves little room for the state to play anything other than a marginal role, supporting those unable to fend for themselves in a competitive market environment with a series of residual, under-funded and stigmatising programs. As the internal contradictions of these programs become increasingly apparent, a new strategy is needed that builds on new formulations of the ends and means of the welfare state.

The central challenge: redistributing income and work

Despite its many significant achievements, persistent inequality remains a central challenge confronting the modern welfare state. It seems unlikely that the foreseeable future will see a reversal of the trend towards increased reliance on market forces and this will continue to impact on all aspects of economic and social life. Increasing marketisation will see a continuation of the trend towards inequality in access to employment and to the income rewards that employment brings for current and future generations.

Against this background, the challenge facing the welfare system is to devise and implement interventions in market processes that moderate the inequalities they produce without creating serious disincentive effects. This will require a set of co-ordinated labour market and tax programs. Labour market intervention is necessary to moderate the trend to inequality at the lower end of the wage and income distributions. Progressive taxation is required to address inequality at the upper end of the distribution and to generate some of the revenue required to fund a modest expansion of the welfare state.

The proposals that follow do not represent a comprehensive program that can address all of the problems identified above. Instead, they try to show what kinds of reforms have the potential to be effective given the available evidence on impacts and can, in light of the evidence produced by the CESC survey, attract broad community support.

Redistributing income

Throughout the post-war period, most OECD countries pursued a combination of tax and transfer policies designed to reduce inequality in the distribution of income. This was achieved through social security transfers that raised the incomes of those with low market incomes and progressive income taxation that lowered the relative incomes of those with high gross incomes. The evidence reviewed in Chapters 5 and 7 confirms that both strategies were remarkably successful in moderating income inequality. Redistribution through the tax-transfer system was often accompanied by policies designed to achieve a more equal distribution of market incomes, including through a range of education programs that reduced the wage premiums for highly skilled workers and direct interventions that set minimum wage levels and moderated wage differentials.

The broad consensus underlying this redistributive strategy began to crumble as a result of three factors. The first was the increasing concern over the adverse disincentive and supply-side effects of taxes and transfers that grew steadily as a proportion of national (and household) income. The second was the emphasis placed on market forces in promoting efficiency and competitiveness and the values of choice and responsibility that underpin the operation of markets. The third was the emergence of mass unemployment, which not only added to inequality, but also undermined the financial viability of the welfare state. In these circumstances, state intervention was perceived as a barrier to market competition because it weakened the price signals that drive market forces.

The key elements of the policy response to these developments were an increased role for market forces, tax cuts that restored economic incentives and placed purchasing power in the hands of consumers, and the linking of social benefit eligibility to participation in paid work. In Australia, these shifts have been accompanied by deregulation of the labour market, a process that has effectively removed one of the central pillars on which its welfare system was based (Castles, 1985; 2001). Yet without a wage system that delivers fair wage outcomes and protects the low-paid, part of the rationale for a highly targeted system of social benefits evaporates. The role of centralised wage determination in protecting the wages and conditions of the low-paid was a key component of Australia's 'welfare settlement' (Kelly, 1992; Maddox, 1998). An effective minimum wage remains important for sustaining community support for welfare targeting and (as explained below) is integral to the success of mutual obligation.

Competitive forces in the labour market have no respect for the needs of workers. This means that as the impact of market forces grows, the effect is either an increase in the numbers of the working poor (as has happened in the United States) or an increased demand for compensating increases in social benefits to provide families with a viable overall income package (as has happened in Australia). The first response accepts that some increase in inequality is the price that has to be paid for increased efficiency, whereas the second response moderates this effect by providing supplementary social support through the budget. Proponents of the first approach stress that it will lead to higher employment, although the evidence suggests that this effect is likely to be small (Nevile, 2001).

It was noted in Chapter 7 that the trend to income inequality has its origins in the labour market, with much of the increase in earnings inequality concentrated at the top of the distribution – particularly at the very top (Table 7.3). This trend has been a consequence of the increased integration of capital and commodity markets associated with globalisation and has been experienced in a wide range of countries. Attempts to control the phenomenal growth in executive salaries (discussed in Chapter 7) are likely to prove futile given the difficulty of enforcement in a world increasingly dominated by multinational companies. A better strategy would be to use the tax system to offset the increase in primary income inequality associated with the boom in executive remuneration. While there may be resistance to higher taxes among the middle class, there is no evidence of widespread opposition to increased taxation on the very rich. A modest increase in marginal tax rates restricted to the top 5 per cent of taxpayers has the potential to offset some of the growth in earnings inequality at the top of the distribution.

Different measures are required at the bottom of the earnings distribution, where an effective minimum wage system is needed to ensure that the increases in labour supply resulting from mutual obligation and other supply-side measures do not drive wages down to socially unacceptable levels. This is all the more important if increases in in-work benefits are shifted backwards onto wages (as discussed below), adding to the increase in earnings inequality (though not to inequality in the distributions of gross and disposable incomes). The United States approach of allowing market forces to drive down wages to a level low enough to make additional employment profitable is not an acceptable option for Australia.

As indicated in Chapter 4, there is very little support for further deregulation of the labour market as a solution to unemployment and there is already widespread insecurity among those in work arising from such moves. Furthermore, Australian research indicates that the elasticity of demand for labour is relatively low, which implies that it would require substantial wage cuts to achieve a significant reduction in unemployment (Gregory, Klug and Martin, 1999; Nevile, 2001).

This still leaves the issue of how to lower unemployment as a way of reducing inequality. The three main options for achieving increased employment at a given level of overall demand are active labour market programs, wage subsidies and direct employment creation. Demand management is obviously also needed to expand demand in order to reduce unemployment, with monetary policy used to ensure that inflation is kept under control. The OECD has argued that active labour market programs have a role to play in the fight against unemployment, but far too little is understood about what works, and too much is often expected of them (Martin, 2000). Australia's past record in the area of labour market programs has been poor. This is largely due to a meagre commitment of resources. In 1997, although Australian spending on labour market programs relative to GDP was only slightly below the OECD average, spending per unemployed person was substantially below average (Martin, 2000, Figure 1 and Table 2). This lack of commitment is reflected in community attitudes, which indicate that the level of public support for labour market programs is not much above that for deregulation of the labour market (Table 4.9).

An important point to emphasise about wage subsidy programs is that, like wage cuts, the effect on labour costs needs to be substantial before they will have a significant impact on unemployment. This implies that the costs to the budget will be high (Piggott and Chapman, 1995). Despite this, wage subsidies (paid through the system of family benefits) are an integral part of the plan developed by the 'five economists' as part of the strategy for reducing unemployment (Dawkins, 1999). The evidence suggests that wage subsidies may be a cheaper way of generating a given number of jobs than labour market programs with the same employment impact (Chapman, 1999). However, Harding and Richardson (1998) and Richardson and Harding (1999) have argued that since many low-wage workers live in families with modest incomes, wage subsidies directed at *low-wage individuals* may not be a very effective device for redistributing income in favour of *low-income families*. While there is some truth in this, there are many workers who are not partnered (including sole parents), and maintaining an adequate minimum wage is crucial in protecting their standards of living.

To the extent that backward shifting of wage subsidies onto wages occurs, it undermines the impact of in-work benefits on workers (though not necessarily on unemployment) by reducing their impact on take home pay. As noted above, this can also exacerbate earnings differentials (since the benefits are generally targeted on those on low wages) and thus add to inequality. If wages do fall, those workers who are not covered by the in-work benefits will be made worse off. These effects suggest that wage subsidies provided in the form of in-work benefits (or employment-conditioned tax credits) may help to stimulate employment, particularly if they are accompanied by the threat of benefit withdrawal, but they are also likely to increase wage inequality at the lower end of the labour market.

The role of public sector job creation in reducing unemployment has been emphasised by Langmore and Quiggin (1994) and Quiggin (2000). They argue that a permanent expansion in public sector employment is an essential component of any full employment strategy. Resistance to this idea by successive governments reflects concerns over past failures, the budgetary cost of new initiatives and the view that only private sector jobs are 'real jobs'. None of these propositions can withstand serious scrutiny. Past policy failings provide lessons for what to avoid in future, while cost is only a problem if conceived in narrow economic terms. Further, the view that only private sector jobs are 'real jobs' is an ideological misconception that has contributed greatly to the unemployment crisis.

In terms of the trends and issues discussed in earlier chapters, there are several advantages to addressing problems of inequality and unemployment through an expansion of public employment. The first is that it is possible to *plan* for the kinds of jobs created, including where they are located. There is scope to target programs so as to increase employment in community (or human) services, including in the areas of health, education and welfare services where there is clear evidence of unmet need (Quiggin, 2000, pp. 218–20). Furthermore, as noted in Chapter 4, these sectors tend to be characterised by low productivity growth and are employment-intensive, so that a switch in demand towards these sectors will increase the level of employment associated with any given level of total demand. Trying to engineer such a switch through the private sector (by expanding the demand for private health, education and welfare services) is more difficult to achieve and likely to involve a substantial cost to the budget if tax concessions are the main vehicle for achieving such a change.

Over the longer term, changes in population structure will increase the demand for aged care and disability services and employment in the industries that provide these services will absorb a growing proportion of the labour force. Employment in the community services is heavily dominated by females (Saunders, 1999b), which implies that a more rapid growth in the human services sector can further reduce the gender disparity in access to employment (though possibly by increasing the gap between families with zero and two earners). Growth in the demand for 'green jobs' in a society that is becoming increasingly aware of the need for environmental sustainability (and demanding more environmentally friendly products and amenities) provides another opportunity to expand the number of public sector jobs.

Finally, there is the issue of Indigenous employment. As noted in Chapter 6, there is strong evidence that Indigenous Australians are exposed to a higher risk of income poverty than non-Indigenous Australians. From this, it follows that any attempt to redistribute income must address the perilous circumstances of the Aboriginal population. Since its establishment on a pilot basis in 1977, the Community Development Employment Projects (CDEP) Scheme has shown remarkable resilience and proved to be popular among the Indigenous community and its leaders (Altman, 1997). It has also been shown to generate *additional* income in the communities reliant on CDEP compared with other indigenous communities (Altman and Gray, 2000). Yet CDEP has not provided the basis for economic renewal in remote Indigenous communities and although Indigenous Australian men have higher incomes than Indigenous men in the United States, Indigenous employment rates are much lower in Australia (Gregory and Daly, 1997). The implication is that CDEP cannot provide a long-run solution to the lack of employment opportunity for Aborigines living in remote communities, whatever its popularity and short-run effectiveness.

This theme has been emphasised by Noel Pearson in his criticisms of 'passive welfare', by which he means welfare provided as 'unconditional cash pay-outs to needy citizens of whom nothing further will be required' (Pearson, 2000a, p.137). Although CDEP requires something of its recipients and provides a modicum of control over local communities, Pearson emphasises that Indigenous Australians have become disconnected from the real economy and their communities excluded as a result of systematic discrimination and dispossession (Pearson 2000b). Welfare reform alone can do little to resolve these problems. What is needed is the development of real productive economic activity in the Indigenous community, and public sector employment creation has an obvious role to play in this process. Expansion of public employment can also have important effects on where jobs are located and this is important in light of the growing spatial inequalities in the distributions of work and income (Chapters 4 and 7).

There are thus many reasons to support a strategy that seeks to expand public sector employment in the services sector. As Quiggin has noted:

> Growth in the demand for services of all kinds and the limited effects of labour-saving technological change in the human services sector imply that growth in employment in the human services is a natural economic response to technological progress and structural change in the economy. (Quiggin, 2000, p. 219)

The costs of such a program need not be prohibitive. Quiggin (2000, p. 226) calculates that it is possible to design an affordable program of public sector job expansion capable of generating almost twice as many extra jobs as can be achieved by a similar increase in private consumption spending. An additional $1 billion of public spending on the human services is estimated to generate about 25,000 additional (average wage) jobs, with a potential claw-back of around one-quarter of the initial (gross) cost resulting from the reduction in welfare benefits and higher tax revenue that accompany the rise in employment.

Building on a platform of economic growth, centralised wage determination to protect low wages within an enterprise bargaining framework, a modest expansion of in-work welfare benefits and growth in public employment in community services has the potential to reduce unemployment to around 5 per cent in the medium term. A supplementary goal would be better integration of the welfare system with the labour market in a situation of high employment to achieve a redistribution of income towards individuals and families at the bottom of the distribution. This would require an increase in income tax for those at the top of the income distribution, accompanied by measures to reduce tax avoidance and a review of the potential introduction of some form of capital transfer or inheritance tax on the very rich.

The program would need to be guided by the development of an explicit and achievable distributional target derived from actual experience. One possible target would be to raise the income share of the bottom decile (or quintile) of workers or families (or both) by a predetermined amount within an agreed timeframe. An example would be to increase the shares of the bottom decile and quintile of full-time wage earners and families by one and two percentage points respectively over a five-year period. Monitoring performance against such targets obviously requires access to reliable and timely distributional data and generating such data would be an essential part of the program.

This strategy reflects a vision in which all members of society are given the option to participate in paid work through the maintenance of a high level of employment and a welfare system that provides an adequate income floor and actively encourages work. The labour market is at the centre of the socioeconomic system, and as many people as possible must be given access to its employment and income benefits. Mutual obligation would be a central element of this approach, serving the dual purpose of reinforcing the work ethic among those out of work and on benefit, while also increasing the community's willingness to incur the cost of the welfare system. But its design would need to reflect the different circumstances of different groups, including their ability to engage in the labour market.

An alternative approach would attempt to achieve a less ambitious goal in relation to employment, accepting that for some, unconditional receipt of social benefits is a more practical option. There is already evidence (summarised in Chapter 8) that public opinion is implicitly supportive of such a strategy for some of the unemployed, particularly those who are older, have responsibility for young children or have a disability. However, the trend is currently in the opposite direction, with receipt of welfare benefits becoming increasingly contingent upon participation in paid work or work-related activity for all welfare recipients.

It may be desirable to try to avoid the current approach to welfare provision, with all its administrative complexity and breaching controversies, by providing a minimal level of social protection on a non-conditional basis. This could take the form of a two-tier system, where the first tier consists of a basic universal benefit subject only to proof of citizenship or permanent residence. This basic benefit would be set at a subsistence level, adequate to cover the costs of the most basic needs only (consistent with community understandings of poverty as subsistence, as discussed in Chapter 6). The second tier would provide a supplementary benefit to those who satisfy an additional set of work-oriented conditions (or mutual obligation requirements). The *sum* of the two benefits would be sufficient to provide a poverty line income adequate to meet living costs at a minimally adequate level for those in employment. This scheme would be similar the guaranteed minimum income (GMI) scheme proposed by the Commission of Inquiry into Poverty (1975) with second-tier benefits made conditional upon participation in some form of work-related activity.

This modified form of basic income scheme in which benefits are made conditional upon participation has been developed by Atkinson (1995b, 1996b) and discussed in the Australian context by Cass and McClelland (1989) and Cass (1994). The underlying idea of making welfare support conditional upon participation is also reflected in the participation support system proposed by the Reference Group on Welfare Reform (2000b). One advantage of a pure unconditional basic income is that it is neutral in its impact on whether to engage in paid work, unpaid (domestic) work or leisure. Against this, there are concerns that basic income could lead to dependency and state-induced exclusion if it induces withdrawal from the labour force (Atkinson, 1998, p. 83). Atkinson goes on to argue that:

> I believe therefore that, in order to secure political support, it may be necessary for the proponents of basic income to compromise – not on the principle of no test of means, nor on the principle of independence, but on the unconditional payment. (Atkinson, 1998b, p. 148)

This is the form of welfare conditionality in which basic income has already been taken up in Australia and the above idea fits within that theme.

Although the idea of basic income receives widespread support (Meade, 1984; van Parijs, 1992), it also has many critics. The detractors, primarily economists, base their criticism on its potentially serious effects on work incentives and cost (Atkinson, 1995b). It is argued that since a basic income scheme provides benefits to which there are no corresponding obligations or eligibility criteria, it will attract large numbers of people prepared to live at taxpayers' expense without having to fulfil any requirements in order to do so.

However, the incentive problems associated with basic income may be less serious in a situation of high unemployment where there is excess supply of labour, since the vacancies created by those who choose to leave the labour force can be filled from the ranks of the unemployed. Indeed, there may be advantages in allowing those with weakest attachment to the world of work to 'opt out', leaving the available jobs to those with a stronger attachment or motivation. The total cost associated with a given level of unemployment will almost certainly be lower. In effect, unconditional basic income provides a self-selection mechanism for job-sharing by encouraging some people to withdraw from the labour force altogether. Another attraction of the scheme is that it, like other universal programs, it is relatively cheap to administer, as there are no eligibility requirements to design and enforce. However, these features will not convince those who argue that unconditional benefits 'send the wrong message' about rights and responsibilities and undermine the integrity and legitimacy of the welfare system.

Finally, there is the important point that the impact of a basic income scheme depends crucially upon the level at which the basic income guarantee is set. If it is set at a level designed to meet the basic costs of subsistence but no more, it is unlikely to provide other than temporary relief to those who have no wish to improve their circumstances by working. A basic income benefit set this low would force those who receive it to economise on their living costs in ways that would be unacceptable to the majority of Australians. There is a trade-off between the level at which the basic income guarantee is set and its impact on incentives and costs. A low basic income benefit may provide an effective way of job-sharing that is not prohibitively expensive, nor likely to encourage permanent dependency. It could also be made time-limited to ensure that it does not have lasting adverse incentive effects.

Redistributing work

Inequalities in the distribution of work need to be addressed alongside inequalities in the distribution of income. Earlier chapters have identified six areas where the distribution of work has evolved in ways that have contributed to growing overall inequality. These relate to: inequality in access to paid work as reflected in unemployment; inequality in the amount of unpaid caring work, where the burden falls disproportionately on women; inequality in the distribution of work between households and locations; inequality in the distributions of earnings; and inequality in hours worked among those who are in employment.

Several of the above proposals designed to redistribute income will have desirable consequences for some of these inequalities in the distribution of work. The combination of demand management policy, increased public employment (particularly in community services) and provision of a modest non-contingent basic income will reduce unemployment by influencing both the demand and supply sides of the labour market. The emphasis given to increased public sector involvement in human services will also ease the pressures on those caring for vulnerable groups such as young children, the frail aged and those with a disability, giving them a greater opportunity to participate in the labour market. The increased commodification of caring work will allow many carers to seek paid work, while others are paid to perform the caring that was previously not remunerated, thus creating new jobs and income opportunities.

Addressing inequality in individual earnings, in the number of earners within households and in average hours worked will require further measures in addition to the minimum wage and tax proposals already canvassed. The growing number of jobless households has not been a direct consequence of the increased number of two-earner households, but reflects a trend decline in the demand for low-skilled labour. That this shift has a locational element to it has meant that both partners in couples in the areas affected have been faced with similarly poor labour market prospects. This may at times have been reinforced by the operation of the social security income test, but changes to the income test have seen a decline in the degree of unemployment concentration within couples since the mid-1990s (Figure 7.1).

Given that these changes have reduced the impact of social security on the concentration of unemployment within households, the growth in the number of jobless households is now likely to reflect local labour market conditions. The problem will only be addressed by tackling the structural conditions that give rise to geographical segmentation of the labour market, for example through regional policies that increase the demand for relatively low-skilled labour. Providing some form of targeted 'job start bonus' may also promote employment among jobless couples, although this kind of supply-side measure will have only a marginal impact, because the main cause of joblessness is inadequate demand, and most effort must therefore concentrate on increasing the level of demand.

The remaining dimension of inequality in the distribution of work relates to the distribution of hours worked among those in the paid workforce. The tendency for average hours of work to increase at a time of high unemployment has been one of the most disturbing of recent labour market trends. Growing inequality in hours worked is of concern in itself, not just because it has contributed to other forms of inequality. If hours worked can be redistributed, there is potential to create additional jobs from which the unemployed and under-employed can benefit. There is already a majority in the community who agree with the view that long hours of work are a factor contributing to unemployment (Table 4.7). At the same time, there is considerable support (matched by a similar level of opposition) for the view that existing work should be shared around more evenly in order to solve the unemployment problem (Table 4.8).

The figures on the distribution of hours worked in Table 4.1 can be used to provide an indication of the potential employment implications of setting an upper limit on the number of hours worked each week. Simple arithmetic calculations imply that if it were possible to set a ceiling of 48 hours on weekly hours worked *without affecting the total amount of work undertaken*, this could create around an additional 126,000 positions working an average of 39 hours a week. If weekly hours worked could be capped at a maximum of 44 hours, a similar calculation suggests that an additional 329,000 jobs could be created. (Both calculations assume that those working over 48 hours work an average of 51 hours, while those working between 45 and 48 hours work an average of 46 hours.) The first calculation is consistent with the estimate of the increase in employment associated with reducing working hours derived by Langmore and Quiggin (1994, p. 246).

These calculations are hypothetical, but they illustrate the potential gains in terms of employment growth (and unemployment reduction) that could result from reductions in hours worked. However, setting an upper limit on the number of hours worked as a way of promoting employment through job-sharing suffers from two problems. The first relates to its acceptability, the second to its practicality. In relation to acceptability, there is evidence that some of those working long hours would prefer to work less (ABS, 1988), although any change would need to be introduced gradually to avoid unexpected and undesirable reductions in income. One possible way of achieving this could be to link reductions in hours worked to increases in productivity, as suggested by Langmore and Quiggin (1994, p. 246). Reductions in hours worked might also be more acceptable if they took the form of reductions in the number of weeks worked each year or in the number of days worked each week, rather than in the number of hours worked each day.

Much of the resistance to reducing hours of work reflects concern over its potential income effects. There are two aspects of this, relating to the impact on the take-home pay of workers and on the labour costs of employers, respectively. For some workers, reducing hours worked will result in lower pay, though for others this will not occur because many of the long hours currently worked are not paid for. In the latter case, the change would thus have no immediate effect on either total earnings or labour costs, aside from any indirect impact on labour productivity. Where lowering hours worked would reduce total earnings, ways would have to be found for sharing the burden by adjusting income and payroll taxes in order to offset the impact on take home pay and labour costs. This approach has been adopted in France and other European countries that have legislated to reduce working hours, suggesting that there is scope for offsetting the direct effects of work sharing on take home pay (OECD, 2000b).

Reductions in hours worked must be accompanied by other changes if they are not to lead to lower earnings and increased labour costs that will be resisted by both employees and employers. There have to be compensating changes designed to reduce these effects, but there are ways of doing this if there is a will to change. There is a body of evidence emerging from those countries that have already introduced limits on working hours that can help to identify the kinds of changes that are required. The details will have to be negotiated between employer groups, the trade unions and government in ways that minimise the effects on earnings and prices and maximise the impact on employment. The problems, though difficult, are not insuperable, particularly if change is introduced gradually to reduce the possibility that earnings fall in absolute terms.

There are two aspects of the practicality issue. The first concerns the mis-match between the skills of those currently working long hours and those under-employed or unemployed. The incidence of long hours of work is concentrated among specific occupations and industries, with the incidence of long working hours highest among those employed in white-collar occupations such as managers, administrators and professionals and among industries such as mining, electricity, gas and water supply, communication and transport. Short hours are common among labourers and elementary and intermediate clerical, sales and service workers and among those employed in cultural and recreational services and retail trades (ABS, 1999b). These differences raise the question of whether reductions in the hours worked by the former groups are capable of generating a chain of labour substitution effects from which the under-employed and unemployed will eventually bene-fit. Although substitution will not occur directly because of skills mis-matches, it is likely that a chain of substitutions will ripple through the workforce, resulting ultimately in increased employment opportunities for those currently working few or no hours.

The second practical aspect relates to enforcement. How can the impact of restrictions on maximum hours worked be monitored in ways that ensure compliance? There are limits to how much can be achieved through legislation and tax schemes that impose penalties on companies that allow their employees to work more than the permitted number of hours. There are no simple solutions to these problems, although it may be possible to use the tax system in imaginative ways that give employers (and employees) a strong financial incentive to comply. Again, there is value in studying the European experience to identify ways of monitoring compliance and promoting enforcement.

The main practical obstacles to job-sharing through restricting hours worked in Australia are outmoded thinking about what can be achieved and an unwillingness to reduce the choices of those currently working long hours. An additional barrier relates to the need for increased state intervention and a commitment to centralised negotiation between employers and employees over the details of any plan to share work. Overcoming these barriers will require reversing the trend towards labour market deregulation. Some form of intervention will be needed to steer the labour market in the right direction. The attitudinal evidence presented in Chapter 4 suggests there is considerable community support for work-sharing as part of the fight against unemployment, which suggests that achieving greater equality in hours worked is within both our aspirations and our capability.

The cost of continuing to pursue current labour market policies is a higher level of unemployment than is necessary given the current level of demand in the economy. A labour market in which some people work very long hours while others are excluded from paid work altogether is fundamentally at odds with the ideal of an egalitarian society. Existing labour market practices, values, institutions and ideas need to be changed to bring about greater equity in access to the many positive outcomes and opportunities that are linked directly to employment. This is one area where market forces left alone will simply not produce a labour market outcome that meets society's need for a fairer distribution of hours worked.

Bringing about change

The ideas outlined in this chapter are designed to achieve a better balance between economic prosperity and social equity. The approach reflects the need to give greater priority to reducing inequalities in the distributions of income and work if economic policy is to produce outcomes that are more consistent with the dominant values and priorities of Australians. It is clear from responses to the CESC survey that many Australians are concerned about what is seen as an imbalance between economic and social objectives and many agree that too much attention has been paid to the economy and too little to society.

Despite the plethora of evidence to the contrary, the vast majority of Australians express support for egalitarian values and believe that they live in a society that has been built upon those values. Most believe that Australian incomes are relatively closely compressed and that their own incomes place them in the middle of the distribution. Virtually everyone thinks that they are part of 'middle Australia'. Relatively few people indicate that they are unable to make ends meet on their income and most express satisfaction with their overall standard of living and a general sense of happiness. At the same time, however, a large section of the population is concerned about the pace of economic and social change and many do not feel that their standard of living has been increasing – despite the growth in real incomes in the 1990s.

There is considerable community sympathy for the poor and many of the unemployed, although there are marked differences in attitudes to different groups of the unemployed. Few people blame the poor or unemployed for their own misfortunes, with many seeing these as resulting from structural features of the economy and the society in which it is embedded. A wide variety of solutions are seen as necessary to solve the unemployment problem that is now accepted by many as a permanent feature of the Australian economy. The welfare system is seen as having a role to play in reinforcing the work ethic among the unemployed, as part of the task of balancing rights and responsibilities. There is strong support for the view that existing levels of support are too high in some cases, but too low in others, suggesting a further move away from standardised benefits.

Intertwined between the layers of experience and knowledge that define public consciousness is a sense of alienation and powerlessness in which a gulf has opened up between the values and priorities of ordinary Australians and those in positions of political power and influence. This general disenchantment with the options that emerge from the political process is reflected in a number of developments that threaten the continued viability of the major political parties. Beneath the unspoken voice of the silent majority lies a sense of disillusionment with politics that reflects a more deeply seated frustration with the ends and means of neo-liberal economic policies. While these concerns are widely shared in the community, the unemployed in particular have missed out on the benefits of employment as a source of prosperity and security, a means of socialisation and an expression of identity.

These problems have been reinforced by the punitive moral overtones of the neo-liberal welfare reform agenda. These are reflected in the idea that getting the unemployed back into work requires changes to the incentive structures and 'morality signals' conveyed by the welfare system, rather than through introducing new policies to create extra jobs through a range of macroeconomic and labour market initiatives. Seen in this light, the idea of mutual obligation, the idea that those who receive social support should be required to 'give something back', is part of a broader attempt to blame the victims for the government's failure to solve the unemployment problem. While there is strong support for many aspects of mutual obligation as it affects the conditions of welfare eligibility, there is also a sense that the idea should be applied selectively and take account of people's circumstances.

Welfare reform alone is not capable of achieving anything other than a marginal impact on unemployment. This suggests that in seeking solutions, it is necessary to look elsewhere. Many of the problems that emerge in the welfare system are a consequence of factors and processes operating in the economy, often in the labour market. Resolving these problems means addressing their causes at source and this will involve reforms that are external to the welfare system – even though they will have implications for aspects of its design and operation.

These ideas reflect an approach that combines welfare reform with changes in the role of government and the institutional structure of the labour market. The ideas set out in this chapter are only sketched in general terms and require further detailed development. Research has an important role to play in highlighting the underlying issues, identifying the size of key parameters, placing reform on the policy agenda and keeping it there. Research findings need to be disseminated in ways that speak to a broad audience without distorting the underlying arguments and ideas. The media have an important role to play in conveying research ideas and in finding ways that can form the basis of a broad reflective evaluation of ideas and arguments. Only when these processes affect community attitudes can a coalition for change be built around a sustainable re-constituted system founded on the legitimacy associated with community support.

This will take time. The successful attainment of the ends of welfare identified here will depend critically upon establishing a practical timetable that reflects the delays and constraints associated with changing attitudes towards work, well-being and the welfare system. A program designed to address these issues does not fit within the normal political cycle and the political process will need to adjust to this reality.

Appendix: Details of the Coping with Economic and Social Change (CESC) Survey

Purpose and structure

The CESC survey was designed to elicit information on Australian attitudes to economic and social change, the causes of a range of social issues such as poverty and unemployment and the policy responses to them, specifically the role of welfare reform. Further information about the survey design, methodology, sampling and administration is provided in Eardley, Saunders and Evans (2000) and Saunders, Thomson and Evans (2001).

The questionnaire contained four main sections, dealing with each of the following topics:

- Standards of living and perceptions of change;
- Perceptions of poverty and its causes;
- The causes of and solutions to unemployment; and
- Personal characteristics of the respondent.

The first section of the questionnaire asked about people's perceptions of changes in their standard of living in the past and future and their overall level of satisfaction with their present standard of living. Questions were asked on the level of happiness, how people were managing on their weekly family income, and their views of whether various items are considered necessary in order to have an acceptable standard of living. The respondents' attitudes towards change were also explored in this section.

The next section of the questionnaire dealt with the issue of poverty. Respondents were asked about their opinions on what it means to be poor, what they thought were the main causes of poverty and how poverty should be alleviated. This was followed by a series of questions concerning perceptions about the causes of unemployment, views on the tasks various groups of unemployed people (and sole parents) should be required to undertake in order to receive welfare benefits, and what the government should do to address the unemployment problem. The final section of the questionnaire collected information on the personal characteristics of the respondents, including age, sex, family status, housing tenure, labour force status, health status, educational attainment, job security, level of income and voting behaviour.

Sampling frame and methods

Initial piloting of the survey instrument took place in Sydney during August and September 1998. This process produced a satisfactory response rate and indicated that respondents, when asked, expressed no great difficulty in completing the questionnaire. After some minor revisions, a random sample of just over four thousand (4041) individuals was extracted from the electoral roll microfiche sheets, and the survey questionnaire was mailed to these people at the end of April 1999. The sampling frame for the CESC survey was the February 1999 microfiche version of the National Electoral Roll. The roll had been updated in the run-up to the federal election held in October 1998 and thus provided a good sampling frame of the adult (aged 18 and over) population, given that voting is compulsory in Australia.

A modified version of Dillman's method was used to conduct the survey (Dillman, 1978). Initially, a questionnaire and an accompanying letter were sent to all selected individuals. One week later, a reminder postcard was sent to the whole sample, to thank those who had returned the survey and to remind others to do so. Three weeks after that, a replacement questionnaire and another reminder letter were sent to the non-respondents.

By the time that the final deadline for receipt of completed responses was reached at the end of August (effectively the end of June, since very few responses were received in July and August), a total of 2403 completed surveys had been returned. A total of 172 questionnaires (4.2 per cent) of those distributed were returned unopened and marked 'Not known at this Address'. Although this might have included some non-respondents, the number is surprisingly high given that the electoral roll had been so recently updated. Deducting these from the original sample gives an adjusted sample of 3869. Of these, a total of 164 people refused to participate in the survey, either by ringing to indicate this or by simply returning an uncompleted questionnaire. The effective response rate was thus just over 62 per cent of the adjusted sample – a fairly high response rate for a postal survey of this kind (Table A.1).

Sample characteristics

The representativeness of the CESC sample was assessed by comparing its characteristics with those of the general population. Table A.2 compares the age–sex profile of the CESC sample described in Table A.1 with that of the population at the time of the 1996 Census. The results indicate that, as compared with the population as a whole, the CESC sample contains fewer younger people

Table A.1 Survey sample and responses

	Number
Questionnaires distributed	4041
Returned 'not known at this address'	172
Adjusted sample	3869
Refusals	164
Completed surveys returned	2403

Response rate = 2403/3869 = 62.1 per cent.

Table A.2 The composition of the CESC sample and the general population

	Males		Females	
Age	Census 1996	Coping with Economic and Social Change	Census 1996	Coping with Economic and Social Change
	Percentages			
18–24	14.3	8.1	13.4	10.0
25–29	10.4	6.9	10.1	11.2
30–34	10.7	8.5	10.4	8.2
35–39	10.8	10.9	10.6	11.7
40–44	10.1	11.7	9.9	11.7
45–49	9.8	10.6	9.3	9.5
50–54	7.7	10.1	7.2	8.8
55–59	6.3	8.4	5.9	5.8
60–64	5.3	6.6	5.1	6.1
65+	14.5	18.3	18.1	17.0
Total	100.0	100.0	100.0	100.0
N	6 431 470	1022	6 732 428	1185

Source: CESC survey and ABS (1997a).

(aged 18 to 34) particularly males, and correspondingly more older people (aged 50 and over). There is also a tendency for the sample to contain a somewhat larger proportion (53.7 per cent) of females than the population percentage of 51.1 per cent.

Table A.3 compares the characteristics of the sample and the general population across a number of dimensions including, in addition to age and sex, labour force status, family type, (gross) family income, birthplace and housing tenure. As well as those differences already highlighted in Table A.2, compared with Census data, the CESC sample contains more people who are not in the labour force and fewer who are either working or unemployed and looking for work. There is also an under-representation of single people and an over-representation of those on very low incomes.

The tendency for the sample to contain too few people in employment and too many outside of the labour force is understandable given the time commitments of people in employment and is a common feature of surveys of this kind (Dillman, 1978; de Vaus, 1995; Papadakis, 1990). It is, however, a feature of the sample that should be kept in mind when assessing some of the results – particularly those relating to the different experiences and attitudes of employed and unemployed people.

Although there are some definitional differences that mean that some of the sample and Census categories included in Table A.1 are not strictly comparable, the evidence suggests that the CESC sample is not equally representative of all groups in the population. (The main area where the difference between Census and CESC survey categories make direct comparisons difficult is household type.

Appendix

Table A.3 Characteristics of the sample compared with 1996 Census data (percentages)

	Census 1996	CESC Survey (unweighted)[a]	CESC Survey (weighted)
Gender			
Male	48.6	47.6	48.6
Female	51.4	52.4	51.4
Age bracket			
18–39 years	45.1	38.0	45.1
40–64 years	38.3	44.4	38.3
65 & over	16.7	17.6	16.7
Labour force status			
Self-employed	5.6	11.6	5.6
Employee	52.9	44.4	52.6
Unemployed	5.6	2.8	5.6
NILF	35.9	41.3	36.2
Household type			
Lives alone	14.8	12.2	13.0
Couple only	24.3	30.5	29.0
Couple & kids	43.1	37.9	35.6
Sole parent	8.0	4.8	5.0
Live with parents	[b]	8.1	9.9
Other	9.8	6.5	7.5
Family income ($ per week)			
< = 0	0.6	1.2	1.0
1–199	6.4	10.3	10.8
200–299	9.4	7.4	6.9
300–399	7.9	11.1	11.0
400–499	8.7	8.9	8.6
500–599	7.1	8.4	8.7
600–699	8.0	6.9	7.2
700–799	6.4	5.7	5.7
800–999	12.2	9.7	9.8
1000–1499	19.0	16.4	16.4
1500–1999	7.3	8.9	9.4
2000+	6.9	5.1	4.5
Birthplace			
Australia	77.7	75.3	76.1
Other English-speaking	6.3	12.0	11.6
Other	16.0	12.7	12.3
Housing tenure			
Owner (or buyer)	70.1	72.2	68.7
Renter	23.1	18.4	20.0
Other	6.8	9.4	11.2

Notes: (a) The unweighted sample size varies between 2,170 and 2,357 according to the variable. (b) Not available from the Census data.

Source: CESC survey and *Census of Population and Housing: Household Sample File*, ABS Catalogue No. 2037.0.

The single question about household type included on the CESC questionnaire produced responses that could not be matched with the more complex Census categories). Table A.3 shows, for example, that people living alone and sole parent households are under-represented in the CESC, as are people living in private rental accommodation. These differences are important, because households containing only a single adult and those renting privately are known to face an above-average risk of poverty and are generally susceptible to low income and/or deprivation (Saunders and Matheson, 1991; Saunders, 1996b).

In order to correct for any biases due to differential response rates, the sample data were weighted using a set of weights constructed from the Census data on which Table A.3 is based. When these weights are applied to the CESC sample, the sample percentages are as shown in the third column of Table A.3. The effect is to bring the composition of the sample much closer to – in some instances identical to – that of the general population, and for this reason the comparisons presented in the remainder of the Appendix (but not those in the main text) are based on the weighted sample.

Income comparisons

Survey respondents were asked to provide information about their incomes and this was used to compare the income distribution among the sample with that for the population as a whole. There is always a danger that seeking information about income will cause a large non-response, not only to the income question itself, but also to the questionnaire as a whole. These effects can be minimised by placing the income question towards the end of the questionnaire and by asking respondents to identify their income within a range rather than providing a precise figure. Although both procedures were followed, the income question still elicited a rather high non-response, with almost 10 per cent of the sample (233 respondents) not answering.

The income question itself asked for information about before-tax (gross) family income from all sources, in brackets of $100 a week up to $1000, $250 a week from there up to $2000, $500 a week between $2000 and $2500, and over $2500 a week. The corresponding annual amounts were also provided in the question. In order to derive an estimate of the income distribution from the responses, the income of each respondent was first set at the mid-point of the relevant income bracket into which their response fell. As a sensitivity check, the income distribution was re-estimated with all responses set at the lower, and then the upper, end of each bracket, although this made little difference to the estimated distribution and does not markedly affect the results. Incomes in the lowest income bracket (less than $100 a week) were set at $50 a week, while those in the top bracket ($2500 a week or more) were set at $3000 a week.

An estimate of the distribution of income among the whole population was derived from data for the distribution of current (weekly) gross income in 1996 as reported in the ABS *Survey of Income and Housing Costs, 1996–97* (ABS, 1999a). These ABS data were updated to the June Quarter 1999 by movements in household income taken from the National Accounts and the two income distributions were then derived and compared. (The ABS distributional data were updated to 1999 by movements in a measure of household income that includes total primary income receivable plus social assistance benefits.)

Table A.4 compares the updated ABS income distribution data with an estimate of income distribution derived from the (weighted) CESC data. At $820 a week, the mean survey income is 17 per cent above the corresponding ABS figure of $698. This upward bias exists across the entire distribution. In part, it reflects the crude way in which actual income has been estimated from the survey data by setting respondents' incomes equal to the mid-point of the bracket into which their reported income falls, combined possibly with the treatment of incomes in the open-ended top bracket.

Despite this difference in mean incomes, Table A.4 shows the two income distributions to be similar in terms of the income shares of each decile. The main difference occurs in the seventh and eighth deciles (where the CESC sample shows a higher income share than the ABS data) and the top decile (where the opposite occurs). The Gini coefficient (a measure of inequality that varies between zero, when there is no inequality and one, where one person has all the income – see Chapter 7) shows that income inequality based on the CESC sample is about six per cent below that indicated by the updated ABS data.

Defining the value framework variables

The approach used to define the three 'value framework' variables (individualist, collectivist and fatalist) is based upon the responses to the questions shown in Table 3.2. This involved assigning a score to each response category and then summing them to give an combined response score that varies between –6 and +6. Those respondents with a combined score of greater or equal to +2 were then

Table A.4 Survey and population estimates of the income distribution

Decile	CESC sample Income share %	CESC sample Minimum income $	CESC sample Mean income $	Updated ABS data Income share %	Updated ABS data Minimum income $	Updated ABS data Mean income $
First	1.5	0	122	1.4	0	96
Second	3.0	150	245	2.9	185	204
Third	4.3	350	354	4.1	232	283
Fourth	5.7	450	467	5.3	325	368
Fifth	7.1	550	580	6.7	417	470
Sixth	8.6	650	709	8.4	530	586
Seventh	11.0	850	909	10.5	659	734
Eighth	14.3	1125	1167	13.4	831	936
Ninth	17.9	1375	1473	17.6	1063	1230
Tenth	26.5	1625	2181	29.7	1446	2070
Overall mean			$820			$698
Gini Coefficient	0.404			0.430		

Sources: See text.

assigned to each value category after eliminating the overlaps between the three categories, as explained in Chapter 3. Setting the cut-off at a combined score of +2 implies that inclusion in a particular value category required respondents to 'Agree' with at least two of the categorising statements shown in Table 3.2 with no 'Disagrees' at all, or for a single 'Disagree' to be offset by at least one 'Strongly agree' response, or for a 'Strongly disagree' to be offset by two 'Strongly agree' responses. It is not possible to disagree with two or more of the statements and exceed the cut-off score of +2.

A stricter definition can be achieved by setting the combined cut-off score at greater or equal to +3. This would exclude anyone who responded with any 'Disagree' or 'Strongly disagree' except where one 'Disagree' was accompanied by two 'Strongly agree' responses. This criteria results in a large loss in the number of usable responses, as indicated in Table A.5. In this case, the numbers decline to 88 individualists, 270 collectivists and 224 fatalists. The number of overlaps among the three value variables (also shown in Table A.5) further reduces the sample size, as indicated.

Table A.5 Numbers satisfying alternative value variable cut-off scores

	Combined score = + 2 or greater	Combined score = + 3 or greater
Individualists (I): total	219	120
Collectivists (C): total	605	367
Fatalists (F): total	538	322
I and C	59	21
I and F	51	22
C and F	236	87
I and C and F	25	11
Neither I nor C nor F	806	1713
Individualists (I*): excluding overlaps[a]	219 – 59 – 51 + 25 = 134	120 – 21 – 22 +11 = 88
Collectivists (C*): excluding overlaps[a]	605 – 59 – 236 + 25 = 335	367 – 21 – 87 +11 = 270
Fatalists (F*): excluding overlaps[a]	538 – 51 – 236 + 25 = 276	322 – 22 – 87 +11 = 224

Note: (a) The numbers in each category after excluding overlaps can be derived from the following formula:
I* = I – {I and C} – {I and F} + {I and C and F}.

References

Abel-Smith, B. (1984), 'The Study and Definition of Poverty: Values and Social Aims', in G. Sarpelloni (ed.), *Understanding Poverty*, Istituto Internazionale, Rome, pp. 68–86.

ACT Poverty Task Group (2000), *Telling the Story. Report on the ACT Poverty Task Group Community Consultation*, ACT Council of Social Service, Canberra.

Aghion, P., Caroli, E. and Garcia-Peñalosa, C. (1999), 'Inequality and Growth: The Perspective of the New Growth Theories', *Journal of Economic Literature*, Vol. XXXVII, pp. 1615–60.

Altman, J. C. (1997), 'The CDEP Scheme in a New Policy Environment: Options for Change?' *CAEPR Discussion Paper No. 148*, Centre for Aboriginal Economic Policy Research, Australian National University, Canberra.

Altman, J. C. and Gray, M. C. (2000), 'The Effects of the CDEP Scheme on the Economic Status of Indigenous Australians: Some Analyses Using the 1996 Census', *CAEPR Discussion Paper No. 200*, Centre for Aboriginal Economic Policy Research, Australian National University, Canberra.

Altman, J. and Hunter, B. (1998), 'Indigenous Poverty', in R. Fincher and J. Niewenhuysen (eds), *Australian Poverty: Then and Now*, Melbourne University Press, Melbourne, pp. 238–57.

Amiel, Y. and Cowell, F. (1999), *Thinking About Inequality. Personal Judgements and Income Distribution*, Cambridge University Press, Cambridge.

Argy, F. (1998), *Australia at the Crossroads. Radical Free Market or a Progressive Liberalism?* Allen & Unwin, Sydney.

Atkinson, A. B. (1970), 'On the Measurement of Inequality', *Journal of Economic Theory*, Vol. 2, pp. 244–63.

Atkinson, A. B. (1989), 'How Should We Measure Poverty? Some Conceptual Issues', in A. B. Atkinson, *Poverty and Social Security*, Harvester Wheatsheaf, London, pp. 7–24.

Atkinson, A. B. (1995a), *Incomes and the Welfare State. Essays on Britain and Europe*, Cambridge University Press, Cambridge.

Atkinson, A. B. (1995b), *Public Economics in Action: The Basic Income/Flat Tax Proposal*, Oxford University Press, Oxford.

Atkinson, A. B. (1996a), 'Seeking to Explain the Distribution of Income', in J. Hills (ed.) *New Inequalities: The Changing Distribution of Income and Wealth in the United Kingdom*, Cambridge University Press, Cambridge, pp. 19–48.

Atkinson, A. B. (1996b), 'The Case For a Participation Income', *Political Quarterly*, Vol. 67, pp. 67–70.

Atkinson, A. B. (1997), 'Bringing Income Distribution in From the Cold', *Economic Journal*, Vol. 107, pp. 297–321.

Atkinson, A. B. (1998a), 'Social Exclusion, Poverty and Unemployment', in A. B. Atkinson and J. Hills (eds), *Exclusion, Employment and Opportunity*, CASEpaper 4, Centre for the Analysis of Social Exclusion, London School of Economics, pp. 1–20.

Atkinson, A. B. (1998b), *Poverty in Europe*, Blackwell, Oxford.

Atkinson, A. B. (1999a), *The Economic Consequences of Rolling Back the Welfare State*, MIT Press, Cambridge, Massachusetts.

Atkinson, A. B. (1999b), 'Is Rising Inequality Inevitable? A Critique of the Transatlantic Consensus', *WIDER Annual Lectures, No. 3*, World Institute for Development Economics Research, Helsinki.

Atkinson, A. B. (1999c), 'Beveridge and the 21st Century', in R. Walker (ed.) *Ending Child Poverty. Popular Welfare for the 21st Century?* Policy Press, Bristol, pp. 29–34.

Atkinson, A. B., Gardiner, K., Lechene, V. and Sutherland, H. (1998), 'Comparing Poverty Rates Across Countries: A Case Study of France and the United Kingdom', in S. P. Jenkins, A. Kapteyn and B. van Praag (eds), *The Distribution of Welfare and Household Production: International Perspectives*, Cambridge University Press, Cambridge, pp. 50–74.

Atkinson, A. B. and Mogensen, G. V. (1993), *Welfare and Work Incentives*, Clarendon Press, Oxford.

Atkinson, A. B., Rainwater, L. and Smeeding, T. M. (1995), *Income Distribution in OECD Countries: The Evidence from the Luxembourg Income Study (LIS)*, OECD, Paris.

Australian Bureau of Statistics (ABS) (1988), *Alternative Working Arrangements Australia 1986*, Catalogue No. 6342.0, ABS, Canberra.

ABS (1992), *The Effects of Government Benefits and Taxes on Household Income, 1988–89*, Catalogue No. 6537.0, ABS, Canberra.

ABS (1995a), *Persons Employed at Home. Australia, 1995*, Catalogue No. 6275.0, ABS, Canberra.

ABS (1995b), *A Provisional Framework for Household Income, Consumption, Saving and Wealth*, Catalogue No. 6549.0, ABS, Canberra.

ABS (1996), *Household Expenditure Survey: The Effects of Government Benefits and Taxes on Household Income, 1993–94*, Catalogue No. 6537.0, ABS, Canberra.

ABS (1997a), *Census of Population and Housing. Selected Social and Housing Characteristics, Australia 1996*, Catalogue No. 2015.0, ABS, Canberra.

ABS (1997b), *Australian Social Trends 1997*, Catalogue No. 4102.0, ABS, Canberra.

ABS (1998), *Australian Social Trends, 1998*, Catalogue No. 4102.0, ABS, Canberra.

ABS (1999a), *Survey of Income and Housing Costs 1996–97*, confidentialised unit record file, ABS, Canberra.

ABS (1999b), *Australian Social Trends, 1999*, Catalogue No. 4102.0, ABS, Canberra.

ABS (1999c), 'Decline of the Standard Working Week', in *Australian Social Trends, 1999*, Catalogue No. 4102.0, ABS, Canberra, pp. 105–8.

ABS (2000a), *Australian Social Trends, 2000*, Catalogue No. 4102.0, ABS, Canberra.

References

ABS (2000b), *1998–99 Household Expenditure Survey, Australia. Summary of Results*, Catalogue No. 6530.0, ABS, Canberra.

ABS (2000c), *Household Expenditure Survey. Australia. User Guide 1998–99*, Catalogue No. 6527.0, ABS, Canberra.

ABS (2001a), *2001 Year Book Australia*, Catalogue No. 1301.0, ABS, Canberra.

ABS (2001b), 'Unemployment and Supplementary Measures of Underutilised Labour', in *The Labour Force. Australia, February 2001*, Catalogue No. 6302.0, pp. 3–10.

ABS (2001c), *1999–2000 Income Distribution Australia*, Catalogue No. 6523.0, ABS, Canberra.

Baldry, E. and Vinson, T. (1998), 'The Current Obsession With Reducing Taxes', *Just Policy*, No. 13, pp. 3–9.

Barrett, G., Crossley, T. and Worswick, C. (2000a), 'Consumption and Income Inequality in Australia', in *Facts and Fancies of Human Development, Occasional Paper 1/2000*, Academy of the Social Sciences in Australia, Canberra, pp. 47–54.

Barrett, G., Crossley, T. and Worswick, C. (2000b), 'Consumption and Income Inequality in Australia', *Economic Record*, Vol. 76, pp. 116–38.

Barry, B. (1998), 'Social Exclusion, Social Isolation and the Distribution of Income', *CASEpaper No. 12*, Centre for the Analysis of Social Exclusion, London School of Economics.

Baumol, W. (1967), 'The Macroeconomics of Unbalanced Growth: The Anatomy of Urban Crisis', *American Economic Review*, Vol. 57, 415–26.

Bean, C. (1991), 'Are Australian Attitudes to Government Different? A Comparison with Five Other Nations', in F. G. Castles (ed.) *Australia Compared. People, Policies and Politics*, Allen & Unwin, Sydney, pp. 74–100.

Beckerman, W. (1979), *Poverty and the Impact of Income Maintenance Programmes in Four Developed Countries*, International Labour Office, Geneva.

Berghman, J. (1997), 'The Resurgence of Poverty and the Struggle Against Exclusion: A New Challenge for Social Security?' *International Social Security Review*, Vol. 50, pp. 3–21.

Beveridge, Lord (1955), *Power and Influence*, The Beechhurst Press, New York.

Bittman, M. (1998), 'The Land of the Lost Weekend? Trends in Free Time Among Working Age Australians, 1974–1992', *Discussion Paper No. 83*, Social Policy Research Centre, University of New South Wales.

Bittman, M., Meagher, G. and Matheson, G. (1998), 'The Changing Boundary Between Home and Market: Australian Trends in Outsourcing Domestic Labour', *Discussion Paper No. 86*, Social Policy Research Centre, University of New South Wales.

Blacklow, P. and Ray, R. (2000), 'A Comparison of Income and Expenditure Inequality Estimates: The Australian Experience, 1975–76 to 1993–94', *Australian Economic Review*, Vol. 33, pp. 317–29.

Blair, T. (1999), 'Beveridge Revisited: A Welfare State for the 21st Century', in R. Walker (ed.), *Ending Child Poverty. Popular Welfare for the 21st Century?* Policy Press, Bristol, pp. 7–18.

Borland, J. (1998), 'Earnings Inequality in Australia: Changes, Causes and Consequences', *Discussion Paper No. 390*, Centre for Economic Policy Research, Australian National University.

Borland, J. (2001), 'Job Stability and Job Security', in J. Borland, B. Gregory and P. Sheehan (eds), *Work Rich, Work Poor. Inequality and Economic Change in Australia*, Centre for Strategic Economic Studies, Victoria University, pp. 142–59.

Borland, J., Gregory, B. and Sheehan, P. (eds) (2001), *Work Rich, Work Poor. Inequality and Economic Change in Australia*, Centre for Strategic Economic Studies, Victoria University.

Borland, J. and Kennedy, S. (1998a), 'Dimensions, Structure and History of Australian Unemployment', in G. Debelle and J. Borland (eds), *Unemployment and the Labour Market*, Reserve Bank of Australia, Sydney, pp. 68–99.

Borland, J. and Kennedy, S. (1998b), 'Earnings Inequality in Australia in the 1980s and 1990s', *Discussion Paper No. 389*, Centre for Economic Policy Research, Australian National University.

Borland, J. and Norris, K. (1996), 'Equity', in K. Norris and M. Wooden (eds), *The Changing Australian Labour Market*, Commission Paper No. 11, Economic Planning Advisory Commission, Canberra, pp. 87–106.

Borland, J. and Wilkins, R. (1996), 'Earnings Inequality in Australia', *Economic Record*, Vol. 76, pp. 7–23.

Bourdieu, P. (1998), *Acts of Resistance. Against the Tyranny of the Market*, The New Press, New York.

Bradbury, B. (1993), 'Added, Subtracted or Just Different? Why Do the Wives of Unemployed Men Have Such Low Employment Rates?' *Australian Bulletin of Labour*, Vol. 21, pp. 48–70.

Bradbury, B. (1998), *Middle Class Welfare in Australia*, Reports and Proceedings No. 138, Social Policy Research Centre, University of New South Wales.

Brennan, G. (1993), 'Economic Rationalism: What Does Economics Really Say?' in S. King and P. Lloyd (eds), *Economic Rationalism. Dead End or Way Forward?* Allen & Unwin, Sydney, pp. 2–11.

Bryson, L. (1977), 'Poverty', *Current Affairs Bulletin*, Vol. 54, No. 5, pp. 4–17.

Bryson, L. and Winter, I. (2002), 'From Job Abundance to Job Scarcity: Unemployment, Social Policy and Community Life, 1960s–1990s', in P. Saunders and R. Taylor (eds), *The Price of Prosperity. The Economic and Social Costs of Unemployment*, University of New South Wales Press, Sydney, forthcoming.

Burbidge, A. and Sheehan, P. (2001), 'The Polarisation of Families', in J. Borland, B. Gregory and P. Sheehan (eds), *Work Rich, Work Poor. Inequality and Economic Change in Australia*, Centre for Strategic Economic Studies, Victoria University, pp. 119–41.

Cass, B. (1986), *The Case for Review of Aspects of the Australian Social Security System*, Background/Discussion Paper No. 1, Department of Social Security, Canberra.

Cass, B. (1994), 'Social Security Policy into the 21st Century', in J. Disney and L. Briggs (eds), *Social Security Policy: Issues and Options*, AGPS, Canberra, pp. 15–27.

Cass, B. and McClelland, A. (1989), 'Changing the Terms of the Welfare Debate: Redefining the Purpose and Structure of the Australian Social Security System', in P. Saunders and A. Jamrozik (eds), *Social Policy for Australia: What Future for the Welfare State?* Reports and Proceedings No. 79, Social Policy Research Centre, University of New South Wales, pp. 55–77.

Castles, F. G. (1985), *The Working Class and Welfare. Reflections on the Political Development of the Welfare State in Australia and New Zealand, 1890–1980*, Allen & Unwin, Sydney.

Castles, F. G. (1994), 'The Wage Earners' Welfare State Revisited: Refurbishing the Established Model of Australian Social Protection, 1893–93', *Australian Journal of Social Issues*, 29, pp. 120–45.

Castles, F. G. (1996), 'Needs-Based Strategies of Social Protection in Australia and New Zealand', in G. Esping-Andersen (ed.), *Welfare States in Transition. National Adaptations in Global Economies*, Sage Publications, London, pp. 88–115.

Castles, F. G. (2001), 'A Farewell to the Australian Welfare State', *Eureka Street*, Vol. 11, pp. 29–31.

Centre for the Analysis of Social Exclusion (2001), *Indicators of Progress. A Discussion of Approaches to Monitor the Government's Strategy to Tackle Poverty and Social Exclusion*, CASEreport No. 13, Centre for the Analysis of Social Exclusion, London School of Economics.

Chapman, B. (1999), 'Could Increasing the Skills of the Jobless be the Solution to Australian Unemployment?' in S. Richardson (ed.), *Reshaping the Labour Market. Regulation Efficiency and Equality in Australia*, Cambridge University Press, Melbourne, pp. 176–99.

Chapman, B. and Kapuscinski, C. A. (2000), *Avoiding Recessions and Australian Long-Term Unemployment*, Discussion Paper No. 29, The Australia Institute, Canberra.

Citro, C. F. and Michael, R. T. (eds) (1995), *Measuring Poverty. A New Approach*, National Academy Press, Washington DC.

Clark, A. E. and Oswald, A. J. (1994), 'Unhappiness and Unemployment', *Economic Journal*, Vol. 104, pp. 648–59.

Commission of Inquiry into Poverty (1975), *First Main Report. Poverty in Australia*, AGPS, Canberra.

Commission on Social Justice (1994), *Social Justice: Strategies for National Renewal*, Vintage Books, London.

Commonwealth Bureau of Census and Statistics (CBCS) (1973), *Income Distribution, 1968–69. Part 1*, Reference No. 17.6, CBCS, Canberra.

Commonwealth of Australia (1994), *Working Nation. Policies and Programs (White Paper)*, AGPS, Canberra.

Cox, E. (1998), 'Measuring Social Capital As Part of Progress and Well-being', in R. Eckersley (ed.), *Measuring Progress. Is Life Getting Better?* CSIRO Publishing, Collingwood, pp. 157–67.

Cox, J. (2001), *Middle Class Welfare*, New Zealand Business Roundtable, Wellington.

Danziger, S. and Weinberg, D. (1986), *Fighting Poverty: What Works and What Doesn't*, Harvard University Press, Cambridge, Massachusetts.

Dawkins, P. (1996), 'The Distribution of Work in Australia', *Economic Record*, Vol. 72, pp. 272–86.

Dawkins, P. (1999), 'A Plan to Cut Unemployment in Australia: An Elaboration on the Five Economists' Letter to the Prime Minister, 28th October 1998', *Mercer Melbourne Institute Quarterly Bulletin of Economic Trends*, pp. 48–57.

Deaton, A. and Muellbauer, J. (1980), *Economics and Consumer Behaviour*, Cambridge University Press, Cambridge.

de Vaus, D. (1995), *Surveys in Social Research* (4th edition), Allen & Unwin, Sydney.
Department of Employment, Education and Training (1995), *Australia's Workforce 2005: Jobs in the Future*, AGPS, Canberra.
Department of Family and Community Services (2001), *Income Support and Related Statistics: A 10-year Compendium 1989–1999*, Occasional Paper No. 1, Department of Family and Community Services, Canberra.
Dillman, D. (1978), *Mail and Telephone Surveys: The Total Design Method*, Wiley, New York.
Donnison, A. (1998), *Policy for a Just Society*, Macmillan, London.
Eardley, T. (2000), 'Working But Poor? Low Pay and Poverty in Australia', *Economic and Labour Relations Review*, Vol. 11, pp. 308–38.
Eardley, T. and Bradbury, B. (1997), 'Not Waving But Drowning? Low Incomes and Poverty Amongst the Self-employed', in M. Bittman (ed.), *Poverty in Australia: Dimensions and Policies*, Reports and Proceedings No. 135, Social Policy Research Centre, University of New South Wales, pp. 39–65.
Eardley, T. and Matheson, G. (1999), 'Australian Attitudes to Unemployment and Unemployed People', *Discussion Paper No. 102*, Social Policy Research Centre, University of New South Wales.
Eardley, T., Saunders, P. and Evans, K. (2000), 'Community Attitudes Towards Unemployment, Activity Testing and Mutual Obligation', *Australian Bulletin of Labour*, Vol. 26, pp. 211–35.
Eardley, T., Saunders, P., Evans, C. and Matheson, G. (2000), *Community Attitudes Towards Unemployment, Activity Testing and Mutual Obligation. Final Report*, Social Policy Research Centre, University of New South Wales.
Eckersley, R. (ed.) (1998), *Measuring Progress. Is Life Getting Better?* CSIRO, Melbourne.
Eckersley, R. (1999), *Quality of Life in Australia: An Analysis of Public Perceptions*, Discussion Paper 23, The Australia Institute, Canberra.
Eckersley, R. (2000), 'The Mixed Blessings of Material Progress: Diminishing Returns in the Pursuit of Happiness', *Journal of Happiness Studies*, Vol. 1, pp. 267–92.
Economic and Social Research Council (1997), *Thematic Priorities Update 1997*, Economic and Social Research Council, London.
Ellwood, D. (1999), 'The Impact of the Earned Income Tax Credit and Other Social Policy Changes on Work and Marriage in the United States', *Australian Social Policy*, 1999/1, pp. 75–113.
Ellwood, D. (2001), 'The US Vision of Work Based Reform: Promise, Prospects and Pitfalls', Plenary Address to the National Social Policy Conference, University of New South Wales, July.
Esping-Andersen, G. (1990), *The Three Worlds of Welfare Capitalism*, Polity Press, Cambridge.
Esping-Andersen, G. (1997), 'Welfare States at the End of the Century: The Impact of Labour Market, Family and Demographic Change', in *Family, Market and Community. Equity and Efficiency in Social Policy*, OECD, Paris, pp. 63–80.
Esping-Andersen, G. (1999), *Social Foundations of Postindustrial Economies*, Oxford University Press, Oxford.

Feagin, J. R. (1972), 'Poverty: We Still Believe That God Helps Those Who Help Themselves', *Psychology Today*, Vol. 6, pp. 101–29.
Feather, N. T. (1974), 'Explanations of Poverty in Australian and American Samples. The Person, Society and Fate', *Australian Journal of Psychology*, Vol. 26, pp. 199–216.
Feather, N. (1990), *The Psychological Impact of Unemployment*, Springer-Verlag, New York.
Feather, N. T. (1997), 'Economic Deprivation and the Psychological Impact of Unemployment', *Australian Psychologist*, Vol. 32, pp. 37–45.
Fincher, R. and Saunders, P. (eds) (2001), *Creating Unequal Futures? Rethinking Poverty, Inequality and Disadvantage*, Allen & Unwin, Sydney.
Flatau, P., Galea, J. and Petridis, R. (2000), 'Mental Health and Wellbeing and Unemployment', *Australian Economic Review*, Vol. 33, pp. 161–81.
Forma, P. (1999), *Interests, Institutions and the Welfare State. Studies on Public Opinion Towards the Welfare State*, Research Report 102, National Research and Development Centre for Welfare and Health (STAKES), Helsinki.
Friedman, M. (1957), *A Theory of the Consumption Function*, Princeton University Press, Princeton.
Galbraith, K. (1996), *The Good Society. The Humane Agenda*, Houghton Mifflin, Boston.
Garfinkel, I. and Haveman, R. (1977), *Earnings Capacity, Poverty and Inequality*, Academic Press, New York.
Giddens, A. (1994), *Beyond Left and Right. The Future of Radical Politics*, Polity Press, Cambridge.
Giddens, A. (1998), *The Third Way. The Renewal of Social Democracy*, Polity Press, Cambridge.
Giddens, A. (2000), *The Third Way and Its Critics*, Polity Press, Cambridge.
Glennerster, H. (2000), 'US Poverty Studies and Poverty Measurement: The Past Twenty-five Years', *CASEpaper No. 42*, Centre for the Analysis of Social Exclusion, London School of Economics.
Goedhart, T., Halberstadt, V., Kapteyn, A. and van Praag, B. (1977), 'The Poverty Line; Concept and Measurement', *Journal of Human Resources*, Vol. 4, pp. 503–20.
Goodin, R. (2001), 'False Principles of Welfare Reform', *Australian Journal of Social Issues*, Vol. 36, pp. 189–205.
Gordon, D. and Pantazis, C. (1997), 'The Public's Perception of Necessities and Poverty', in D. Gordon and C. Pantazis (eds), *Breadline Britain in the 1990s*, Ashgate, Aldershot, pp. 71–96.
Gregory, R. G. (1993), 'Aspects of Australian and US Living Standards: The Disappointing Decades 1970–1990', *Economic Record*, Vol. 69, pp. 61–76.
Gregory, R. G. (1999), 'Children and the Changing labour Market: Joblessness in Families With Dependent Children', presented to the Conference on *Labour Market Trends and Family Policies: Implications for Children*, Australian National University, Canberra.
Gregory, R. G. and Daly, A. E. (1997), 'Welfare and Economic Progress of Indigenous Men of Australia and the US 1980–1990', *Economic Record*, Vol. 73, pp. 101–19.

Gregory, R. G. and Hunter, B. (1995), 'The Macroeconomy and the Growth of Ghettos and Urban Poverty in Australia' *Discussion Paper No. 325*, Centre for Economic Policy Research, Australian National University.

Gregory, R. G. and Hunter, B. (1996), 'Increasing Regional Inequality and the Decline of Manufacturing', in P. Sheehan, B. Grewal and M. Kumnick (eds), *Dialogues on Australia's Future. In Honour of the Late Professor Ronald Henderson*, Centre for Strategic Economic Studies, Victoria University of Technology, pp. 307–24.

Gregory, R. G., Klug, E. and Martin, Y. M. (1999), 'Labour Market Deregulation, Relative Wages and the Social Security System', in S. Richardson (ed.), *Reshaping the Labour Market. Regulation Efficiency and Equality in Australia*, Cambridge University Press, Melbourne, pp. 200–22.

Gregory, R. G. and Sheehan, P. (1998), 'Poverty and the Collapse of Full Employment', in R. Fincher and J. Niewenhuysen (eds), *Australian Poverty: Then and Now*, Melbourne University Press, Melbourne, pp. 103–26.

Gruen, F. (1989), 'Australia's Welfare State: Rearguard or Avant Garde?' in P. Saunders and A. Jamrozik (eds), *Social Policy for Australia: What Future for the Welfare State?* Reports and Proceedings No. 79, Social Policy Research Centre, University of New South Wales, pp. 33–54.

Gruen, F. (1996), 'The Quality of Life and Economic Performance', in P. Sheehan, B. Grewal and M. Kumnick (eds), *Dialogues on Australia's Future. In Honour of the Late Professor Ronald Henderson*, Centre for Strategic Economic Studies, Victoria University of Technology, pp. 363–84.

Hagenaars, A. (1986), *The Perception of Poverty*, North Holland, Amsterdam.

Harding, A. (1995), 'Non-cash Benefits and the Measurement of Poverty, May 1995', paper presented to the *24th Conference of Economists*, Adelaide.

Harding, A. (1997), 'The Suffering Middle: Trends in Income Inequality in Australia, 1982 to 1993–94', *Australian Economic Review*, Vol. 30, pp. 341–58.

Harding, A., Lloyd, R. and Greenwell, H. (2001), *Financial Disadvantage in Australia 1990 to 2000: The Persistence of Poverty in a Decade of Growth*, The Smith Family, Sydney.

Harding, A. and Richardson, S. (1998), 'Unemployment and Income Distribution', in G. Debelle and J. Borland (eds), *Unemployment and the Labour Market*, Reserve Bank of Australia, Sydney, pp. 139–64.

Harding, A. and Szukalska, A. (2000a), *Financial Disadvantage in Australia – 1999*, The Smith Family, Sydney.

Harding, A. and Szukalska, A. (2000b), 'Trends in Child Poverty in Australia, 1982 to 1995–96', *Economic Record*, Vol. 76, pp. 236–54.

Harper, R. J. A. (1967), 'Survey of Living Conditions in Melbourne – 1966', *Economic Record*, Vol. 43, pp. 262–88.

Harris, E. and Morrow, M. (2001), 'Unemployment is a Health Hazard: the Health Costs of Unemployment', *Economic and Labour Relations Review*, Vol. 12, pp. 18–31.

Haveman, R. (2000), 'Poverty and the Distribution of Economic Well-Being Since the 1960s', in G. L. Perry and J. Tobin (eds), *Economic Events, Ideas and Policies: The 1960s and After*, The Brookings Institute, Washington DC.

Haveman, R. (2001), 'Welfare Reform in the US: Objectives, Structure and Potential', *The F. H. Gruen Lecture Series*, Australian National University, 14 March.

Haveman, R. and Buron, L. F. (1993), 'Escaping Poverty Through Work – The Problem of Low Earnings Capacity in the United States', *Review of Income and Wealth*, Vol. 39, pp. 141–58.

Headey, B. and Wearing, A. (1992), *Understanding Happiness. A Theory of Subjective Well-Being*, Longman Cheshire, Melbourne.

Henderson, R. F., Harcourt, A. and Harper, R. J. A. (1970), *People in Poverty. A Melbourne Survey*, Institute of Applied Economic and Social Research, Melbourne.

Henman, P. (1999), 'Deconstructing Welfare Dependency: The Case of Australian Welfare Reform', mimeo, Sociology Department, Macquarie University.

Henman, P. (2000), 'What is Welfare Dependency and What are its Causes? An Examination of Current Government Thinking on Welfare Reform', mimeo, Sociology Department, Macquarie University.

Hills, J. (1998), 'Does Income Mobility Mean that We Do Not Need to Worry about Poverty? in A. B. Atkinson and J. Hills (eds), *Exclusion, Employment and Opportunity*, CASEpaper No. 4, Centre for the Analysis of Social Exclusion, London School of Economics, pp. 31–54.

Hills, J. and Lelkes, O. (1999), 'Social Security, Selective Universalism and Patchwork Redistribution', in R. Jowell et al. (eds), *British Social Attitudes 15th Report*, Ashgate, Aldershot.

Hirsch, F. (1978), *Social Limits to Growth*, Routledge, London.

Howard, J. (1999), 'Building a Stronger and Fairer Australia: Liberalism in Economic Policy and Modern Conservatism in Social Policy', Address to the *Australia Unlimited Roundtable*, Canberra, 4 May.

Howarth, C., Kenway, P., Palmer, G. and Miorelli, R. (1999), *Monitoring Poverty and Social Exclusion, 1999*, New Policy Institute/Joseph Rowntree Foundation, York.

Hunter, B. (1995), *Changes in the Geographic Dispersion of Urban Employment in Australia 1976–1991*, unpublished PhD thesis, Australian National University.

Hunter, B. (2001), 'Tackling Poverty Among Indigenous Australians', in R. Fincher and P. Saunders (eds), *Creating Unequal Futures? Rethinking Poverty, Inequality and Disadvantage*, Allen & Unwin, Sydney, pp. 129–57.

Ignatieff, M. (1994), *The Needs of Strangers*, Vintage, London.

Ingles, D. (1998), 'Older Workers, Disability and Early Retirement in Australia', Background Paper prepared for the Conference on *Income Support, Labour Markets and Behaviour: Research Agenda*, Department of Family and Community Services, Canberra.

Ironmonger, D. (1994), 'The Value of Care and Nurture Provided by Unpaid Household Work', *Family Matters*, No. 37, Australian Institute of Family Studies, Melbourne, pp. 46–51.

Ironmonger, D. (1996), 'Counting Output, Capital Input and Caring Labour: Estimating Gross Household Product', *Feminist Economics*, Vol. 2, pp. 37–64.

Jarvis, S. and Jenkins, S. P. (1995), 'Do the Poor Stay Poor? New Evidence About Income Dynamics from the British Household Panel Survey', *Occasional Paper No. 95*, ESRC Research Centre for Micro-Social Change, University of Essex.

Jarvis, S. and Jenkins, S. P. (1997), 'Low Income Dynamics in 1990s Britain', *Fiscal Studies*, Vol. 18, pp. 123–42.

Jenkins, S. P. (1991a), 'Poverty Measurement and the Within-Household Distribution: Agenda for Action', *Journal of Social Policy*, Vol. 20, pp. 357–83.
Jenkins, S. P. (1991b), 'The Measurement of Income Inequality', in L. Osberg (ed.), *Readings on Economic Inequality*, M. E. Sharpe, New York, pp. 3–38.
Johnson, D. (1998), 'Incorporating Non-cash Income and Expenditure in the Measurement of Inequality and Poverty', in R. Eckersley (ed.), *Measuring Progress. Is Life Getting Better?* CSIRO, Melbourne, pp. 255–66.
Johnson, D., I. Manning, I. and O. Hellwig (1995), *Trends in the Distribution of Cash Income and Non-Cash Benefits. Report to the Department of Prime Minister and Cabinet*, AGPS, Canberra.
Johnson, J. and Taylor, J. (2000), *Growing Apart. A New Look at Poverty in Australia*, Brotherhood of St Laurence, Melbourne.
Jones, A. and Smyth, P. (1999), 'Social Exclusion: A New Framework for Social Policy Analysis', *Just Policy*, Vol. 17, pp. 11–20.
Jones, B. (1990), *Sleepers Wake! Technology and the Future of Work*, Oxford University Press, Melbourne.
Jones, F. L. (1975), 'The Changing Shape of the Australian Income Distribution, 1914–15 to 1968–69', *Australian Economic History Review*, Vol. 15, pp. 21–34.
Kalisch, D. W. (1991), 'The Active Society', *Social Security Journal*, August, pp. 3–9.
Kelley, J., Evans, M. and Dawkins, P. (1998), 'Job Security in the 1990s: How Much is Job Security Worth to Employees?' *Australian Social Monitor*, Vol. 1, pp. 1–7.
Kelley, J. and Zagorsky, K. (1999), 'Changing Attitudes Toward Income Inequality in East and West', *Australian Social Monitor*, Vol. 2, pp. 5–8.
Kelly, P. (1992), *The End of Certainty. The Story of the 1980s*, Allen & Unwin, Sydney.
Kelly, P. (2000), 'Rhetoric is no Remedy for Inequity', *The Australian*, 21 June, p. 13.
King, A. (1991), 'Poverty Measurement in Australia: Towards a New Consensus', *Australian Quarterly*, Vol. 63, pp. 235–46.
Korpi, W. (1985), 'Economic Growth and the Welfare System: Leaky Bucket or Irrigation System?' *European Sociological Review*, Vol. 1, pp. 97–118.
Kwon, H.-J. (1998), *The Welfare State in Korea. The Politics of Legitimation*, Macmillan, Basingstoke.
Lampman, R. J. (1965), 'Approaches to the Reduction of Poverty', *American Economic Review*, Vol. 55, pp. 521–29.
Langmore, J. and Quiggin, J. (1994), *Work For All. Full Employment in the Nineties*, Melbourne University Press, Melbourne.
Latham, M. (1998), *Civilising Global Capital: New Thinking for Australian Labor*, Allen & Unwin, Sydney.
Le Grand, J. (1982), *The Strategy of Equality. Redistribution and the Social Services*, George Allen & Unwin, London.
Lewis, J. (2000), 'Funding Social Science Research in Academia', *Social Policy & Administration*, Vol. 34, pp. 365–76.
Lydall, H. (1968), *The Structure of Earnings*, Oxford University Press, Oxford.
Lyons, M. (2001), *Third Sector. The Contribution of Nonprofit and Cooperative Enterprises in Australia*, Allen & Unwin, Sydney.

Mack, J. and Lansley, S. (1985), *Poor Britain*, George Allen & Unwin, London.
Maddox, G. (1998), 'The Australian Settlement and Australian Political Thought', in P. Smyth and B. Cass (eds) (1998), *Contesting the Australian Way, States, Markets and Civil Society*, Cambridge University Press, Melbourne, pp. 57–68.
Manning, I. (1982), 'The Henderson Poverty Line in Review', *Social Security Journal*, June, pp. 1–13.
Manning, I. (1998), 'Policies: Past and Present', in R. Fincher and J. Niewenhuysen, (eds), *Australian Poverty: Then and Now*, Melbourne University Press, Melbourne, pp. 10–32.
Manning, I. and de Jonge, A. (1996), 'The New Poverty: Causes and Responses', in P. Sheehan, B. Grewal and M. Kumnick (eds), *Dialogues on Australia's Future. In Honour of the Late Professor Ronald Henderson*, Centre for Strategic Economic Studies, Victoria University of Technology, pp. 351–62.
Manning, I. and Saunders, P. (1978), 'On the Reform of Taxation and Social Security in Australia', *The Australian Economic Review*, 1st Quarter, pp. 51–57.
Martin, J. (2000), 'What Works Among Active Labour Market Policies: Evidence from OECD Countries' Experiences', *OECD Economic Studies*, No. 30, pp. 79–113.
McColl, R., Pietsch, L. and Gatenby, J. (2001), 'Household Income, Living Standards and Financial Stress', *Australian Economic Indicators. June 2001*, Catalogue No. 1350.0, ABS, Canberra, pp. 13–32.
McDonald, P. and Brownlee, H. (1994), 'Australian Living Standards: The Next Decade', in J. Disney and L. Briggs (eds), *Social Security Policy: Issues and Options*, AGPS, Canberra, pp. 49–62.
McLean, I. W. and Richardson, S. (1986), 'More or Less Equal? Australian Income Distribution in 1933 and 1981', *Economic Record*, Vol. 62, pp. 67–81.
Mead, L. (ed.) (1997), *The New Paternalism: Supervisory Approaches to Poverty*, The Brookings Institute, Washington DC.
Mead, L. (2000), 'Welfare Reform and the Family: Lessons for America', in Peter Saunders (ed.), *Reforming the Australian Welfare State*, Australian Institute of Family Studies, Melbourne, pp. 44–61.
Meade, J. E. (1984), 'Full Employment, New Technology and the Distribution of Income', *Journal of Social Policy*, Vol. 13, pp. 129–46.
Melbourne Institute of Applied Economic and Social Research (2001), *Australian Social Monitor*, University of Melbourne.
Midgley, J. (1999), 'Growth, Redistribution and Welfare: Toward Social Investment', *Social Service Review*, Vol. 73, pp. 3–21.
Millar, J. (2001), 'Lone Parents, Employment and Welfare Reform in the UK', mimeo, Centre for the Analysis of Social Policy, University of Bath.
Miller, P. (1997), 'The Burden of Unemployment on Family Units: An Overview', *Australian Economic Review*, Vol. 30, pp. 16–30.
Mishel, L., Bernstein, J. and Schmitt, J. (1999), *The State of Working America, 1998–99*, Cornell University Press, Ithaca.
Mitchell, D. (1991), *Income Transfers in Ten Welfare States*, Avebury, Aldershot.
Morrell, S., Page, A. and Taylor, R. (2001), 'Unemployment and Youth Suicide', *Economic and Labour Relations Review*, Vol. 12, pp. 4–17.
Nevile, J. (1998), 'Economic Rationalism: Social Philosophy Masquerading as Economic Science', in P. Smyth and B. Cass (eds) (1998), *Contesting the*

Australian Way, States, Markets and Civil Society, Cambridge University Press, Melbourne, pp. 169-79.

Nevile, J. (2001), 'Should Award Wages Be Frozen?' *Economic Papers,* Vol. 20, pp. 26-35.

Nevile, J. and Saunders, P. (1998), 'Globalization and the Return to Education in Australia', *Economic Record,* Vol. 74, pp. 279-85.

Newman, J. (1999a), *The Future of Welfare in the 21st Century,* Telstra Address to the National Press Club, Canberra, 29 September.

Newman, J. (1999b), *Discussion Paper. The Challenge of Welfare Dependency in the 21st Century,* Department of Family and Community Services, Canberra.

Newton, K. (1998), 'The Welfare State Backlash and the Tax Revolt', in H. Cavanna (ed.), *Challenges to the Welfare State. Internal and External Dynamics for Change,* Edward Elgar, Cheltenham, pp. 98-122.

Nolan, B. (2000), 'Targeting Poverty – The Irish Example', *Australian Social Policy,* 2000/1, pp. 25-41.

Norris, K. and Wooden, M. (eds) (1996), *The Changing Australian Labour Market,* Commission Paper No. 11, Economic Planning Advisory Commission, Canberra.

O'Connor, J. S., Orloff, A. S. and Shaver, S. (1999), *States, Markets, Families. Gender, Liberalism and Social Policy in Australia, Canada, Great Britain and the United States,* Cambridge University Press, Melbourne.

Office of the Economic Planning Advisory Council (1987), *The Social Wage: A Review of Social Expenditures and Redistribution,* Council Paper, No.27, Office of EPAC, Canberra.

Okun, A. (1975), *Equality and Efficiency: The Big Tradeoff,* The Brookings Institution, Washington DC.

Onyx, J. and Bullen, P. (2000), 'Sources of Social Capital', in I. Winter (ed.), *Social Capital and Public Policy in Australia,* Australian Institute of Family Studies, Melbourne, pp. 105-34.

Organisation for Economic Cooperation and Development (OECD) (1981), *The Welfare State in Crisis,* OECD, Paris.

OECD (1982) *The OECD List of Social Indicators,* OECD, Paris.

OECD (1985), *Social Expenditure 1960-1985: Problems of Growth and Control,* OECD, Paris.

OECD (1993), 'Earnings Inequality, Low-paid Employment and Earnings Mobility', in *OECD Employment Outlook July 1993,* OECD, Paris, pp. 59-108.

OECD (1997a), 'Is Job Insecurity on the Increase in OECD Countries?' *OECD Employment Outlook, July 1997,* OECD, Paris, pp. 130-60.

OECD (1997b), *Family, Market and Community. Equity and Efficiency in Social Policy,* OECD, Paris.

OECD (1998a), 'Income Distribution and Poverty in Selected OECD Countries', *OECD Economics Department Working Paper No. 189,* OECD, Paris.

OECD (1998b), *Employment Outlook June 1998,* OECD, Paris.

OECD (1999), *OECD Economic Surveys 1998-99.* Australia, OECD, Paris.

OECD (2000a), *OECD Social Expenditure Database 1960-1997,* OECD, Paris.

OECD (2000b), *OECD Economic Outlook* No. 68, December 2000, OECD, Paris.

OECD (2001), *OECD in Figures. Statistics on the Member Countries*, OECD, Paris.
Osberg, L. (1995), 'The Equity/Efficiency Tradeoff in Retrospect', *Canadian Business Economics*, Vol. 3, pp. 5–20.
Osberg, L. (1998), 'Economic Insecurity', *Discussion Paper No. 88*, Social Policy Research Centre, University of New South Wales.
Papadakis, E. (1990), *Attitudes to State and Private Welfare*, Reports and Proceedings No. 88, Social Policy Research Centre, University of New South Wales.
Pappas, N. (2001), 'Family Income Inequality', in J. Borland, B. Gregory and P. Sheehan (eds), *Work Rich, Work Poor. Inequality and Economic Change in Australia*, Centre for Strategic Economic Studies, Victoria University, pp. 21–39.
Parham, D., Barnes, P., Roberts, P. and Kennett, S. (2000), *Distribution of the Economic Gains of the 1990s*, Productivity Commission, Melbourne.
Pearson, N. (2000a), 'Passive Welfare and the Destruction of Indigenous Society in Australia' in Peter Saunders (ed.), *Reforming the Australian Welfare State*, Australian Institute of Family Studies, Melbourne, pp. 136–55.
Pearson, N. (2000b), *The Light on the Hill. Ben Chifley Memorial Lecture*, Bathurst Panthers League Club, 12 August 2000.
Perry, J. (2000), 'One Language, Three Accents. Welfare Reform in the United States, the United Kingdom and Australia', *Family Matters*, No. 56, pp. 40–47.
Persson, T. and Tabellini, G. (1994), 'Is Inequality Harmful for Growth?' *American Economic Review*, Vol. 84, pp. 600–21.
Piggott, J. and Chapman, B. (1995), 'Costing the Job Compact', *Economic Record*, Vol. 71, pp. 313–28.
Ploug, N. (1995), 'The Welfare State in Liquidation?' *International Social Security Review*, No. 2, pp. 61–71.
Pusey, M. (1991), *Economic Rationalism in Canberra. A Nation-Building State Changes Its Mind*, Cambridge University Press, Melbourne.
Pusey, M. (1993), 'Reclaiming the Middle Ground ... From New Right "Economic Rationalism"', in S. King and P. Lloyd (eds), *Economic Rationalism. Dead End or Way Forward?* Allen & Unwin, Sydney, pp. 12–27.
Pusey, M. (1998), 'Incomes, Standards of Living and Quality of Life: Preliminary Findings from the Middle Australia Project', in R. Eckersley (ed.), *Measuring Progress. Is Life Getting Better?* CSIRO Publishing, Collingwood, pp. 183–97.
Putnam, R. D. (1993), *Making Democracy Work. Civic Traditions in Modern Italy*, Princeton University Press, Princeton, New Jersey.
Putnis, P. (2001), 'Popular Discourses and Images of Poverty and Welfare in the News Media', in R. Fincher and P. Saunders (eds), *Creating Unequal Futures? Rethinking Poverty, Inequality and Disadvantage*, Allen & Unwin, Sydney, pp. 70–101.
Quiggin, J. (2000), 'Human Services and Employment in the Post-industrial Labour Market', in I. O'Connor, P. Smyth and J. Warburton (eds), *Social Work & the Human Services. Challenges and Change*, Longman, pp. 30–44.

Radner, D. (1997), 'Noncash Income, Equivalence Scales, and the Measurement of Economic Well-Being', *Review of Income and Wealth*, Vol. 43, pp. 71–88.

Ramia, G. (1998), *Wage Earners and 'Wage-Earners' Welfare States'. Industrial Relations, Social Policy and Social Protection in Australia and New Zealand, 1890 to 1996*, unpublished PhD thesis, School of Industrial Relations and Organisational Behaviour, University of New South Wales.

Ravallion, M. (1996), 'Issues in Measuring and Modelling Poverty', *Economic Journal*, Vol. 106, pp. 1328–43.

Redmond, G. (1999), 'Income Sharing and Income Distribution', in *Australian Social Trends 1999*, Catalogue No. 4102.0, ABS, Canberra, pp. 129–33.

Reference Group on Welfare Reform (2000a), *Interim Report: Participation Support for a More Equitable Society*, Department of Family and Community Services, Canberra.

Reference Group on Welfare Reform (2000b), *Participation Support for a More Equitable Society. Full Report*, Department of Family and Community Services, Canberra.

Reich, R. B. (1993), *The Work of Nations. Preparing Ourselves for 21st Century Capitalism*, Simon & Schuster, London.

Richardson, S. (1998), 'Progress in the Workplace', in R. Eckersley (ed.), *Measuring Progress. Is Life Getting Better?* CSIRO Publishing, Collingwood, pp. 201–21.

Richardson, S. and Harding, A. (1999), 'Poor Workers? The Link between Low Wages, Low Family Income and the Tax and Transfer Systems', in S. Richardson (ed.) (1998), *Reshaping the Labour Market. Regulation Efficiency and Equality in Australia*, Cambridge University Press, Melbourne, pp. 122–58.

Ringen, S. (1987), *The Possibility of Politics. A Study in the Political Economy of the Welfare State*, Clarendon Press, Oxford.

Room, G. (1995), *Beyond the Threshold: The Measurement and Management of Social Exclusion*, Policy Press, Bristol.

Ross, R. and Mikalauskas, A. (1996), 'Income Poverty among Aboriginal Families with Children: Estimates from the 1991 Census', *Discussion Paper No. 110*, Centre for Aboriginal Economic Policy Research, Australian National University, Canberra.

Ross, R. and Whiteford, P. (1992), 'Poverty in 1986: Aboriginal Families with Children', *Australian Journal of Social Issues*, Vol. 27, pp. 91–111.

Rowntree, B. S. (1901), *Poverty. A Study of Town Life*, Macmillan, London.

Ruggles, R. (1990), *Drawing the Line: Alternative Poverty Measures and Their Implications for Public Policy*, The Urban Institute, Washington DC.

Saunders, P. (1976), 'A Guaranteed Minimum Income Scheme for Australia? Some Problems', *The Australian Journal of Social Issues*, Vol. 11, pp. 174–86.

Saunders, P. (1987), *Growth in Australian Social Security Expenditures, 1959–60 to 1985–86*, Background Discussion Paper No. 19, Social Security Review, Department of Social Security, Canberra.

Saunders, P. (1991) 'Selectivity and Targeting in Income Support: The Australian Experience, *Journal of Social Policy*, Vol. 20, pp. 299–326.

Saunders, P. (1993a), 'The Economy, Economists and the Welfare State: Crisis or Crusade?' in P. Saunders and S. Graham (eds), *Beyond Economic*

Rationalism: Alternative Futures for Social Policy, Reports and Proceedings No. 105, Social Policy Research Centre, University of New South Wales, pp. 33–70.

Saunders, P. (1993b), 'Longer Run Changes in the Distribution of Income in Australia', *Economic Record*, Vol. 69, pp. 353–66.

Saunders, P. (1994), *Welfare and Inequality: National and International Perspectives on the Australian Welfare State*, Cambridge University Press, Melbourne.

Saunders, P. (1995), 'Improving Work Incentives in a Means-Tested Welfare System: The 1994 Australian Social Security Reforms, *Fiscal Studies*, Vol. 16, pp. 45–70.

Saunders, P. (1996a), 'Income, Health and Happiness', *Australian Economic Review*, 4th Quarter, pp. 353–66.

Saunders, P. (1996b), 'Poverty and Deprivation in Australia', in *1996 Year Book Australia*, ABS Catalogue No. 1301.0, ABS Canberra, pp. 226–40.

Saunders, P. (1996c), 'Poverty in the 1990s: A Challenge to Work and Welfare' in P. Sheehan, B. Grewal and M. Kumnick (eds), *Dialogues on Australia's Future. In Honour of the Late Professor Ronald Henderson*, Centre for Strategic Economic Studies, Victoria University of Technology, pp. 325–50.

Saunders, P. (1996d), 'Unpacking Inequality: Wage Incomes, Disposable Incomes and Living Standards, in *The Industry Commission Conference on Equity, Efficiency and Welfare. Conference Proceedings*, The Industry Commission, Melbourne, pp. 225–55.

Saunders, P. (1997a), 'Living Standards, Choice and Poverty', *Australian Journal of Labour Economics*, Vol. 1, pp. 49–70.

Saunders, P. (1997b), 'The Meaning of Poverty', *SPRC Newsletter*, No. 65, pp. 1–5.

Saunders, P. (1998a), 'Reflections on the Australian Poverty Debate', *Social Security Journal*, 1998/1, pp. 9–36.

Saunders, P. (1998b), 'The Re-emergence of Poverty as a Research and Policy Issue', in *Wealth, Work, Well-being*, Occasional Paper 1/1998, Academy of the Social Sciences in Australia, Canberra, pp. 54–78.

Saunders, P. (1998c), 'Setting the Poverty Agenda. The Origins and Impact of the Henderson Report', in R. Fincher and J. Niewenhuysen (eds), *Australian Poverty: Then and Now*, Melbourne University Press, Melbourne, pp. 52–70.

Saunders, P. (1999a), 'The Perception of Inequality', *SPRC Newsletter*, No. 75, pp. 1–6.

Saunders, P. (1999b), 'Changing Work Patterns and the Community Services Workforce', in *Australia's Welfare 1999. Services and Assistance*, Australian Institute of Health and Welfare, Canberra, pp. 38–87.

Saunders, P. (1999c), 'Social Security in Australia and New Zealand: Means-tested or Just Mean?' *Social Policy & Administration*, Vol. 33, pp. 493–515.

Saunders, P. (2000a), 'Global Pressures, National Responses: The Australian Welfare State in Context', in I. O'Connor, P. Smyth and J. Warburton (eds), *Social Work & the Human Services. Challenges and Change*, Longman, pp. 12–29.

Saunders, P. (2000b), 'Defining Poverty and Identifying the Poor', in J. Bradshaw and R. Sainsbury (eds), *Experiencing Poverty*, Ashgate, Aldershot, pp. 5–25.

Saunders, P. (2000c), 'Trends in Earnings Distribution', in *Australian Social Trends, 2000*, Catalogue No. 4102.0, ABS, Canberra, pp. 145–8.

Saunders, P. (2001a), 'Household Income and Its Distribution', *Australian Economic Indicators, June 2001*, Catalogue No. 1350.0, ABS, Canberra, pp. 33–55.

Saunders, P. (2001b), 'Household Income and Its Distribution', *2001 Year Book Australia*, Catalogue No. 1301.0, ABS, Canberra, pp. 280–95.

Saunders, P. (2001c), 'Welfare Reform, Work and the Labour Market', *Economic and Labour Relations Review*, Vol. 12, pp. 151–64.

Saunders, P. (2001d), 'Reflections on Social Security and the Welfare Review', *Australian Economic Review*, Vol. 34, pp. 100–8.

Saunders, P. (2002a), 'Mutual Obligation, Participation and Popularity: Social Security Reform in Australia', *Journal of Social Policy*, Vol. 30, pp. 21–38.

Saunders, P. (2000b), 'Getting Poverty Back onto the Policy Agenda', *Briefing Paper No. 10*, The Smith Family, Sydney.

Saunders, P., Bradshaw, J. and Hirst, M. (2002), 'Using Household Expenditure Data to Develop an Income Poverty Line', *Social Policy & Administration*, Vol. 36, forthcoming.

Saunders, P., Hallerod, B. and Matheson, G. (1994), 'Making Ends Meet in Australia and Sweden: A Comparative Analysis Using the Subjective Poverty Line Methodology', *Acta Sociologica*, Vol. 37, pp. 3–22.

Saunders, P. and Hobbes, G. (1988), 'Income Inequality in Australia in an International Comparative Perspective', *Australian Economic Review*, 3rd Quarter, pp. 25–34.

Saunders, P. and King, A. (1994), *Immigration and the Distribution of Income*, Bureau of Immigration and Population Research, Melbourne.

Saunders, P. and Klau, F. (1985), *The Role of the Public Sector. Causes and Consequences of the Growth of Government*, OECD Economic Studies (Special Issue), Vol. 4, OECD Paris.

Saunders, P. and Matheson, G. (1991), 'An Ever Rising Tide? Poverty in Australia in the Eighties', *Economic and Industrial Relations Review*, Vol. 2, pp. 143–71.

Saunders, P. and Matheson, G. (1992), *Perceptions of Poverty, Income Adequacy and Living Standards in Australia*, Reports and Proceedings No. 99, Social Policy Research Centre, University of New South Wales.

Saunders, P., I. O'Connor and T. Smeeding (1998), 'The Distribution of Welfare: Inequality, Earnings Capacity and Household Production in Comparative Perspective', in S. P. Jenkins, A. Kapteyn and B. van Praag (eds), *The Distribution of Welfare and Household Production: International Perspectives*, Cambridge University Press, Cambridge, pp. 75–110.

Saunders, P. and Taylor, R. (eds) (2002), *The Price of Prosperity. The Economic and Social Costs of Unemployment*, University of New South Wales Press, Sydney.

Saunders, P., Thomson, C. and Evans, C. (2001), 'Social Change and Economic Prosperity: Attitudes to Growth and Welfare', *Just Policy*, No. 23, pp. 4–15.

Saunders, P. and Whiteford, P. (1987), *Ending Child Poverty: An Assessment of the Government's Family Package*, Reports and Proceedings No. 69, Social Policy Research Centre, University of New South Wales.

Saunders, Peter (2000), 'Issues in Australian Welfare Reform', in Peter Saunders (ed.), *Reforming the Australian Welfare State*, Australian Institute of Family Studies, Melbourne, pp. 1–43.

References

Sawyer, M. (1976), *Income Distribution in OECD Countries*, OECD, Paris.
Scarth, W. (2001), 'Growth and Inequality: A Review Article', *Review of Income and Wealth*, Vol. 46, pp. 389–97.
Scherer, P. (1997), 'Socio-economic Change and Social Policy', in *Family, Market and Community. Equity and Efficiency in Social Policy*, OECD, Paris, pp. 13–61.
Sen, A. K. (1985), *Commodities and Capabilities*, North Holland, Amsterdam.
Sen, A. K. (1987), *The Standard of Living*, Cambridge University Press, Cambridge.
Sen, A. K. (1995), *Inequality Re-examined*, Clarendon Press, Oxford.
Sen, A. K. (2000), *Development as Freedom*, Anchor Books, New York.
Sheehan, P. (1998), 'The Changing Nature of Work', *Australian Bulletin of Labour*, Vol. 24, pp. 317–32.
Sheehan, P. (2001), 'The Causes of Increased Earnings Inequality: The International Literature', in J. Borland, B. Gregory and P. Sheehan (eds), *Work Rich, Work Poor. Inequality and Economic Change in Australia*, Centre for Strategic Economic Studies, Victoria University, pp. 40–59.
Slesnick, D. T. (1993), 'Gaining Ground: Poverty in the Postwar United States', *Journal of Political Economy*, Vol. 101, pp. 1–38.
Slesnick, D. T. (2001), *Consumption and Social Welfare. Living Standards and Their Distribution in the United States*, Cambridge University Press, New York.
Smeeding T. M. (2000), 'Changing Income Inequality in OECD Countries: Updated Results from the Luxembourg Income Study (LIS)', in R. Hauser and I. Becker (eds), *The Personal Distribution of Income in an International Perspective*, Springer-Verlag, Berlin, pp. 205–24.
Smith, A. [1776] (1976), *An Enquiry into the Nature and Causes of the Wealth of Nations*, R. Campbell, A. Skinner and W. Todd (eds), Clarendon Press, Oxford.
Smyth, P. and Cass, B. (eds) (1998), *Contesting the Australian Way, States, Markets and Civil Society*, Cambridge University Press, Melbourne.
Snooks, G. D. (1994), *Portrait of the Family Within the Total Economy: A Study in Long Run Dynamics*, Cambridge University Press, Melbourne.
Solow, R. M. (1998), *Work and Welfare*, Princeton University Press, Princeton.
St Vincent de Paul Society (1999), *The 'Hidden Faces' of Poverty. Identifying Poverty Issues in Australia*, St Vincent de Paul Society, Sydney.
St Vincent de Paul Society (2001), *Two Australias: Addressing Inequality and Poverty*, St Vincent de Paul Society, Sydney.
Stanton, D. (1973), 'Comprehensive Inquiry into Poverty', *Social Security Journal*, Winter, pp. 26–32.
Stone, W. and Hughes, J. (2000), 'What Role for Social Capital in Family Policy?' *Family Matters*, No. 56, pp. 20–7.
Sullivan, L. (2000), *Behavioural Poverty*, Centre for Independent Studies, Sydney.
Tann, T. and Sawyers, F. (2001), 'Survey of FaCS Unemployed People: Attitudes Towards the Activity Test', presented to the conference on *The Path to Full Employment*, University of Newcastle, June.
Taxation Review Committee (1975), *Full Report*, AGPS, Canberra.
Taylor-Gooby, P. (1985), *Public Opinion, Ideology and State Welfare*, Routledge & Kegan Paul, London.

Thompson, E. (1994), *Fair Enough. Egalitarianism in Australia*, University of New South Wales Press, Sydney.
Thurow, L. (1980), *The Zero-Sum Society*, Penguin Books, Harmondsworth.
Titmuss, R. M. (1958), 'The Social Division of Welfare', in *Essays on the Welfare State*, Unwin University Books, London, pp. 34–55.
Tobin, J. (1999), 'A Liberal Agenda', in R. B. Freeman (ed.), *The New Inequality*, Beacon, Boston, pp. 58–61.
Townsend, P. (1979), *Poverty in the United Kingdom*, Penguin Books, Harmondsworth.
Townsend, P. (1987), 'Deprivation', *Journal of Social Policy*, Vol. 16, pp. 125–46.
Travers, P. (1996), 'Deprivation Among Low Income DSS Australian Families: Results from a Pilot Study', in R. Thanki and C. Thomson (eds), *Mortgaging Our Future? Families and Young People in Australia*, Reports and Proceedings No. 129, Social Policy Research Centre, University of New South Wales, pp. 27–45.
Travers, P. and Richardson, S. (1993), *Living Decently. Material Well-Being in Australia*, Oxford University Press, Melbourne.
Travers, P. and Robertson, F. (1996), 'Relative Deprivation Among DSS Clients. Results of a Pilot Survey', *Monograph No. 2*, National Institute of Labour Studies, Flinders University.
Tsumori, K., Saunders, Peter and Hughes, H. (2002), 'Poor Arguments. A Response to The Smith Family Report on Poverty in Australia', *Issue Analysis*, No. 21, pp. 1–12.
van Oorschot, W. (2000), 'Who Should Get What and Why? On Deservingness Criteria and Conditionality of Solidarity Among the Public', *Policy and Politics*, Vol. 28, pp. 33–48.
van Oorschot, W. and Halman, L. (2000), 'Blame or Fate, Individual or Social? An International Comparison of Popular Explanations of Poverty', *European Societies*, Vol. 2, pp. 5–28.
van Parijs, P. (ed.) (1992), *Arguing for Basic Income. Ethical Foundations for a Radical Reform*, Verso, London.
Vanstone, A. (2001), *Media Release: Unemployed Support Government's Mutual Obligation and Breaching Rules*, Department of Family and Community Services, Canberra.
Veit-Wilson, J. (1998), *Setting Adequacy Standards. How Governments Define Minimum Incomes*, The Policy Press, Bristol.
Walker, R. (1987), 'Consensual Approaches to the Definition of Poverty: Towards an Alternative Methodology', *Journal of Social Policy*, Vol. 17, pp. 213–26.
Walker, R. (1994), *Poverty Dynamics: Issues and Examples*, Avebury, Aldershot.
Walker, R. and Park, J. (1998), 'Unpicking Poverty', in C. Oppenheim (ed.), *An Inclusive Society. Strategies for Tackling Poverty*, Institute for Public Policy Research, London, pp. 29–51.
Watson, I. and Buchanan, J. (2001), 'Beyond Impoverished Visions of the Labour Market', in R. Fincher and P. Saunders (eds), *Creating Unequal Futures? Rethinking Poverty, Inequality and Disadvantage*, Allen & Unwin, Sydney, pp. 194–228.
Watts, M. (2000), 'The Dimensions and Costs of Unemployment in Australia', in S. Bell (ed.), *The Unemployment Crisis in Australia. Which Way Out?* Cambridge University Press, Melbourne, pp. 21–48.

Watts, R. (1999), 'Australia's Welfare Policy and Latham's Third Way: A Critical Commentary', *Just Policy*, No. 17, pp. 21–31.

Weatherburn, D. (2002), 'The Impact of Unemployment on Crime', in P. Saunders and R. Taylor (eds), *The Price of Prosperity. The Economic and Social Costs of Unemployment*, University of New South Wales Press, Sydney, forthcoming.

Weiss, C. H. (1986), 'The Many Meanings of Research Utilisation', in M. Bulmer (ed.) *Social Science and Social Policy*, Allen & Unwin, London, pp. 31–40.

Western Australian Poverty Task Force (1998), *Report*, Task Force on Poverty in Western Australia, Perth.

Whelan, C. T. and McGinnity, F. (1999), 'Unemployment and Satisfaction: A European Analysis', presented to *the 4th European Conference of Sociology*, Vrije Universiteit, Amsterdam, 18–21 August.

White, G. (1998), 'Social Security Reforms in China: Towards and East Asian Model?' in R. Goodman, G. White and H.-J. Kwon (eds), *The East Asian Welfare Model. Welfare Orientalism and the State*, Routledge, London, pp. 175–97.

Whiteford, P. (1997), 'Measuring Poverty and Income Inequality in Australia', *Agenda*, Vol. 4, pp. 39–50.

Whiteford, P. (1998), 'The Australian System of Social Protection: What (Overseas) Economists Should Know', Background Paper prepared for the Conference on *Income Support, Labour Markets and Behaviour: A Research Agenda*, Department of Family and Community Services, Canberra.

Whiteford, P. (2000), *The Australian System of Social Protection – An Overview*, Policy Research Paper No. 1, Department of Family and Community Services, Canberra.

Whiteford, P. (2001), 'Understanding Poverty and Social Exclusion: Situating Australia Internationally', in R. Fincher and P. Saunders (eds), *Creating Unequal Futures? Rethinking Poverty, Inequality and Disadvantage*, Allen & Unwin, Sydney, pp. 38–69.

Whiteford, P. and Bond, K. (2000), *Trends in the Incomes and Living Standards of Older People in Australia*, Policy Research Paper No. 6, Department of Family and Community Services, Canberra.

Williams, T., Hill, M. and Davies, R. (1999), *Attitudes to the Welfare State and the Response to Reform*, Research Report No. 88, Department of Social Security, London.

Winter, I. (ed.) (2000), *Social Capital and Public Policy in Australia*, Australian Institute of Family Studies, Melbourne.

Withers, G., Throsby, D. and Johnston, K. (1994), *Public Expenditure in Australia*, Commission Paper No. 3, Economic Planning Advisory Commission, AGPS, Canberra.

Wolfe, B. L. (2001), 'Public Programs Create Private Incentives and Disincentives Toward Work', in E. Schokkaert (ed.), *Ethics and Social Security Reform*, Ashgate, Aldershot, pp. 203–41.

Wooden, M. (1996), 'Hidden Unemployment and Underemployment: Their Nature and Possible Impact on Future Labour Force Participation and Unemployment', *Working Paper No. 40*, National Institute of Labour Studies, Flinders University.

Wooden, M. (1998), 'Is Job Stability Really Declining?' *Australian Bulletin of Labour*, Vol. 24, pp. 186–9.

Wooden, M. (1999), 'Job Insecurity and Job Stability: Getting the Facts Straight', *BCA Papers*, Vol. 1, pp. 14–18.

Yates, J. (1991), *Australia's Owner-Occupied Housing Wealth and Its Impact on Income Distribution*, Reports and Proceedings No. 92, Social Policy Research Centre, University of New South Wales.

Yeatman, A. (2000), 'Mutual Obligation: What Kind of Contract is This?' in Peter Saunders (ed.), *Reforming the Australian Welfare State*, Australian Institute of Family Studies, Melbourne, pp. 156–76.

Index

Abel-Smith, B. 143
absolute poverty 149
active society 63, 226, 247
activity/work test 231, 235
adequacy 20, 222 *see also* income adequacy, public opinion about income adequacy
affluence 3, 4, 31, 45, 47, 90, 92, 121, 135, 249 *see also* wealth
Aghion, P. 183
Altman, J. 168, 255
Amiel, Y. 186
arbitration 3, 23, 49, 196 *see also* wage determination
Argy, F. 9, 15, 24, 78
assets test 226
assets *see* wealth
Atkinson, A.B. 43, 56, 171, 172, 181, 183, 185, 186, 203, 206, 208, 224, 258
attitudes *see* public opinion
Australian Bureau of Statistics (ABS) 94, 95, 117, 119, 121, 128, 204, 261
  data 4, 33, 34, 35, 89, 90, 93, 95, 130, 131, 159, 187, 194, 198, 205, 215, 262, 270
  studies 39, 130, 132, 135, 158, 188, 192
Australian Capital Territory (ACT) Poverty Task Group 143
Australian Institute of Family Studies (AIFS) 128, 129

Baldry, E. 74
Barnes, P. 41
Barrett, G. 119, 192
Barry, B. 172, 175
basic income 257–9
Baumol, W. 50, 90
Bean, C. 60, 203
Beckerman, W. 56
beliefs 3, 65, 67–8, 113 *see also* values
benefit fraud 64, 68, 95, 224, 237, 248
Berghmann, J. 171
Bernstein, J. 197, 228
Beveridge, Lord 250

Bittman, M. 127
Blacklow, P. 193
Blair, T. 224
Bond, K. 158
Borland, J. 34, 88, 93, 94, 98, 100, 193, 195, 196
Bourdieu, P. 24, 25, 44
Bradbury, B. 59, 89, 116, 197
Bradshaw, J. 146
Brennan, G. 9
breaching 257 *see also* penalties
British Household Panel Study 98, 170
Brownlee, H. 128, 129
Bryson, L. 98, 169
Buchanan, J. 88
budget deficit 42
Bullen, P. 173
Burbidge, A. 196, 199
Buron, L.F. 120

capabilities 147
capital gains 117, 122
Caroli, E. 183
Cass, B. 23, 247, 258
Castles, F.G. 23, 49, 223, 229, 252
categoricalism 221–2
Centre for Independent Studies 143
Centre for the Analysis of Social Exclusion 249
Chapman, B. 34, 94, 253, 254
child care 90, 120
child poverty 57 *see also* poverty
Citro, C.F. 157
Clark, A.E. 98
collectivists 109, 112, 237, 240–1, 271–2
  identification of 78–9
  characteristics of 79–83
Commission of Inquiry into Poverty *see* Poverty Commission
Commonwealth Bureau of Census and Statistics 187
Community Development Employment Projects (CDEP) Scheme 255
community opinion *see* public opinion

competition 23–4
conditionality 221–2, 225, 258
consensual poverty 160–5, 167
consumption 30–1, 117, 118, 145–6, 187, 191–3, 256
Coping with Economic and Social Change (CESC), 243, 266–7
  focus of questions 17–19, 270–1
  methodology 266–7
  purposes 16, 266
  responses 76–83, 98–113, 134–42, 148–51, 153–57, 163–68, 173–5, 203–5, 232–41, 244–5, 248, 251, 263
  sample 267–70
  value framework 271–2
Cowell, F. 186
Cox, E. 8
Cox, J. 59
cross-national studies 182–3, 196–7, 202–3, 205–11
Crossley, T. 119, 192

Dalton, H. 183
Daly, A.E. 255
Danziger, S. 158
Davies, R. 75
Dawkins, P. 37, 100, 253
Deaton, A. 124
de-industrialisation 52, 205
de Jonge, F. 145
Department of Family and Community Services (FaCS) 95
deprivation 5, 41, 147, 161, 173, 200, 249
Department of Social Security (DSS) 151, 173–4
deregulation 23, 36, 97, 191, 211
deservingness 113, 231
disappearing middle 19, 191
discrimination 179–80
Donnison, A. 171, 172, 173
durable goods 118–19

Eardley, T. 76, 89, 110, 116, 155, 235, 239
earnings capacity 120
earnings inequality 128, 193–6, 202, 252, 254, 259, 261
Eckersley, R. 5, 37, 39, 41, 47, 203
economies of scale 124, 185
economic inequality 178, 183 *see also* income inequality
economic insecurity 37, 100–2
economic outcomes 178–9
economic performance *see* economic policy
Economic Planning Advisory Commission 73
economic policy 10, 23, 41–5, 66, 97, 256, 264

economic rationality 8, 9
economic reform 24–5, 27, 44
Economic and Social Research Council (ESRC) (UK) 172
effectiveness 10, 53–6, 57–8, 63
efficiency 44, 53, 55–6, 181, 182, 222, 247, 248, 251, 252
egalitarianism 3, 77, 78, 196, 202–3, 206, 208, 229, 263
eligibility criteria *see* social security transfers, eligibility for
Ellwood, D. 228
employment 16, 146, 198 *see also* unemployment
  access to 55, 87, 250, 257, 259, 263
  casual 87
  distribution 89–90, 91–2
  female 92
  insecurity 83, 93–4, 100–1
  instability 100
  in manufacturing 89, 90, 195
  in services *see* service sector
  part-time 87, 91, 97
  regional distribution of 91, 94, 200–1, 256, 260
  self 89
entitlements 49, 87, 97, 123, 221, 225
equality 54–6
  of opportunity 68, 175, 178–81, 184, 263
  of outcomes 179, 181, 263
equivalence scales 124–5, 132, 185, 190, 208
Esping-Andersen, G. 50, 75, 90, 218–9, 245
European Community Household Panel 98
Evans, C. 47, 76, 235, 239
Evans, M. 37, 100
exclusion *see* social exclusion
executive packages 127

fair go 3, 5, 202, 229
families 52, 188, 197
  dual-earner 90, 121
fatalists 109, 112, 237, 241, 271–2
  identification of 78–9
  characteristics of 79–83
Feagin, J.R. 78
Feather, N.T. 78, 98, 152, 153
financial stress 39–40
Fincher, R. 170
fiscal stringency 96
Flatau, P. 98
Forma, P. 59
Friedman, M. 116
fringe benefits tax 127
functionings 146

Index

Galbraith, K. 6, 176, 182
Galea, J. 98
Garcia-Peñalosa, C. 183
Gardiner, K. 125
Garfinkel, T. 120
Gatenby, J. 39, 40, 135
Giddens, A. 9, 61, 80, 172, 228, 249–50
Gini coefficient 186, 188, 190, 191, 192, 208–11
Glennerster, H. 158
globalisation 25, 29, 36, 87, 211, 252
Goedhart, T. 161
Goodin, R. 220, 221, 231
goods and services tax (GST) 132, 218
Gordon, D. 173
government expenditure 27–30, 248 *see also* social expenditure
Greenwell, H. 143
Gregory, R.G. 88, 94, 125, 127, 191, 199, 200, 201, 253, 255
Gruen, F. 9, 73
GST *see* good and services tax
guaranteed minimum income (GMI) 246, 257

Hagenaars, A. 161
Hallerod, B. 161
Halman, L. 78
Harcourt, A. 146
Harding, A. 117, 128, 143, 158, 191
Harper, R.J.A. 69, 146
Harris, E. 98
Haveman, R. 120, 144, 152, 153, 158, 245
Hawke government 17, 57
Headey, B. 47, 98
health status 83, 99, 123, 136–7, 141–2, 183
Hellwig, O. 46
Henderson, R.F. 69, 146
Henderson poverty line 157 *see also* poverty line
Henman, P. 227
Hill, M. 75
Hills, J. 71, 170
Hirst, M. 146
Hobbes, G. 117
home ownership 127–8
home purchase 121
hours worked *see* work patterns
household consumption 119
household expenditure 118–9
household needs 132
household size 32, 115, 185
Howard, J. 230
Howard government 57, 64, 75, 247
Howarth, C. 173
Hughes, H. 143
Hughes, J. 173

human capital 120, 182
human/community services *see* social programs
Hunter, B. 94, 168, 201

ideology *see* politics
Ignatieff, M. 51
imputed rent 119–20, 121–2, 129
incentives/disincentives 20, 44, 51, 54, 58, 63, 66, 68, 96, 109, 131, 181, 182, 216–22, 226, 251–2, 258, 259, 264
income 4, 16–18, 45, 46–7, 116, 117–8, 124–7, 146, 184
  current 116, 127
  deferred 127
  disposable 30–1, 117, 188, 190, 191, 253
  earned 46, 115, 125
  equivalent 124
  from capital *see* unearned
  from self-employment 116
  from transfers 122, 125 *see also* social security transfers
  full 46, 122
  gross 117, 126, 187–8, 190, 251, 253
  household 40, 114, 125–6, 127, 128
  lifetime 115–6, 118, 127
  market 38, 117, 122, 188, 190, 191, 206, 251
  non-cash 62, 119–22, 127, 130–1
  permanent *see* lifetime
  primary 117, 252
  unearned 46, 125
income adequacy 138, 156–7, 165, 222, 225, 244
income churning 59
income contingency 221–2
income distribution 19, 37–8, 39, 133, 158, 175, 176, 177, 183, 185–96, 202, 206, 209
income dynamics *see* poverty dynamics
income inequality 115, 129, 175, 178, 183–4, 188, 193–6, 210, 252, 259, 263
income insecurity 36–7
income maintenance 49, 221
income mobility 180
income poverty 159, 249
income redistribution 55, 245, 251
income replacement 49
income sharing 123, 185
income support *see* social security transfers
income test 199
indicators 16–7, 25, 26, 38
  objective 4–5, 16, 45, 47
  subjective 4–5, 16, 45, 47, 137, 155, 157
Indigenous Australians 4, 168–9, 179, 202, 255–6

individualists 109, 112–3, 237, 240–1, 271–2
　identification of 78–9
　characteristics of 79–83
inequality 3, 4–5, 15, 16, 37, 38, 39, 63, 88, 175, 219, 249–50, 254, 260
　adverse effects of 183, 201
　of earnings 100
　index/measures 177, 186
　trends in 191
inflation 26–7
Ingles, D. 92
in-kind benefits *see* income, non–cash
international studies *see* cross–national studies
Ironmonger, D. 120

Jarvis, S. 170
Jenkins, S.P. 123, 170, 186
job creation 106, 146, 253–4 *see also* employment
job rich/poor households 125, 199–200 *see also* workless households
job search 64, 102, 220,
job sharing 106, 259–63
Johnson, D. 46, 121, 123, 128
Johnson, J. 143
Johnston, K. 73, 74, 128, 248
Jones, A. 172
Jones, B. 89
Jones, F.L. 187

Kalisch, D.W. 226
Kapuscinski, C.A. 34, 94
Kelley, J. 37, 100
Kelly, P. 23, 133, 252
Kennedy, S. 34, 93, 193, 195, 196
Kennett, S. 41, 129
Keynesian policy 23, 50
King, A. 57, 180
Klau, F. 30
Klug, E. 253
Korpi, W. 182
Kwon, H.-J. 59

labour force 198
　participation 92, 102, 227, 233, 252, 257
labour market 25, 36, 87–90, 91–2, 96, 216, 219, 222, 228, 245, 252, 256, 257, 264–5
　programs 64, 109, 228, 230, 253
　deregulation 23, 229, 252–3, 262
　discrimination 55
　research 100
　segmentation 91
　trends 17, 26, 34, 91–4, 97, 201–2
labour/occupational mobility 180

Lampman, R.J. 152
Langmore, J. 254, 261
Lansley, S. 147
Latham, M. 249
'leaky bucket' 181–2
Lechene, V. 125
legitimacy *see* social policy, legitimacy of
Le Grand, J. 62
leisure 120, 127, 129
Lelkes, O. 71
Lewis, J. 14
Leyden research group 161
life satisfaction 47, 98, 136–7, 139–42, 248 *see also* living standards, well–being
living standards 4–5, 16–17, 25, 30, 32–3, 41, 46, 64, 89, 117–8, 123, 146, 245, 249, 263 *see also* well–being
　of households 114
　relative 38
Lloyd, R. 143
Lorenz curve 186, 188
Luxembourg Income Study (LIS) 207, 208–11
Lydall, L. 202
Lyons, M. 52

Mack, D. 147
Maddox, G. 252
Manning, I. 46, 128, 145, 157, 246
market forces 9, 10, 15, 23–4, 43, 54, 88, 97, 102, 178, 190–1, 211, 220, 223, 229, 245, 250–3
market sector 8, 52–3 *see also* policy, market-oriented
Martin, D. 253
Martin, Y.M. 253
Matheson, G. 110, 127, 161
McDonald, P. 128, 129
McClean, I.W. 187
McClelland, A. 258
McClure report 8
McColl, R. 39, 40, 135
McGinnity, F. 98
Mead, L. 68, 217, 227
Meade, J.E. 258
Meagher, G. 127
means testing *see* targeting
measurement of consumption 117–19
　of economic and social conditions 15–16
　of inequality 177, 183–6, 193–6
　of income 46, 116–7, 119–24, 126
　of living standards 128–30
　of poverty 17, 56–7, 143–5, 158
media 6, 11, 48, 65, 68, 69, 243, 265
Melbourne Institute of Applied Economic and Social Research 12
Michael, R.T. 157

Index

middle Australia 3, 77, 133, 205, 217, 245, 263
middle class welfare 59, 62, 223–4
Midgley, J. 55, 250
Mikalauskas, A. 168
Millar, J. 228
Miller, P. 98, 197, 199
minimum income question (MIQ) 161–3, 165
Mishel, L. 197, 228
Mitchell, D. 56
Mogenson, G.V. 181
moral authority 173
Morrell, S. 98
Morrow, M. 98
Muellbauer, J. 124
Murray, C. 217
mutual obligation 16, 19, 64, 75, 77, 97, 122, 229–40, 247, 250, 252–3, 257, 264
   requirements (MOR) 234–7

National Social Science Survey 203
necessities *see* needs
needs 123–5, 142, 146, 147, 171, 174, 185, 229, 252 *see also* household needs
neo-liberalism 8–10, 23–4, 27, 54–5, 59, 60, 62, 78, 96, 102, 147, 175, 179, 180–1, 202, 217, 219, 233, 249–50, 264
Nevile, J. 9, 195, 252, 253
Newman, J. 58, 227, 230
Newspoll 133
Newton, K. 48, 60
Nolan, B. 144
non-government welfare sector 52–3, 59, 247
normative judgment 173
Norris, K. 94, 193
Nuffield Foundation 13

O'Connor, I. 120
O'Connor, J.S. 56
Okun, A. 181
Onyx, J. 173
Organisation for Economic Cooperation and Development (OECD) 37, 50–1, 57, 63, 100, 190, 207, 216, 219, 253, 261
   cross-country comparisons 25–30, 57, 92–3, 196–7, 206 *see also* cross-national studies
   data 26, 29, 197, 216
Orloff, A.S. 56
Osberg, L. 100, 182, 245
Oswald, A.J. 98

Page, A. 98

Pantazis, C. 173
Pappas, N. 191
Parham, D. 41, 129
Park, J. 169
participation *see* labour force participation, social participation
participation support system 258
passive welfare 255
paternalism 68, 217
Pearson, N. 255–6
penalties 223, 237, 239–40
percentile ratio 186, 188–9, 192, 193–7, 205, 209, 210
perceptions *see* public opinion
Persson, T. 182
Perry, J. 228
Petridis, R. 98
Pietsch, L. 39, 40
Piggott, J. 253
Ploug, N. 48
policy instruments 42
policy, market-oriented 5, 32, 61–2, 97
politics, role of 5–6, 61, 96, 216, 248
   party 11–12
politics of welfare 50, 75, 218, 222–5
positional goods 63
poverty 3, 16, 18, 62, 63, 96, 143–176
   causes of 152–7, 169
   consensual 160–5, 167
   impact of 143–6, 148
   meaning of 148–52
   perceptions of 160–1
   primary 157–9
   subjective 160, 165–8
poverty alleviation 56, 57–8, 221, 246
Poverty Commission 57, 69, 96, 144, 146, 157, 169, 246, 257
poverty dynamics 169–70
poverty line 17, 57, 143–4, 146, 157, 158–9, 168, 225–6
poverty research 146, 169
poverty statistics 145
poverty trap 66, 97, 217, 219, 221, 226–8
private sector 195, 223, 254–5
productivity 3, 261
Productivity Commission 129
prosperity *see* affluence
psychological stress 98
public opinion 3, 5, 6, 11, 15–16, 19–20, 37, 38, 47, 48, 60–2, 64, 65–80, 99–100, 224, 242–4, 248, 257, 262, 263–5
   about causes of poverty 152–7
   about health 136–8
   about income 138–42
   about income adequacy 111, 166
   about income distribution 203–5
   about inequality 203

public opinion *cont'd*
  about labour market programs 253–4
  about living standards 134–7
  about mutual obligation and penalties 237–40
  about poverty 147–52, 160–1, 163–5, 167–8
  about social security system 232–4, 239–41
  about unemployment 103–13
  demographic differences in 101–3
  trends 72–3
public policy 7, 15, 184, 191 *see also* social policy
public provision/services *see* social programs
public sector 10, 195, 255
  employment 90–1, 254–6, 259
Pusey, M. 9, 24, 37, 77, 133
Putnam, R.D. 8
Putnis, P. 69

Quiggin, J. 254, 256, 261

Radner, D. 124
Rainwater, L. 117, 203, 208
Ramia, G. 223
Ravallion, M. 143
raw data 207
Ray, R. 193
reciprocal obligation *see* mutual obligation
Redmond, G. 123
reform strategies 19, 20
Reference Group on Welfare Reform 8, 57, 227, 230, 231, 247, 258
Reich, R.B. 89
relative income 191
relative poverty 145, 147
research 14, 69, 128–30, 132–4, 152, 173, 192–5, 219, 243, 265 *see also* CESC, OECD, ABS, social research
  attitudinal 70–5
  impact of 15, 48
  role of 6
  utilisation of 13–14, 207
research funding 13–14
Richardson, S. 46, 47, 118, 120, 128, 184, 187, 254
Ringen, S. 60, 72
Roberts, P. 41, 129
Robertson, F. 174
Room, G. 171
Ross, R. 168
Rowntree Foundation 13, 14
Rowntree, S. 145
Ruggles, R. 157

St Vincent de Paul Society 143

Saunders, P. 17, 24, 35, 47, 49, 50, 52, 56, 57, 64, 69, 74, 76, 90, 95, 96, 117, 120, 121, 124, 126, 128, 132, 137, 143, 144, 145, 146, 148, 151, 158, 159, 161, 170, 180, 187, 189, 192, 193, 195, 199, 203, 207, 218, 221, 222, 228, 235, 239, 246, 255
Saunders, Peter 52, 143, 218
savings *see* wealth
Sawyer, M. 202, 206
Sawyers, F. 75
Scarth, W. 245
Scherer, P. 92
Schmitt, J. 197, 228
Sen, A.K. 56, 114, 145, 146, 147, 171, 178, 184
service sector 89, 90, 195
services *see* social programs
Shaver, S. 56
Sheehan, P. 88, 92, 127, 193, 196, 199, 201
simplicity 222
Slesnick, D.T. 116
Smeeding, T.M. 117, 120, 203, 208, 209
Smith, Adam 147
Smith Family 143
Smyth, P. 23, 172
Snooks, G.D. 90
social assistance 221–2, 223, 246
social capital 8, 173, 249
social exclusion 16, 96, 170–6, 184, 200, 219, 249
social expenditure 28, 51, 52, 58, 73, 74–5, 97, 130, 215–6, 218, 226 *see also* government expenditure
social insurance 49, 221, 223, 245–7
social justice 55, 178, 243, 248
social participation 8, 64
social policy 10, 20, 24, 41, 43, 44, 45, 53, 54, 56, 61, 63, 77, 93, 96–7, 115, 178, 215, 217, 249, 250
  legitimacy of 15, 16, 48, 59–60, 70, 75, 218, 224, 225, 244, 259
Social Policy Research Centre (SPRC) 16, 75–6
social programs 10, 44, 50, 51, 54, 74–5, 95, 175–6, 181, 247
  employment in 254–5
social progress 7
social research 12–15, 55, 63, 215 *see also* research
Social Security Act 237
social security benefits *see* social security transfers
social security programs 43, 219
Social Security Review 247
social security system 19, 49, 184, 191, 215, 245

Index

social security transfers 28, 34, 49, 50, 56, 63, 71, 95, 122, 130–1, 132, 146, 190, 215, 220, 221, 231, 251–2, 256, 260
   eligibility for 49–50, 63, 68, 92, 122, 127, 199, 207, 216, 221, 224, 225, 226–7, 231, 246, 252, 264
social solidarity 218, 243
social wage 121, 127, 130–2
sole parents 63, 121, 122, 159, 163, 166, 168, 199, 230, 254
Solow, R. 244–5
standard of living *see* living standards
Stanton, D. 144
state intervention 9, 27, 43, 109, 182
stigmatisation 122, 127, 225, 250
Stone, W. 173
subjective poverty 160, 165, 166–8
Sullivan, L. 158
superannuation 115, 127, 247
sustainability 7, 50, 51, 59, 223–4, 251
Sutherland, H. 125
Szukalska, A. 143, 158

Tabellini, G. 182
targeting 20, 28, 29, 49, 56, 57, 63, 122, 216–9, 221, 223–5, 227, 247–8, 250, 252, 254
Tann, T. 75
Taylor, J. 143
Taylor, R. 35, 96, 98
Taylor-Gooby, P. 72
taxation 42, 51, 59, 63, 73–4, 117, 119, 178, 222, 233, 246–8, 251–2, 256, 262
   as a redistributive instrument 38, 184, 190, 256
   concessions 116, 255
   cuts 24, 176, 182, 252
   level of 28–30
   marginal 57
Taxation Review Committee 246–7
taxpayers 218, 223, 233, 252
tax-transfer system 122, 130–2, 191, 206
technological change 87, 88, 89, 206
Third Way 20, 62, 249–50
Thompson, E. 202, 231
Thomson, C. 47, 76, 137
Throsby, D. 73, 74, 248
Thurow, L. 179
Titmuss, R.M. 223
Tobin, J. 181
Townsend, P. 147, 171
trade unions 89–90, 106
training 64, 90, 230
transfer system *see* social security system
Travers, P. 47, 118, 120, 128, 173, 174

'trickle down' theory 181–2
trust 8
Tsumori, K. 143

underclass 96
unemployment 4, 15, 16, 23, 26–7, 32–5, 36, 42, 44, 51, 62, 63, 66, 67, 68, 97–100, 229, 242, 247–8, 251, 253, 258–9, 264 *see also* employment
   consequences of 97–8, 100, 220, 232
   concentration of 96, 98, 199, 260
   female 34, 197, 259
   incidence of 94
   long-term 34, 35, 71, 91, 94, 95
   of older workers 71
   statistics 33, 93–4
unemployment benefit *see* social security transfers
unit of analysis 123, 124–5, 185–6
universal benefits 218, 223, 246, 257

values 10, 16, 18, 47, 65–8, 78–9, 80–3, 92, 113, 144–5
van Oorschot, W. 78, 111, 113
van Parijs, P. 258
Vanstone, A. 75
Veit-Wilson, J. 144
Vinson, T. 74

wage bargaining 196, 256
wage determination 229, 252, 256
wage earner's welfare state 223
wage subsidies 253–4
Walker, R. 161, 169
War on Poverty (US) 144
Watson, I. 88
Watts, M. 94
Watts, R. 229, 249
wealth 115–16, 122, 176, 178 *see also* affluence
Wealth of Nations, The 147
Wearing, M. 47, 98
Weatherburn, D. 98
Weinberg, D. 158
welfare beneficiaries 218, 220
welfare cheats *see* benefit fraud
welfare dependency 57, 63, 102, 169, 222, 226–7, 230, 233, 266
welfare programs *see* social programs
welfare reform 61, 64, 75, 122, 215–41, 242–3, 246, 249, 264
welfare services 90–1
welfare state 9, 10, 24, 49–56, 127, 229, 242–3, 245
   budget *see* social expenditure
welfare support *see* welfare dependency
welfare system 215, 219–25, 228–9, 242, 245, 249, 264

well-being 5, 23, 25, 30, 45, 97, 98, 119, 129, 183–5 *see also* living standards
   subjective 80, 82–3, 99–100
Weiss, C.H. 13
Western Australian Poverty Taskforce 143
Whelan, C.T. 98
White, G. 61
Whiteford, P. 17, 29, 34, 50, 57, 145, 158, 168, 171, 225
Wilkins, R. 193
Williams, T. 75
Winter, I. 98, 173
Withers, G. 73, 74, 248
Wolfe, B.L. 230
Wooden, M. 37, 94, 100, 193
work ethic 92, 244–5, 257, 264

work/activity test 231, 235
work as an end 227–8
work distribution *see* employment, access to
work for the dole 75
work patterns/hours 87, 88–9, 91–3, 259–63
Working Nation 247
working poor 155, 229, 252
workless households 125–7, 260
   children in 199–200, 202
Worswick, C. 119, 192

Yates, J. 46
Yeatman, A. 231

Zagorski, K. 203

For EU product safety concerns, contact us at Calle de José Abascal, 56–1°, 28003 Madrid, Spain or eugpsr@cambridge.org.

www.ingramcontent.com/pod-product-compliance
Ingram Content Group UK Ltd.
Pitfield, Milton Keynes, MK11 3LW, UK
UKHW010859060825
461487UK00012B/1231